THE
WOODWORKERS
VISUAL HANDBOOK

Professional Edition

THE WOODWORKERS
VISUAL HANDBOOK

**From Standards to Styles, from Tools to Techniques:
The Ultimate Guide to Every Phase of Woodworking**

Jon Arno

Reader's®
Digest

THE READER'S DIGEST ASSOCIATION, INC.
Pleasantville, New York/Montreal

The author and editors who compiled this book have tried to make all
of the contents as accurate and correct as possible. Plans, illustrations,
photographs, and text have all been carefully checked and cross-checked.
However, due to the variability of local conditions, construction materials,
personal skill and so on, neither the author nor Reader's Digest assumes
any responsibility for any injuries suffered or for damages or other losses
incurred that result from the material presented herein. All instructions
and plans should be carefully studied and clearly understood before
beginning construction.

Library of Congress Cataloging in Publication Data

Arno, Jon.
   The woodworkers visual handbook : from standards to styles, from
   tools to techniques : the ultimate guide to every phase of woodworking / Jon Arno. – Professional ed.
        p.   cm.
    ISBN 0-7621-0226-8
    1. Woodwork Handbooks, manuals, etc. I. Title.
   TT180.A74   1999
   684'.08–dc21   99-24914

READER'S DIGEST ILLUSTRATED REFERENCE BOOKS
Editor-in-Chief: Christopher Cavanaugh
Art Director: Joan Mazzeo
Operations Manager: William J. Cassidy
Director, Trade Publishing: Christopher T. Reggio

Address any comments about *The Woodworkers Visual Handbook* to:
   Reader's Digest
   Editor-in-Chief, Illustrated Reference Books
   Reader's Digest Road
   Pleasantville, NY 10570

Visit our website at: www.readersdigest.com

Printed in the United States of America
Second Printing, February 2001

CONTENTS

INTRODUCTION

One problem all woodworkers face is finding reliable information about their craft. Certainly, good information abounds: in magazines and books, in workshops and seminars, and on television. But it's not always easy to locate the exact answer to a particular question quickly.

This book was inspired by the hope of including between two covers *all* of the essential information woodworkers need to complete their projects successfully. The goal was to produce a book that would guide woodworkers from the idea stage to assembly and finishing and help alleviate the guesswork in between, from designing and sizing a project, equipping the shop, and using tools properly to choosing the right stock, cutting the appropriate joints, and applying the best finish. Whether you are just starting out or are seasoned at this craft, *The Woodworkers Visual Handbook* will put the information you need at your fingertips.

There are several ways to use this book. As a reference guide, you can turn to its pages for the answers to hundreds of specific woodworking questions. For example, how large should a dining table be? What types of router bits and accessories are available and which ones best meet your needs? Or which wood is stronger—butternut or birch?

The thirteen chapters of *The Woodworkers Visual Handbook* are also organized to guide you through a typical project from start to finish. Each chapter explores a different phase of the process and provides a wealth of ideas and inspiration. The opening chapter, Furniture Dimensions and Design, will help you design your projects and determine their dimensions. The Furniture Styles chapter surveys four centuries of American cabinetmaking tradition and will help you distinguish among the various styles. The next four chapters deal with how to lay out and equip a workshop and how to use and care for the plethora of hand and power tools available to woodworkers. The Lumber and Veneer chapter will help you select stock for your projects. It explores the types and properties of wood and includes a color-photo gallery of over 60 wood species favored by cabinetmakers. The Encyclopedia of Joinery chapter discusses the strengths and weaknesses of the most commonly used woodworking joints and describes how to cut many of them.

The remaining chapters tackle the subject of building furniture—from assembling your projects (Cabinetmaking Techniques) and gluing them up (Gluing and Clamping) to installing hardware and applying a finish. The final chapter is a treasure trove of jigs that will no doubt make your woodworking safer and more efficient.

Whenever you have a woodworking question, *The Woodworkers Visual Handbook* is the first resource you should look to for an answer.

FURNITURE
DIMENSIONS AND DESIGN

Once you have learned to build projects from published plans, you will probably want to start experimenting with your own designs. To do this, you will need to understand a few basic principles and master some easy-to-learn drawing skills. This chapter will tell you what you need to know to create your own pieces of furniture from scratch and adapt existing plans to suit your individual needs.

Some pieces of furniture, such as chairs, tables, and desks, have special requirements dictated by human anatomy. A table, for example, has to be built at a certain height to accommodate the legs of whoever will be sitting at it. Charts offering suggested dimensions are provided for different types of chairs (page 3), tables (page 6), desks and other office furniture (page 7), and beds (page 10). Still, there is plenty of room for style and creativity. Use the standards in the charts as guidelines. Doing it yourself allows you to design and make furniture that is tailored to your particular circumstances.

Even types of furniture that do not involve the human body have their own requirements. For example, the spacing, depth, and load capacity of shelves in a bookcase must be designed around the anticipated size and weight of the books they will support. The maximum span of a shelf will be influenced by these considerations and also by the strength of the wood you select to build it. Plywood, hardwood, softwood, and particleboard each have substantially different properties in this respect; the tables on pages 8 and 9 present their load-carrying capacities and the potential deflection for various spans.

While the charts and tables in this chapter offer guidance, it is important to recognize that few design rules are mandatory. Also, there is rarely only one solution to a problem. To make the most of the design process, it helps to explore all the options. A drawing board and some basic drafting tools will help you evaluate them before sawing your first piece of wood. Starting on page 13 is an explanation of how to use drafting tools and how to convert plans to cutting patterns.

Knowing how to design your own furniture will free you from relying on plans devised by other woodworkers. Take the time to understand the information in this chapter. It will add a whole new dimension to your woodworking.

CHAIRS

**PRINCIPLES
OF CHAIR
DESIGN**

A chair's design inevitably evolves from a series of compromises. Style is important, but it should not override the requirements of human anatomy and the specific purpose the chair will perform. The height of the seat, for example, should allow the soles of the feet to rest on the floor. For chairs designed for use with tables, the table height also influences how high the chair seat should be. Generally, seats that slope toward the back, as shown below, help position body weight more comfortably. Level seats are more functional for eating or working at a table.

A well-designed chair should be able to accommodate off-center loads. One way to incorporate this in chair design is to splay the back legs outward beyond the back of the seat. This will enable someone to lean back in the chair and lift the front legs off the floor without toppling the chair.

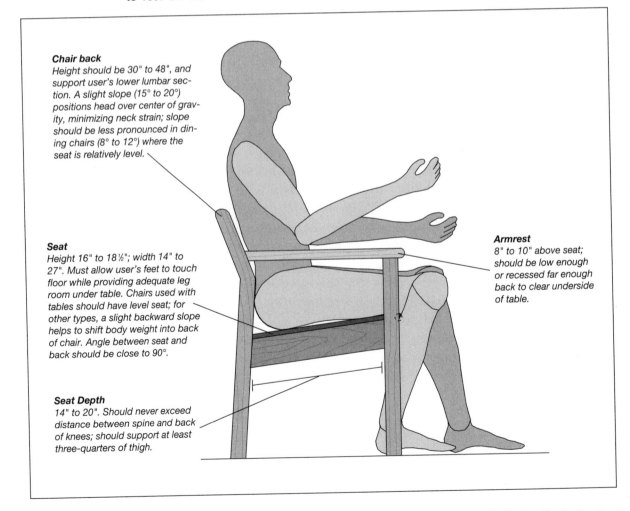

Chair back
Height should be 30" to 48", and support user's lower lumbar section. A slight slope (15° to 20°) positions head over center of gravity, minimizing neck strain; slope should be less pronounced in dining chairs (8° to 12°) where the seat is relatively level.

Seat
Height 16" to 18½"; width 14" to 27". Must allow user's feet to touch floor while providing adequate leg room under table. Chairs used with tables should have level seat; for other types, a slight backward slope helps to shift body weight into back of chair. Angle between seat and back should be close to 90°.

Seat Depth
14" to 20". Should never exceed distance between spine and back of knees; should support at least three-quarters of thigh.

Armrest
8" to 10" above seat; should be low enough or recessed far enough back to clear underside of table.

Because chairs are intended to support a human body, their dimensions are crucial. Chairs must be large enough to accept the human form, but even very small excesses quickly detract from a chair's comfort, utility, and appearance. A certain amount of bulk is necessary to provide sufficient strength, but most types of chairs also need to be somewhat portable, so compact size and light weight are important virtues. The chart below offers the range of dimensions traditionally used for various types of chairs.

TYPE OF CHAIR	SEAT WIDTH	SEAT DEPTH	SEAT HEIGHT	BACK HEIGHT
Kitchen	14" to 16"	14" to 16"	17" to 18½"	30" to 36"
Dining (side)	18" to 21"	16" to 20"	18" to 18½"	40" to 48"
Dining (arm)	20" to 27"	16" to 20"	18" to 18½"	40" to 48"
Rocker	18" to 22"	16" to 20"	16" to 17"	36" to 42"
Writing chair	18" to 20"	16"	17"	42"
Counter stool	16" to 18"	16" to 18"	Up to 30" (foot rest 20" below seat)	36" to 42"
Baby high chair	12" to 14"	12" to 14"	22" to 28"	36" to 40"

Unlike dining chairs, rocking chairs need not be designed to accompany a table. They are leisure seats; design considerations can be shifted toward maximizing comfort. Since the user does not have to be held forward, the slope of both the seat and back can be substantially increased. These adaptations, however, require some dimensional adjustments. As the slope of the seat is increased, the height of its front edge should be lowered to keep the user's feet in firm contact with the floor. Also, as the backrest is angled back, it should be lengthened to provide support for the user's shoulders and head. The angle formed by the seat and the back may be as much as 115 degrees. However, this angle affects the chair's center of gravity and, consequently, the appropriate positioning of the rockers. As the center of gravity shifts to the back, so must the rockers. The diagram below offers proportions for a typical rocker.

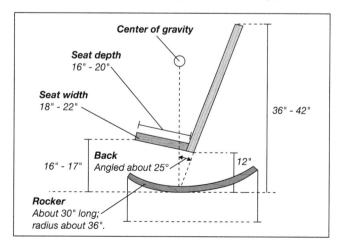

Center of gravity

Seat depth
16" - 20"

Seat width
18" - 22"

36" - 42"

Back
Angled about 25°

16" - 17"

12"

Rocker
About 30" long;
radius about 36".

TABLES

ROUND DINING TABLES

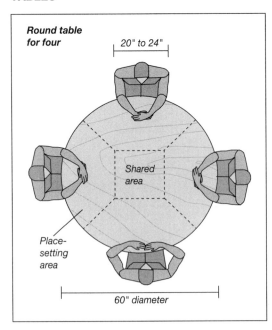

Round table for four

20" to 24"

Shared area

Place-setting area

60" diameter

Courtesy Julius Panero, Human Dimensions and Interior Space, Watson-Guptill Publications, 1979

Viewed from the top, tables designed for dining demand that careful consideration be given to minimum area requirements. As with other furniture that must accommodate the human form, table design is based on the normal dimensions of the human body. Starting with a shoulder breadth of from 20 to 24 inches and adding additional clearance for the upper arms and elbows, most adults need approximately 30 inches of linear space to eat in comfort. With round tables, this is seldom a problem since the curvature of the table affords ample room. As shown in the illustrations on this page, the problem with round tables is that the place-setting areas taper as they extend inward to the table's center. This restricts the space available for a complete, formal service-setting with side plate, cup, and two glasses. At the same time, the depth of the place-setting area should not exceed about 18 inches so that the entire service is within easy reach without leaning forward. These two competing requirements become increasingly unmanageable as the diameter of the table decreases. In fact, it is difficult to accommodate a dinner for four people around a circular table that is less than 40 inches in diameter, even though each setting can be allocated more than 30 inches of the table's circumference. As the diameter of the table increases, the taper of the place-setting area decreases and the table can accommodate more settings. However, the shared area in the center of a table with a diameter of more than about 60 inches becomes difficult to reach.

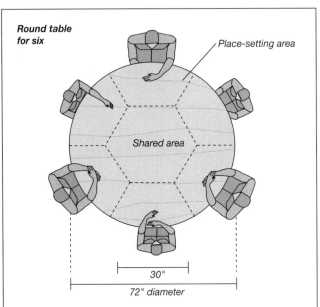

Round table for six

Place-setting area

Shared area

30"

72" diameter

Courtesy Julius Panero, Human Dimensions and Interior Space, Watson-Guptill Publications, 1979

Square dining tables present many of the same place-setting constraints as small-diameter round tables. As the illustration at right shows, the place-setting areas afforded by a 42-inch square table taper sharply inward, leaving little room for a formal setting. Although acceptable for informal dining, the shared area at the center of such a table all but disappears, leaving little space for dishes.

As a table's length is extended *(right, below)*, additional place settings become possible and the shared area expands to provide adequate space for dishes. A table 42 inches wide by 80 inches long will comfortably serve a party of six. Extending the table's length to 96 inches allows it to accommodate eight people. The place-setting areas at the ends will be less than ideal, but the rectangular shape provides adequate elbow room for everyone. Increasing the table's width from 42 to 48 inches expands the central, shared area and relieves congestion at the corners. However, keep in mind that a table's maximum dimensions are limited by the size of the room and other furnishings. You must allow for a minimum of 24 inches of free space behind the chairs. Remember too that the longer a table extends, the more difficult it will be for people to communicate and pass dishes.

Courtesy Julius Panero, Human Dimensions and Interior Space, Watson-Guptill Publications, 1979

Courtesy Julius Panero, Human Dimensions and Interior Space, Watson-Guptill Publications, 1979

FOUR-SIDED DINING TABLES

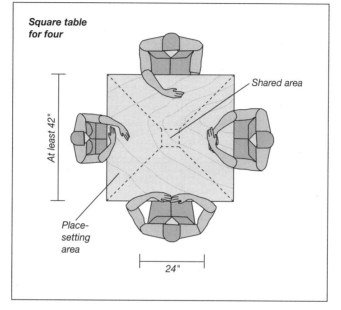

Square table for four

Shared area

At least 42"

Place-setting area

24"

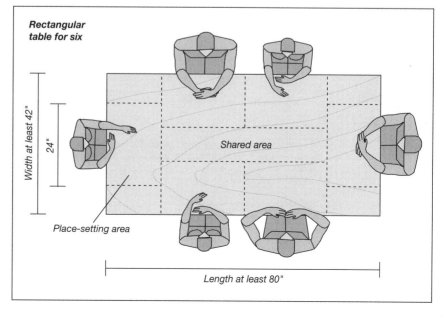

Rectangular table for six

Width at least 42"

24"

Shared area

Place-setting area

Length at least 80"

TABLES

TABLES : STANDARD DIMENSIONS

TABLES	LENGTH	WIDTH	TOP HEIGHT
Coffee	As desired	18" to 30"	16" to 18"
Serving	36" to 48"	20"	32" to 36"
Small bedside	14"	14"	24" to 30"
Night	18"	18"	24" to 30"
End	24"	18"	21" to 24"
Candle stand	12" to 21"	12" to 21"	25" to 31"
Trestle	48" to 120"	30" min.	29" to 31"
Round dining	—	40" min.	29" to 31"
Rectangular dining	42" min.	42" min.	29" to 31"
Dining with leaves	40"	40"	29" to 31"
Leaves	—	12" to 16"	—

PRINCIPLES OF DINING TABLE DESIGN

Before building a dining table, you must consider how it will relate to the chairs around it. The specifications of the two are interrelated. As shown in the illustration below, you need to allow at least 7½ inches between the chair seat and the underside of the tabletop to provide sufficient room for the thighs. There should also be from 15 to 18 inches of clearance from the edge of the table to any obstruction, such as a central pedestal, to accommodate the knees.

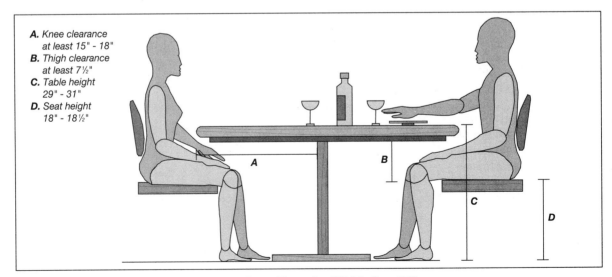

A. Knee clearance
at least 15" - 18"
B. Thigh clearance
at least 7½"
C. Table height
29" - 31"
D. Seat height
18" - 18½"

Courtesy Julius Panero, Human Dimensions and Interior Space, Watson-Guptill Publications, 1979

OFFICE FURNITURE	LENGTH	WIDTH	TOP HEIGHT
Office desk	60"	30"	29"
Secretarial desk	60" to 66"	30" to 32"	30"
Executive desk	72" to 84"	30" to 36"	30"
Workstation	48"	30"	26" to 30"
Personal computer desk	48" to 50"	24" to 30"	20" to 26"
Printer table	24" to 30"	21" to 24"	26" to 29"
Credenza	69"	19"	29"
Home computer desk	50"	24" to 28"	29"

OFFICE FURNITURE: STANDARD DIMENSIONS

COMPUTER FURNITURE DESIGN

As in the cockpit of an airplane, the various components of a personal computer in a well-designed workstation are laid out for easy access and visibility. The diagram below shows some of the factors that need to be considered. The dimensions cited can be tailored to your individual needs, which are often determined by the type and brand of computer. Adjustability is important, especially if the workstation will be used by more than one person or the equipment may be upgraded or expanded.

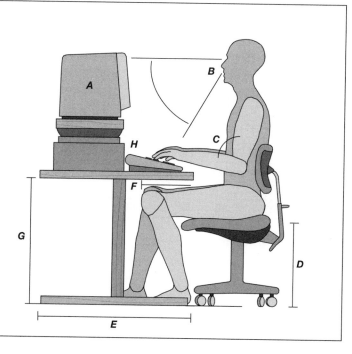

A. Monitor height, adjustable in 5" range
B. Angle of vision from keyboard to top of monitor should not exceed 60°
C. Angle formed by upper and lower arm should be between 70° and 135°
D. Adjustable seat height 16" - 20"
E. Work surface at least 20" wide and deep
F. Minimum knee clearance 12" - 15"
G. Knee space height 20" - 26"
H. Keyboard height 23" - 28"

Data from American National Standard for Human Factors Engineering of Visual Display Terminal Workstations (ANSI/HFS 100-1988), 1988. Santa Monica, CA: Human Factors and Ergonomics Society.

BOOKSHELVES

The size and strength of shelves are two critical factors in bookcase design. Standard dimensions for shelving are helpful, but they leave a lot of room for latitude. The depth of the shelves can range from 10 to 14 inches. The height of the bookcase should not be less than 36 inches, and can be as high as you want. Shelf length, or span, can normally fall anywhere between 16 and 40 inches, while the vertical distance between shelves should be in the 8- to 14-inch range.

Given these guidelines and the information in the tables below and on page 9, you can make some decisions about shelf span, thickness, and material. First, you need to estimate the weight of the books that the shelves will support. You can do this using a bathroom scale, but as a rough guide, paperbacks generally weigh about 30 to 35 pounds per cubic foot, while hardcover books may weigh up to 60 pounds per cubic foot. So, 1 linear foot of hardcover books with a cover size of 7 x 10 inches could weigh as much as 30 pounds. Depending on the span, shelves should only sag by a certain amount, as listed in the second column in the tables. The longer the span, the greater the allowable sag. The material you use is also crucial. Hardwoods are generally a little stronger than softwoods, and solid wood shelves can support much heavier loads than either plywood or particleboard of equal span and thickness. For example, a ½-inch plywood shelf with a 24-inch span will support 80 pounds per square foot (PSF), while a shelf of the same size made of black cherry can hold 137 PSF. Once you know the approximate weight of your books in pounds per square foot (PSF) of shelf surface, you can choose the right combination of material, thickness, and span that will support at least that weight.

MAXIMUM LOADS FOR SHELVING: HARDWOOD	SPAN* (in inches)	MAXIMUM DEFLECTION (in inches)	HARDWOOD (BLACK CHERRY)		
			1/2"	3/4"	1"
			MAXIMUM LOAD (in PSF)		
	16	0.089	465	1575	3728
	20	0.111	237	804	1904
	24	0.133	137	465	1100
	28	0.156	86	294	696
	32	0.178	58	196	466
	36	0.200	40	138	326
	40	0.222	29	100	238

*Single span shelf

SOFTWOOD

SPAN* (in inches)	MAXIMUM DEFLECTION (in inches)	SOFTWOOD (EASTERN WHITE PINE)		
		1/2"	3/4"	1"
		MAXIMUM LOAD (in PSF)		
16	0.089	387	1311	3102
20	0.111	197	669	1584
24	0.133	114	387	915
28	0.156	72	245	579
32	0.178	48	163	387
36	0.200	33	114	272
40	0.222	24	83	198

*Single span shelf

PLYWOOD

Chart courtesy American Plywood Association

SPAN* (in inches)	MAXIMUM DEFLECTION (in inches)	PLYWOOD				
		3/8"	1/2"	5/8"	3/4"	1"
		MAXIMUM LOAD (in PSF)				
16	0.089	110	205	295	355	575
20	0.111	65	135	195	240	385
24	0.133	30	80	120	150	240
32	0.178	10	30	50	80	130
36	0.200	10	20	35	55	100
40	0.222	5	15	25	40	80

*Single span shelf

PARTICLEBOARD

Chart courtesy National Particleboard Association

SPAN* (in inches)	MAXIMUM DEFLECTION (in inches)	LAMINATE PARTICLEBOARD			
		1/2"	5/8"	3/4"	1"
		MAXIMUM LOAD (in PSF)			
16	0.089	110	190	300	570
20	0.111	55	95	150	325
24	0.133	30	55	85	185
28	0.156	15	30	50	115
32	0.178	10	20	35	75
36	0.200	7.5	12.5	20	50
40	0.222	—	7.5	15	35

*Single span shelf

BEDS

Some flexibility exists in bed design with respect to height off the floor—18 to 20 inches is ideal—but the width and length of beds are very much dictated by the standard sizes of box springs and mattresses. Traditionally, the "twin" bed accommodates a single individual and derives its name from the practice of furnishing a bedroom with two such beds. The "full" bed is the standard size for two individuals.

Queen- and king-sized beds have become much more popular in recent years, the result perhaps of higher standards of personal comfort and a gradual increase in the average height of adults. The chart at left provides standard dimensions for all four sizes of mattresses.

	TWIN	FULL	QUEEN	KING
Length	78"	75"	80"	80"
Width	39"	54"	60"	76"

DESIGNING BUNK BEDS

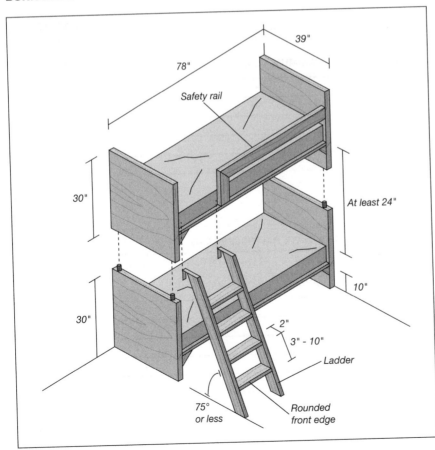

39"

78"

Safety rail

30"

30"

At least 24"

10"

2"

3" - 10"

Ladder

75"
or less

Rounded
front edge

Bunk beds are normally two twin beds, one stacked on top of the other. Their length and width should accommodate twin-bed mattresses. Head space for both bunks depends on the age and size of the children—24 to 30 inches is a good guideline. As illustrated at left, access must be provided to the upper bunk and should take the form of a sturdy and stable ladder, which hooks to the bed frame. A safety rail made from stock at least 3 inches wide is necessary on the upper bunk; the gap between the top of the mattress and the lower edge of the rail should be narrow enough to prevent the child from slipping beneath the rail. Designing the bunks so that they can be easily separated and used as individual twin beds is a handy option, but the fittings connecting them must be very sturdy.

CHESTS OF DRAWERS

The height, width, and depth of a chest of drawers have practical limitations, but as shown in the illustration below, only one of these, the height, relates directly to human anatomy. The top drawer of a chest of drawers should be below the user's eye level so that its contents can be seen without removing the drawer. Although most adult men would not be inconvenienced by a height of 60 inches, a practical limit of about 54 inches makes the chest of drawers more universally acceptable for both men and women.

If the width of the drawers exceeds about 24 inches, they should be equipped with two pulls; if the opening is greater than about 36 inches, it is generally best to divide it and install two drawers side-by-side. A depth of between 10 and 15 inches provides adequate drawer capacity for storing most articles typically kept in a chest of drawers. These dimensions are not absolute, but be careful about exceeding them. The larger the drawer, the more weight it can contain. This not only makes the drawer more difficult to open and close, it also strains the structure of the chest when fully extended.

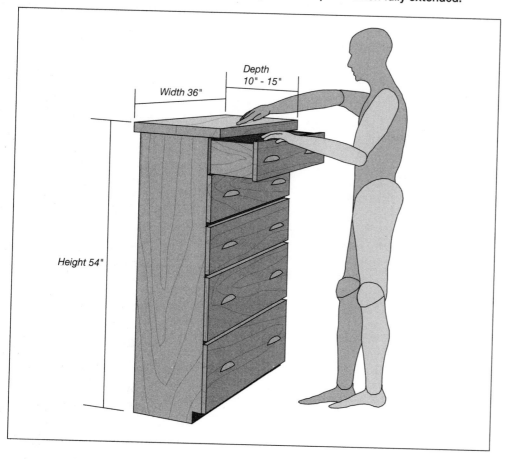

Depth 10" - 15"

Width 36"

Height 54"

KITCHEN CABINETS

KITCHEN CABINETS: STANDARD DIMENSIONS

Kitchen cabinets are a type of stand-up workstation. Today, most of these units are prefabricated at factories and shipped to the building site. To simplify installation, the units are modular and can be ordered in various lengths, such as 2, 4, and 6 feet, and then joined to create various combinations. Custom cabinets and counters for individuals with handicaps or who are remodeling older homes can be ordered at a premium price.

If you are building and installing your own counter and cabinets, refer to the illustration at left for basic standard dimensions. The depth of the base cabinet is typically 24 inches and the depth of the upper cabinets is 12 inches. The upper cabinets will accept 10-inch-diameter dinner plates, while larger pots and pans fit comfortably in the lower units. The height from floor to countertop is 36 inches; a 3-inch-deep and 4-inch-high notch, known as a toe kick, should be installed along the bottom front edge so the user can stand close to the counter. Countertops may be ordered flat or contoured, with built-in splash backs, and they average 25 to 26 inches deep. Since the upper cabinets are separate units, you have some flexibility as to the clearance between the top of the counter and the bottom of the upper cabinets. A distance of 16 to 18 inches allows ample room for most appliances without putting the cabinets too high to reach. The area over the stove and sinks is normally provided with lighting to enhance visibility.

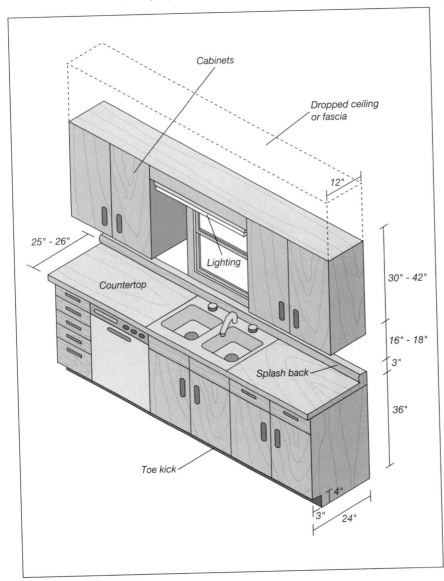

Cabinets

Dropped ceiling or fascia

12"

25" - 26"

Countertop

Lighting

30" - 42"

16" - 18"

3"

Splash back

36"

Toe kick

4"

3"   24"

DESIGN TOOLS

One of the most rewarding parts of woodworking is furniture design. Cultivating this skill frees you from relying on someone else's plans, and expands the possibilities of the craft toward truly creative achievements. Unfortunately, many woodworkers view the design process as an art form requiring rare and special talent. This is not the case. While mechanical drawing does require some perceptual ability, you do not need the hand-eye skills of a brush-and-canvas artist to get the job done. The goal is simply to convey the shape and structure of an object so that its dimensions and parts can be understood and then built. The illustrations below show the basic tools you need to get started.

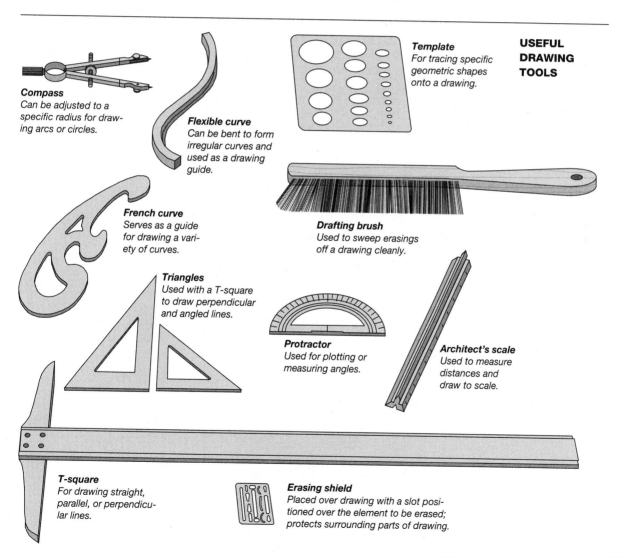

USEFUL DRAWING TOOLS

Compass
Can be adjusted to a specific radius for drawing arcs or circles.

Flexible curve
Can be bent to form irregular curves and used as a drawing guide.

Template
For tracing specific geometric shapes onto a drawing.

French curve
Serves as a guide for drawing a variety of curves.

Drafting brush
Used to sweep erasings off a drawing cleanly.

Triangles
Used with a T-square to draw perpendicular and angled lines.

Protractor
Used for plotting or measuring angles.

Architect's scale
Used to measure distances and draw to scale.

T-square
For drawing straight, parallel, or perpendicular lines.

Erasing shield
Placed over drawing with a slot positioned over the element to be erased; protects surrounding parts of drawing.

DESIGN TOOLS

USING A PANTOGRAPH TO ENLARGE A PATTERN

Provided the difference in scale is not too great, you can enlarge a drawing with a pantograph. The pantograph is a mechanically simple device that requires little experience to use properly. The results, however, are amazingly accurate. As shown below, the pantograph is an interlocked grid of four flat bars. The bottom end of the first bar is attached to a fixed pivot while the joint connecting the second and third bars features a tracing pin which follows the outline of the original drawing. The bottom of the fourth bar holds a graphite marker that reproduces the drawing. By adjusting the pivot points connecting the bars, the pantograph can be used to either enlarge or reduce the original. Most commercial models provide adjustments for up to a 1:10 enlargement or a 10:1 reduction.

To use a pantograph, set the pivot points to the desired scale and place the tracing pin at a point on the original drawing. As you trace along the lines of the original drawing with the tracing pin, the graphite marker at the end of the fourth bar reproduces the drawing at the preset scale.

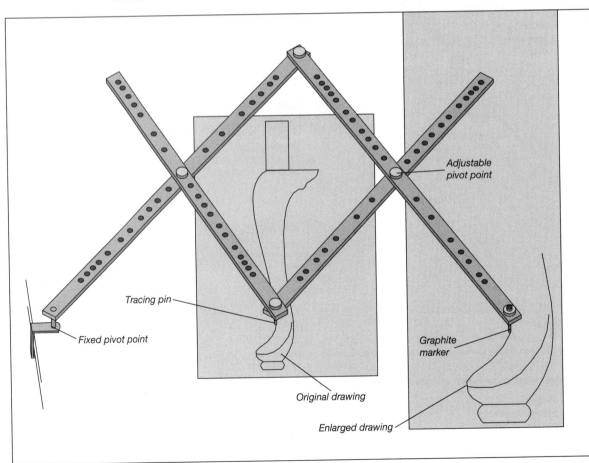

Adjustable pivot point

Tracing pin

Fixed pivot point

Original drawing

Graphite marker

Enlarged drawing

DESIGNING FURNITURE

One of the cornerstones of this chapter is that design is heavily influenced by the intended purpose of a piece of furniture. The dimensions of various kinds of furniture, for example, depend on their need to interact with the human form. However, form does not slavishly follow function. The proportions of a well-designed piece should also be pleasing to the eye. This aspect of design is totally discretionary, but there are some time-honored principles that generally result in attractive and graceful proportions.

Mathematical relationships are often incorporated as design elements. Their main advantage over haphazard dimensions is that these relationships lend a certain logic to the appearance of furniture. At either the conscious or subliminal level, observers sense at first glance that the elements of the piece were put together in an orderly and balanced fashion.

Among these relationships is the so-called Golden Mean, which dates back to ancient Greece. The Golden Mean is a proportioning technique achieved by bisecting a line so that the relationship between the length of its smaller segment and its larger segment is the same as the relationship between the larger segment and the original line. In the example below, the relationship between BC and AB is the same as the one between AB and AC:

```
A               B       C
├───────────────┼───────┤
```

Reduced to a ratio, the Golden Mean is 1:1.6. It is illustrated in practice in the drawing of a table below. The turning on the legs is located so that the leg section below the turning is 1.6 times longer than the section above. Similarly, the tabletop is 1.6 times longer than the height of the table. This forms what is called a Golden Rectangle.

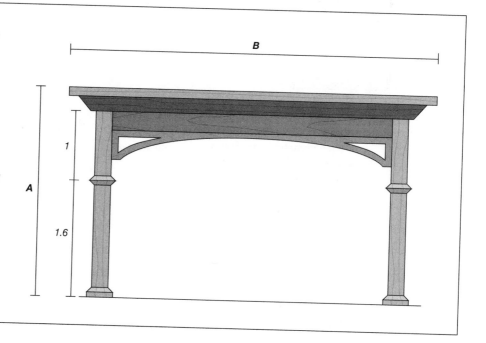

Based on the Golden Mean, the top part of the table leg could be about 12 inches long and the lower leg portion a little over 19 inches long.

The ratio between the height of the table (A) and the length of the tabletop (B) is 1:1.6, forming a Golden Rectangle.

DESIGNING FURNITURE

DESIGN PRINCIPLES: GEOMETRIC, ARITHMETIC, AND HARMONIC PROGRESSION

Geometric progression is another system of mathematical relationships often used in designing furniture. The basic principle is that one part of a piece relates to a second part in the same ratio that the second relates to the third, and so on. A typical geometric progression—2, 4, 8, 16—is illustrated in the drawing of a table 1. In this example, each element after the first is twice as long as the preceding one.

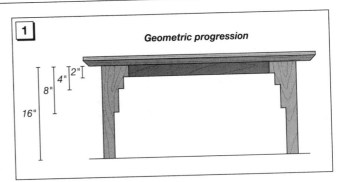

1 | Geometric progression

top's length gives you the height of the chest (39 inches). Both types of progression are useful ways of proportioning the various elements of a piece. Arithmetic progression also works well in modular furniture, since the size increase between parts is constant.

Harmonic progression is similar, except that the recip-rocals of the various dimensions in a piece form an arithmetic progression. (The reciprocal of a number equals 1 divided by the number.) Harmonic progression is illustrated in drawing 3. This principle is worth trying when you want the sizing of various parts or the spacing between them to decrease gradually.

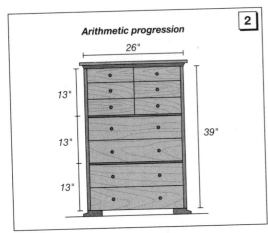

2 | Arithmetic progression

An arithmetic progression, on the other hand, is created by increasing the dimensions of the elements in a piece by a constant amount. In the drawing of the chest of drawers 2, for example, the drawer segments are each 13 inches high. The length of the top (26 inches) is obtained by adding 13 to this base amount. Adding 13 to the

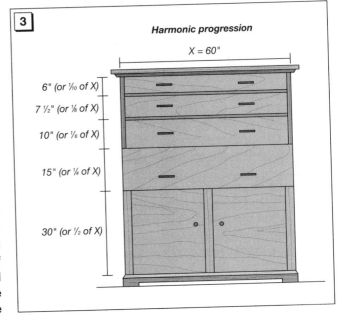

3 | Harmonic progression

There are several ways to draw a piece of furniture. Three common methods are shown in the illustration below; each has its own strengths and weaknesses. The isometric technique enables you to render all three dimensions of an object in a single drawing. Portrayal of the object centers on one corner; on the table shown, this is the central corner in the foreground. The three planes are then drawn 120 degrees apart. Since all the lines in the same plane are parallel, dimensions are to scale. This is the main advantage of the isometric approach, but isometric drawings often look distorted.

With the perspective technique, the image of the object is much the same as the eye would see it in its three-dimensional form. Again, the portrayal of the object centers on a corner, but the dimensions to the left and right of the corner recede so that more distant parts of the piece appear smaller in scale.

The third technique—orthographic drawing—is the two-dimensional technique used in most blueprints and engineering plans. No attempt is made to portray the depth of the object in a single drawing. Instead, two or more individual drawings, each illustrating the object from a dif-

ferent direction, are used to accurately convey all dimensions to scale. To produce an orthographic drawing, start by drawing the front view. Use vertical and horizontal extension lines to develop the top and side views. To show the relationship between the top and side views, draw a deflection line at a 45 degrees angle between the two. Then extend lines at 90 degrees from key elements of the top view to the deflection line.

Drop these lines down at 90 degrees to locate the corresponding elements in the side view. While not as visually expressive as perspective drawings, orthographic drawings are very useful because they are easy to translate into cutting patterns.

If you own a computer you can buy a software program that converts an object's dimensions into a three-dimensional rendering from any angle.

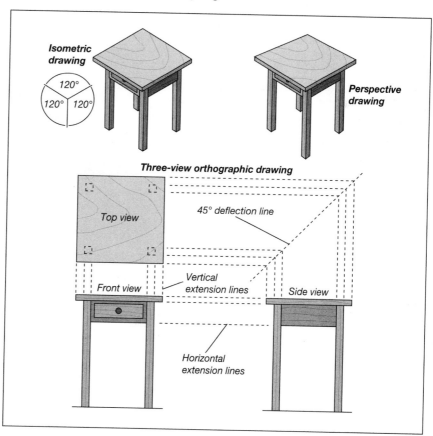

Isometric drawing

120°
120° 120°

Perspective drawing

Three-view orthographic drawing

Top view

45° deflection line

Vertical extension lines

Front view

Side view

Horizontal extension lines

READING FURNITURE PLANS

Reading blueprints and plans is not difficult, but you must be able to look at several separate views of an object and imagine its three-dimensional form and true scale. You also need to understand the standard drafting symbols and conventions commonly used on blueprints and plans. These symbols are a form of shorthand that keep a drawing from becoming cluttered with descriptive text. Each notation and symbol has a specific meaning. For example, a dotted line indicates details within an object that would ordinarily be hidden from view when looking at the object from the direction illustrated in the drawing. Some of the more commonly used notations and symbols are shown below.

INTERPRETING SYMBOLS

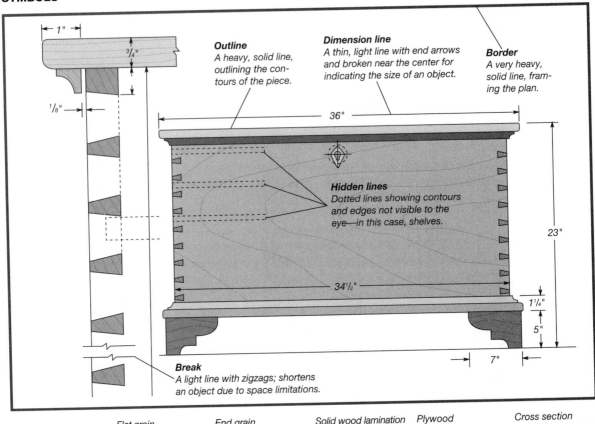

Outline
A heavy, solid line, outlining the contours of the piece.

Dimension line
A thin, light line with end arrows and broken near the center for indicating the size of an object.

Border
A very heavy, solid line, framing the plan.

Hidden lines
Dotted lines showing contours and edges not visible to the eye—in this case, shelves.

Break
A light line with zigzags; shortens an object due to space limitations.

Flat grain   End grain   Solid wood lamination   Plywood   Cross section

Illustrations of symbols courtesy Lee Valley Tools Ltd.

SHOP GEOMETRY

The principles of geometry used in woodworking are seldom more complicated than what is taught in the typical high school geometry class. The problem is that unless you go on to pursue a career in engineering or architecture, you may forget these more technical skills. It is worth taking a few minutes to brush up on some of the basic principles. Some of the more useful ones are shown below and on the following page.

One of the handiest drafting tools for putting geometry into practice in the shop is the compass. Drawing circles is an obvious application, but the compass has many other uses. For example, rounding corners is a problem often encountered in woodworking. A few strokes with a compass is all it takes to define your cutting line. A couple of examples are shown below and on the folling page.

ROUNDING CORNERS

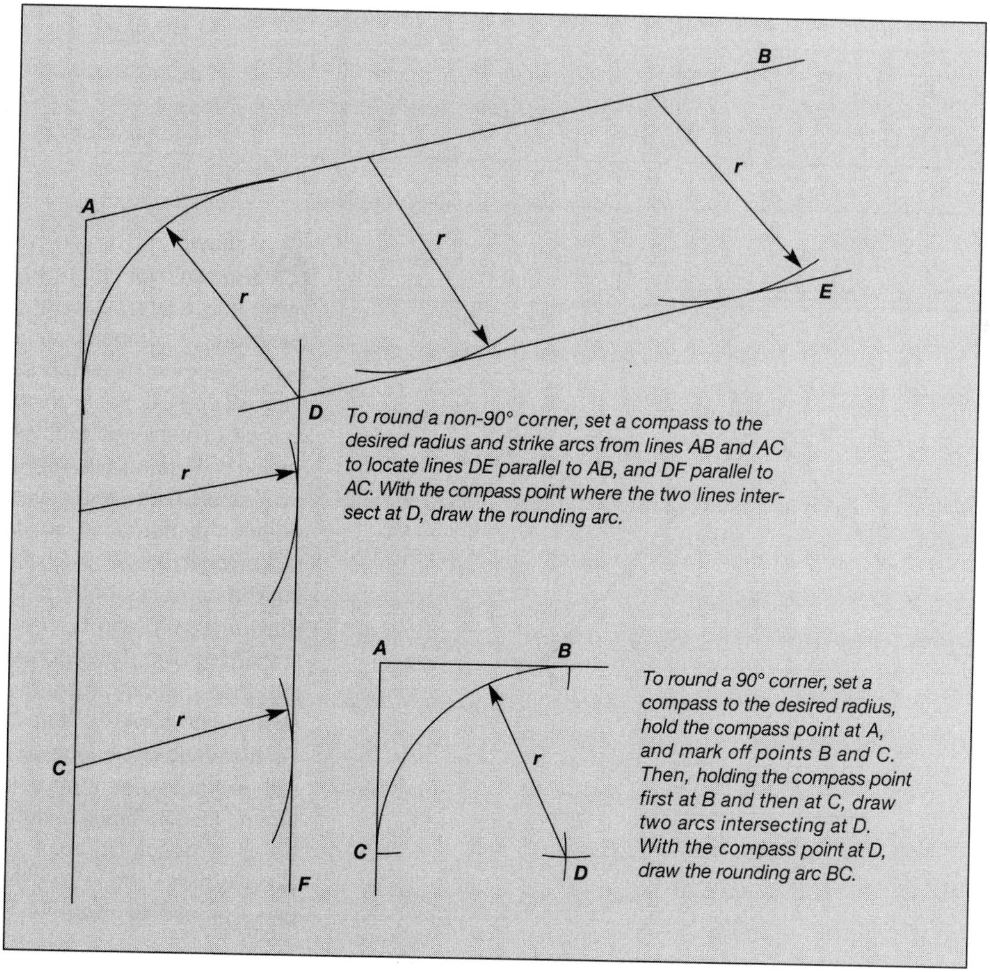

To round a non-90° corner, set a compass to the desired radius and strike arcs from lines AB and AC to locate lines DE parallel to AB, and DF parallel to AC. With the compass point where the two lines intersect at D, draw the rounding arc.

To round a 90° corner, set a compass to the desired radius, hold the compass point at A, and mark off points B and C. Then, holding the compass point first at B and then at C, draw two arcs intersecting at D. With the compass point at D, draw the rounding arc BC.

SHOP GEOMETRY

MORE USES FOR THE COMPASS

To draw a line at a right angle to a line **1**, set a compass to a convenient radius, hold the compass point at A, and mark off points B and C. Then, holding the compass point first at B and then at C, draw two arcs intersecting at D. To find the midpoint of a line **2**, hold the compass point first at B and then at C to draw arcs intersecting at D and E. Line DE will divide line BC at its center, point A. To bisect an angle **3**, mark off points B and C from A. Then, holding the compass point first at B and then at C, draw two arcs intersecting at D. Line AD will bisect angle BAC.

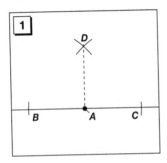

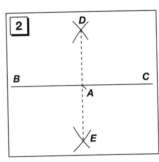

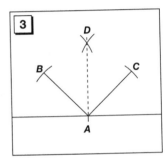

DRAWING AN OVAL

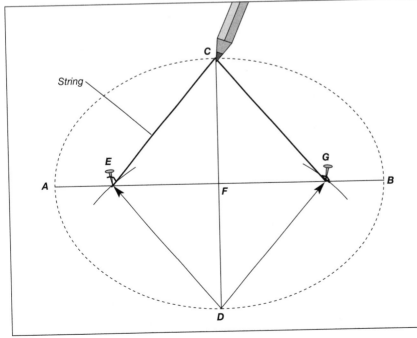

As shown at left, you can draw an oval of any size using only a length of string, two brads, a compass, and a pencil. Draw two perpendicular lines AB and CD that intersect at their centers—point F. AB should be the long axis of your oval, and CD the short axis. Adjust the compass so its radius equals line AF and, holding the compass point at D, draw arcs at E and G. Drive brads into points E and G, leaving their heads protruding about ¼ inch above the surface. Tie the string into a loop so it will be tight when stretched around the two brads and the tip of a pencil at point C. Keeping the loop taut, draw the pencil around the oval.

FURNITURE STYLES

The American furniture tradition, like American culture itself, is a blend of outside influences so thoroughly mixed as to be identifiable in its own right. We have borrowed a great deal from others, but we have also contributed innovations that are uniquely American. Historians and museum curators are often able to trace individual pieces to their place of origin and date the time of manufacture with surprising accuracy by examining structural elements or minor decorative details.

To these specialists, there are meaningful differences between Chippendale pieces produced in Philadelphia versus Newport or Boston—and indeed there are. But for identifying broad trends in furniture styles, it is important to be able to spot the design elements that differentiate, for example, a style such as Chippendale from the Queen Anne that preceded it or the Hepplewhite that followed. In this chapter, we will survey almost four centuries of cabinetmaking progress, concentrating on the major style transitions, where they originated, and how they contributed to the American tradition.

Although the periods examined are presented in their approximate chronological order, styles come and go and return again as "revivals" or lend subtle decorative elements to subsequent styles that are otherwise substantially different. For example, French provincial and Chippendale share a common heritage, inspired by the courtly rococo style of Bourbon France, while Hepplewhite and Sheraton represent interpretations of the neoclassical movement. In addition, some styles have remained popular while never attaining dominance over other styles. American country furniture is a good example of this phenomenon; its comfortable informality has always enjoyed a following.

Perhaps the purest and only truly American style is Shaker. Its utter lack of decoration and extreme utility set it apart. Although often considered pared-down Sheraton, it is indebted to no prior tradition and spawned no progeny. The Shaker style can be reproduced, but it cannot be embellished and still be Shaker. Aside from this one immutable style, however, the design concepts presented in this chapter are intended to stimulate creativity and experimentation. Knowing that even the great masters borrowed freely from each other reminds us that, when it comes to style, there are no absolute rules about what can and cannot be done.

17TH CENTURY

The American furniture tradition began with the founding of the Jamestown Colony in 1607 and the arrival of the Pilgrims in 1620. For most of the 17th Century, what little furniture existed in the struggling new settlements consisted of two quite different types: The few precious pieces the colonists had brought with them from England and the more rustic but functional items they were able to fashion themselves. From a style perspective, the latter are perhaps best characterized as early examples of American Country furniture, although it is sometimes referred to as "Pilgrim." Early on, these primitive pieces were made by carpenters pressed into finer work than their skills and training warranted. Surviving examples include plank-topped trestle tables, pine settles, benches, stools, and pewter cupboards.

In stark contrast to these primitive pieces, the more fortunate early colonists might also have had a prized chair, chest, or table from the Old World. These professionally made pieces were predominately of the Jacobean style, named after the early 17th-Century ruler of Great Britain, James I. At that time, Italian fashions were in vogue and the Jacobean style had a Mediterranean look characterized by heavy, rectangular construction; plentiful bracing in the form of spindles and stretchers; dark finishes; and ornate carvings. Made almost exclusively of oak, Jacobean furniture

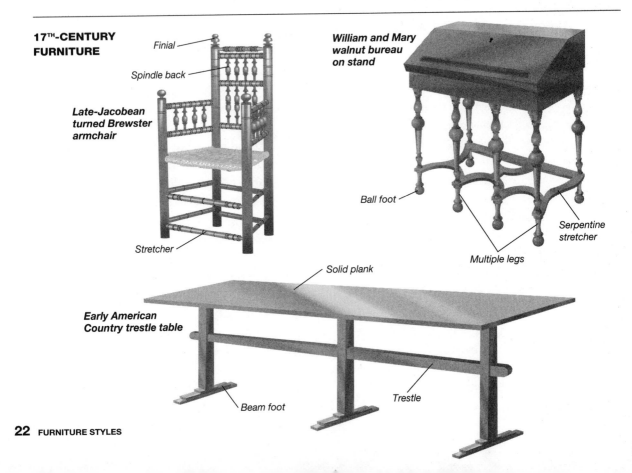

17TH-CENTURY FURNITURE

Finial

Spindle back

Late-Jacobean turned Brewster armchair

Stretcher

William and Mary walnut bureau on stand

Ball foot

Serpentine stretcher

Multiple legs

Solid plank

Early American Country trestle table

Beam foot

Trestle

generally had a rigid quality both in terms of appearance and lack of comfort. Like the Tudor style that preceded it, Jacobean designs and methods of construction were decidedly medieval in comparison to the rapid advancements achieved by cabinetmakers in the following century. Relatively easy to execute, the simple, large dovetail shown below is typical of 17th-Century furniture.

The transition toward finer, more graceful furniture began in England during the reign of William and Mary (1689-1702). During this period, religious persecution on the continent had caused many Dutch and French craftsmen to emigrate to England, bringing with them new designs and decorative treat-ments. The resulting William and Mary style was characterized by high-backed chairs, scrolled aprons, serpentine stretchers, and chest-on-frame construction. Straight legs with inverted cup turnings and ball- or bun-shaped feet were commonly used on dressers, tables, and desks, with the larger pieces often supported by six legs.

Typical hardware consisted of inconspicuous teardrop-shaped pulls with small, round, back plates. Oak remained a popular cabinetwood, but some of the finer pieces were made of walnut. Although colonial cabinetmakers adopted these new decorative elements, most American pieces in the William and Mary style actually date from the early 18th Century.

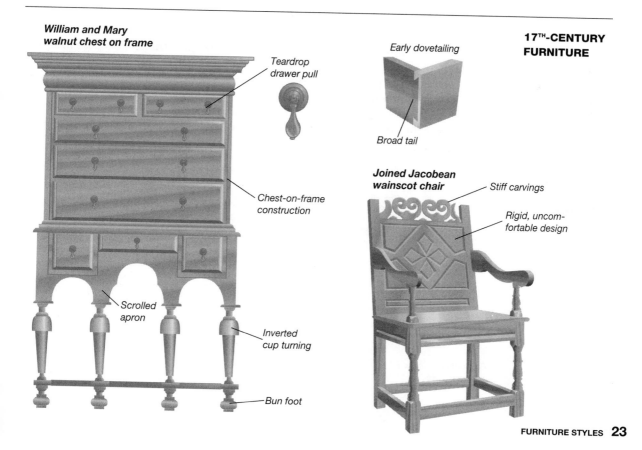

William and Mary walnut chest on frame

Teardrop drawer pull

Chest-on-frame construction

Scrolled apron

Inverted cup turning

Bun foot

Early dovetailing

Broad tail

17ᵀᴴ-CENTURY FURNITURE

Joined Jacobean wainscot chair

Stiff carvings

Rigid, uncomfortable design

QUEEN ANNE

The style named for Queen Anne, sovereign of England from 1702 to 1714, became popular in the American colonies shortly after her reign. Compared to the heavy, box-like designs of the 17th Century, Queen Anne style furniture appeared more graceful and refined, exemplified in the flowing lines of one of its defining elements—the cabriole leg.

The popularity of Queen Anne furniture grew with an increasing sophistication in America. By 1720, after a century of struggle to tame the wilderness, the eastern seaboard of North America was becoming more civilized. The plantation owners of the South and the wealthier merchants of the North could afford larger homes and more elegant furniture, both for personal comfort and for entertaining. The Queen Anne style met these demands. Upholstered furniture appears at this time in the form of easy chairs, settees, and side chairs with padded slip seats. Reflecting a growing interest in entertaining in 18th-Century America, Queen Anne accent pieces included tea and card tables, dining tables, and corner chairs.

Queen Anne furniture varied from region to region in America. There are marked differences in the construction of pieces crafted in New England compared to those built in New York or Philadelphia, but the similarities are sufficient to make up a reasonably well-defined style. The primary wood used in most Queen Anne pieces is walnut; the darker color of the native black walnut helps to distinguish American Queen Anne pieces from their European counterparts. Other features to look for are cabriole legs with simple pad feet and single-piece, vase-shaped splats in chair backs that were often bent to fit the curvature of the spine. S-shaped curves adorn the aprons and pediments with urn-and-flame finials and ogee-molded edges for added decoration. The simple teardrop pulls of the William and Mary style gave way to larger brass back plates with bails. Although intricate carving is a hallmark of the later Chippendale period, shell carvings and the occasional claw-and-ball foot are seen on some of the more elaborate Queen Anne pieces, which are sometimes referred to as "Georgian." Many of these elements survive in the formal, high-quality furniture manufactured today.

QUEEN ANNE FURNITURE

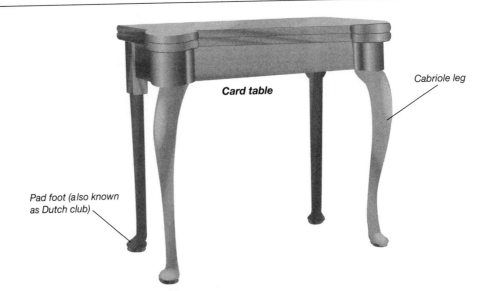

Card table

Cabriole leg

Pad foot (also known as Dutch club)

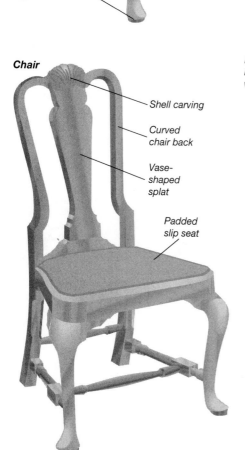

Corner chair

Padded slip seat

Pad foot

Tall chest

Large brass back plate with bail

Chair

Shell carving

Curved chair back

Vase-shaped splat

Padded slip seat

FRENCH PROVINCIAL

At first glance, French Provincial furniture looks very much like Chippendale (*page 28*). Although less bulky and less ornately carved, it possesses the same flowing curves, cabriole legs, and floral motifs. Both styles borrowed elements from the rococo designs popular in France during the reign of Louis XV. The French Provincial style is a more direct descendant of French Rococo and came into being as cabinetmakers in rural France copied the fashionable styles then being commissioned by the monarchy. Less ornate and less costly to make, this style became the furniture of the French middle class who migrated to French colonies in the New World. A very fluid and curved style, rococo is generally characterized by vegetative decoration like leaves and vines.

The role of French Provincial in the American furniture tradition is basically that of a regional style that became popular in the Deep South as French settlements expanded up the Mississippi River from New Orleans.

Although European French Provincial furniture was usually made of walnut or chestnut, American examples were almost always built of pecan, a very hard, light, tan-colored species of hickory that was plentiful in the lower Mississippi valley. Whether the extreme density of pecan made it difficult to carve, or the early French settlers simply preferred less decoration, American examples of this style tend to be less ornate than their Old World counterparts, as shown in the pieces illustrated. Even in its simplified form, a complete dining room or bedroom set of French Provincial furniture is impressive.

The style seems to lend itself well both to delicate tables and chairs and also larger storage pieces such as armoires, dressers, and china cupboards. A dull, rubbed oil finish is traditional and very attractive on pecan, but the style has also experienced periods of revival when it was more fashionable to paint it a translucent creamy white with gold highlights and striping.

FRENCH PROVINCIAL FURNITURE

Table

Integrated apron

Delicate cabriole leg

Armchair

Raised
bead
edging

Armoire

Scrolled top

Scroll foot

Small settee

Floral motif

CHIPPENDALE

Traditionally, furniture styles are associated with the monarch who ruled when the style was first popularized. Keeping to that convention, several styles of 18th-Century English furniture might well have become known as Georgian, in honor of George I through George III (1714-1820). But the work of three great cabinetmakers so dominated the styles of that period that most historians give them special recognition. The first of these masters was Thomas Chippendale (1718-1779), both a fine cabinetmaker and an outstanding carver. Furniture produced in his shop gained a following among London's aristocracy, and with the publication in 1754 of his design book, *The Gentlemen and Cabinet-Maker's Director*, Chippendale became the most imitated craftsman of his time.

Chippendale borrowed heavily from the Queen Anne, or "Georgian," style and blended in French rococo elements such as shell carvings, intricate fretwork, piecrust edging, and beautifully flowing curves. Cabriole legs with shell or floral carvings at the knees and claw-and-ball feet are typical of his basic design. To please his upper-class clientele, Chippendale also dabbled in radically different styles. The expansion of British trade with the Orient and a growing taste in England for tea, porcelain, and art from the Far East led

CHIPPENDALE FURNITURE

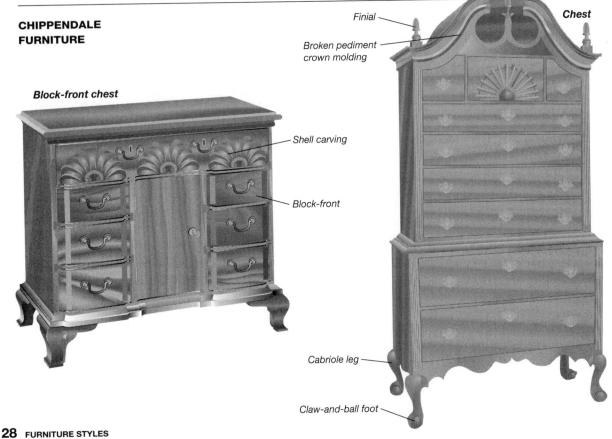

Block-front chest

Finial

Broken pediment crown molding

Chest

Shell carving

Block-front

Cabriole leg

Claw-and-ball foot

to the development of Chinese Chippendale furniture. A total departure from his rococo style, Chinese Chippendale tea tables and chairs exhibit a clean, rectangular look with light, geometric fretwork. To achieve delicate detail without sacrificing strength, fretted panels and chair splats were glued up in what was essentially the forerunner of plywood, using a horizontally grained core stock sandwiched between vertically grained front and back veneers.

As a master carver, Chippendale appreciated mahogany, one of the world's best carving woods. The colonization of Jamaica and Honduras made this New World timber readily available in London by Chippendale's

time and most English furniture of that period was made of mahogany. In North America, cherry was often used as a less expensive substitute. Chippendale's design book immediately popularized his styles in the colonies and they dominated the American furniture scene from about 1755 until the American Revolution. In fact, some of the finest examples of Chippendale furniture are of American origin. Well-known colonial masters like Rhode Island's Job Townsend and John Goddard augmented the style with innovations such as the block-front on dressers and desks. A block-front is characterized by drawer fronts that are raised, often by means of add-on blocks.

CHIPPENDALE FURNITURE

Chinese Chippendale chair

Geometric
fretwork

Fall-front desk

HEPPLEWHITE

Following Chippendale, the second of England's trio of great 18th-Century cabinetmakers was George Hepplewhite. Hepplewhite borrowed very little from Chippendale. Instead, his style was heavily influenced by the architect Robert Adam, who in turn was inspired by the ruins of ancient Greece and Rome. Excavations of sites such as Herculaneum and Pompeii during the latter half of the 18th Century kindled an interest in classical motifs, and the resulting neoclassical movement in furniture design represented a sharp departure from the rococo style of Chippendale.

The new look that Hepplewhite helped to establish was a light and graceful blend of straight lines and gentle curves. Typical Hepplewhite style elements included straight, square, and tapered legs ending in spade-shaped feet. Chair backs were often oval or shield-shaped and not connected to the center of the back seat frame. Relief carvings and marquetry provided decoration without dominating the clean lines of the structural parts. Both inlays and painted surfaces were

**HEPPLEWHITE
FURNITURE**

Wardrobe

Curved apron

Oval brass pull
(common on Hepplewhite carcases)

Chair

Shield back

Decorative tacking

Carving

sometimes employed using rosettes, urns, and other classical designs.

Proud of the fact that the Prince of Wales was one of his distinguished patrons, Hepplewhite incorporated the three feather plumes of the Welsh coat-of-arms in some of his work. On carcase furniture, the typical hardware consisted of brass bails with simple oval back plates. The upholstery used in seat covers was stretched down to conceal the seat frame and anchored with closely spaced decorative tacks. The overall appearance of the Hepplewhite style is one of extreme delicacy.

Unfortunately, his furniture was also very fragile. There are no surviving pieces that can be certainly identified as having been made in his shop.

Like Chippendale, Hepplewhite's enduring fame is in large part due to the fact that his designs were eventually published. Although Hepplewhite died in 1786, his wife, Alice, carried on the business. Approximately 300 of his works were published over a period of years, enabling his designs to influence the development of neoclassical furniture well into the 19th Century.

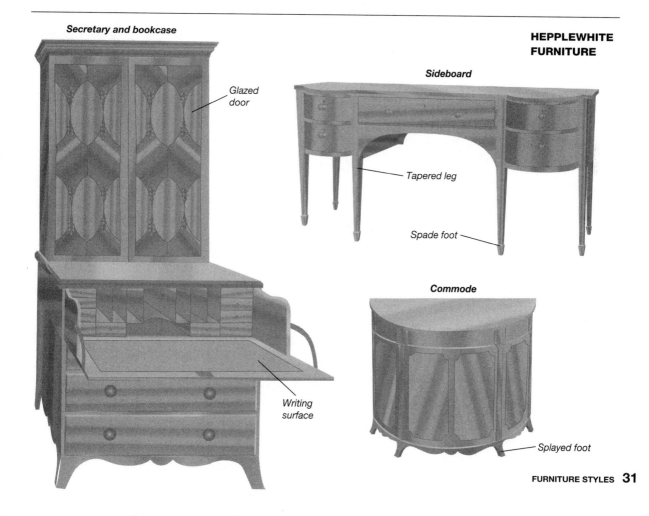

Secretary and bookcase

Glazed door

Writing surface

HEPPLEWHITE FURNITURE

Sideboard

Tapered leg

Spade foot

Commode

Splayed foot

SHERATON

The last of the great Georgian furniture designers, Thomas Sheraton (1751-1806), came to London in 1790, four years after Hepplewhite's death. There is no evidence that Sheraton ever opened a shop of his own, but he was an accomplished draftsman with impressive conceptual skills. By 1794 he had published his *Cabinet-Maker and Upholsterer's Drawing Book,* which contained some 100 illustrations. Although a creative designer in his own right, it is obvious that Sheraton borrowed heavily from the Hepplewhite style. In fact, the two are sometimes difficult to tell apart.

Among the differences, Sheraton chairs tend to have rectangular backs, occasionally with armrests sloping down toward the front. In most instances, at least a portion of the seat frame is exposed below the fabric. Like Hepplewhite, Sheraton employed decorative elements of classical origin such as urns, swags, fans, and ornamental disks; among his favorites was the lyre. Intricate inlays using vividly colored woods adorn many Sheraton pieces. Round, fluted legs were also commonly used and sometimes tied together with diagonal, X-shaped stretchers which lent

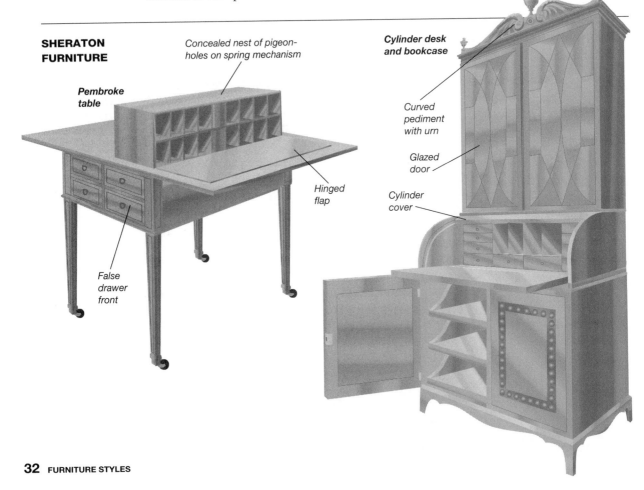

SHERATON FURNITURE

Concealed nest of pigeon-holes on spring mechanism

Pembroke table

Hinged flap

False drawer front

Cylinder desk and bookcase

Curved pediment with urn

Glazed door

Cylinder cover

considerable strength to what was otherwise an exceptionally delicate style.

What set Sheraton apart, however, was not his graceful interpretation of the neoclassical style, but rather his remarkable ingenuity in introducing practical and often very clever mechanical elements into his designs. The London of his time was an overcrowded place and furniture had to occupy limited living space. Sheraton answered this need with designs that were not only attractive, but also compact and functional. His Pembroke tables employed springs and weights to raise and lower a box of pigeon-holes, while Sheraton writing tables and secretary desks made efficient use of drawers and hidden compartments.

Sheraton is also credited with having popularized the concept of twin beds and even his accent pieces, such as small tables and shaving mirrors, were created both to lend beauty to the decor and perform an important function. Virtually all surviving examples of Sheraton-style furniture were built by other craftsmen. We therefore have no way of measuring his skills as a cabinetmaker, but there is no doubt that his designs were ingenious—and beautiful.

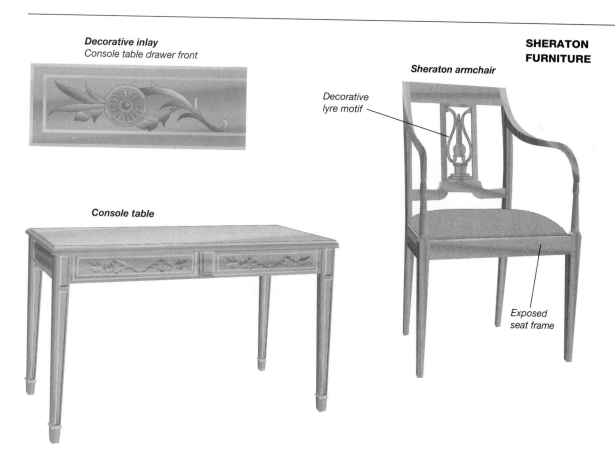

Decorative inlay
Console table drawer front

SHERATON FURNITURE

Sheraton armchair

Decorative lyre motif

Console table

Exposed seat frame

FEDERAL PERIOD

Prior to the American Revolution, colonial cabinetmakers catered to English styles, but the bitterness of that conflict led to the first truly American period in furniture design. It is usually referred to as the Federal style because it appeared in the 1790s while the former colonies were establishing their new federal government. The style could also be called "Federal/Empire" or "American Neoclassical." However it is termed, the style evolved slowly and lasted well into the 1840s. In fact, Federal furniture was a continuation of the neoclassical movement and its structural components differ very little from those of Hepplewhite and Sheraton. The difference is that American cabinetmakers were no longer intentionally trying to give their creations an English look.

French assistance in the American Revolution led to growing French influence in American designs. Elements of the French Directoire and Empire styles of the Napoleon-

**FEDERAL
PERIOD
FURNITURE**

Military motif

Dressing table

ic Era introduced military motifs such as spears, swords, flags, and ribbons into furniture inlays and carvings. These were, in turn, altered and Americanized with the symbols of the new nation including stars, stripes, and spread eagles. To the modern eye, Federal furniture can appear stiff and excessively patriotic, but a few masters of the time were able to translate the style with graceful results. Perhaps the best known of these was the New York cabinetmaker Duncan Phyfe (1768-1854), who also worked extensively in the Directoire style. Phyfe employed many of Sheraton's decorative elements such as reeding, fluting, shallow relief carvings, and the lyre. He also used brass-tipped legs, often cast to look like animal claws. Working almost exclusively in mahogany, Phyfe made the most of the wood's distinctive figure, complemented by well-executed inlays of satinwood and rosewood, while still maintaining lustrous, glass-smooth surfaces.

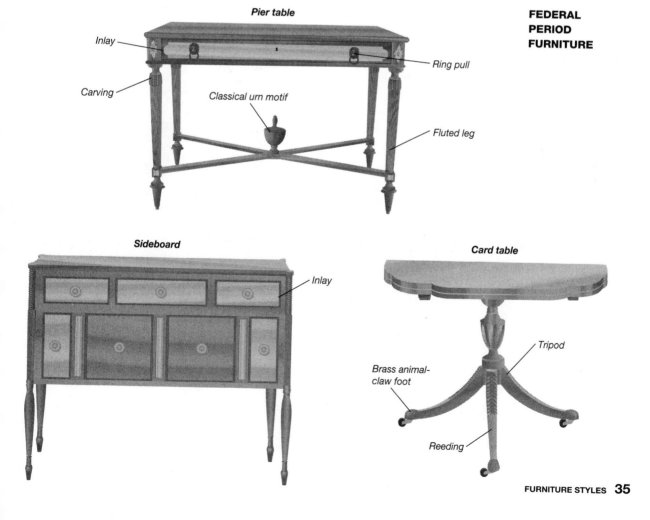

FEDERAL PERIOD FURNITURE

Pier table

Inlay

Carving

Classical urn motif

Ring pull

Fluted leg

Sideboard

Inlay

Card table

Tripod

Brass animal-claw foot

Reeding

AMERICAN COUNTRY

American Country furniture springs from the melting pot of American society. It incorporates such an incredible mix of styles from the 17th through the 19th Centuries that it has gained a certain individuality as a style in its own right. While furniture making became an apprenticed trade in the cities, settlers out on the frontier were obliged to furnish their homes almost exclusively with what they could make themselves. In fact, the one cohesive element in the American Country style is its amateurish innocence. While professional cabinetmakers back East were using mahogany, walnut, cherry, and maple, most frontier furniture makers worked with pine. This easily worked wood appealed to part-time craftsmen with limited tools and skills, but it also required design adaptations to give the furniture adequate strength. As a result, most American Country furniture has a heavy look, with thicker tabletops, wider framing, and stockier legs.

Because metal was precious on the frontier, hardware was used sparingly. This led to novel and charming wooden latches, leather hinges, and carved pulls. Even on the more prestigious pieces, locally forged wrought-iron hinges and pinned bails were substitut-

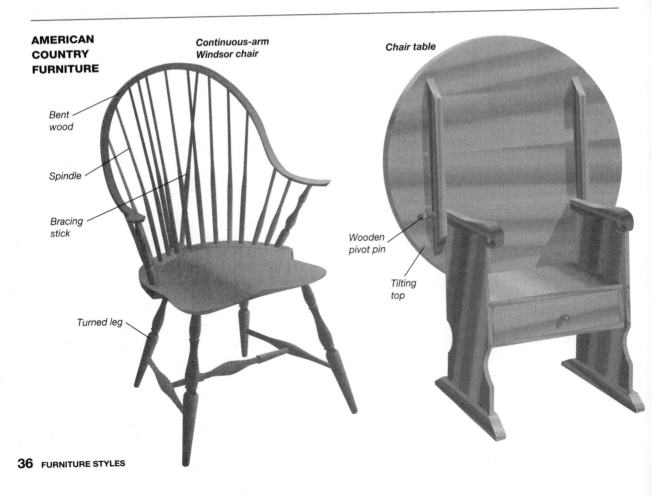

AMERICAN COUNTRY FURNITURE

Continuous-arm Windsor chair

Bent wood

Spindle

Bracing stick

Turned leg

Chair table

Wooden pivot pin

Tilting top

ed for the fine brass hardware seen on contemporary professional furniture. Because American Country furniture was produced over such a long period of time and by homesteaders with diverse cultural backgrounds, there is no continuity with respect to decorative motifs. In general, decoration consisted of simple moldings, scrolled aprons, and occasionally turned legs or spindles.

The Windsor Chair is often included in the American Country category because it fits so well with this informal style. However, it is neither American nor Country. Originating in 16th-Century England and later mass-produced in the colonies, Windsor chairs were portable enough to be taken along as the settlers moved West. They became one of the few professionally made furnishings commonly seen on the frontier.

In most cases, American Country furniture was originally painted in vivid colors such as soldier blue, Indian red, or various greens and yellows. So many surviving pieces have been stripped and varnished to reveal the natural, soft orange patina of pine that it is easy to forget how bright and cheerful this style of furniture was meant to be.

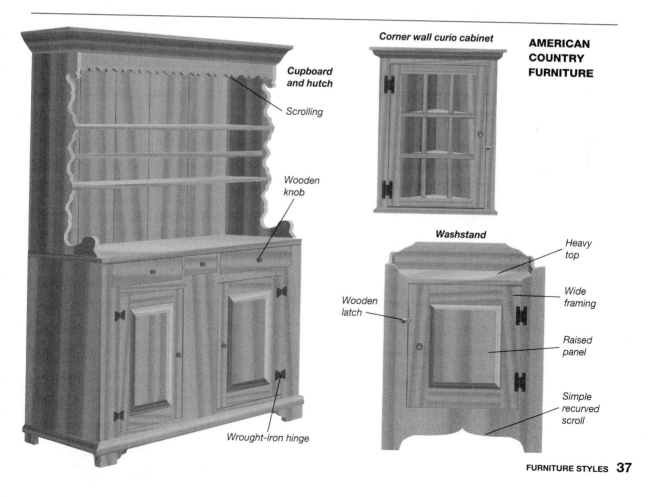

AMERICAN COUNTRY FURNITURE

Corner wall curio cabinet

Cupboard and hutch

Scrolling

Wooden knob

Wrought-iron hinge

Washstand

Heavy top

Wide framing

Wooden latch

Raised panel

Simple recurved scroll

SHAKER

K nown to her followers as "Mother Ann," an English mill worker named Ann Lee brought eight members of her religious sect to America in 1774. Formally called the United Society of Believers, the group first settled at Watervliet, New York. Because of the frenzied dancing performed at their prayer meetings, they became known as "Shaking Quakers," or Shakers, and the sect soon expanded to establish settlements throughout New England and the Midwest. The Shakers believed in celibacy, communal ownership of all property, and hard work in the service of God. Adornment of any kind was shunned and their furniture, initially made to supply their own settlements, was strictly austere and functional.

Credited with having invented circular saws and steel cut nails, the Shakers were industrious people, and once their own needs were met, they manufactured furniture for sale outside of their communities. Cane-seated ladderback chairs, candle sconces, and oval boxes were made in great quantity, but some of their finest pieces included clocks, desks, tables, and dressers. Although a few subtle

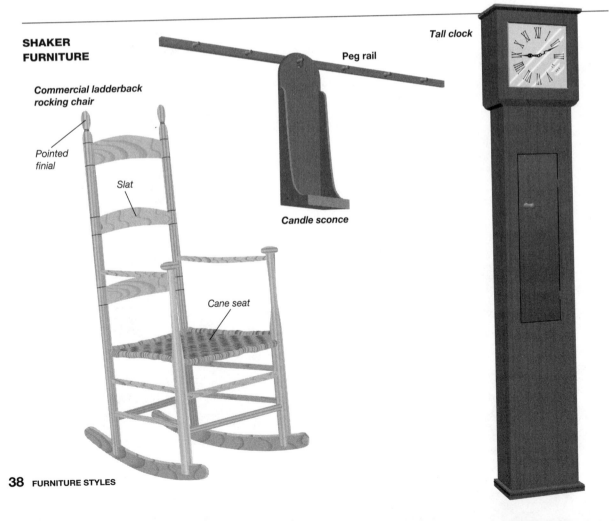

SHAKER FURNITURE

Commercial ladderback rocking chair

Pointed finial

Slat

Cane seat

Peg rail

Candle sconce

Tall clock

decorative elements such as ball finials and scrolled aprons crept into their commercial creations, for the most part every aspect of a Shaker design had a utilitarian purpose.

The Shakers' creed "That which has the highest use possesses the greatest beauty" is reflected in the furniture they built. Shaker pieces were most commonly made from pine, poplar, maple, and other woods with relatively modest figure; walnut and cherry were occasionally used. Imported timbers were avoided and even some plentiful domestic species with somewhat flamboyant figure such as ash and oak seem to have been used only when their great strength served a structural purpose. Metal hinges were sometimes used because of their rugged durability, but simple mushroom-shaped wooden knobs served as the standard "hardware." Although early Shaker doctrine dictated very regular designs, many later pieces are asymmetrical, with doors and drawers located off center and in unexpected places. Perhaps the enduring beauty of the Shaker style rests in the fact that its appearance was meant to be utterly unimportant.

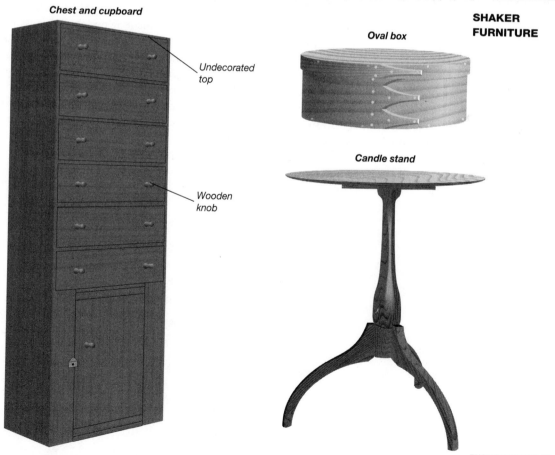

SHAKER FURNITURE

Chest and cupboard

Undecorated top

Wooden knob

Oval box

Candle stand

VICTORIAN

The 63-year reign of Queen Victoria (1837-1901) was one of the longest and most prosperous in English history. During that time there was a continuous evolution in furniture styles that might best be characterized as a series of revivals. Beginning with the Gothic revival, fashions progressed through the Egyptian, Elizabethan, and Renaissance periods to end in a more ornate rococo style by the close of the 19th Century. The more enduring phases of this evolution—and those most associated with the reign of Queen Victoria—are perhaps the latter designs of the Gothic revival and the incredibly ornate gingerbread-encrusted pieces of the final rococo period.

From an American point of view, the creations of the English designer and author Charles Eastlake were most influential in defining a tasteful interpretation of the Gothic look, with arched panels, rectangular frames, and well-executed mortise-and-tenon joinery. The Eastlake Gothic style enjoyed a sudden popularity in the 1880s and is now much sought after by antique collectors. By the 1890s, however, fashions had shifted toward the flowing curves and intricate orna-mentation of an exaggerated French rococo style. Furniture of this late Victorian period tended to be imposingly large, dark, and ostentatious. Marble-topped tables, purple velvet upholstery, ottoman cushions, and overstuffed settees gave the late Victorian decor a rich but overfurnished appearance. The predominant use of naturally dark woods such as mahogany, walnut, and rosewood also added a formal, yet often somber, mood to the typical Victorian interior.

In terms of methods of construction, Victorian furniture represented a sharp change from previous periods. By the late 19th Century, the Industrial Revolution had mechanized the manufacture of furniture. New machines made it possible to mass produce intricately detailed decorative parts, and the designers of the time seem to have been overly eager to exploit this technology. Another by-product of the Industrial Revolution was a sharp decline in the cost and scarcity of metal. As a result, decorative castings became common tack-on embellishments and even complete pieces, such as chairs and tables, were made of cast iron. By today's interior decorating standards, a little Victorian goes a long way.

VICTORIAN FURNITURE

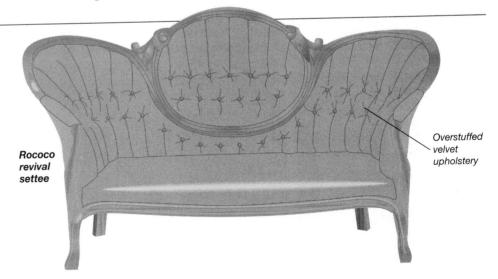

Rococo revival settee

Overstuffed velvet upholstery

Gothic revival table

Arch

VICTORIAN FURNITURE

Gothic revival library bookcase

Late Victorian Rococo revival chair

Rococo fret carving

20ᵀᴴ CENTURY

The task of characterizing the furniture styles of the 20th Century rests more properly with historians not yet born. Much as contemporaries of the Victorian era would have viewed the furniture styles of their time as a series of revivals rather than as a distinct Victorian style, today's observers lack the perspective to make final judgments regarding the age in which they live. There is some evidence to suggest the evolution of furniture designs in the 20th Century will be viewed as merely a continuation of this parade of revivals that began with the Age of Mechanization in Victorian times. The individual craftsmanship of the great masters of the 18th Century spawned experimentation and creative new designs. Today, a greater proportion of the population can afford quality reproduction furniture with its vague similarities to the works of craftsmen such as Chippendale, Sheraton, and Phyfe.

In retrospect, the 20th Century has produced the prototypes of what might have been major styles. The Mission style, inspired by the heavy oak furniture of the Spanish Colonial period, was popularized by Gustav Stickley around the turn of the century, but it was never made in large numbers. Also, the French Art Nouveau and the English Arts and Crafts movements, although not well

20ᵀᴴ-CENTURY FURNITURE

Carving

Oak rolltop desk

Rolltop

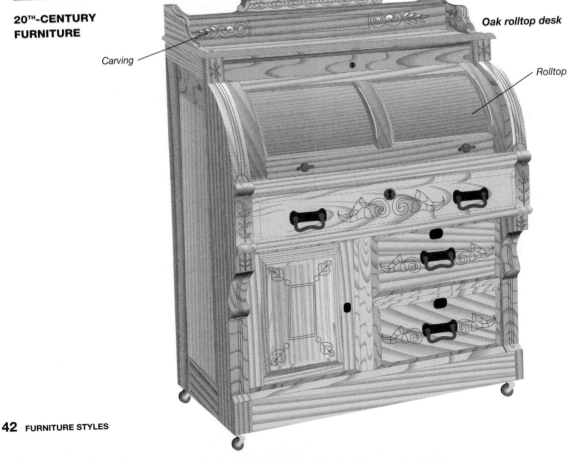

focused in terms of definable styles, succeeded in contributing fresh new designs that might have become major trends. The Arts and Crafts movement has done a great deal to foster continued interest in "Art" furniture. Designers like Charles Eames, Frank Lloyd Wright, and Charles Rennie Mackintosh have had considerable influence on modern furniture making.

Massive, honey-colored "golden oak" pedestal tables and rolltop desks were popular in the early 1900s. The art deco style of the 1920s and 1930s also had a distinctive look, with its curved veneer surfaces and banded inlays. Made in large quantities, it is just now becoming old enough to be of special interest to antique dealers. In addition, there has been a strong Scandinavian influence, such as the Danish modern style, with its oiled teak finish, clean lines, and rugged construction.

Golden oak desk/bookcase

Glass door

Drop-front writing surface

Mission sofa

20TH CENTURY

*Art deco
dressing table*

Art deco chair

Curved
veneer
surface

Inlay

Tapered legs

Wrapped
veneers

Danish modern chair

Wall unit

Plastic-
covered
steel legs

THE WORKSHOP

This chapter will provide you with a wealth of ideas and useful information to make your shop work well. It will help you choose a suitable location, control dust, lay out your shop so that tools do not interfere with each other, and satisfy your electrical requirements without overloading circuits. Satisfying all of these needs in the average family house takes planning and some compromise. And because each woodworker's demands are unique, there is no one way to set up a shop.

For a start, however, you need to make some decisions about the location and size of the shop, the tools it will house, and the type of woodworking projects you intend to do. Although these choices are personal, it helps to approach them in a rational and orderly manner.

Woodworkers generally house a shop in a basement, garage, attic, or separate building. Each location has its advantages and disadvantages. Basements are usually spacious, easy to heat, and convenient. Because they are close to the main electrical box, upgrading the wiring, lighting, and ventilation is relatively simple. But basements are relatively dark and subject to high seasonal fluctuations in humidity. Bringing material into a basement and conveying finished furniture out

can also be difficult. And, because they are situated directly below living areas, the noise from basement shops can be a problem. Garages do not generally have the access and lighting problems of basements, but they are humid, and are often unheated and inadequately wired. Cars, bicycles, and lawn mowers can cause space and storage problems. A separate building can be constructed to your specifications, but is expensive to heat, wire, maintain, and secure. Attics are generally a poor choice. Lighting and ventilation are usually inadequate, and the sloping ceilings typical of most attics encroach on usable floor space. Finally, attics are often inconvenient, even dangerous, to access.

Once you have decided on a location, draw a floor plan to scale, as described on page 46. Next, select your tools and determine their space requirements, as summarized in the chart on page 48. Next, determine your electrical, lighting, ventilation, and dust control needs. As the layout develops, safety considerations, discussed on pages 52 to 55, can be brought into the equation. The heart of a well-designed shop, the workbench, is discussed on page 56. Work surfaces and storage space are discussed beginning on page 58.

DESIGN AND LAYOUT

Being able to design and construct a workshop as a separate, freestanding building is a luxury few woodworkers can enjoy. Typically, a shop is a partitioned-off section of the basement or garage. As a result, the floor plan is seldom ideal and the amount of space that can be dedicated to the shop is often limited. Each situation is unique, but there are some general shop layout principles that enhance productivity and safety. Ideally, you should lay out the shop to complement your work flow. As illustrated in the diagram below, locate stock preparation tools, such as the table saw or radial arm saw and the planer, close to the entrance. As a safety feature, align these tools so that their direction of feed is toward the door. For one thing, facing the door will protect you from unexpected interruptions; it also allows you to feed long boards into the doorway, if necessary, when ripping or planing. You can increase the outfeed clearance around stationary tools by offsetting the table heights of your machines so that a workpiece on one tool's table clears the table of another.

If your shop is cramped, mount your tools on movable stands with lock casters to enable you to shift the machines out of the way when they are not needed. A final tip: Isolate the finishing area from the rest of the shop, which is likely to be dusty. And, a window in the finishing area is a definite plus, both as a source of ventilation and natural light.

TOOL PLACEMENT

A: Jointer
B: Band saw
C: Router table or shaper
D: Drill press
E: Planer
F: Table saw
G: Lathe
H: Workbench
I: Assembly table
J: Storage shelves

→

Direction of feed: whenever possible, orient major power tools so that they feed toward the door.

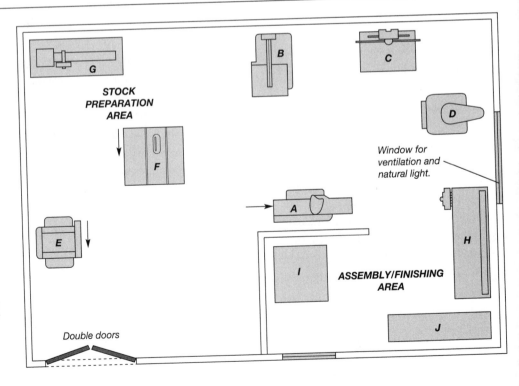

One simple way to choose the best locations for your shop fixtures and tools is to use graph paper and scale silhouettes, like the ones shown below. Begin by drawing a floor plan of the proposed shop on graph paper with ¼-inch squares. Use a scale of ¼ inch = 1 foot. Any of the power tools and fixtures shown can then be photocopied or traced on a second sheet of paper and cut out so they can be positioned on the floor plan drawing. Minor details are not critical, but if you plan to include fixtures or equipment that do not conform to these silhouettes, simply measure them and produce your own ¼-inch to 1-foot scale cutouts. Move the cutouts around on the floor plan and experiment with various layouts until you come up with the best combination. It is important to keep in mind that each power tool has necessary clearance requirements, as described in the chart on page 48.

STATIONARY TOOLS: SCALE DRAWINGS

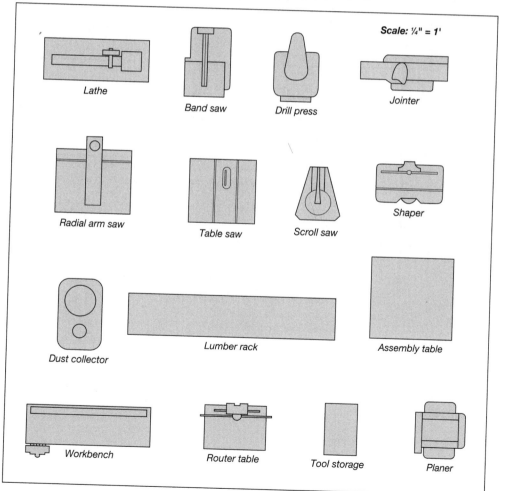

Scale: ¼" = 1'

Lathe

Band saw

Drill press

Jointer

Radial arm saw

Table saw

Scroll saw

Shaper

Dust collector

Lumber rack

Assembly table

Workbench

Router table

Tool storage

Planer

DESIGN AND LAYOUT

TOOL	CLEARANCE	LIGHTING
Table saw	Should be freestanding near center of shop to provide access from all sides, and accommodate long boards and 4' x 8' panels.	From above, directly over, or slightly behind blade.
Radial arm saw	Align perpendicular to the long axis of the shop to facilitate cutting long boards. Should be positioned against a wall.	From above, front, and to both sides of blade.
Band saw	Provide access to front and both sides, and about 4' to 6' of clearance all around. May be positioned against a wall or in front of a corner.	Light blade with a spotlight.
Router table or shaper	Provide access to front and both sides. Mount on a stand with lock casters.	Flood table with light from above.
Lathe	Provide minimum of 3' of front clearance. May be positioned against a wall, no side clearance required.	Light from above and slightly behind.
Drill press	Provide access in front. Can be positioned against a wall, but provide 3' to 4' of clearance on sides to accommodate longer workpieces.	Point a light at bit.
Planer	Provide access of 3' on three sides or more for long boards. Position above level of other work surfaces, if possible.	Light from above to flood both infeed and outfeed tables.
Jointer	May be positioned against a wall and above level of other work surfaces. Provide access to front and both sides.	Light from above and slightly to the outfeed side of cutters.
Scroll saw	May be positioned against a wall. Provide access in front and at least 3' of clearance all around.	Light the blade with a dedicated spotlight.
Stationary disc/belt sander	Provide access to the front and left of the disc. May be positioned near a wall.	Light from above so that no shadows are cast on belt or disc.
Workbench	Clearance requirements vary with type of bench. Most may be positioned against a wall. Typical benches require access on three sides.	Light from above and slightly to the rear of the work surface.
Work tables	Vary depending on application.	Flood work surface from above. Natural or full spectrum lighting preferred for finishing tables.

If you are setting up a shop in your home, you will probably have to adapt the shop's floor plan to the existing structure. It is seldom worth moving staircases, doors, and windows, so you will have to make the most of what is already there. The design and layout techniques discussed on pages 46 and 47 provide a good starting point for organizing your shop around work flow, but a well-designed shop must also address power, light, and dust collection requirements. The diagram below illustrates how these elements can be integrated into a typical shop. Power and lighting circuits should be separate, and for safety reasons, the lighting should be supplemented by at least some natural light in the event of a power outage. Make sure that any new wiring you have installed conforms to local building and electrical codes. Run dust collection ducting along the ceiling, using metal brackets to fix the ducts in place. Ventilation and dust collection are discussed in more detail on pages 50 and 51.

TYPICAL SHOP LAYOUT

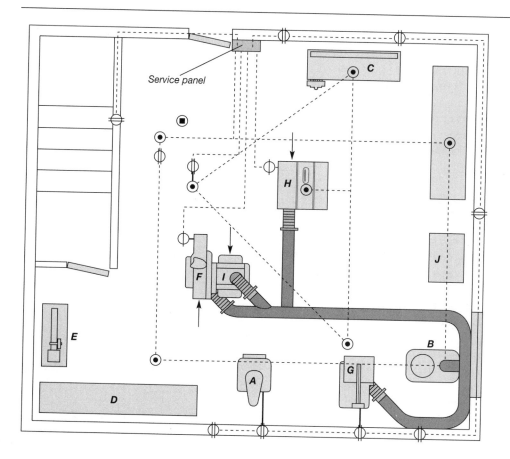

Service panel

ELECTRICAL AND DUST COLLECTION LAYOUT

A: Drill press or scroll saw
B: Dust collector
C: Workbench
D: Wood storage racks
E: Lathe
F: Jointer
G: Band saw
H: Table saw
I: Planer
J: Work table/ tool cabinet

LEGEND

⏀ 240 V outlet
⏀ 120 V outlet
⊙ Light fixture
▣ Overhead switch for stationary tools (page 53)
▥ Flexible duct connector with blast gate

DUST COLLECTION SYSTEMS

The dust created by power tools is both a health hazard and a nuisance. Prolonged exposure to wood dust can cause serious health problems *(page 185)*. Larger particles end up cluttering the shop floor, making it slippery.

You cannot eliminate dust, but you can certainly reduce the amount in your shop. Keeping windows open while you work will help a little; a better answer is to buy a dust collection system and hook your tools up to it. There are several kinds of stationary and portable collectors. Three options are shown below and on page 51.

A drop box system collects debris from a tool in a high-speed air stream and directs it to a large drop box. Gravity then separates out the larger particles. A cyclone system is similar except that the high-speed air stream enters a separator in such a way that the air inside spins rapidly. Centrifugal force separates out the larger particles, which remain in the separator. In both systems, air flow speed is critical. Efficiency is lost if the flow is too fast to allow the particles to settle out in the separator or drop box. But the air flow must be sufficient to aid centrifugal separation. Stationary systems, like the one shown, usually include a second phase in which the air stream is conducted through semipermeable polyester bags which allow air to escape while filtering fine particles.

Determining the size of the collector depends on the volume of air flow needed at each dust-producing tool (measured in cubic feet per minute, or CFM), and some other factors, such as the length and diameter of the ductwork. However, as a rule of thumb, a dust collector in the 350 to 600 CFM range will efficiently extract dust from the machines in the typical shop, like jointers, table saws, and shapers. This assumes only one machine is being operated at a time. Most manufacturers of dust collection equipment will provide you with the charts and calculations needed to choose the right collector for your needs.

QUICKTIP

Increasing the capacity of a dust collector

Shop vacuums and small portable dust collectors can sometimes be swamped by high volumes of chips and shavings, and must be emptied frequently. One way to increase the capacity of such a system is to add a 55-gallon drum or a large barrel as an extra reservoir. Cut two holes in the lid of the drum to accept vent pipe connectors, one for the intake leading from the power tool and one for the exhaust going on to the shop vacuum or commercial dust collector. Installing a 90° elbow on the intake pipe inside the drum, aimed at the sides, makes the unit more efficient by causing the air to cyclone inside the drum. Make sure all connections are airtight.

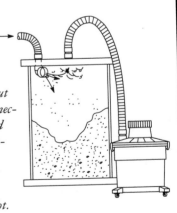

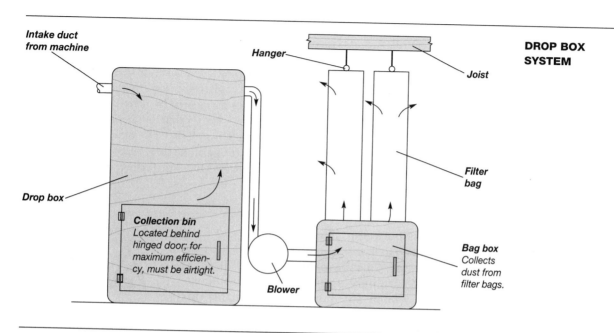

Intake duct from machine

Hanger

DROP BOX SYSTEM

Joist

Drop box

Filter bag

Collection bin
Located behind hinged door; for maximum efficiency, must be airtight.

Blower

Bag box
Collects dust from filter bags.

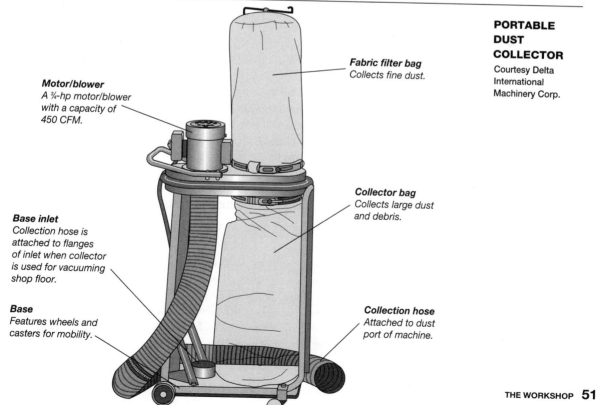

PORTABLE DUST COLLECTOR
Courtesy Delta International Machinery Corp.

Fabric filter bag
Collects fine dust.

Motor/blower
A ¾-hp motor/blower with a capacity of 450 CFM.

Collector bag
Collects large dust and debris.

Base inlet
Collection hose is attached to flanges of inlet when collector is used for vacuuming shop floor.

Base
Features wheels and casters for mobility.

Collection hose
Attached to dust port of machine.

FIRE PREVENTION

In a typical home, the shop is perhaps second only to the kitchen in terms of fire hazard. The risks are many: fine particles of wood in the air; chips and sawdust on the floor; electrical circuits; heat from motors, friction, and a host of flammable adhesives and finishing chemicals. Keeping the shop clean and disposing of oil-soaked rags that can cause spontaneous combustion help to reduce the risk. However, you should also be prepared to fight a fire if it can be caught in the early stages. Keep a fire extinguisher handy and check it regularly to make sure it is properly charged. As explained below, there are three types of fires designated by national safety organizations; each type is represented by a symbol or the letter A, B, or C. Since most shops can have any of the three types of fires, be sure to buy an ABC extinguisher. It will be rated for all three classes.

DIFFERENT TYPES OF FIRE EXTINGUISHERS

Fire extinguishers are rated according to three basic types of fires. Class A fires involve "ordinary combustibles," such as wood, paper, cloth, rubber, household rubbish, and many plastics. Class B fires involve flammable liquids such as oils, greases, tars, oil-based paints, lacquers, flammable gases, and some plastics. Class C fires involve "energized" (that is, plugged in) electrical equipment. An extinguisher rated ABC can safely be used on fires involving any of these materials.

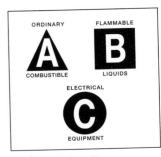

Courtesy National Fire Protection Association

USING A FIRE EXTINGUISHER

Most fire extinguishers consist of a metal canister, handle, valve, hose, nozzle, breakaway strap, and safety pin. Familiarize yourself with the operating instructions provided on the label. When the extinguisher is needed, you will not want to waste valuable seconds learning how to use it. Keep the extinguisher in a readily accessible place, preferably on the wall near the shop entrance.

To use the extinguisher, hold it upright and aim for the base of the flames. Crouching down, position yourself between the fire and a sure route of escape at a safe distance from the fire—6 to 10 feet. Sweep the nozzle and spray in a side-to-side motion. If the fire progresses beyond the capacity of the extinguisher, leave the area immediately and call the fire department.

Tips
- *Keep the shop clean; sweep the floor and work surfaces at the end of each work session.*
- *Submerge oil-soaked rags in water in a metal can double-lined with heavy-duty garbage bags.*
- *Periodically inspect electrical systems for loose connections, exposed wire, or frayed insulation.*
- *Store flammables in a metal cabinet away from potential sources of heat or ignition.*

ELECTRICAL SAFETY

The electrical requirements of a fully equipped woodshop can easily exceed the capacity of the original wiring installed by the builder. For example, the only existing circuits in unfinished basements and garages, especially in older homes, are likely to be 15-amp, 14-gauge lighting circuits. Since lighting circuits should never be tapped or extended to include power outlets, your shop should be wired with dedicated circuits directly from the main power box. Their number and type should be based on the power requirements of the equipment and a familiarity with local building codes. Installation of shop circuits is a task best handled by a professional electrician.

A drop in line voltage can be caused by using an extension cord of insufficient gauge. The result will be a loss of power, excessive heat, and tool burnout. To determine the minimum wire gauge for a power tool, refer to the chart at right. If, for instance, your tool has a 5-amp motor and you need a 50-foot-long extension cord, its minimum wire gauge should be 18. Only buy round-jacketed extension cords approved by Underwriters Laboratory (UL).

AMPERAGE RATING OF TOOL	MINIMUM GAUGE FOR DIFFERENT LENGTH CORDS		
	25'	50'	75'
0 - 2.0	18	18	18
2.1 - 3.4	18	18	18
3.5 - 5.0	18	18	16
5.1 - 7.0	18	16	14
7.1 - 12.0	18	14	12
12.1 - 16.0	16	12	10

MINIMUM WIRE GAUGE FOR EXTENSION CORDS

Chart courtesy Delta International Machinery Corp.

Electrical safety tips

• *Never modify a three-pronged, grounded plug by cutting off the ground prong to fit into an ungrounded receptacle.*
• *Never replace a fuse or circuit breaker with one that is rated for a higher amperage.*
• *Never extend a circuit with lighter-gauge wire than that used in the original installation.*
• *Replace any receptacle or switch that is loose or shows any signs of malfunction.*

• *Do not allow power tools to overheat.*
• *Never overload a circuit. When acquiring new equipment or reorganizing your shop, make sure the electrical system can accommodate the tools.*
• *Install an overhead switch for turning stationary machines on and off when tool switches are out of reach. Wire the switch so that both it and original switches can start and stop machines; do not disable original switches.*

PERSONAL SAFETY GEAR

While the workshop is often seen as a retreat or sanctuary from the hurly-burly of everyday life, it is also a potentially dangerous place. Safety gear is essential to help you reduce or eliminate risks such as noise, dust, pressure-treated wood (page 185), and flying debris. Dust masks and respirators, for instance, can protect you from a variety of airborne hazards, depending on the filter material you use. Refer to the chart directly below to help you distinguish these various hazards and choose the appropriate filter.

Still, do not rely on safety gear alone to keep your work environment safe. No equipment can counteract careless work habits. Caution, concentration, and common sense are the most important prerequisites of safe woodworking.

PHYSICAL FORMS OF MATERIALS
Chart courtesy National Institute for Occupational Safety and Health

DUSTS	Particles of various shapes and sizes. Produced by cutting, grinding, and sanding.
FUMES	Small, solid particles which form above molten metal by chemical reactions like oxidation (example: welding or soldering fumes).
GASES	Compressible, formless fluids which occupy a space or enclosure.
MISTS	Droplets which become airborne through boiling, bubbling, spraying, splashing, or other agitation; also form from liquids at room temperature (such as aerosol spray can mist).
VAPORS	Gaseous forms of substances which are normally liquids or solids.

PERMISSIBLE EXPOSURE TIMES TO NOISE WITHOUT HEARING PROTECTION
Chart courtesy National Institute for Occupational Safety and Health

MACHINE	SOUND LEVEL IN DECIBELS*	MAXIMUM DAILY EXPOSURE	MACHINE	SOUND LEVEL IN DECIBELS*	MAXIMUM DAILY EXPOSURE
5-hp radial arm saw	110	30 min.	5-hp jointer	98	1½ hrs.
1-hp saber saw	108	30 min.	½-hp router	98	2 hrs.
1.5-hp router	108	30 min.	2-hp belt sander	96	3 hrs.
2-hp circular saw	108	30 min.	¾-hp band saw	95	4 hrs.
1-hp router	103	1 hr.	2-hp shaper	95	4 hrs.
3-hp planer	102	1½ hrs.	2-hp table saw	92	6 hrs.
¾-hp radial arm saw	102	1½ hrs.	½-hp drill press	87	8 hrs.

Highest decibel reading while cutting or sanding hardwood

Face shield
Clear plastic shield protects face from flying debris and splashes; features adjustable head strap.

Safety glasses
Protect eyes from flying wood chips and other debris; frames are fitted with shatterproof lenses.

Disposable dust mask
Provides protection against inhalation of dust or mist; features a cotton or fiber shield with an elastic head strap and a metal nose clip for close fit.

Reusable dust mask
Protects against dust and mist. Features a neoprene rubber or soft plastic frame with an adjustable head strap and a replaceable cotton fiber or gauze filter.

Safety goggles
Flexible molded plastic goggles protect eyes. Type with vent holes guards against impact injury and sawdust; type with baffled vents shields against chemical splashes. Nonvented type also available.

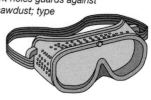

Dual-cartridge respirator
Protects against inhalation of vapors, mists, and dusts; interchangeable filters and chemical cartridges guard against specific hazards (see chart on page 54). Cartridges purify air.

Work gloves
Used for handling rough lumber. Feature leather or thick fabric palms and fingertips, along with elasticized or knitted wrists.

Rubber gloves
Household rubber gloves or disposable vinyl gloves are adequate when working with mild chemicals; wear neoprene rubber gloves when using caustic finishing products.

Earplugs with neck band
Feature detachable foam rubber plugs, which are compressed and inserted into ear canals; plastic band fits around neck.

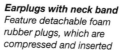

Hearing protectors
Cushioned muffs feature adjustable head strap.

Foam earplugs
Made of compressible foam; when inserted in ears, they expand to fit the shape of the ear canal. Can be worn comfortably for long periods; washable.

Premolded earplugs
Made of a pliable material that is formed to fit the ear canal. Some are made with different sized flanges to fit a variety of ear canal sizes.

WORKBENCHES

The workbench is perhaps the most personal fixture in the shop. Although many experienced woodworkers believe a bench should be custom-built, most people buy standard commercial models. Making a workbench is time-consuming, but if you plan to build one, buy a good set of detailed plans from a woodworking supply store. If you are buying one already made, look for quality construction and vises that suit the work you plan to do.

A good bench provides a sturdy work surface and useful hold-down devices. The bench shown below illustrates some of these. Hardware for custom-built workbenches comes in a wide variety of types and brands. In choosing among various components, keep the intended task in mind. Standard machinist's vises can be adapted for some woodworking applications, but the greater throat capacities and wider jaws of vises designed specifically for woodworking make them generally more useful.

ANATOMY OF A WORKBENCH
Courtesy Veritas Tools

Tray
Recessed area in the work surface for placing tools, fasteners, or other supplies so they are within easy reach without cluttering the work surface.

Work Surface
Ideally constructed of thick, fine-textured, and dense wood, such as maple, capable of taking considerable abuse.

Bench dog
A stop pin that fits into sockets in the bench; works with the face and tail vises to hold a workpiece.

Bench hold-down
Traditional device for clamping a workpiece to the top of the bench. Fits into dog holes; can be rotated 360°. Clamping mechaninsm may be cam type, as shown, or screw type (page 57).

Adjustable screw dog

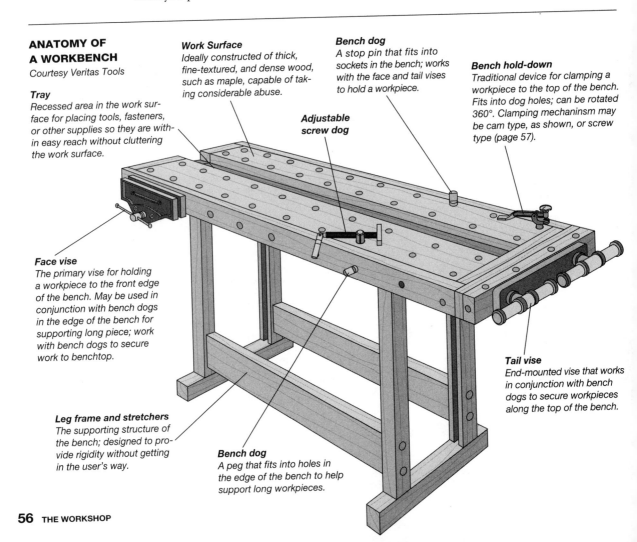

Face vise
The primary vise for holding a workpiece to the front edge of the bench. May be used in conjunction with bench dogs in the edge of the bench for supporting long piece; work with bench dogs to secure work to benchtop.

Leg frame and stretchers
The supporting structure of the bench; designed to provide rigidity without getting in the user's way.

Bench dog
A peg that fits into holes in the edge of the bench to help support long workpieces.

Tail vise
End-mounted vise that works in conjunction with bench dogs to secure workpieces along the top of the bench.

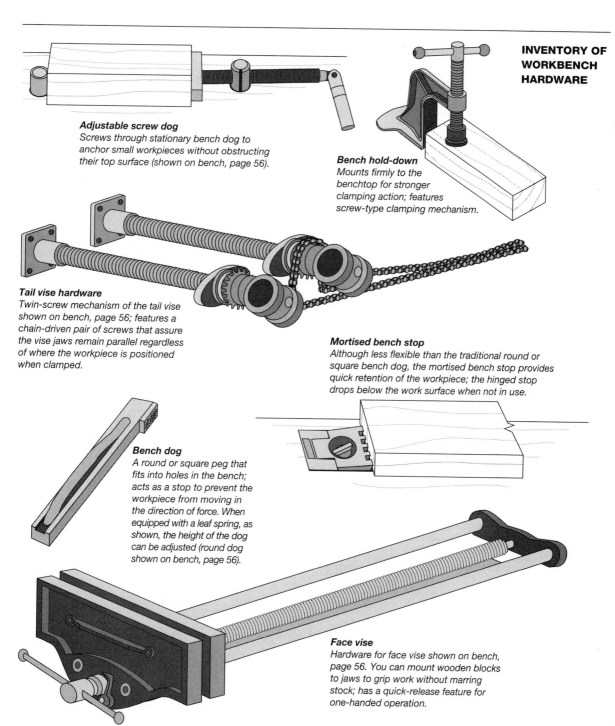

Adjustable screw dog
Screws through stationary bench dog to anchor small workpieces without obstructing their top surface (shown on bench, page 56).

Bench hold-down
Mounts firmly to the benchtop for stronger clamping action; features screw-type clamping mechanism.

Tail vise hardware
Twin-screw mechanism of the tail vise shown on bench, page 56; features a chain-driven pair of screws that assure the vise jaws remain parallel regardless of where the workpiece is positioned when clamped.

Mortised bench stop
Although less flexible than the traditional round or square bench dog, the mortised bench stop provides quick retention of the workpiece; the hinged stop drops below the work surface when not in use.

Bench dog
A round or square peg that fits into holes in the bench; acts as a stop to prevent the workpiece from moving in the direction of force. When equipped with a leaf spring, as shown, the height of the dog can be adjusted (round dog shown on bench, page 56).

Face vise
Hardware for face vise shown on bench, page 56. You can mount wooden blocks to jaws to grip work without marring stock; has a quick-release feature for one-handed operation.

WORK SURFACES AND TOOL STANDS

Planning an efficient workshop starts with an effective floor plan, as discussed on pages 47 to 49. But do not forget that a shop is a three-dimensional work space. The height of tool tables and work surfaces is critical in planning infeed and outfeed clearances. Tools like the table saw, the jointer, and the planer need considerable space in front and behind to handle long boards, but the space is only required while the tools are in use. A tool stand with casters enables you to move a tool out of the way when it is not needed. Similarly, many projects require a large work surface for assembly and fin-

ishing, but only while the project is ongoing. By varying the height of work surfaces and tool tables, and planning your projects carefully, you can make a little space go a long way.

The remaining pages of this chapter illustrate a number of useful space-saving devices and ideas. Shown below is a knock-down sawhorse you can make yourself. Page 59 shows a shop-built multiple-height work surface and a commercial tool stand designed to convert a benchtop tool into a stationary one. Two efficient wood storage systems are described on page 60.

KNOCKDOWN SAWHORSE

Sawhorses are invaluable in the shop. The knock-down version shown below can be built in a few minutes with only a few scraps of lumber and plywood. Begin by cutting the two 30-inch-high legs from ¾-inch ply-

wood, then saw a notch 3 inches deep in the top of each leg. Next, cut the crosspiece from 1 x 6 lumber. Saw a 1½-inch-deep slot 8 inches in from each end of the crosspiece to fit into the leg notches. Angle the slots

approximately 5 degrees from the vertical so the legs will spread slightly outward. You can make the sawhorse more stable by screwing 4-inch-long 1 x 2 cleats to the crosspiece on each side of the slots.

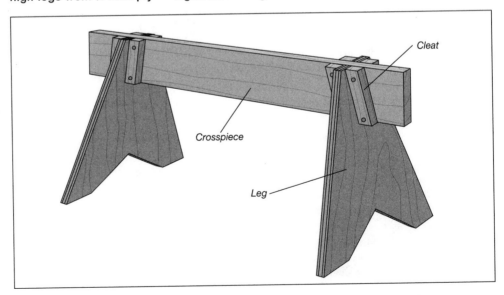

Cleat

Crosspiece

Leg

It is helpful to have several work surfaces at different heights, but most shops lack the space for more than one or two work tables. One simple solution is the shop-built workbox shown at right, made from 1 x 4 lumber. Depending on how the box is positioned, it will provide you with a work surface at one of three heights. If you wanted a box with heights of 24, 32, and 40 inches, as shown in the illustration, you would cut eight 33-inch-long boards, four 32-inch-long pieces, eight 22½-inch-long boards, and four 23½-inch-

long pieces. Join the boards into six rectangular frames with biscuit joints *(page 258)*.

Then nail or screw the frames together to form a lightweight but sturdy platform.

MULTIPLE-HEIGHT WORKBOX

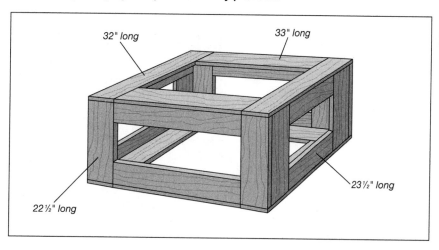

32" long
33" long
23½" long
22½" long

Your first concern in selecting a tool stand is to provide solid, stable support for the tool without introducing obstructions that might get in the way as you operate it. The stand shown at right fits the bill. It features a simple, but sturdy design, and a heavy-gauge steel top with a series of predrilled holes that enable you to fasten a number of benchtop tools to the stand: from scroll saws and miter saws to band saws and sanders. Larger versions can be used to accommodate stationary power tools such as drill presses and contractor's saws.

If you have several tools mounted on stands, consider models with adjustable

legs. This feature allows tools that require considerable infeed and outfeed clearances to be positioned

at different heights. Stands with lock casters allow you to wheel a tool out of the way when it is not needed.

COMMERCIAL TOOL STANDS

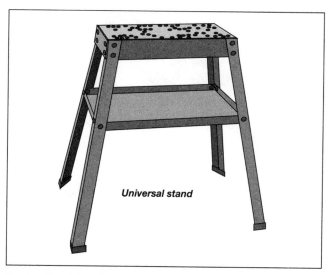

Universal stand

Courtesy Delta International Machinery Corp.

WOOD STORAGE

TWO STORAGE RACKS

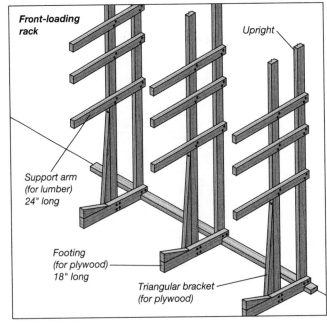

Front-loading rack

Upright

Support arm (for lumber) 24" long

Footing (for plywood) 18" long

Triangular bracket (for plywood)

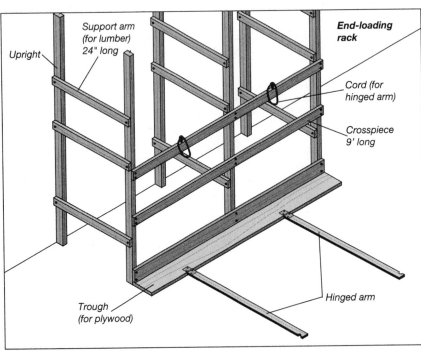

Support arm (for lumber) 24" long

Upright

End-loading rack

Cord (for hinged arm)

Crosspiece 9' long

Trough (for plywood)

Hinged arm

Making the most of space in a shop is critical for storing wood, especially if you end up buying more wood than you need just for the next project. If your shop is in a garage or unfinished basement, you can store cut-offs, moldings, and other short lengths of stock in the space between wall studs, roof rafters or joists. The wall racks at left, made largely from 2 x 4 stock, provide the capacity for larger inventories of lumber and plywood.

The front-loading rack requires no extra space to load and unload lumber. If you have the extra space in your shop, you can go with an end-loading rack, which includes a trough in the front with hinged arms to hold plywood.

Both racks are made from frameworks of vertical uprights and horizontal support arms. They are each about 9 feet across and span from floor to ceiling. Carriage bolts join the pieces together. The tops of the uprights should be fastened to the joists in the floor above, if possible, and the back uprights should be anchored to a wall stud. The footings in the front-loading rack should be nailed to the shop floor.

HAND TOOLS

A common misconception among beginning woodworkers is that the only way to work wood quickly and accurately is by acquiring a lot of expensive power tools. While there is no denying the precision and labor-saving capacities of power tools, they are certainly not indispensable to the craft. The great master woodworkers of the 18th Century worked solely with hand tools that were often much more primitive and less effective than those available today. In addition, the set-up time required for power tools often makes them inconvenient for small projects. Setting up a router jig to cut dovetails, for example, makes a lot of sense when you are constructing a large carcase, but for a single drawer, a dovetail saw, a chisel, and a mallet can get the job done much more quickly.

This chapter focuses on the broad array of hand tools on the market. It will help you decide which tools you need for the kind of woodworking projects you do. The chapter also describes how hand tools are used and maintained in top working order.

Measuring and marking tools are shown on pages 62 to 68. Although these tools may seem utterly basic, do not discount their importance. A professional-quality piece of furniture starts with using these tools properly. Along with step-by-step guidelines for

marking and scribing straight, accurate, and recognizable layout lines, the chapter presents several not-so-obvious tips that can help you perform measuring and marking tasks that are otherwise awkward or difficult to do. Measuring the inside of a carcase is one example, as shown on page 64.

The section on saws (*page 69*) features a sampling of traditional, modern, and Japanese saws. Japanese saws differ from their Western counterparts, cutting on the pull stroke, rather than the push stroke. Japanese blades are much thinner and more flexible than Western saws, making them ideal for certain tasks. For example, the Japanese *kugihiki* is excellent for flush-cutting dowel pegs.

The chapter follows with sections on planes and scrapers (*page 82*); shaping tools (*page 92*), such as files and rasps; boring tools, which include items like hand drills and bits (*page 95*); and striking and fastening tools such as hammers, mallets, and screwdrivers (*page 97*).

The performance of most of these hand tools rests heavily on keeping them sharp. Periodic sharpening will keep your saws, chisels, planes, and other cutting tools working the way they should. It will also make them safer: Cutting tools that are dull tend to skip off the wood instead of biting cleanly into it.

61

MEASURING AND MARKING TOOLS

The starting point of good craftsmanship is proper measuring and marking. Accurate cutting and shaping will be wasted if the project has not been laid out with precision. Some general rules of thumb apply to all measuring and marking tasks. Whether you are using a rule or a square, measure from as few reference surfaces as possible to minimize repeating an error or adding to it. Also, read scales from a straight-on eye position, rather than on an angle, to prevent parallax error, which leads to imprecise readings. And, when

TAPES AND RULES

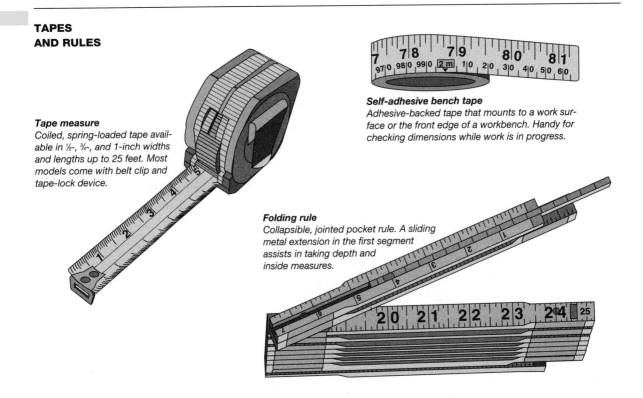

Tape measure
Coiled, spring-loaded tape available in ½-, ¾-, and 1-inch widths and lengths up to 25 feet. Most models come with belt clip and tape-lock device.

Self-adhesive bench tape
Adhesive-backed tape that mounts to a work surface or the front edge of a workbench. Handy for checking dimensions while work is in progress.

Folding rule
Collapsible, jointed pocket rule. A sliding metal extension in the first segment assists in taking depth and inside measures.

Straightedge
Available in various lengths up to several feet; usually made of steel or aluminum. Used for scribing straight lines; may also be used on edge to check whether a surface is flat.

scribing the end line of a measurement, use a V-shaped mark, rather than a simple dot or line, to locate your endpoint exactly.

The inventories and step-by-step instructions presented here and on the following six pages group measuring and marking tools into three categories: tapes and rules; marking and scribing tools; and squares and gauges. Although most are designed to perform only one task, a few tools—the compass, the carpenter's square, and the combination square, for example—are useful in many ways.

TAPES AND RULES

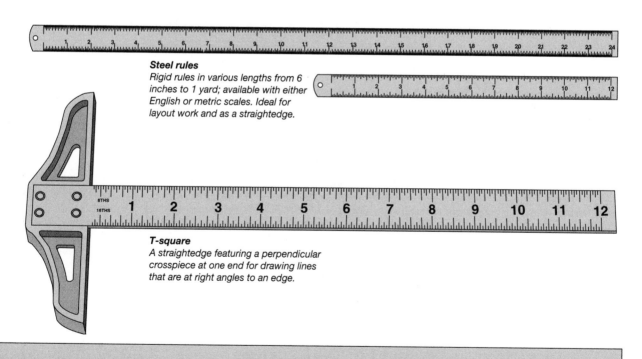

Hook rule
Usually scaled in both directions. The hook at one end facilitates accurate outside measures from an edge; inside measures can be taken from the straight end.

Steel rules
Rigid rules in various lengths from 6 inches to 1 yard; available with either English or metric scales. Ideal for layout work and as a straightedge.

T-square
A straightedge featuring a perpendicular crosspiece at one end for drawing lines that are at right angles to an edge.

MEASURING AND MARKING TOOLS

**TAKING
AN INSIDE
MEASUReMENT**

Despite its convenience, a tape measure can be hard to read when taking an inside measure. For more accurate results, use a ruler with the tape measure as shown at right. Butt the tape against one side and the ruler against the other. Check where the end of the ruler aligns with the tape and simply add the two measurements together.

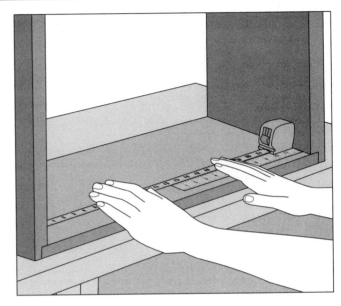

QUICKTIP

Sliding measuring sticks

You can take inside measures with a jig consisting of two sticks each slightly shorter than the length to be measured. The sticks must be square so that they can slide against each other smoothly; the sticks shown in the jig below mesh together with a router-cut joint, but this is not necessary. Place the sticks side by side and slide them outward until their ends touch the inside walls of the case. Clamp the sticks together, remove them from the case, and measure between their ends to obtain your inside measurement.

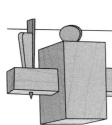

Cutting gauge
Useful for marking shoulder lines parallel to an end (see page 66); similar to the marking gauge and mortise gauge, except the scriber is parallel to the guide fence for scribing sharp lines across the grain.

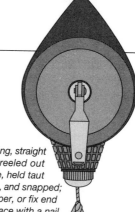

Chalk line
Used to mark long, straight lines. String is reeled out from chalk case, held taut over the surface, and snapped; work with a helper, or fix end of string to surface with a nail.

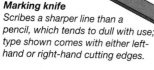

Marking knife
Scribes a sharper line than a pencil, which tends to dull with use; type shown comes with either left-hand or right-hand cutting edges.

Trammels
Used for scribing large arcs and circles (see page 66). Can be attached to any point on a straightedge; distance between points equals circle radius.

Pounce wheel
Used for transferring paper patterns onto a workpiece. Pattern is positioned atop workpiece and spurred wheel follows pattern and penetrates the paper, leaving indentations in the wood.

Marking gauge
Features a sharp point for marking lines along the grain parallel to an edge or face; to adjust marking distance, slide shaft through guide fence and lock it in place with the setscrew. Can also be used as a "slitting gauge" to cut thin stock.

Compass
Used to draw arcs and circles. Available in several sizes for circles up to 16 inches in radius.

Awl
A sharp-pointed tool used to make starting holes for drills, screws, or nails. Also better than a pencil for scribing layout lines.

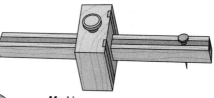

Mortise gauge
Designed for laying out mortises and tenons (see page 276); adjusted in same way as marking gauge, except that one of the pins is adjustable for setting the width of the mortise or tenon.

Center punch
Marks starting holes for drill bits or screws. Some models must be tapped with a hammer, while others are spring-loaded.

MEASURING AND MARKING TOOLS

SCRIBING A LINE WITH A CUTTING GAUGE

Scribing a line across the face of a board is commonly done with a cutting gauge to mark the shoulder line of a joint, such as a dovetail. Loosen the thumbscrew to release the guide fence [1]. Slide the fence along the shaft and use a rule (or the thickness of the workpiece, if appropriate) to adjust the distance between the fence and the cutter. Tighten the thumbscrew. Next, hold the board flat, butt the fence of the gauge against its end, and scribe the line with the tool angled slightly forward [2].

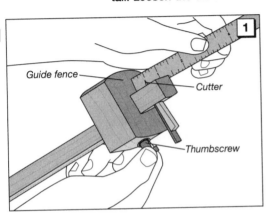

Guide fence

Cutter

Thumbscrew

MARKING A CIRCLE

Trammels are ideal for drawing circles larger than the capacity of a standard compass. Insert a sharpened pencil lead in the chuck of one trammel and a pivot pin in the chuck of the other, then slip the trammels onto a metal straightedge or rule. Lock the pivot pin trammel in position. Then slide the other trammel out to the desired radius of the circle and tighten its clamping handle. Press the pivot pin down at the center of the circle as you guide the other trammel to draw the circumference (below).

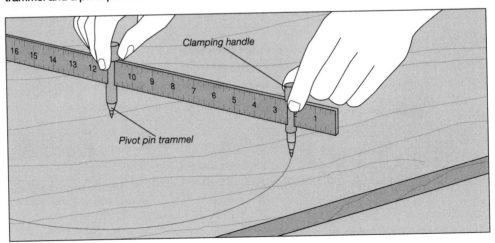

Clamping handle

Pivot pin trammel

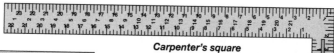

Carpenter's square
A rigid steel square usually 16 inches by 24 inches; each arm is calibrated along both edges. Used for checking and marking 90° angles.

Combination gauge
Used to measure and mark angles from 0 to 360°; can also be used to adjust power tools.

Try square
A metal blade mounted at precisely 90° to the handle; used for marking perpendicular lines or checking right angles. Available in a variety of blade lengths.

Steel protractor
For marking, checking, or transferring angles; blade pivots to read angles from 0 to 180°.

Combination square
One of the handiest of woodworking devices; used to mark and verify both 90° and 45° angles. Handle features a bubble rule for checking level and plumb; removable blade functions as straightedge and ruler. Some models include a detachable scribing pin in the handle.

Sliding bevel
Used to transfer angles (from a protractor to a table saw blade for bevel cutting, for example) or to compare angles; the blade slides and pivots and may be locked at any angle.

Caliper
For taking precise inside and outside measurements. For outside measurement, long fingers are adjusted to grip item to be measured; for inside measurement, short fingers are spread until they contact sides. Dial provides reading; available with English or metric scales.

Miter square
Similar to the try square, except that the blade is fixed to the handle at 45°; used to scribe and verify miter and bevel angles.

Contour gauge
Used to copy and transfer curved profiles. Closely spaced sliding pins duplicate the contour when the gauge is pressed against the surface.

Carpenter's level
Used to check whether surfaces are level (horizontal) or plumb (vertical); available in various lengths with either traditional bubble gauges or an electronic display.

MEASURING AND MARKING TOOLS

FINDING THE CENTER OF A CIRCULAR PIECE

Clamped together, a carpenter's square and a combination square can be used to locate the center of a circle. Set the 45° face of the combination square's handle against the outside edge of the carpenter's square so that its blade bisects the angle formed by the carpenter's square. Clamp the two squares together. Set the assembly against the workpiece so that both arms of the carpenter's square contact its circumference. Then scribe a line along the blade of the combination square. Rotate the circle and scribe a second line as shown below. The two lines will intersect at the center of the circle.

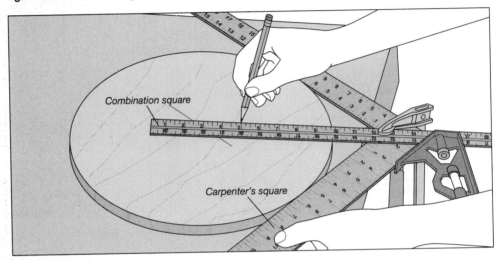

Combination square

Carpenter's square

QUICKTIP

A jig for mitering edge banding

Installing edge banding around the perimeter of a plywood panel requires precise miter cuts for the corners. Mark the cuts using the simple jig shown at right. Fasten a 45° drafting triangle to the end of a scrap board the same thickness as the plywood. To use the jig, butt the edge banding along one side of the plywood and position the jig along an adjoining side so that an edge of the triangle bisects the corner of the panel. Scribe your cutting line along the triangle. Tape the edging in place so it will not move as the jig is positioned to mark the miter cut at the opposite end.

HANDSAWS

Although most woodworkers rely on power tools for cutting, handsaws have a legitimate place in the modern workshop. One-of-a-kind cuts that require lengthy set-up time on a power tool are often quicker and easier to do with the appropriate handsaw. Also, if you are involved in authentic reproduction work, there is no substitute for executing the joinery with traditional methods. For example, the large tails, widely spaced pins, and subtle lack of symmetry in some dovetail joints can only be done by hand.

The key to mastering handsaws rests in learning what saw is appropriate for a given task, and keeping their blades sharp and in good working order. This section covers both topics.

USEFUL HANDSAWS

Crosscut saw
Designed to cut wood smoothly across the grain; typically shorter than a rip saw and with finer teeth, spaced 8 to 12 per inch of blade length. Rip saws (not shown) cut parallel to the grain; the typical rip saw is 26 inches long with 5 teeth per inch. Rip saw teeth angle forward and are chisel-shaped to tear the wood fibers and quickly remove debris from the kerf.

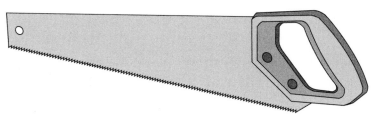

Toolbox saw
A general purpose saw with "combination" teeth (for ripping or crosscutting) and a short blade, typically 15 inches long; the teeth are knife-shaped to crosscut wood fibers without tearout, but are also longer, like rip saw teeth, to facilitate quick rip cuts.

Backsaw
A fine-toothed saw with 12 to 15 teeth per inch used for cutting joints that require fine tolerances, such as miters and tenons (see page 276); the blade is reinforced with a spine along its upper edge to prevent flexing.

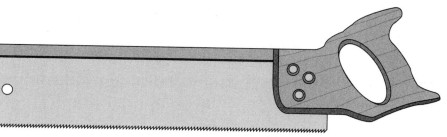

HANDSAWS

**USEFUL
HANDSAWS**

Frame saw
Available in various sizes and with interchangeable blades, this traditional handsaw performs many of the tasks of the modern band saw, such as resawing and ripping; handy when width of stock exceeds the maximum depth of cut of band saw. Saw shown is fitted with a rip blade; blades are held in tension by means of a tourniquet at the top of the frame (see page 74).

Coping saw
Smallest of the frame saws, the coping saw is used for fine curved cuts in thin stock (see page 76); the blade can be detached from the frame, inserted into a starter hole, and reattached to the frame.

Flush cutter
Commonly used for trimming dowel pegs flush with the surface; the offset handle pivots to lock in place at either end of the blade.

Dovetail saw
A fine-toothed, lightweight version of the backsaw with a straight handle, used for cutting fine joints such as dovetails (see pages 282 and 284).

Bowsaw
A smaller version of the frame saw used for curved cuts (see page 76); features a narrower, shorter blade, typically 12 inches long.

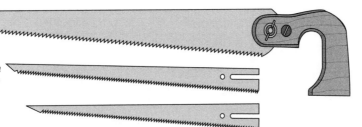

Three-in-one saw
Features an open-grip handle
and interchangeable crosscut,
compass, and keyhole blades; a
notch enables the blades to slip
into place in the handle and a
wing nut holds them in place.

Compass saw
Designed for making interior cuts;
the blade is sufficiently narrow to be
inserted into a starter hole. The keyhole
saw is a version of the compass saw
with a smaller and narrower blade; it is
used for curved interior cuts.

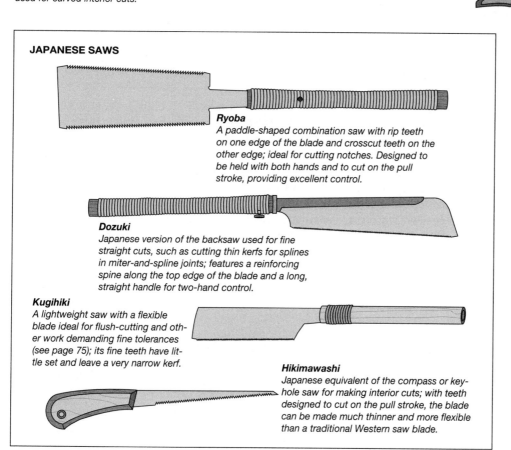

JAPANESE SAWS

Ryoba
A paddle-shaped combination saw with rip teeth
on one edge of the blade and crosscut teeth on the
other edge; ideal for cutting notches. Designed to
be held with both hands and to cut on the pull
stroke, providing excellent control.

Dozuki
Japanese version of the backsaw used for fine
straight cuts, such as cutting thin kerfs for splines
in miter-and-spline joints; features a reinforcing
spine along the top edge of the blade and a long,
straight handle for two-hand control.

Kugihiki
A lightweight saw with a flexible
blade ideal for flush-cutting and other work demanding fine tolerances
(see page 75); its fine teeth have little set and leave a very narrow kerf.

Hikimawashi
Japanese equivalent of the compass or keyhole saw for making interior cuts; with teeth
designed to cut on the pull stroke, the blade
can be made much thinner and more flexible
than a traditional Western saw blade.

HANDSAWS

**TUNING
A SAW**

TECHNIQUE	PURPOSE	REQUIRED	RECOMMENDED
Jointing	Makes the teeth the same height.	If the teeth have been damaged by improper use of the saw.	After several filings; ensures the teeth are same height.
Setting	Makes kerf wider than blade by bending alternate teeth in opposing directions so that blade will not bind.	When teeth have been jointed.	After several filings not preceded by jointing.
Filing	Sharpens the teeth.	When teeth have been jointed and set.	If teeth are dull.

**SHARPENING
SAW TEETH**

Clamp the saw in a vise [1] between two strips of wood to protect the blade and hold it rigid. Hold a commercial saw jointer fitted with a flat mill bastard file against one side of the blade and run it gently along the entire length of the blade. Two or three passes may be required to cut down any high teeth and even them all out. To set the teeth, adjust a commercial saw set [2] to the same TPI (teeth per inch) setting as the blade. Work from one end of the blade to the other, setting all the teeth that are bent away from you. Then,

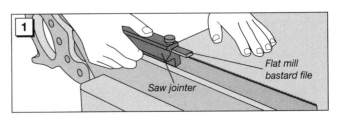

Flat mill bastard file

Saw jointer

turn the saw around in the vise and set all the remaining teeth. To set each tooth, place the saw set over the tooth and squeeze the handle. To sharpen the cutting edges of the teeth, use a slim-taper triangular file [3]. Place the file in the gullet between the teeth. For crosscut saws, like the one in the illustration, hold the file at

both ends at a 60 degree angle to the blade and file in a slightly upward direction. For rip saws, hold the file perpendicular to the blade. As when setting the teeth, file in every other gullet, then turn the saw around in the vise and repeat the procedure on the remaining teeth. Try to establish a rhythm so that you file each tooth equally.

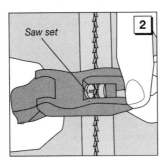

Saw set

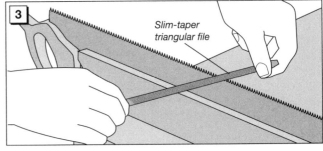

Slim-taper triangular file

A saw is a series of cutting edges. The size and shape of each tooth affects a saw blade's performance and the tasks for which it is suited. For example, the teeth on a rip saw function like miniature chisels or adzes that chip out the wood. This enables a rip saw to cut quickly with the grain. The teeth on crosscut saws are angled and sharpened like knives to shear the wood fibers cleanly on each side of the kerf. This makes a crosscut saw ideal for cutting across the grain. The small, finely set teeth of a dovetail saw make it a good choice for fine cutting.

With any type of blade, small chips and dust collect in the gullets between the teeth as the blade makes its cut. As a result, the spacing between the teeth also affects how a blade will perform in different materials of various thicknesses. Saw blades are measured in TPI—the number of teeth per inch of blade length. An alternate way of measuring blades is in PPI, or points per inch; the PPI of a blade is always one unit more than the TPI. As a general rule, saws with fewer TPI can cut more quickly, but more roughly, than those with more TPI. In thick material, small, closely spaced teeth may produce more debris than the gullets can carry. The blade will tend to clog and bind. On the other hand, since small, closely spaced teeth cut smoothly, they perform well in thin stock or hard material where the rate of feed is reduced. The chart below suggests appropriate TPI for various kinds of materials and thicknesses.

THE SHAPE AND NUMBER OF SAW TEETH

SAW TOOTH AND MATERIAL GUIDE

TYPE OF MATERIAL	THICKNESS OF MATERIAL			
	1/4"	1/4" - 5/8"	5/8" - 1 1/4"	Over 1 1/4"
SOLID WOOD	NUMBER OF TEETH PER INCH (TPI)			
Soft	8 - 12	6 - 8	6	4
Medium	12	6 - 8	6	6
Hard	12	8	6 - 8	6 - 8
PLYWOOD	10 - 12	6 - 8	6 - 8	—
FIBERBOARD				
Medium density fiberboard	8	6 - 8	6	— —
Hardboard	8 - 12	8	6	—
PARTICLEBOARD				—
Soft and medium	8 - 12	6 - 8	6	—
Hard	8 - 12	6 - 8	6 - 8	—

HANDSAWS

CUTTING ANGLES

The angle at which you hold a saw affects both the speed and the quality of the cut. Begin any cut at a low angle. This establishes a kerf on the surface of the board that guides the blade into the wood on the first few strokes (see QuickTip, below). Once the kerf is deep enough, raise the angle of the saw. A shop-made jig, such as a cutting board (*page 388*), can help you make square cuts. As shown below, a rip saw cuts efficiently at an angle of about 60 degrees while a crosscut saw performs best at about 45 degrees. An angle of about 20 degrees will minimize splintering, but slows the rate of feed.

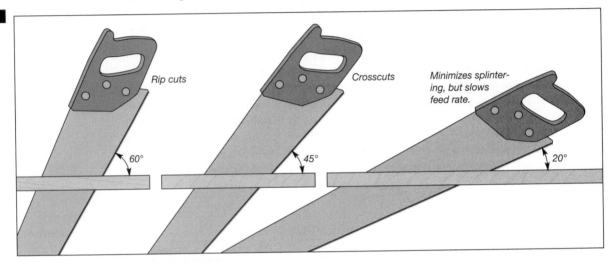

Rip cuts

60°

Crosscuts

45°

Minimizes splintering, but slows feed rate.

20°

*QUICK*TIP

Lining up a saw blade

The first few strokes of a saw cut are critical: They must be perfectly lined up with the cutting mark. One simple way to improve your accuracy is to rest the side of the blade against the thumb of one hand to guide the cut, as shown at right. Start sawing at a low angle and slowly raise the handle as the blade establishes its kerf in the wood. Shown at right is a frame saw making a rip cut.

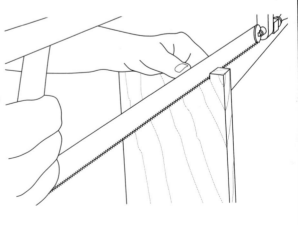

The best way to cut a miter by hand is with a miter box. To use the commercial model shown at right, first fasten it to a plywood panel and clamp the panel to a work surface. Adjust the blade to the desired angle; 45 degrees is typical for miter cuts. Raise the saw assembly and slide the workpiece into the box flush against the fence so that the cutting mark is directly below the blade. Gently set the blade down and draw it back across the workpiece a few times to establish the kerf. Continue the cut with the blade parallel to the surface of the workpiece at all times. Allow the weight of the saw assembly to do the work, applying force only to move the blade back and forth.

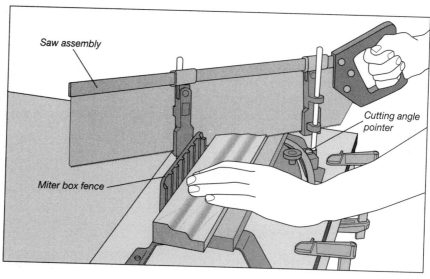

Saw assembly

Cutting angle pointer

Miter box fence

FLUSH CUTS

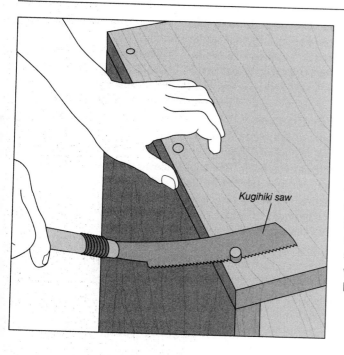

Kugihiki saw

The Japanese kugihiki saw, shown at left, is the best handsaw for trimming dowel pegs flush with a surface. Its blade is knife-thin and exceptionally flexible. The saw has very little set to the teeth, so there is little risk of marring the stock. To make the cut, butt the teeth against the base of the protruding dowel. Press down on the handle to flex the blade flat on the surface on the pull stroke and relax the pressure when pushing the blade back through the kerf.

HANDSAWS

CURVED CUTS WITH A BOWSAW

To change the blade on a bowsaw, unwind the handle rod to slacken the tourniquet and release tension on the blade. Once the new blade is installed, wind the handle rod until the blade is sufficiently taut, and rest the rod on the stretcher to prevent the tourniquet from loosening. To make a cut, grip the handle in both hands with the index finger of one hand resting on the edge of the blade, as shown at left. Start the cut slowly, keeping the blade square to the workpiece as it penetrates the wood. Hold the saw level throughout, turning the handle to follow the curve and maneuvering the frame clear of the workpiece. In soft, relatively thin stock, the weight of the saw's frame will apply adequate pressure on the blade. In harder, thicker material, you will need to apply gentle pressure. If the blade loses its tautness during a cut, tighten the handle rod to restore proper tension.

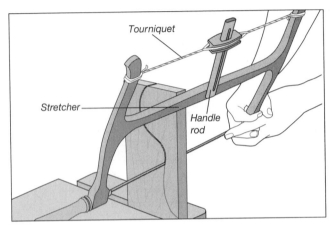

Tourniquet

Stretcher

Handle rod

INTERIOR CUTS WITH A COPING SAW

Fretwork is often used as a decorative element on furniture. The coping saw is the best hand tool for cutting its intricate interior curves. First lay out the pattern on the workpiece, then drill starter holes through the waste areas large enough to accept a coping saw blade. (Place a backup board on the back face of the workpiece as you drill to prevent tearout.) Clamp the panel 1 in a vise, remove the blade from the saw, and insert it through one of the starter holes. Remount the blade, making sure its teeth are pointing away from the handle. To make each cut, hold the blade perpendicular to the face of the workpiece 2 and cut along the waste side of the pattern lines until the waste piece breaks free. Work with even, long strokes, applying gentle pressure only on the push stroke. This will minimize the amount of sanding you will have to do later. Disassemble the blade and repeat the process to clear the remaining waste areas. On some cuts, you may have to turn the fitting levers so the frame clears the edge of the panel.

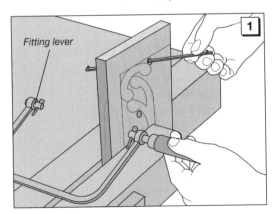

Fitting lever

1

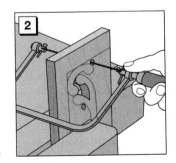

2

CHISELS

Chisels are basically sharpened wedges. So, too, are most cutting tools. The hand plane, for example, was originally little more than a mortised wooden block that held a chisel at a preset angle. Today, chisels come in many forms and sizes for a host of specific tasks. To use them properly, you must know how to select the right one for the job at hand. You also have to know how to keep the tool sharp. This section will help you do both.

ESSENTIAL WOODWORKING CHISELS

Paring chisel
As the name indicates, the ideal chisel for paring to a line (see page 81); features a relatively long blade with beveled sides. Almost always used with the bevel up; its length makes it easy to change the angle of attack. Available in widths from ¼ inch to 2 inches.

Framing chisel
Also known as a firmer chisel; a more rugged, rectangular-bladed version of the paring chisel. For added strength, its handle is separated from the blade by a ferrule and leather washer; designed to be struck with a mallet. Available in widths from ⅛ inch to 2 inches.

Lock mortise chisel
Also known as a swan-neck chisel; features a curved blade for smoothing the bottom of mortises. Available in widths from ⅜ inch to ⅝ inch.

Mortising chisel
Struck with a mallet to chop out mortises (see page 277); rectangular in cross section, the blade is strong and shaped to make it easy to get into corners. Available in widths from ⅛ inch to 2 inches; it is best to outline the width of a mortise according to the chisel blade width.

Drawer lock chisel
Designed to be struck with a hammer for cutting recess mortises for lock plates and hinges; the cutting edges at opposite ends of the blade are perpendicular to each other. Available in widths from ⅜ inch to ⅝ inch.

Corner chisel
The L-shaped blade and two perpendicular cutting edges are designed to remove waste from the corners of mortises; available in various widths starting at ⅜ inch.

Skew chisel
The 60° angle of the blade's cutting edge makes this chisel useful for cleaning out corners and shearing off end grain, as in trimming dovetails; comes in both right- and left-angle versions. Available in widths from ½ inch to 1 inch.

CHISELS

Bevel-edged chisel
*Also known as a cabinetmaker's or bevel-edged firmer chisel;
used to cut hinge mortises. Can be used with hand pressure only
for fine cutting, but sturdy enough to be struck with a mallet.*

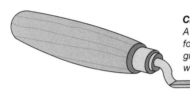

Cranked-neck paring chisel
*A specialized chisel with an offset handle, ideal
for paring the bottoms of long dadoes and
grooves; the blade remains flat on the stock
with the handle elevated above it.*

**PROS AND CONS
OF VARIOUS
SHARPENING
STONES**
(Chart information
courtesy Diamond
Machining
Technology Inc.)

TYPE OF STONE	ADVANTAGES	DISADVANTAGES
Oilstones	• Slurry not necessary • Relatively inexpensive • Available in a variety of sizes and shapes • Easy to flatten • Will not cause tools to rust • Resist damage from tools • Uniform grit	• Wear quickly • Finer grits are moderately expensive • Residual oil can stain wood
Waterstones	• Cut more quickly than oilstones • Synthetic stones are inexpensive • Available in a wide range of grits • Larger sizes are less expensive than oilstones or diamond stones	• Wear very quickly • Water can cause tools to rust • Require a slurry before use • Must be kept wet during use • Must be protected from freezing • Relatively fragile
Ceramic stones	• Easy to clean up, since lubricant is not necessary • Remain flat • Long-lasting • Available in extra-fine grits	• Expensive • Cut slowly • Load quickly • Limited grits available • Fragile
Diamond stones	• Cut quickly • Do not require lubricant • Durable and long-lasting • Flattest and truest of sharpening stones	• Expensive • Limited grits available

USES OF OILSTONES AND WATERSTONES

OILSTONES	BASIC GRINDING OR EDGE-SHAPING	INITIAL SHARPENING	MIDDLE-LEVEL SHARPENING	FINAL SHARPENING	HONING OR POLISHING	STROPPING
Crystolon (oil-impregnated silicon carbide)						
100 coarse	Yes	No	No	No	No	No
180 medium	Yes	Yes	No	No	No	No
280 fine	No	Yes	No	No	No	No
India (oil-impregnated aluminum oxide)						
100 coarse	Yes	No	No	No	No	No
240 medium	No	Yes	No	No	No	No
280-300 fine	No	No	Yes	No	No	No
Soft Arkansas	No	Yes	Yes	No	No	No
Hard Arkansas	No	No	Yes	Yes	No	No
Hard Black Arkansas	No	No	No	Yes	Yes	No
WATERSTONES						
Japan No. 800	No	Yes	No	No	No	No
Japan No. 1000	No	Yes	Yes	No	No	No
Japan No. 1200	No	No	Yes	Yes	No	No
Japan Finish	No	No	No	Yes	Yes	No
Japan Super	No	No	No	No	Yes	No
Strope Wheels	No	No	No	No	No	Yes

USES OF CERAMIC AND DIAMOND STONES

TYPE OF STONE	GRIT	USES
Ceramic	Medium	Removing burrs and other damage; initial sharpening
	Fine	Sharpening and refining edges
	Ultra-fine	Honing and polishing
Diamond	Extra-coarse	Dressing damaged blades
	Coarse	Rapid sharpening
	Fine	Honing and refining edges
	Extra-fine	Polishing

(Chart information courtesy Diamond Machining Technology Inc.)

CHISELS

**SHARPENING
A CHISEL**

If the cutting edge of a chisel is chipped, or repeated sharpenings have worn away the primary bevel, regrind the bevel on a bench grinder. The procedure is similar to that shown for plane irons on page 85. Otherwise, honing is all that is required to keep a chisel in good working order. Honing involves two steps: The first creates a microbevel on the

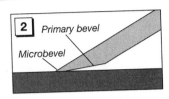

2 Primary bevel

Microbevel

blade's leading edge and the second removes the resulting burr from the back face of the chisel. Start by securing a combination stone 1 coarse-side up on a work surface and lubricating it with a puddle of the appropriate lubricant—either oil or water. Then place the primary bevel of the chisel flat on the stone, raise the handle about 5 degrees, and slide the blade on the surface with an elliptical motion. Continue until a microbevel 2 forms. Repeat the process on the fine side of the stone. The

burr, or fine curl, that forms along the back of the cutting edge must be removed in a process called "lapping." With the fine side of the stone still facing up, hold the back of the chisel flat on the stone 3 and hone it with a circular motion. A few strokes is normally all it takes. Test to be certain you have removed the burr by sliding a thumb along the back of the blade. It should be smooth to the touch.

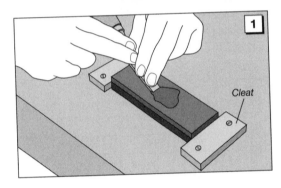

1

Cleat

3

QUICKTIP

A sharpening-stone holder

One of the biggest problems with sharpening stones is that their surfaces eventually become uneven with repeated use. This is because woodworkers generally hone near the center of the stone to ensure that blades are not damaged by slipping off the ends. The shop-made holder shown at right will enable you to hone in long strokes and utilize the entire surface of the stone, resulting in more even wear. To make the holder, screw two wood blocks to a wood base to hold the stone in place. The blocks should be the same thickness as the stone and their grain should run parallel to its length.

The illustrations on this page, which show cutting a hinge mortise, demonstrate proper use of the chisel for many typical woodworking applications. Secure the workpiece and use the hinge as a template to outline the mortise. The first step involves scoring the outline. Start by making a cut at both ends just on the waste side of the line with a bevel-edged chisel about the same width as the hinge 1 . Hold the chisel vertically with the bevel facing the waste and tap the handle with a mallet, scoring the wood to the desired depth, up to a maximum of about ⅛ inch. Repeat this process around the perimeter of the mortise. To simplify removal of the waste, use the same technique to score a row of cuts at ¼-inch intervals from one end of the mortise to the other. Next, hold the chisel blade horizontally with the beveled side up 2 between your thumb and index finger. Pare out the waste by pressing the cutting edge into the face of the workpiece and moving the handle back and forth in a shearing motion. If the mortise is deeper than about ⅛ inch, remove the waste in a series of layers, scoring the mortise outline before each pass.

USING A CHISEL

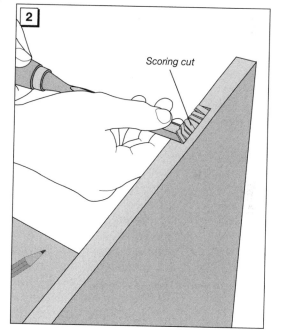

Scoring cut

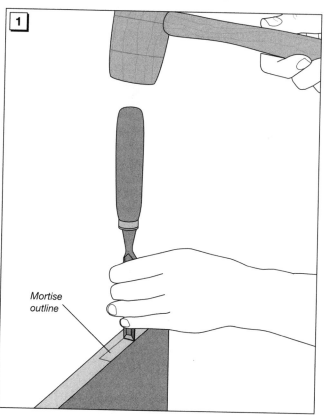

Mortise outline

PLANES AND SCRAPERS

As the beginning woodworker collects tools, it is remarkable how many of them relate to smoothing wood. Preparing projects for a finish can be tedious work—which explains the rise of timesaving devices such as sanding blocks, electric drill sanding attachments, and belt sanders. As their experience grows, however, many woodworkers tend to gravitate toward planes and scrapers for smoothing wood. Long before sandpaper was invented, these were the tools that craftsmen used and, in

ANATOMY OF A BENCH PLANE

STEEL-BODIED SMOOTHING PLANE
A general purpose plane for smoothing faces and edges; the sole is 2 to 2½ inches wide and 8 to 10 inches long.

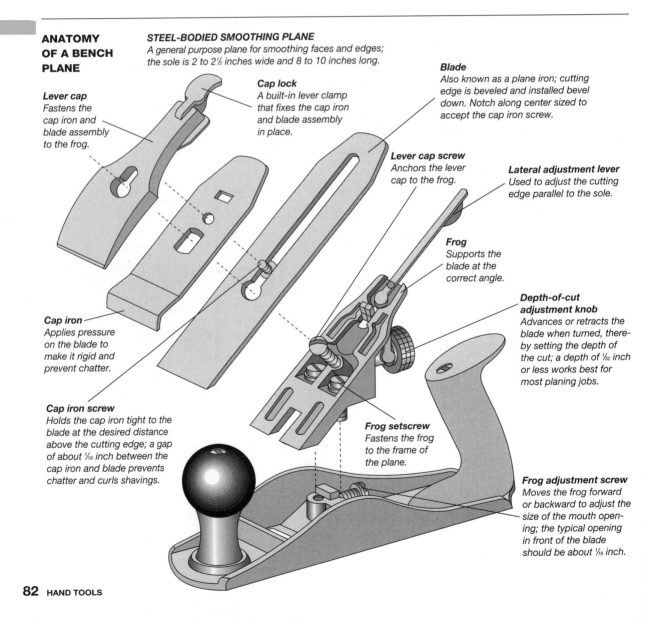

Lever cap
Fastens the cap iron and blade assembly to the frog.

Cap lock
A built-in lever clamp that fixes the cap iron and blade assembly in place.

Blade
Also known as a plane iron; cutting edge is beveled and installed bevel down. Notch along center sized to accept the cap iron screw.

Lever cap screw
Anchors the lever cap to the frog.

Lateral adjustment lever
Used to adjust the cutting edge parallel to the sole.

Frog
Supports the blade at the correct angle.

Depth-of-cut adjustment knob
Advances or retracts the blade when turned, thereby setting the depth of the cut; a depth of ¹⁄₃₂ inch or less works best for most planing jobs.

Cap iron
Applies pressure on the blade to make it rigid and prevent chatter.

Cap iron screw
Holds the cap iron tight to the blade at the desired distance above the cutting edge; a gap of about ¹⁄₁₆ inch between the cap iron and blade prevents chatter and curls shavings.

Frog setscrew
Fastens the frog to the frame of the plane.

Frog adjustment screw
Moves the frog forward or backward to adjust the size of the mouth opening; the typical opening in front of the blade should be about ¹⁄₁₆ inch.

skilled hands, they perform very well. Also, the results are often superior: A planed or scraped surface reveals a wood's grain and figure with far greater clarity than a sanded surface, no matter how fine the grit used. To perform properly, planes require careful adjustment, and both planes and scrapers demand periodic sharpening, but these tasks can be mastered quickly. Planes are generally expensive, but they are durable, efficient and, in the long run, economical to use and maintain.

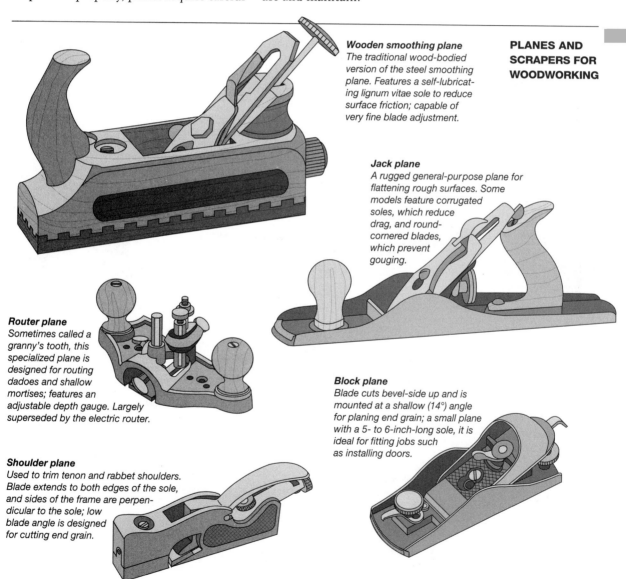

Wooden smoothing plane
The traditional wood-bodied version of the steel smoothing plane. Features a self-lubricating lignum vitae sole to reduce surface friction; capable of very fine blade adjustment.

Jack plane
A rugged general-purpose plane for flattening rough surfaces. Some models feature corrugated soles, which reduce drag, and round-cornered blades, which prevent gouging.

Router plane
Sometimes called a granny's tooth, this specialized plane is designed for routing dadoes and shallow mortises; features an adjustable depth gauge. Largely superseded by the electric router.

Block plane
Blade cuts bevel-side up and is mounted at a shallow (14°) angle for planing end grain; a small plane with a 5- to 6-inch-long sole, it is ideal for fitting jobs such as installing doors.

Shoulder plane
Used to trim tenon and rabbet shoulders. Blade extends to both edges of the sole, and sides of the frame are perpendicular to the sole; low blade angle is designed for cutting end grain.

PLANES AND SCRAPERS

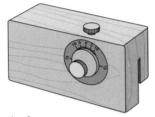

Burnisher
Used to turn the burr, or hook, on scrapers. Its smooth blade may be round, oval, or triangular, depending on the shape of the scraper; the blade of the tri-burnisher shown can be used on most scrapers regardless of their shape.

Variable burnisher
Used for turning the burr on scrapers; this model can be preset to the required angle of the hook, anywhere between 0 and 15°.

Jointing plane
Used for jointing board edges in preparation for glue up and leveling large surfaces; the sole, typically 20 inches or longer, allows the blade to shave down high spots. A must for purists, but largely superseded by the jointer (page 162).

Circle plane
Used to smooth concave or convex curves; flexible spring steel sole adjusts to curved surface.

Hand scraper
Steel blade for smoothing flat or curved surfaces, depending on shape of cutting edge. Available in various thicknesses; the thinnest scrapers are highly flexible and provide excellent control.

Cabinet scraper
Used for leveling high spots and touch-up work, typically after planing; ideal for smoothing knots and removing dried glue. The blade is mounted at a high angle and cuts extremely fine shavings; side handles provide excellent control.

Rabbet-and-filister plane
For planing rabbets either with or across the grain. The body provides two blade-mounting positions for smoothing the bottoms of through and stopped rabbets; the front-mounted position permits use as a bullnose rabbet plane. Features a depth stop and an adjustable guide fence to ensure square cuts. Largely superseded by the router.

Bullnose rabbet plane
The small body of this plane makes it ideal for work in tight places, such as trimming stopped rabbets. As with the shoulder plane, the blade extends to both edges of the sole, but is mounted close to the front; model shown has a removable nose which converts plane into a chisel plane.

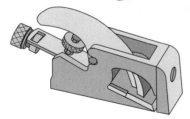

Normally, honing the microbevel and lapping the burr are all you need to do to sharpen a plane blade. However, if the blade is nicked, its primary bevel must be reground. The best way to do this is with a bench grinder 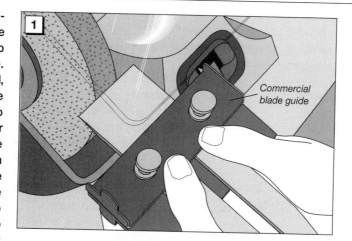 and a commercial blade guide. Position the blade in the guide and set the guide on the tool rest so that the edge of the blade is square to the grinding wheel. Adjust the rest so that the blade will meet the wheel at the proper angle, typically 30 degrees. Then, with the blade clear of the wheel, turn on the grinder, advance the blade, and gently slide it back and forth across the wheel. A few passes will usually restore the bevel. Periodically dip the blade in water to prevent it from overheating.

The procedure for honing a plane blade is essentially the same as for a chisel (page 80). It helps to use a commercial honing guide  to keep the blade at the proper angle on the sharpening stone. Anchor the stone, coarse-side up, on a work surface and lubricate it. Insert the blade in the honing guide and adjust it so that the primary bevel rests flat on the stone. Slide the blade back and forth across the entire length of the stone. To create the microbevel, turn the stone over and

Commercial
blade guide

Commercial
honing guide

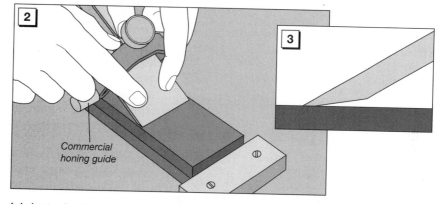

lubricate the fine side. Next, raise the blade in the guide about 5 degrees and hone it until a slight burr appears along the upper edge.

To remove the burr and polish the back of the blade, take the blade out of the honing guide and place it bevel-side up on the fine stone . Holding the blade absolutely flat, hone it gently in a circular motion. After a few light strokes, lift the blade and confirm that the burr is gone by sliding your thumb across the back of the edge.

PLANES AND SCRAPERS

**ADJUSTING
A PLANE**

To perform well, a plane must be assembled and adjusted to relatively tight tolerances. Begin by screw-

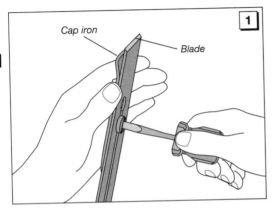

Cap iron

Blade

1

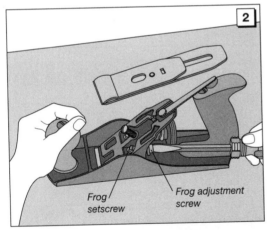

2

Frog setscrew

Frog adjustment screw

ing the cap iron 1 to the blade so that the blade's cutting edge extends about 1/16 inch beyond the front of the cap iron. Make sure the blade and cap iron are parallel to each other as you tighten the cap iron screw. Next, position the blade/cap iron assembly on the frog. The gap be-

tween the leading edge of the blade and the front of the mouth should be about 1/32 to 1/16 inch. If not, remove the blade/cap iron assembly and adjust the frog by loosening the frog setscrews and turning the frog adjustment screw 2. Once you have the correct gap, tighten the frog setscrews, and fasten the blade/cap iron assembly and the lever cap in place.

The next step is to set the depth of cut and center the blade in the mouth. Holding the plane upside down 3, sight down the sole, and turn the depth-of-cut adjustment knob to advance or retract the blade. The depth-of-cut depends on the workpiece: 1/32 inch works well for straight-grained softwoods, but highly figured hardwoods demand an even shallower cut. Finally, move the lateral adjust-

ment lever to the right or left to adjust the cutting edge parallel to the sole of the plane.

There are a variety of plane blades on the market that can give an older tool new life. If you are looking for a replacement blade, a critical consideration is the quality of the metal used in the blade. The softer the steel, the easier it is to sharpen, but the more often it must be sharpened. Conversely, harder blades hold their edge, but tend to be brittle and more heat-sensitive when the primary bevel is reground. Laminated blades provide a workable compromise. They feature a layer of high-tempered steel bonded to softer steel. One disadvantage is their high price. Extra-hard blades are thicker than standard blades, which makes them easier to sharpen and more stable in use.

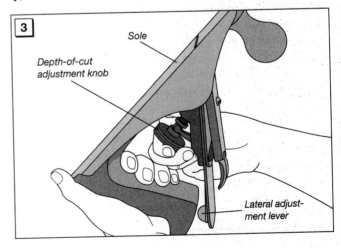

3

Sole

Depth-of-cut adjustment knob

Lateral adjustment lever

Hand planing is best done in a direction that is "uphill" in relation to the wood fibers on the surface. However, the visible figure in the wood grain is a poor indicator of wood fiber direction. Experienced woodworkers determine the best planing direction by making a pass on a workpiece and examining the cut surface. If the planing direction is appropriate, the blade will lift a thin wood shaving; planing in the wrong direction will cause tearout.

Depending on fiber orientation, some boards may need to be planed from the ends toward the middle or from the middle toward the ends. In some cases, you will have to reduce the depth of cut and hold the plane at an oblique angle to the planing direction.

To smooth a board edge [1], secure the workpiece and set the sole of the plane flat on the surface so that the blade is beyond the end. Hold the plane with both hands and guide the tool in a continuous stroke along the edge. Begin the stroke by applying pressure down on the front of the plane. Gradually shift pressure to the back of the plane to keep the sole flat on the board. Continue the process until the surface is smooth.

To smooth a board face [2], follow the same procedure as you would for smoothing an edge, making a series of overlapping side-by-side passes until the surface is smooth. Holding the plane at a slight angle to the planing direction, as shown, will minimize tear-out. Check for high spots with a straightedge and reduce the plane's cutting depth before planing down any uneven areas.

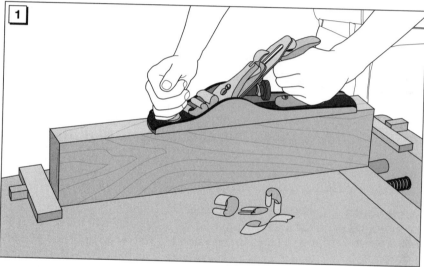

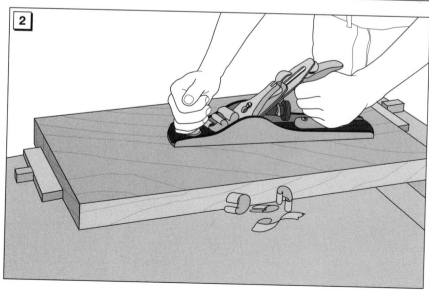

PLANES AND SCRAPERS

PRINCIPLES OF SHARPENING A HAND SCRAPER

Sharpening a hand scraper involves three steps: Filing, honing, and burnishing. Filing removes all traces of the previous burr. Honing prepares the edge by removing any flaws left by filing and flattening the edges of the scraper so that they are square to the face, as shown below *(left)*. Burnishing first raises a burr *(center)*, and then turns it over into a hook *(right)*. The scraper is now ready to be used. Step-by-step instructions for sharpening a scraper are provided below and on the following page.

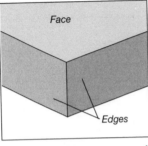
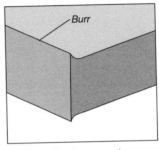
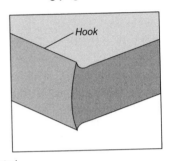

The thickness of the scraper, as well as the burr and hook, are greatly exaggerated for clarity. In practice, the burr and hook are not nearly as visible or pronounced. Their presence is usually confirmed with the touch of a finger rather than by eye.

TECHNIQUES FOR SHARPENING A HAND SCRAPER

Clamp the scraper in a vise supported by a wood block on one side to hold it rigid ☐1. Install a flat mill bastard file in a commercial saw jointer and, holding the jointer against one side of the scraper, file the edge until it is perfectly flat. Turn the scraper over in the vise and repeat the process on the opposite edge. Next, anchor a sharpening stone fine-side up on a work surface and lubricate it with water or oil ☐2. Pressing the scraper flat on the stone, hone both faces using a gentle circular motion. This will remove file marks and ensure the edge is square to the faces. Repeat with the other cutting edge.

To complete the sharpening process, you must create a burr on both sides of each cutting edge and then roll the burrs into hooks, as shown in the illustrations above. Clamp the scraper in a vise and apply a thin film of oil on the edge as a lubricant. Pass a bur-

Wood block

Saw jointer

Flat mill bastard file

nisher along the edge, hold-ing the tool at a 90-degree angle to the scraper's edge. Applying firm downward pres-sure, make several passes to create a burr on each side of the edge. To roll each burr over into a "hook," continue bur-nishing, gradually inclining the handle of the burnisher down until it is tilted at an angle of about 10 degrees to the edge of the scraper 3. Repeat along the other side of the edge of the scraper with the burnisher's handle tilted up by about 10 degrees. Turn the scraper over in the vise and repeat the process to roll the burrs and the hooks on the opposite edge.

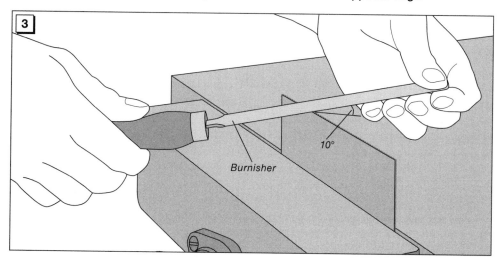

Burnisher

10°

PLANES AND SCRAPERS

**USING
A HAND
SCRAPER**

The hand scraper is one of the most versatile of all smoothing tools. Although it is sometimes used across the grain when leveling varnished surfaces, it performs best on raw wood when the direction of travel is with the grain. To cut properly, the blade must be flexed slightly. Grip the scraper in both hands with your thumbs pressing against the back to bow the blade in the direction of travel and push it across the surface, as shown at right. Tilt the blade forward until it bites into the stock. The depth of cut depends on how much you tilt the blade. Lift the scraper off the workpiece toward the end of the stroke to prevent the hook from marring the surface. You can also cut with a scraper on the pull stroke by reversing the tilt, moving your fingers together, and applying pressure with your fingers to bow it in the direction of travel.

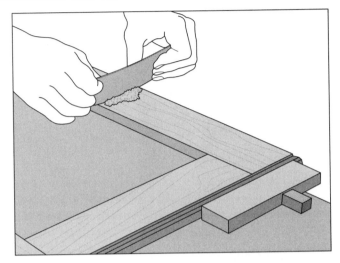

**SHARPENING
A CABINET
SCRAPER**

Cabinet scraper blades are sharpened in much the same way as hand scrapers. Remove the blade from the scraper and clamp it in a vise. File the blade with a flat mill bastard file, drawing the file along the bevel to remove the old burr. Hold the file at an angle to the blade to avoid gouging the bevel. Then hone the bevel on a sharpening stone as you would a hand scraper *(page 89)*. To form a burr and turn it over into a hook, return the blade to the vise and use a burnisher. To create the burr, start at a steep angle of about 45 degrees, pulling the burnisher along the bevel with light pressure. Make several passes. To create the hook, gradually decrease the angle and increase the pressure, until the burnisher is at an angle of about 15 degrees to the blade, as shown above. Many cabinet scrapers have a double-edged blade. With these, sharpen both edges the same way.

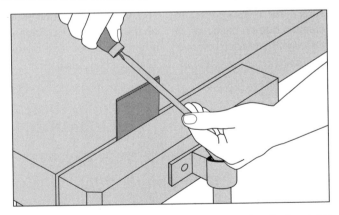

1

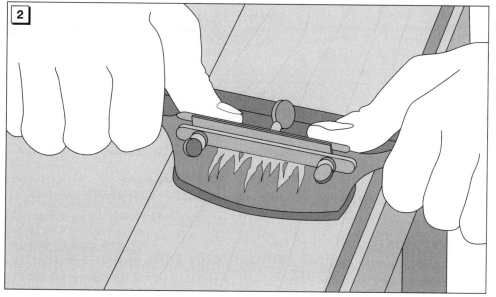

Thumbscrew

Slip the blade into the scraper with the beveled edge facing the back. With the scraper upside down, position the blade for the desired depth of cut, typically between $\frac{1}{32}$ and $\frac{1}{64}$ inch. Holding the blade with one hand, tighten the two thumbscrews on the front of the tool to secure the blade in place $\boxed{1}$. The cabinet scraper cuts with the top of the blade tilted in the direction of travel. To smooth a board, grip the scraper in both hands with your thumbs pressed against the back of the tool $\boxed{2}$. Then push the scraper along the surface, keeping the sole flat on the workpiece. At the end of each pass, lift the tool off the stock and empty out the shavings.

USING A CABINET SCRAPER

2

SHAPING TOOLS

Because shaping wood often involves curved or irregular surfaces, few shaping tools have been superseded by automation. Most of the tools shown below and on page 93 would be recognized by an 18th-Century craftsman. A few, such as the shaver or planer rasp, use modern blades, but their purpose is so obvious that using them poses little mystery.

Shaping tools are generally designed for coarse work and the quick removal of waste stock, but a few perform multiple tasks. Files, for example, are indispensable for shaping wood and sharpening bits and blades. On flat, half-round, and triangular files, as well as patternmaker's and concave rasps, mount a handle for greater control and comfort.

As shown on page 94, a file has one of three types of teeth and one of three grades of coarseness. The types of teeth are rasp-cut, single-cut, and double-cut. The grades of coarseness are bastard cut (coarsest), second cut (moderately smooth), and smooth cut (smoothest).

FILES AND RASPS

Flat file
Coarse, general-purpose file for smoothing wood and sharpening tool blades and scrapers.

Half-round file
Features both flat and curved cutting faces for smoothing similar-shaped surfaces.

Triangular file
Used to clean out angles, cut grooves or notches, and sharpen tools; available with coarse or fine teeth and in various sizes from 6 to 10 inches.

Patternmaker's rasp
Used for shaping irregular surfaces; similar in profile to the half-round file. Its teeth provide smoother cutting than with a standard rasp.

Concave rasp
Staggered rows of teeth on this knife-shaped rasp allow it to cut smoothly on concave surfaces.

Round file
Also known as a rat-tail file; used for filing tight curves and smoothing or enlarging holes. Tapers toward the tip.

Needle rasp
Ideal for detailed shaping work and carving; typically about 6 inches long and available in a variety of shapes.

Planer rasp
Useful for shaping curved surfaces; its stamped tubular blade cuts with rasp-like action, but allows debris to pass through perforations without clogging. Different profiles are available.

Shaping plane
Ideal for rough-shaping work in soft wood; stamped replaceable blade cuts quickly. Similar in cutting action to the shaver, but larger; handles provide two-handed control.

Inshave
Designed for scooping out hollows, as on chair seats; like the drawknife, the inshave is a two-handed tool that cuts on the pull stroke.

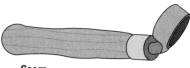

Drawknife
Used for quickly removing large amounts of stock when rough-shaping a wood blank; shaving square blanks into round chair legs or rungs is a typical application. The beveled cutting edge cuts on the pull stroke; the angle at which the handle is held controls the depth of cut.

Spokeshave
Shapes flat or curved edges, such as rungs, spokes, and spindles; the spoke-shave is used with both hands and may be pushed or pulled. Available in both flat-face and round-face models.

Scorp
Used with one hand to shape con-cave surfaces, such as spoons and small bowls; similar to the inshave but the blade features a tighter curve.

Japanese planer-rasp
Used for shaping, this versatile tool has a tapered blade for getting into tight places; the double handle can be mounted to expose the fine teeth on one side of the blade or the coarse teeth on the other.

File card
A flat brush with short steel bris-tles used to remove debris from the teeth of files and rasps.

Riffler
Coarse-tooth versions are ideal for shaping irregular surfaces and getting into tight spots; the ends of the file are tapered and curved.

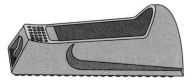

Pocket plane
Shapes and smooths wood much like a rasp, but cuts more quickly and is less likely to clog; the stamped grate-like blade covers the entire sole.

Shaver
Used to shape curved edges; the perforated stamped blade cuts like a rasp, but allows debris to escape through the blade.

SHAPING TOOLS

**WOODWORK-
ING FILES**
(Illustrations cour-
tesy CooperTools,
makers of Nicholson
Files & Rasps)

TYPE AND CROSS SECTION		COARSENESS AND TYPE OF TEETH	TYPICAL USES
Auger bit	▬	Bastard, second cut, and smooth; single-cut.	For sharpening bits; with safe, or uncut, edges at one end and safe sides at other end, surfaces adjacent to those being sharpened will not be damaged.
Cabinet	◖	Bastard, second cut, and smooth; double-cut.	For smoothing wood.
Flat	▬	Usually bastard, but also second cut and smooth; double-cut on sides and single-cut on edges.	For removing material quickly; handy for shaping grooves, squaring holes, and working in corners.
Half-round	◖	Usually bastard, but also second cut and smooth. Flat sides are double-cut; backs of bastard files are double cut, while backs of smooth files are single-cut.	Flat side is used on flat or convex surfaces; half-round side is ideal for concave surfaces.
Hand	▬	Bastard, second cut, and smooth; double-cut.	With one safe, or uncut, edge, this file is ideal for working in corners with an adjoining surface that should not be filed.
Mill	▬	Bastard, second cut, and smooth; single-cut.	For jointing and sharpening handsaw blades and sharpening scrapers; for shaping and smoothing wood.
Pillar	▪	Bastard; double-cut.	For filing slots and keyways.
Round	●	Usually bastard, but also second cut and smooth; single- and double-cut.	For filing circular openings or concave surfaces.
Triangular	▲	Bastard, second cut, and smooth; single-cut.	For sharpening 60° handsaw teeth.
Wood	◖	Bastard; double-cut.	For shaping wood without clogging.

COARSENESS OF FILE TEETH

Bastard cut
(relatively rough)

Second cut
(medium smooth)

Smooth cut
(relatively smooth)

TYPES OF FILE TEETH

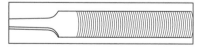

Rasp-cut files
Consist of individual teeth used to rough-shape wood.

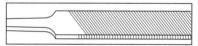

Single-cut files
Feature a single set of teeth with parallel rows arranged diagonally; typically used with light pressure to smooth wood surfaces or sharpen saws.

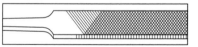

Double-cut files
Have two sets of teeth with parallel rows arranged diagonally. The second set is laid over the first at about a 90° angle; typically used with heavy pressure to remove more material from a workpiece.

TOOLS FOR BORING

The vital role once played by the brace-and-bit and other traditional hand-powered boring tools has been much reduced. The electric drill and the drill press have minimized the drudgery involved in boring pilot holes for nails and screws, and other repetitive tasks such as boring round mortises for chair making. The modern variable-speed reversible power drill has become the preferred tool not only for boring holes, but also for driving screws. Still, there are occasions when hand-powered boring tools outperform their modern counterparts. The great leverage afforded by a brace-and-bit, for example, can prove indispensable for boring large-diameter holes or cranking down a heavy screw. Other tools, such as the gimlet, countersinks, and screw starter, shown on the following page, deserve a place in the modern shop simply because they are so quick and handy.

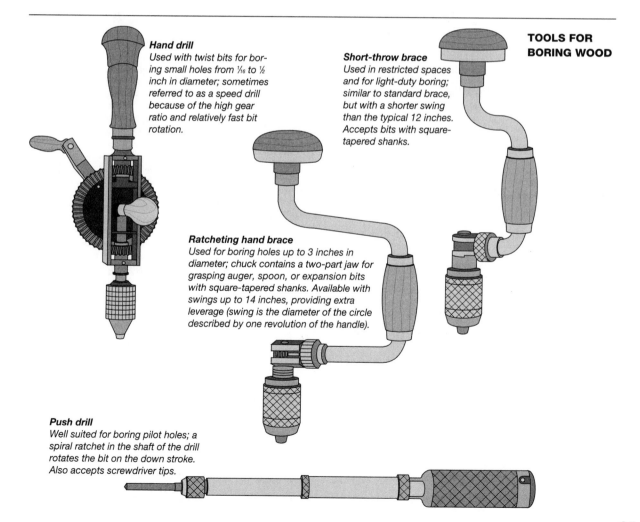

TOOLS FOR BORING WOOD

Hand drill
Used with twist bits for boring small holes from 1/16 to 1/2 inch in diameter; sometimes referred to as a speed drill because of the high gear ratio and relatively fast bit rotation.

Short-throw brace
Used in restricted spaces and for light-duty boring; similar to standard brace, but with a shorter swing than the typical 12 inches. Accepts bits with square-tapered shanks.

Ratcheting hand brace
Used for boring holes up to 3 inches in diameter; chuck contains a two-part jaw for grasping auger, spoon, or expansion bits with square-tapered shanks. Available with swings up to 14 inches, providing extra leverage (swing is the diameter of the circle described by one revolution of the handle).

Push drill
Well suited for boring pilot holes; a spiral ratchet in the shaft of the drill rotates the bit on the down stroke. Also accepts screwdriver tips.

TOOLS FOR BORING

BORING TOOLS FOR WOOD-WORKING

Hand countersink
Bores cone-shaped holes so that flat head screws can be driven flush with the surface of the wood.

Screw starter
Used to center and start holes for screws; large-diameter wooden handle provides adequate leverage.

Countersink bit
Performs the same function as the hand countersink; available diameters from ½ to ¾ inch. Bits with round shanks are designed for drills; square-tapered shanks are for use with braces.

Solid-center auger bit
The standard bit for use with a brace; the lead screw draws the two cutting spurs into the wood. Available in various shaft lengths and diameters.

Spoon bit
Used for boring dowel holes in frame construction and round mortises for chair legs and rails; shaped like a round-tipped gouge, the spoon bit is an ancient design.

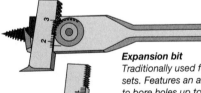

Double-twist auger bit
Used in braces; available in ¼- to 1½-inch diameters. The tight continuous spiral of this bit facilitates removal of debris; sometimes referred to as the Jennings Pattern Auger.

Brad-point wood bit
Used with hand drill; the brad point centers the hole while two spur-type cutters penetrate the surface, leaving a sharp-edged hole with less tearout than is produced by twist drills.

Expansion bit
Traditionally used for drilling holes in doors for lock sets. Features an adjustable cutter that can be set to bore holes up to 3 inches in diameter; most models come with second cutter for smaller holes.

Screwdriver bit
Ideal for driving large screws where high torque is required. Tip designed for driving slotted screws; square-tapered shank fits the two-jawed chuck of a standard brace.

Twist drill
The standard bit for use with the hand drill; the spiral shaft ends in a cone-shaped tip, forming two cutters. Available in sizes up to ½ inch in diameter; diameters greater than ⅜ inch generally have reduced shanks to accommodate ¼-, ⅜-, or ½-inch chucks.

Drill point
Used with the hand drill or push drill for boring pilot holes; fluted, rather than spiral, cutters allow this bit to bore holes very quickly.

Ring-handled gimlet
A primitive but very handy tool that makes pilot holes for screws or nails; the threaded tip pulls bit into the wood. Inserting a stick or screwdriver shaft in the handle ring improves leverage.

STRIKING AND FASTENING TOOLS

The purpose of most striking and fastening tools—hammers, mallets, and screwdrivers—seems pretty obvious, but choosing the right one for the job at hand is not always clearcut. Differences in the weight, size, and shape of various tools can be both subtle and significant. Refer to the information on the following pages to help choose the right tool for the job. Always buy good-quality tools. Whether you are driving nails or screws or striking a chisel, you will appreciate a tool that is well balanced, comfortable to hold, and capable of delivering the needed force with precision.

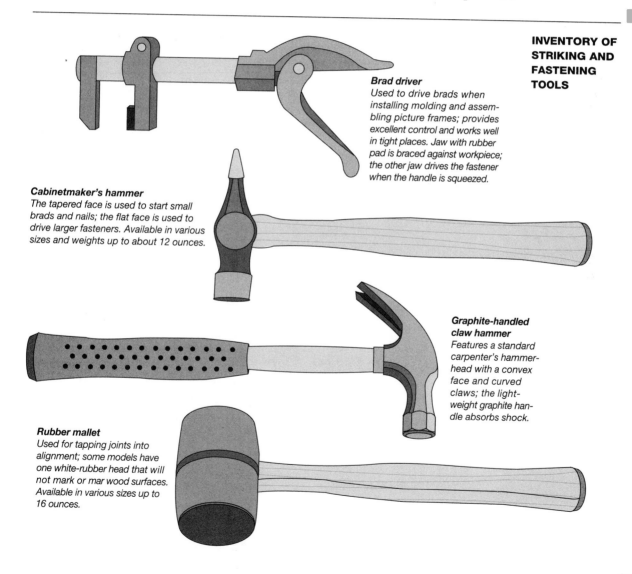

Brad driver
Used to drive brads when installing molding and assembling picture frames; provides excellent control and works well in tight places. Jaw with rubber pad is braced against workpiece; the other jaw drives the fastener when the handle is squeezed.

Cabinetmaker's hammer
The tapered face is used to start small brads and nails; the flat face is used to drive larger fasteners. Available in various sizes and weights up to about 12 ounces.

Graphite-handled claw hammer
Features a standard carpenter's hammer-head with a convex face and curved claws; the lightweight graphite handle absorbs shock.

Rubber mallet
Used for tapping joints into alignment; some models have one white-rubber head that will not mark or mar wood surfaces. Available in various sizes up to 16 ounces.

STRIKING AND FASTENING TOOLS

INVENTORY OF STRIKING AND FASTENING TOOLS

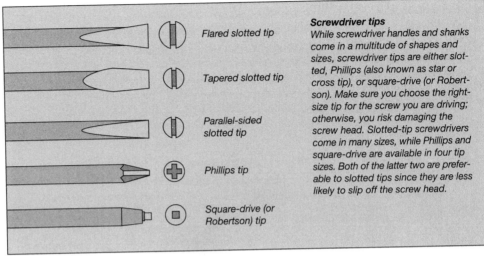

Flared slotted tip

Tapered slotted tip

Parallel-sided slotted tip

Phillips tip

Square-drive (or Robertson) tip

Screwdriver tips
While screwdriver handles and shanks come in a multitude of shapes and sizes, screwdriver tips are either slotted, Phillips (also known as star or cross tip), or square-drive (or Robertson). Make sure you choose the right-size tip for the screw you are driving; otherwise, you risk damaging the screw head. Slotted-tip screwdrivers come in many sizes, while Phillips and square-drive are available in four tip sizes. Both of the latter two are preferable to slotted tips since they are less likely to slip off the screw head.

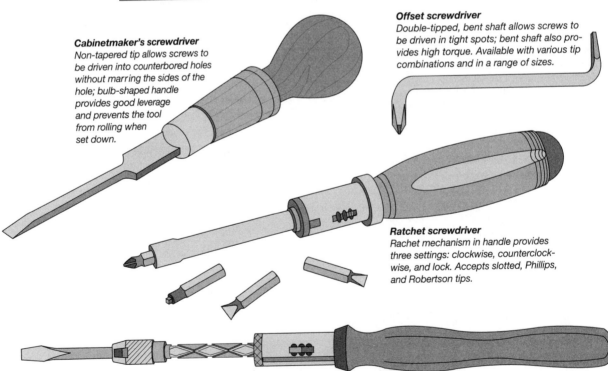

Cabinetmaker's screwdriver
Non-tapered tip allows screws to be driven into counterbored holes without marring the sides of the hole; bulb-shaped handle provides good leverage and prevents the tool from rolling when set down.

Offset screwdriver
Double-tipped, bent shaft allows screws to be driven in tight spots; bent shaft also provides high torque. Available with various tip combinations and in a range of sizes.

Ratchet screwdriver
Rachet mechanism in handle provides three settings: clockwise, counterclockwise, and lock. Accepts slotted, Phillips, and Robertson tips.

Spiral ratchet screwdriver
Similar to the basic ratchet screwdriver, but the tip rotates when the handle is pushed.

Magnetizer/Demagnetizer
Used to magnetize a screwdriver tip so that it will hold steel screws. To magnetize a screwdriver, shank is inserted through hole in device, which is then rubbed back and forth several times along shank and tip; to demagnetize, use one of the slots on the sides of the device.

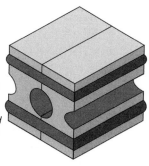

Nail set
Used to drive the heads of brads and finishing nails below the surface of a workpiece; conical, concave-cupped tip helps center the tool on the nail head. Serrated shaft provides sure grip.

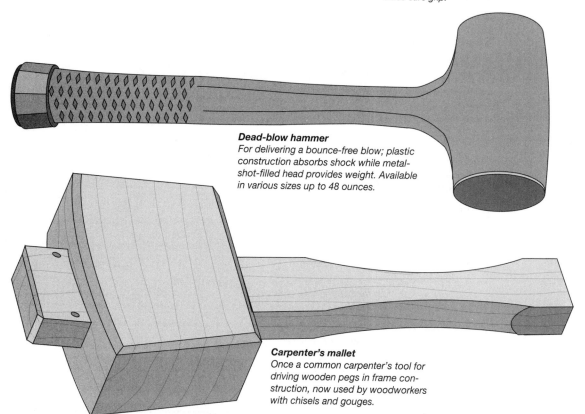

Dead-blow hammer
For delivering a bounce-free blow; plastic construction absorbs shock while metal-shot-filled head provides weight. Available in various sizes up to 48 ounces.

Carpenter's mallet
Once a common carpenter's tool for driving wooden pegs in frame construction, now used by woodworkers with chisels and gouges.

STRIKING AND FASTENING TOOLS

REPAIRING A DAMAGED SCREWDRIVER TIP

A screwdriver with a damaged tip can be repaired on a bench grinder. Using the grinder's coarse-grit wheel, set the tip on the tool rest, as shown at right. Hold the shaft between the thumb and index finger of one hand with the tip clear of the wheel. Turn on the grinder. With your index finger braced against the tool rest, slide the screwdriver forward until the tip touches the wheel. Slide the tip across the wheel from side to side, keeping the tip square to the wheel. Check the tip periodically, continuing until it is square. After every two or three passes across the wheel, cool the tip in a can filled with water.

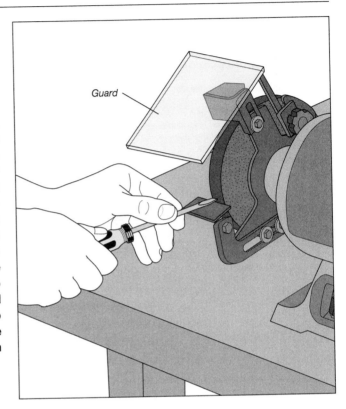

Guard

_QUICK_KTIP_

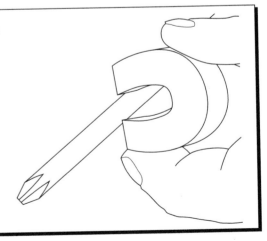

Magnetizing a screwdriver tip

Installing screws in tight spots can be made easier with a magnetized screwdriver, which will hold the screw until it is started. If you do not have a commercial magnetizer/demagnetizer, you can magnetize any steel screwdriver by rubbing a magnet along its shaft a few times. Make each stroke in the same direction. To demagnetize the screwdriver, simply rub it with the magnet in the opposite direction.

PORTABLE POWER TOOLS

Portable power tools are essential in a modern shop. While stationary tools such as the table saw can perform with great accuracy and convenience on parts that are small enough to maneuver and manipulate, portable tools are better when the workpiece is large and bulky. For example, a portable circular saw is often more convenient and safer than a table saw for cutting up full-size sheets of plywood. Some tools, like finish sanders, don't have a stationary counterpart.

Another advantage of portable power tools is versatility; the router and the drill are good examples. The router is arguably the single most important woodworking invention of the 20th Century. It can mold edges and perform a host of milling operations such as rabbeting and dadoing. Teamed up with a jig, the router can form flawless dovetails or cut perfect circles. And mounted upside down in a router table, it can become a mini-shaper.

The drill is another versatile tool. In addition to boring holes, it can be outfitted with a wide array of accessories to shape and sand wood.

Although the saber saw is less capable than its stationary equivalent—the band saw—it is the best portable power tool for cutting inside curves and following intricate fret patterns. Other portable power tools, such as the circular saw and various power sanders, simplify and speed up otherwise tedious tasks.

The plate joiner and the portable planer are more recent arrivals on the power tool scene. The plate joiner may well be destined to revolutionize production joinery, enabling you to assemble a carcase or add a row of shelves to a bookcase in a few minutes. The joint it creates is invisible, durable, and simple to cut.

The portable planer can remove stock more quickly than any hand plane. While traditionalists believe that it does little more than motorize the joy out of one of woodworking's most time-honored and pleasant tasks, the portable planer's speed offers undeniable advantages to someone hanging a door or planing a large surface like a tabletop.

ROUTER

Before the invention of the router in the early part of the 20th Century, cabinetmakers had to rely on molding planes for rabbeting and edging work. Today, the router has made molding planes virtually obsolete; it not only performs these functions with greater speed and less labor, it also can be used on curved edges much more easily. In addition, the router is faster than the mallet and chisel in cutting mortises and dadoes. Although slower than the table saw, the router can cut wider grooves and leave smoother surfaces. In fact, as shown on page 270, it is the preferred tool for making stopped dadoes because the bit leaves less waste to clean out at the stopped end of the dado.

Many woodworkers think of the router as a central power source for a system of tools. It accepts a broad array of bits, works either hand-held or mounted in a table, and can be used with a template or jig to cut hinge mortises or dovetails.

Give careful consideration to selecting a router; you will want it to fit your current and anticipated needs. If most of your routing

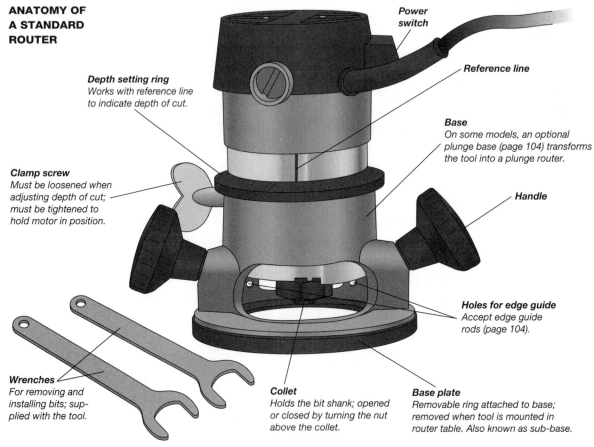

ANATOMY OF A STANDARD ROUTER

Power switch

Depth setting ring
Works with reference line to indicate depth of cut.

Reference line

Base
On some models, an optional plunge base (page 104) transforms the tool into a plunge router.

Clamp screw
Must be loosened when adjusting depth of cut; must be tightened to hold motor in position.

Handle

Holes for edge guide
Accept edge guide rods (page 104).

Wrenches
For removing and installing bits; supplied with the tool.

Collet
Holds the bit shank; opened or closed by turning the nut above the collet.

Base plate
Removable ring attached to base; removed when tool is mounted in router table. Also known as sub-base.

will be hand-held, for example, it is better to sacrifice some size and power in favor of lightweight comfort and portability. A standard router *(page 102)* provides these features and will normally accommodate edge guides and other fixtures that make it a flexible all-purpose tool. A standard router is also the best choice for router table work because adjusting the cutting depth on a plunge router is difficult when the tool is mounted in a table. If you will be doing less edging and more mortising and dadoing, however, a plunge router *(below)* has significant advantages. The best solution might be to

equip your shop with one of each type. In any case, select a tool with at least 1 horsepower. Adjustable speed is another worthwhile option, since small-diameter bits work best at high speeds and larger-diameter bits operate better at slower speeds.

A modern router turning at 20,000 or more rpm can be quite frightening to a woodworker who has never held one. When running and held in midair, it even feels somewhat like a gyroscope. If you have never used a router before, you might be more comfortable buying one with big elongated handles.

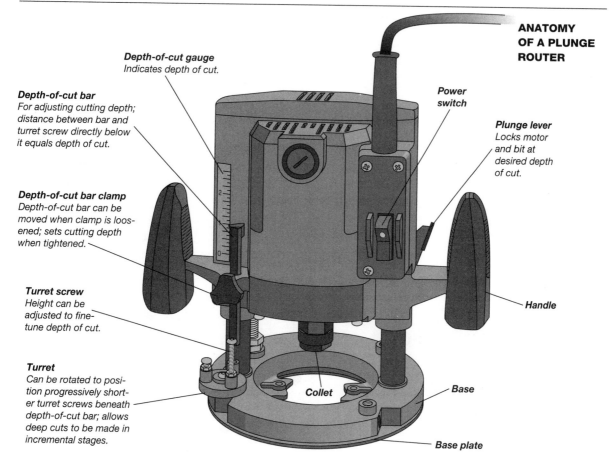

ANATOMY OF A PLUNGE ROUTER

Depth-of-cut gauge
Indicates depth of cut.

Depth-of-cut bar
For adjusting cutting depth; distance between bar and turret screw directly below it equals depth of cut.

Depth-of-cut bar clamp
Depth-of-cut bar can be moved when clamp is loosened; sets cutting depth when tightened.

Turret screw
Height can be adjusted to fine-tune depth of cut.

Turret
Can be rotated to position progressively shorter turret screws beneath depth-of-cut bar; allows deep cuts to be made in incremental stages.

Power switch

Plunge lever
Locks motor and bit at desired depth of cut.

Handle

Collet

Base

Base plate

ROUTER ACCESSORIES

The versatility of the router is a function of the wide variety of accessories that are available for it. They enable the router to perform a multitude of cutting, shaping, and smoothing tasks quickly and accurately, from plowing rabbets and stopped dadoes to fashioning perfect-fitting mortises for hinges. Dovetail jigs can help you rout precise through and half-blind dovetails in a fraction of the time it takes to cut them by hand. Three of the most popular dovetail jigs are shown on pages 281 and 285. Some other useful router accessories are illustrated below.

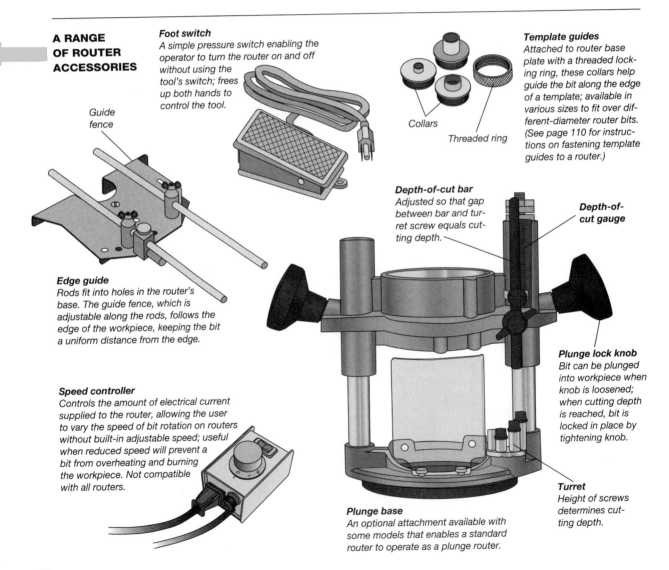

A RANGE OF ROUTER ACCESSORIES

Foot switch
A simple pressure switch enabling the operator to turn the router on and off without using the tool's switch; frees up both hands to control the tool.

Guide fence

Template guides
Attached to router base plate with a threaded locking ring, these collars help guide the bit along the edge of a template; available in various sizes to fit over different-diameter router bits. (See page 110 for instructions on fastening template guides to a router.)

Collars

Threaded ring

Depth-of-cut bar
Adjusted so that gap between bar and turret screw equals cutting depth.

Depth-of-cut gauge

Edge guide
Rods fit into holes in the router's base. The guide fence, which is adjustable along the rods, follows the edge of the workpiece, keeping the bit a uniform distance from the edge.

Plunge lock knob
Bit can be plunged into workpiece when knob is loosened; when cutting depth is reached, bit is locked in place by tightening knob.

Speed controller
Controls the amount of electrical current supplied to the router, allowing the user to vary the speed of bit rotation on routers without built-in adjustable speed; useful when reduced speed will prevent a bit from overheating and burning the workpiece. Not compatible with all routers.

Turret
Height of screws determines cutting depth.

Plunge base
An optional attachment available with some models that enables a standard router to operate as a plunge router.

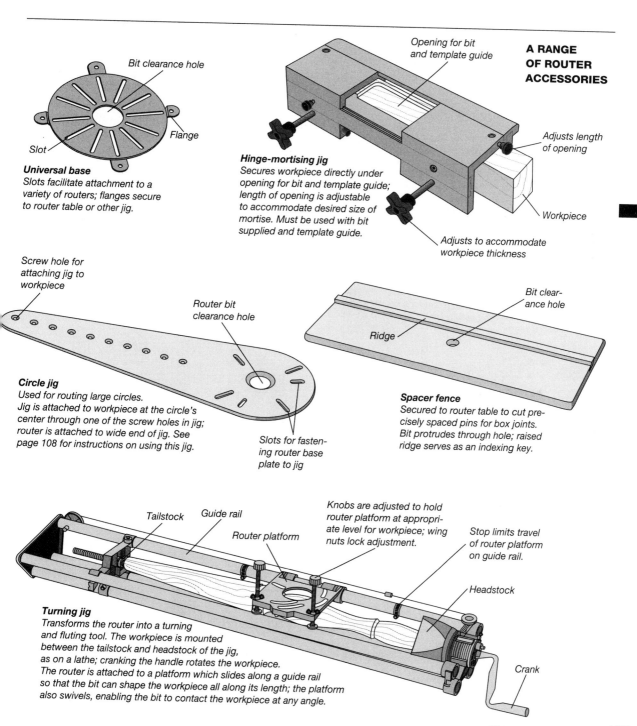

Universal base
Slots facilitate attachment to a variety of routers; flanges secure to router table or other jig.

Bit clearance hole

Slot

Flange

Opening for bit and template guide

Adjusts length of opening

Workpiece

Hinge-mortising jig
Secures workpiece directly under opening for bit and template guide; length of opening is adjustable to accommodate desired size of mortise. Must be used with bit supplied and template guide.

Adjusts to accommodate workpiece thickness

Screw hole for attaching jig to workpiece

Router bit clearance hole

Bit clearance hole

Ridge

Circle jig
Used for routing large circles. Jig is attached to workpiece at the circle's center through one of the screw holes in jig; router is attached to wide end of jig. See page 108 for instructions on using this jig.

Slots for fastening router base plate to jig

Spacer fence
Secured to router table to cut precisely spaced pins for box joints. Bit protrudes through hole; raised ridge serves as an indexing key.

Tailstock

Guide rail

Router platform

Knobs are adjusted to hold router platform at appropriate level for workpiece; wing nuts lock adjustment.

Stop limits travel of router platform on guide rail.

Headstock

Crank

Turning jig
Transforms the router into a turning and fluting tool. The workpiece is mounted between the tailstock and headstock of the jig, as on a lathe; cranking the handle rotates the workpiece. The router is attached to a platform which slides along a guide rail so that the bit can shape the workpiece all along its length; the platform also swivels, enabling the bit to contact the workpiece at any angle.

ROUTER BITS

Router bits come in hundreds of different profiles and sizes. As shown below, a bit's design and shape enable it to be used for a specific application. For example, bits are either plunging or non-plunging. Plunging bits are typically used to cut deep mortises, stopped dadoes, or decorative beads in the middle of a workpiece where the bit does not start or end at the edge. All piloted bits, like the round-over bit, are non-plunging types. Most router bits are designed to be guide—by an edge guide *(page 109)*, a template *(page 110)*, or a pilot on the bit itself. There are two basic types of bit pilots: Ball-bearing and fixed. Most bearing pilots are located below the cutters, but top-piloted bits have specific applications. Bottom-piloted bits are used for edge-shaping the upper edge of a workpiece; the pilot runs along the workpiece or along a template positioned underneath the workpiece. In either case, the pilot keeps the cutting depth uniform.

A RANGE OF ROUTER BITS

PLUNGING AND NON-PLUNGING BITS

Efficient plunging bits are designed so the cutting edges continue around the bottom and are ground to a sharp edge. Bits lacking this feature will tend to spin and chatter.

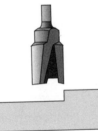

Round-over
A non-plunging bit used to mill a curve along the edge or end of a workpiece; the depth of cut may be adjusted to produce a shoulder. In a rule joint (page 288), a round-over bit shapes the edge of the table-top while a matching cove bit cuts the drop leaf to fit.

Core-box or round-nose
A plunging bit; cuts a round-bottomed channel. Available in various diameters up to 1 inch.

Hinge mortising
A non-plunging bit designed to start a cut at an edge; similar to a straight bit, but more effective in removing waste from shallow mortises.

FLUTE DESIGNS

Single-flute bits are designed for high feed rates and relatively fibrous materials like plastic. The most predominant configuration is the two-flute bit, which usually offers the best cutting performance and balance. Triple-flute bits, such as the three-wing slotting cutter, are used in trimming and finishing operations that require a cleaner cut.

Single-flute bit

Double-flute bit

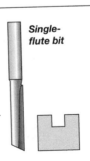

Double-flute bit features a double-flute design for clean cuts, particularly on end grain.

Top-piloted bits can be used for shaping or pattern routing, provided a template is positioned above the workpiece *(page 110)*. For this application, top-piloted bits are easier to use than unpiloted bits and template guides. Since the pilot is usually the same diameter as the cutter, you need not compensate for the difference between the bit and guide diameter when sizing a template.

Another important feature of a router bit is the number of cutting edges, or flutes, it has. Bits can have up to four flutes. The more flutes a bit has, the smoother the cut.

Many bits, such as the solid spiral straight bit shown below, are manufactured as cast bodies or machined from solid bar stock. Other bits are compiled by assembling two or more cutters on a single arbor. One example of an assembled cutter is the three-wing slotting cutter, also shown below, in which several cutters can be stacked to produce a groove of the desired width.

PILOTED AND UNPILOTED BITS

Ball-bearing pilots are typically attached to bits with cap screws. While this enables worn or damaged pilots to be replaced, the pilots can fail should the screw loosen or bend. The main benefit of this type, however, is that the bearings spin independently of the cutters, producing less heat and friction and no compression of the edge they are following. Fixed-bearing bits are less expensive, but heat, friction, and compression are drawbacks—except with laminate trimming. In this application, the laminates can withstand the heat buildup and there is no bearing to clog up with contact cement residue.

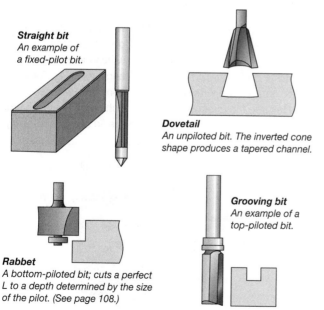

Straight bit
An example of
a fixed-pilot bit.

Dovetail
An unpiloted bit. The inverted cone shape produces a tapered channel.

Grooving bit
An example of a
top-piloted bit.

Rabbet
A bottom-piloted bit; cuts a perfect L to a depth determined by the size of the pilot. (See page 108.)

A RANGE OF ROUTER BITS

SOLID AND ASSEMBLED BITS

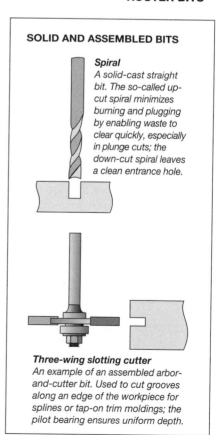

Spiral
A solid-cast straight bit. The so-called up-cut spiral minimizes burning and plugging by enabling waste to clear quickly, especially in plunge cuts; the down-cut spiral leaves a clean entrance hole.

Three-wing slotting cutter
An example of an assembled arbor-and-cutter bit. Used to cut grooves along an edge of the workpiece for splines or tap-on trim moldings; the pilot bearing ensures uniform depth.

ROUTER

FIVE COMMON ROUTER CUTS

Operating a router may seem as simple as grabbing it by the handles and turning it on, but it takes experience to become comfortable with the balance of the

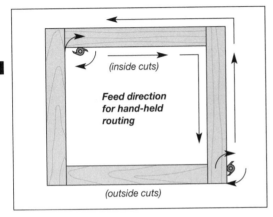

(inside cuts)

Feed direction for hand-held routing

(outside cuts)

tool and develop a feel for controlling it. Its cutting action is quick and unforgiving. The router demands a two-handed grip and an even rate of feed to ensure a smooth cut. It is also crucial to install a bit properly. To ensure that the collet gets a good grip on the shank, never let the shank

bottom out in the collet. Rather, insert the bit all the way in, then retract it about 1/16 inch before tightening the collet.

For any cut, particularly when edge-shaping, the direction of feed should always be against the direction of bit rotation. For hand-held routing *(left, top)*, move the tool clockwise to shape an inside edge and counterclockwise to shape an outside edge. Reverse the direction of feed when the tool is mounted

upside down in a router table *(left, bottom)*. Feeding the router in the wrong direction will cause it to scoot away from you as the bit pushes the tool away from the stock.

Although the router can be used freehand, a jig or guide will keep the bit on track for precision cuts. One task at which the router excels is cutting circles [1]. For this operation, you will need a circle-cutting jig. Fasten the router to the jig and screw the jig to the

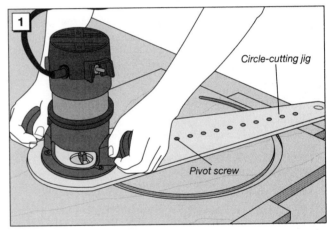

1

Circle-cutting jig

Pivot screw

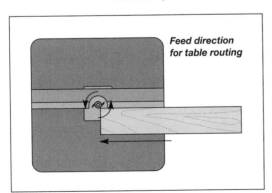

Feed direction for table routing

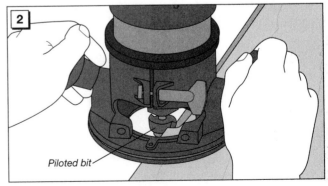

2

Piloted bit

center of the circle so that the distance between the screw and the bit equals the desired radius. Then plunge the bit into the stock and make the cut. The pivot screw will hold the bit at a constant radius throughout.

Shaping the edge of a workpiece is best done with a piloted bit [2], which uses the workpiece edge itself as a guide. Although a straight cut is shown, piloted bits can also rout curved edges.

Unpiloted bits can also be used to shape straight edges or cut dadoes, but an edge guide is required [3]. For a dado, align the bit with the cutting mark, butt the guide against the router base plate, and clamp the guide in place. Keep the base plate butted against the guide as you make the cut. If you are routing dadoes for shelves, you can plow facing dadoes in the two side panels at the same time. Clamp down the panels edge to edge, making certain their ends are aligned. This will ensure that the two dadoes line up perfectly.

3

Edge guide

QUICKTIP

Offset distance formula
It is handy to know the distance that a guide board has to be offset to align the router bit with a cutting mark. This offset depends on the diameters of both the router base and the bit. To calculate the offset, subtract the bit diameter from the router base diameter, then divide the difference by two.

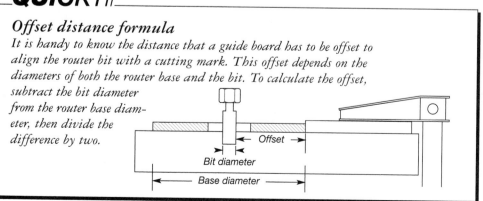

Offset

Bit diameter

Base diameter

ROUTER

Routing a mortise is much like routing a dado that is stopped at both ends. A narrow workpiece, however, may not provide enough support for the router to prevent it from rocking. The best way to compensate for this is to clamp down the workpiece with a support board 4 butted against it. Make sure the top edges of the two boards are level. To cut the mortise, attach a commercial edge guide to the router and install a straight bit the same diameter as the width of the mortise. Adjust the guide to position the bit over one end of the mortise and plunge the bit into the stock. Continue the cut to the other end, then square up the corners with a chisel. If the mortise width

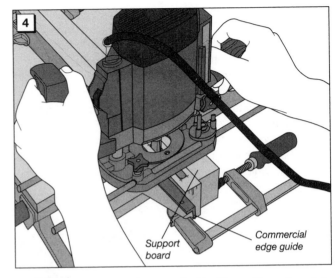

Support board

Commercial edge guide

exceeds the diameter of your largest bit, or the mortise depth exceeds ½ inch, make multiple passes to rout the mortise.

Another routing technique woodworkers consider a time-saver is one known as pattern routing. It enables you to produce several copies of the same contoured shape much more efficiently than if you routed the pieces individual-

ly. Start by cutting a template that reproduces your pattern exactly. Position the template over the workpiece and clamp both to a work surface. You can now make the cut with a top-piloted straight bit 5. You can also use a non-piloted bit and a template guide if you cut the template smaller than the desired pattern to compensate for the difference between the diameters of the guide and the bit. As shown in the inset, install the guide by removing the base plate from the router and slipping it through the center of the base plate. Fasten the guide in place with the threaded ring. The collar of the template guide functions as a pilot that tracks along the edge of the template.

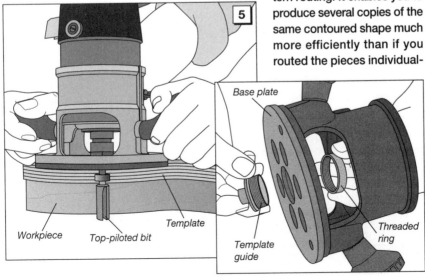

Workpiece

Top-piloted bit

Template

Base plate

Template guide

Threaded ring

A router table is probably the single most valuable accessory for your router. Because it frees up both hands outfeed half of the fence can be offset to support the stock when you are removing the entire edge of a board.

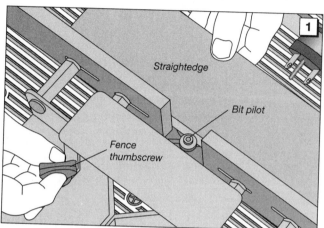

Straightedge

Bit pilot

Fence thumbscrew

to feed the stock, a router table greatly increases your control over the operation and saves setup time. For most models, mount your router by attaching its base to the underside of the table. Install a bit in the router, set the cutting depth, and lock the router securely in the base. Mount the fence to allow correct feed direction, as explained on page 108.

The commercial router table shown on this page is equipped with a two-piece fence. This feature offers several advantages. First, the two halves of the fence can be adjusted close to the bit, regardless of its diameter, providing maximum support for the workpiece. Also, the

If you are using a piloted bit [1], you need to make sure that both sections of the fence are in line with the edge of the bit pilot. Place a straightedge against the pilot, loosen the thumbscrews behind the fence, advance both sections of the fence against the straightedge, and tighten the thumbscrews.

To keep the workpiece butted against the fence and flat on the table as you make a cut, use featherboards [2]. Clamp one featherboard to the fence above the bit so that it applies gentle downward pressure on the workpiece. Clamp another to the table so that it presses the stock against the fence. As the trailing end of the workpiece approaches the bit, use a push stick to feed it past the bit.

USING A ROUTER TABLE

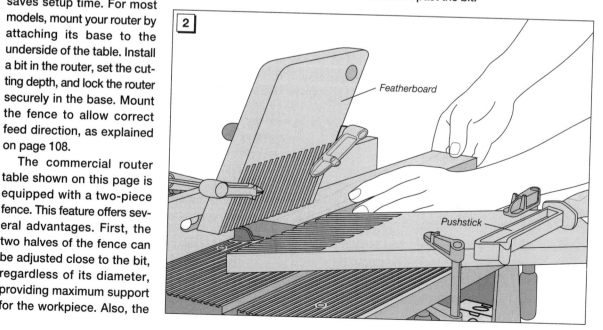

Featherboard

Pushstick

ROUTER

USING A ROUTER TABLE

The table-mounted router can cut a variety of joints, including the rabbet and the sliding dovetail. One of the disadvantages of using the router table, however, is that the precise location of the bit is often hidden by the workpiece. With a stopped rabbet, for example, this makes it difficult to know when to stop feeding the stock. One solution is to place a piece of tape across the table in line with the contact point between the bit and the

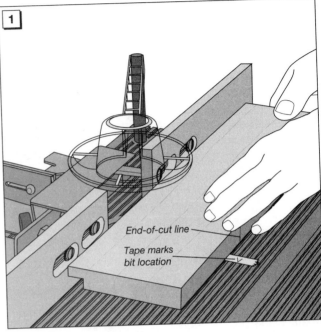

End-of-cut line

Tape marks bit location

Dovetail bit

Featherboard

workpiece **1**. Also mark a line on the outside edge of the workpiece where the rabbet should end. Feed the workpiece along the table until the line on the stock reaches the edge of the tape, and then pivot the stock away from the bit.

For a sliding dovetail, rout the groove in the panels with a hand-held router. The technique is the same as for cutting a dado (*page 270*), except that you should rout the groove in two passes, first using a straight bit to remove most of the waste and then finishing off the cut with a dovetail bit. Make sure the diameter of the straight bit

does not exceed the diameter of the narrowest part of the dovetail bit. Cutting the matching dovetail in the shelves involves some trial and error **2**. Mount the router in the table and position the fence so that only about one-half the bit's diameter projects beyond the fence. Clamp a featherboard to the table to support the stock. Make a test cut on a scrap piece: Rout one side of the tail, then turn the workpiece around and rout the other side. Check the fit and adjust the fence position and the height of the bit as necessary until the joint slides together smoothly.

DRILL

Electric drills come in both corded and battery types and in a multitude of sizes. In selecting the right drill or (drills) for the shop, consider chuck capacity and the size, weight, and maneuverability of the tool. A ¼-inch chuck is too limited for most purposes; a ½-inch drill supplies plenty of power but is fairly heavy. Most cabinetmakers opt for a ⅜-inch model, like the one shown below. Some valuable optional features include keyless chucks, which help speed up bit changes, side-mounted handles for two-handed control, and variable-speed reversible (VSR) capability.

Cordless battery-powered drills are growing in popularity. Available in 7.2-, 9.6-, 12-, 13.2-, and 14.4-volt models, the main benefit of these drills is their capacity to work without a nearby electrical outlet and with no cord to get in the way. Their quiet operation and pistol-like feel make them pleasant to use. On the down side, the battery's limited ability to hold a charge limits the tool's endurance. Although battery technology has improved greatly since these drills were first introduced, their ability to sustain high torque is limited. On projects requiring prolonged use, keep a fully charged backup battery on hand.

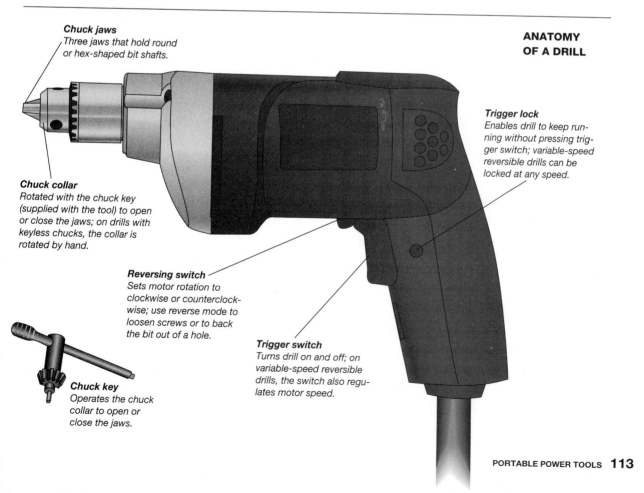

ANATOMY OF A DRILL

Chuck jaws
Three jaws that hold round or hex-shaped bit shafts.

Trigger lock
Enables drill to keep running without pressing trigger switch; variable-speed reversible drills can be locked at any speed.

Chuck collar
Rotated with the chuck key (supplied with the tool) to open or close the jaws; on drills with keyless chucks, the collar is rotated by hand.

Reversing switch
Sets motor rotation to clockwise or counterclockwise; use reverse mode to loosen screws or to back the bit out of a hole.

Trigger switch
Turns drill on and off; on variable-speed reversible drills, the switch also regulates motor speed.

Chuck key
Operates the chuck collar to open or close the jaws.

DRILL

Accessories that expand a drill's capacity to bore holes with precision, like those shown below, significantly expand its woodworking applications. Some enable the tool to perform tasks that would otherwise be difficult, such as boring pocket holes or centering dowel holes on the edge of a workpiece. Others, such as the flexible shaft, allow a drill to work in areas that would normally be difficult to access.

DRILL
ACCESSORIES

Self-centering doweling jig
Centers dowel holes on edge of workpiece; also ensures that holes are perpendicular to edge. Jig is self-centering when it is clamped to the stock. (See page 118 for instructions on using this jig to bore dowel holes.)

Stop collars
Attached to a bit to limit hole depth. Setscrew is tightened with hex wrench provided to fasten collar to bit; available in various sizes to match common bit diameters.

Transparent guide

Metal bushing

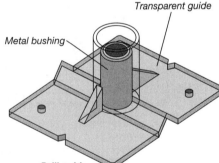

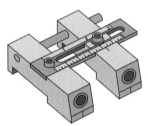

Pocket-hole drill guide
Used to guide a drill bit at the correct angle for boring pocket holes; model shown features two pocket hole guides mounted to an adjustable gauge to facilitate spacing the holes.

Jig   Drill bit

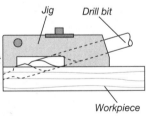

Workpiece

Drill guide
Positioned on workpiece over hole location to drill perpendicular holes into flat or round workpieces; interchangeable bushings slip into the barrel to accommodate different diameter drill bits.

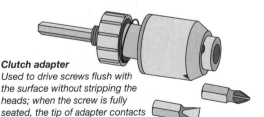

Clutch adapter
Used to drive screws flush with the surface without stripping the heads; when the screw is fully seated, the tip of adapter contacts the surface, releasing the built-in clutch so that the screwdriver bit stops rotating.

Flexible shaft
Mounts in chuck of drill to transfer the drill's rotation to a lightweight chuck at the other end of the flexible cable; handy for carving and for drilling in tight spaces.

When it was first introduced, the electric drill could not be used with conventional auger-type bits with screw pilots because of the unregulated high speed of the tool. The drill was limited to twist bits. The development of the variable-speed reversible (VSR) drill has changed that. But in the meantime, several new bit designs have emerged, notably the brad-point and spade bit, both of which are self-centering. The sensitive control provided by the VSR drill has also made it a very convenient tool for driving screws and operating other bits that perform best at lower speeds. Shown below are some of the bits woodworkers consider essential.

Brad-point bit
Bores clean holes in wood with minimum tearout; generally preferred to twist bit for woodworking. The sharp, brad-type pilot helps to prevent the bit from skipping as the cutter spurs contact the surface; not suitable for drilling into metal.

Tapered bit
Ideal for drilling pilot holes for screws because bit matches shapes of screws to improve grip of screw threads.

Twist bit
The traditional bit used for boring small-diameter holes in wood or metal; cone-shaped tip provides two cutting edges, while the spiral shaft removes debris.

Screwdriver bit
Converts the drill into a power screwdriver; available in various sizes with tips that accommodate either slotted-, square-, or Phillips-head screws.

Spade bit
For boring holes up to 1½ inch in diameter; bores quickly and performs well at high rotation speeds. Relatively inexpensive and easy to sharpen.

Hole saw
Cuts large-diameter holes around a piloting twist drill. Two-piece assembly provides for interchangeable outer saw sleeves, depending on desired diameter of hole; available individually and in sets.

Counterbore bit
Also known as combination bit. Adjusts to bore pilot holes, screw shank clearance holes, and counterbore holes in one operation. (See page 117 for details on using this bit.)

DRILL

SCREW SIZE	TRADITIONAL WOOD SCREWS			CUT-THREAD SCREWS		
	Clearance hole	Pilot hole (Hardwood)	Pilot hole (Softwood)	Clearance hole	Pilot hole (Hardwood)	Pilot hole (Softwood)
0	1/16"	1/32"	1/64"	1/16"	3/64"	1/32"
1	5/64"	1/32"	1/32"	5/64"	1/16"	3/64"
2	3/32"	3/64"	1/32"	3/32"	5/64"	1/16"
3	7/64"	1/16"	3/64"	7/64"	3/32"	5/64"
4	1/8"	1/16"	3/64"	1/8"	7/64"	3/32"
5	1/8"	5/64"	1/16"	1/8"	7/64"	3/32"
6	9/64"	5/64"	1/16"	9/64"	1/8"	3/32"
7	5/32"	3/32"	1/16"	5/32"	9/64"	7/64"
8	5/32"	3/32"	5/64"	11/64"	5/32"	1/8"
9	11/64"	7/64"	5/64"	3/16"	11/64"	9/64"
10	3/16"	7/64"	3/32"	13/64"	3/16"	5/32"
12	7/32"	1/8"	7/64"	7/32"	13/64"	11/64"
14	1/4"	3/16"	7/64"	1/4"	7/32"	3/16"
16	17/64"	3/16"	9/64"	9/32"	1/4"	7/32"

Chart information courtesy Lee Valley Tools Ltd.

With woodworkers no longer confined to the traditional wood screws commonly available at hardware stores, drilling clearance and pilot holes for screws is not as straightforward as it once was. Drywall screws, for example, have been used for quite some time to assemble furniture. They offer several advantages. In addition to being relatively inexpensive, drywall screws feature a Phillips head, a small-diameter shaft, and an aggressive thread, which makes them easy to drive. However, drywall screws are not the best fastener for all woodworking projects. They are only available in five sizes (No. 4, 6, 8, 10, and 12) and they are threaded right up to the head; screws with shanks are better for holding two pieces of wood tightly together. In addition, the small-diameter shaft together with the threaded shank makes drywall screws more prone to snapping in two. More recently, a new generation of screws has become available to woodworkers. Depending on where they are sold, these screws are known by names like "Hi-lo double-thread" screws, steel screws, "lo-root" screws, "cut-thread" screws, "deep-thread" screws, and so on. Refer to page 365 for illustrations of several types. In general, these modern screws are specially manufactured with the same aggressive thread and small-diameter shaft of drywall screws with the added advantage of an unthreaded shank. Many come with square (Robertson) drive or combination (Square/Phillips) heads for easier driving. Like traditional wood screws, they also feature an 82-degree-angle head, which facilitates countersinking. Other features of some modern screws include corrosion resistance, heat processing for additional strength, double-threading for faster driving, and threads with serrated edges or auger tips for greater holding power in harder stock. Some screws are also available in brass or other alloys, depending on the needs of your project. The chart on page 116 suggests the appropriate diameter of clearance and pilot holes for traditional wood screws and one type of modern screw—the cut-thread—in both hardwood and softwood. Drilling pilot holes for screws, particularly in hardwood, is a must. It will help prevent the stock from splitting and tearing out. In dense wood, clearance and pilot holes lessen the chance that the screw head will be stripped or snapped off—a common weakness of brass screws. Further, a screw can wander off line without a guiding hole, often following the wood grain. With a pilot hole, a screw will end up exactly where you want it.

CLEARANCE AND PILOT HOLES FOR SCREWS

A s shown at right, a screw can be counterbored into a workpiece and covered with a plug *(near right)*, or countersunk so that its head is driven flush with the surface *(center)*. A counterbore bit *(far right)* can be used to drill either type of hole. In both cases, a counterbore bit drills a pilot hole for the threaded part of the screw and a clearance hole for the shank. Depending on where the stop collar is positioned on the bit, it will also bore either a counterbore or a countersink hole.

Make sure the diameters of the clearance and pilot holes you drill are appropriate for the type and size of screw you will be driving. Refer to the chart on page 116. For example, to drive a No. 6 cut-thread screw, bore a ⁹⁄₆₄-inch clearance hole and a ³⁄₃₂-inch pilot hole in softwood or a ⅛-inch pilot hole in hardwood.

COUNTER-BORED AND COUNTER-SUNK HOLES

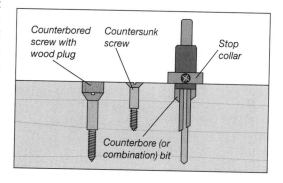

Counterbored screw with wood plug

Countersunk screw

Stop collar

Counterbore (or combination) bit

*QUICK*TIP

Shop-made depth stop
Commercial stop collars limit the depth to which a bit can drill. If you do not have a stop collar of the correct diameter, use a strip of masking tape. Measure the desired depth of the hole from the tip of the bit and wrap the tape around the shank at your end-point, as shown at right. Stop drilling when the tape contacts the surface of the workpiece.

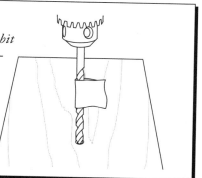

DRILL

DRILLING Although straight holes can be bored freehand, when "close" is not good enough, it is best to use a commercial drill guide *(page 114)* or a simple guide block 1. You can fashion such a block by cutting a 90-degree

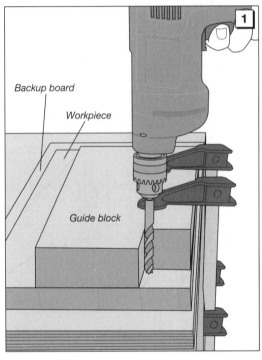

Backup board

Workpiece

Guide block

notch out of one corner of a scrap piece of 2 x 4. If you are drilling through the face of a workpiece, set it on a backup board to minimize tearout as the bit exits the wood. To use the jig, center the bit over the hole location and butt the guide block against the bit. Keep the bit aligned with the corner of the block as you bore the hole.

When boring holes for a dowel joint *(page 256)*, a commercial doweling jig 2 will ensure that the holes are centered between the board edges. For the panel joint shown, first align the boards edge to edge and mark the hole locations across the seam. Then secure one of the boards in a vise and set the jig on the workpiece; with the model of jig shown, align the appropriate diameter hole over the first hole location mark and tighten the handle to clamp the jig in place. Insert the bit into the hole in the jig and bore the hole. Loosen the handle to reposition the jig and bore the remaining holes the same way. Once all the holes are drilled, spread some glue in the holes and insert the dowels 3. Clamp the joint as you would a plate joint *(page 135)*.

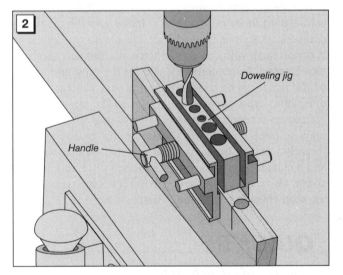

Doweling jig

Handle

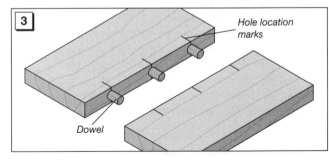

Hole location marks

Dowel

SABER SAW

The saber saw is often compared to the band saw because both tools are used for cutting curves. Although the band saw can cut faster and handle thicker stock, the saber saw has the advantage of being portable. Lacking a stationary table and a throat column, it can be used to cut large workpieces that would be unwieldy on the band saw. And as shown on page 122, the saber saw's blade can be plunged into a workpiece to make interior cuts.

The cutting actions of the two saws are substantially different. The band saw cuts continuously as its blade passes down through the table. The saber saw cuts only on the up stroke. On older saber saws, the blade moves straight up and down, which tends to push the stock away on the down stroke, causing the tool to vibrate and kick. Most recent-model saws have overcome this problem by shifting the blade slightly forward on the up stroke and then back away from the direction of travel on the down stroke, giving the blade what is termed "orbital action." As shown in the illustration below, some saber saws are equipped with a selector switch that can vary the blade's orbital action.

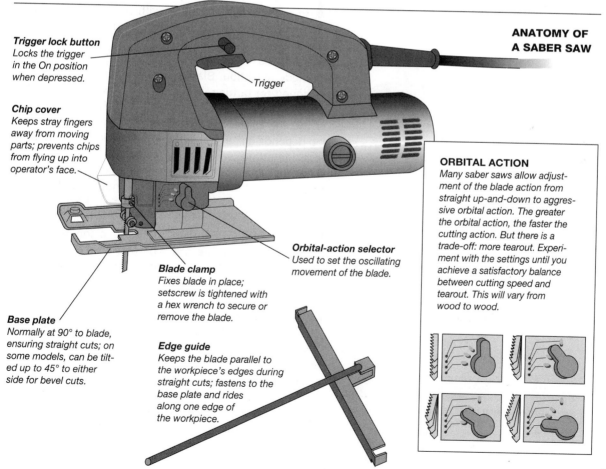

ANATOMY OF A SABER SAW

Trigger lock button
Locks the trigger in the On position when depressed.

Chip cover
Keeps stray fingers away from moving parts; prevents chips from flying up into operator's face.

Trigger

Base plate
Normally at 90° to blade, ensuring straight cuts; on some models, can be tilted up to 45° to either side for bevel cuts.

Blade clamp
Fixes blade in place; setscrew is tightened with a hex wrench to secure or remove the blade.

Edge guide
Keeps the blade parallel to the workpiece's edges during straight cuts; fastens to the base plate and rides along one edge of the workpiece.

Orbital-action selector
Used to set the oscillating movement of the blade.

ORBITAL ACTION
Many saber saws allow adjustment of the blade action from straight up-and-down to aggressive orbital action. The greater the orbital action, the faster the cutting action. But there is a trade-off: more tearout. Experiment with the settings until you achieve a satisfactory balance between cutting speed and tearout. This will vary from wood to wood.

SABER SAW

SABER SAW BLADES FOR WOODWORKING

Combination blade
A general-purpose blade for straight and curved cuts.

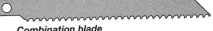

Knife-edge blade
A toothless blade used for cutting veneers.

Offset blade
Projects the teeth beyond the front of the saw's base plate, allowing cuts to be made right up to a vertical surface; also a good blade for making plunge cuts (page 122).

Grit blade
A knife-type blade with carbide abrasives bonded to the cutting edge for sawing thin wood, veneer, and laminates; available in various grits.

Reverse-tooth blade
Teeth cut on the downstroke to minimize tearout on the upper surface of the stock; useful for cutouts in countertops.

Metal-cutting blade
A fine-tooth blade—typically 24 to 32 TPI—for cutting metal and making smooth cuts in thin plywood.

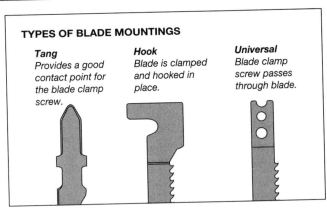

TYPES OF BLADE MOUNTINGS

Tang
Provides a good contact point for the blade clamp screw.

Hook
Blade is clamped and hooked in place.

Universal
Blade clamp screw passes through blade.

The saber saw's capacity to cut smoothly through materials as diverse as solid wood, particleboard, metal, and ceramics hinges on careful blade selection. Blades designed for cutting wood are illustrated at left. Choosing the right blade for a given job depends on several factors, including workpiece thickness, the curvature of the intended cut, and the desired feed rate. For starters, the blade must be longer than the thickness of the stock. Blades are typically 3 to 4 inches long, but 12-inch-long blades are available. The width of a blade dictates how tight a curve you can cut: The tighter the curve, the narrower the blade must be.

Feed rate is directly related to the number of teeth per inch (TPI) of a blade. It is also important how the teeth are set, or bent. For example, a relatively coarse 7 TPI blade with set teeth cuts quickly but produces a rough kerf. A toothless grit blade, on the other hand, leaves a smooth kerf but cuts about three times slower. Because fine-toothed blades are less effective in removing debris from the kerf than coarser blades, they tend to heat up more quickly and require a slower rate of feed. It is better to select the proper blade for the job than attempt to force a blade to perform beyond its intended capabilities. Most saber saw blades are relatively inexpensive, but they rarely last very long; plan on replacing them frequently.

Aside from selecting the correct tooth configuration for a given task, you have to be sure that the blade-mounting method is the right one for your saw. As shown above, there are three different types: Tang, hook, and universal.

Cutting a tight curve places a great deal of stress on a saber saw blade. The blade may be too wide for the radius of the curve, or the feed rate may be too rapid. Slowing the feed rate helps to some degree, but that increases the risk of burning the wood or breaking the blade. Making straight release cuts [1] through the waste from the edge of the stock to the cutting line relieves pressure on the blade when cutting curves. The tighter the curve, the closer together the release cuts should be. Then saw along the cutting line; as the blade reaches each release cut, a waste piece will fall away, releasing pressure on one side of the blade.

The saber saw is an excellent tool for cutting circles quickly. To ensure an accu-

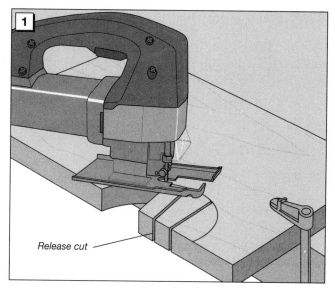

Release cut

rate cut, attach a circle-cutting guide [2] to the saw's base plate. Adjust the distance between the guide's pivot point and the blade to the radius of the circle. Clamp the workpiece down, butt the blade against an edge of the workpiece, and screw the pivot point into the stock at the center of the circle. Keeping the saw's base plate flat on the workpiece, cut the circle, repositioning the workpiece as necessary.

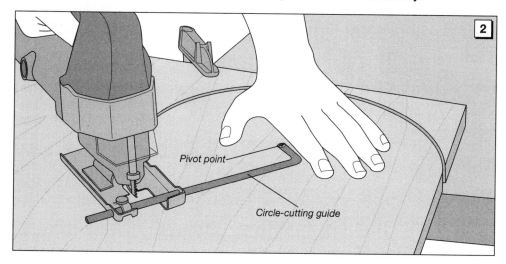

Pivot point

Circle-cutting guide

SABER SAW

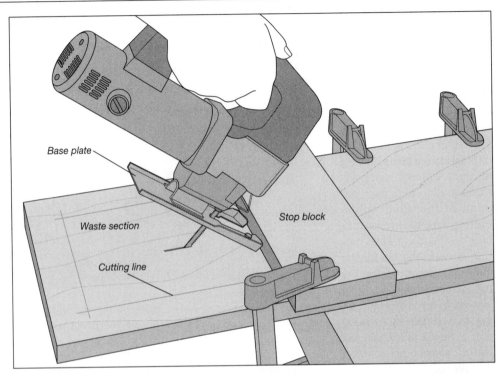

Base plate

Waste section

Cutting line

Stop block

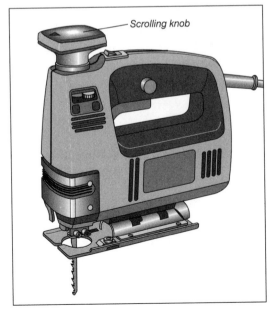

Scrolling knob

The saber saw shown at left has a scrolling feature that is well suited to intricate contour cuts. The blade can be rotated 360° within its housing by the simple turn of a knob or by exerting steering pressure on the handle. This feature enables the tool to cut curves in tight areas where the body of the saw has little room to move.

There are two ways to start an interior cut with a saber saw. One method is to bore a hole through the waste large enough to insert the blade. Another technique is the plunge cut, which involves pivoting the blade through the stock. For a plunge cut, clamp down the workpiece so that it overhangs the work surface; also clamp a stop block to the board, as shown above. Then butt the front of the saber saw's base plate against the stop block and tip the tool forward so the blade is clear of the workpiece. Gripping the saw firmly, turn it on and slowly pivot the blade down into the stock until the base plate rests flat on the surface. Keep a firm grip on the handle; otherwise, the blade will skip off the stock at the start of the plunge.

CIRCULAR SAW

The circular saw is commonly dismissed as a construction-trade tool, too imprecise for fine woodworking. This neglects two points. First, the circular saw excels at rough sizing unwieldy stock, such as 4 x 8-foot panels. In a fraction of the time it would take to wrestle such pieces onto a table saw, a circular saw can reduce them to manageable size.

The saw's portability allows you to size stock outdoors, if necessary, saving the inconvenience of carrying materials down stairways and through doors. Second, the circular saw can cut accurately, as long as you do not try to do the job freehand. As shown on page 124, there are several useful accessories that enable the saw to make precise cuts.

ANATOMY OF A CIRCULAR SAW

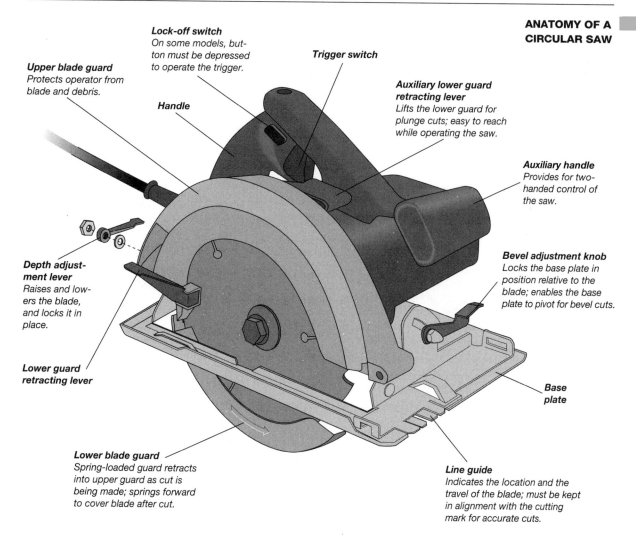

Lock-off switch
On some models, button must be depressed to operate the trigger.

Trigger switch

Upper blade guard
Protects operator from blade and debris.

Handle

Auxiliary lower guard retracting lever
Lifts the lower guard for plunge cuts; easy to reach while operating the saw.

Auxiliary handle
Provides for two-handed control of the saw.

Depth adjustment lever
Raises and lowers the blade, and locks it in place.

Bevel adjustment knob
Locks the base plate in position relative to the blade; enables the base plate to pivot for bevel cuts.

Lower guard retracting lever

Base plate

Lower blade guard
Spring-loaded guard retracts into upper guard as cut is being made; springs forward to cover blade after cut.

Line guide
Indicates the location and the travel of the blade; must be kept in alignment with the cutting mark for accurate cuts.

CIRCULAR SAW

The circular saw was designed to take most of the elbow grease out of hand-sawing lumber. Used freehand, the saw's accuracy depends solely on the skill of the operator. With experience, you can become very proficient with the tool. However, to cut with absolute precision, you should rely on one of the various accessories that have evolved to take the guesswork out of using the circular saw.

These accessories range from simple clamp-on edge guides to complete systems that help the saw make long cuts in panels. The accessories shown below span the range from simple to complex and provide only a sampling of the multitude of devices on the market. See the Table Saw section in the next chapter (*page 143*) for a full range of the blades that can be used on the circular saw.

CIRCULAR SAW ACCESSORIES

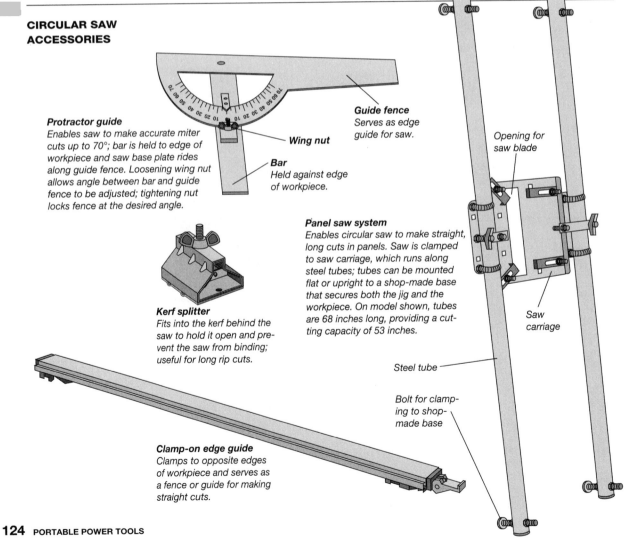

Protractor guide
Enables saw to make accurate miter cuts up to 70°; bar is held to edge of workpiece and saw base plate rides along guide fence. Loosening wing nut allows angle between bar and guide fence to be adjusted; tightening nut locks fence at the desired angle.

Guide fence
Serves as edge guide for saw.

Wing nut

Bar
Held against edge of workpiece.

Kerf splitter
Fits into the kerf behind the saw to hold it open and prevent the saw from binding; useful for long rip cuts.

Panel saw system
Enables circular saw to make straight, long cuts in panels. Saw is clamped to saw carriage, which runs along steel tubes; tubes can be mounted flat or upright to a shop-made base that secures both the jig and the workpiece. On model shown, tubes are 68 inches long, providing a cutting capacity of 53 inches.

Opening for saw blade

Saw carriage

Steel tube

Bolt for clamping to shop-made base

Clamp-on edge guide
Clamps to opposite edges of workpiece and serves as a fence or guide for making straight cuts.

To rip a large panel with a circular saw, support the workpiece on a grid of support boards. This will prevent the panel from sagging and the blade from binding in the kerf as the cut proceeds.

In the illustration below, four support boards are set on sawhorses and the panel is clamped to the boards. Make sure that none of the boards obstructs your cutting line, and protect the face of the panel with wood clamping pads.

Hold the saw at one end of the panel. Align the blade with your cutting line. Pull the switch and make the cut slowly and steadily, holding the saw with a firm, two-handed grip.

RIPPING LARGE PANELS

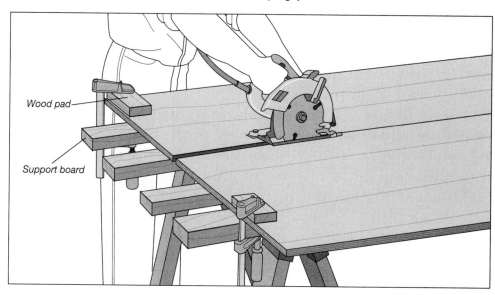

Wood pad

Support board

The maximum depth of cut of a circular saw depends on the size of the blade and the brand and model of the saw. Think twice before buying the largest saw available to maximize the depth of cut. Comfort and ease of handling are also important factors. Saws limited to 7¼-inch-diameter blades will easily saw through 1½-inch-thick stock—even when bevel cutting at a 45-degree angle *(right)*.

MAXIMUM DEPTH OF CUT

CIRCULAR SAW

USING THE CIRCULAR SAW

The best way to make an accurate rip cut or cross-cut is to use an edge guide. A commercial guide that attaches to the saw works well for a cut near the edge of the workpiece, as shown in the Tip on page 127. But for a cut that is farther from the edge, joint the edge of a board perfectly straight and use it to guide your cut. The board should be at least a few inches longer than the length of the cut to provide enough support for the saw. To position the edge guide, you need to know the distance between the edge of the saw's base plate and the blade [1]. Be sure to take this measurement from one of the teeth that is set *toward* the edge of the base plate. This distance will differ from blade to blade, so take a new measurement when you change blades. As a reminder, mark the distance on a strip of masking tape and attach it to the saw.

To make the cut, clamp the edge guide [2] atop the workpiece. Make sure that it is square to the edge of the stock and offset from your cutting line by the distance you measured. Keep the base plate of the saw butted against the guide as you make the cut.

Edge guides also enable the circular saw to make quick work of cutting wide dadoes.

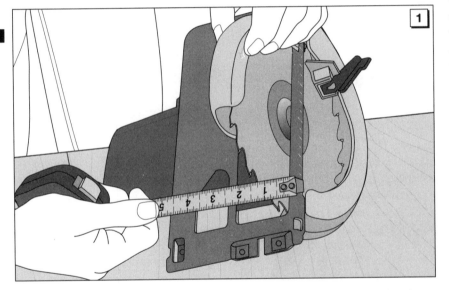

Edge guide

Clamp two edge guides 3 atop the workpiece. Position one as you would for a straight cut. To position the second edge guide, measure the distance from the other edge of the saw's base plate to the blade, choosing a tooth that is set toward this edge. The two edge guides ensure that the blade will not cut outside the dado outline. Set the depth of cut. Saw the two shoulders of the dado, riding the saw's base plate along each edge guide in turn. Break up the waste with kerfs about ¼ inch apart, then remove the remaining waste with a chisel and mallet 4.

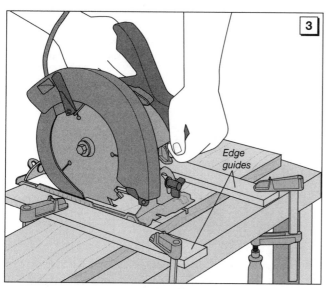

Edge guides

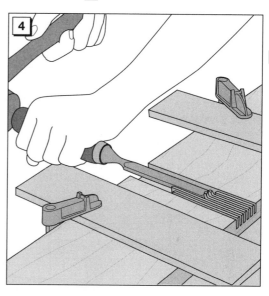

*QUICK*TIP

Extending a commercial edge guide
Commercial edge guides work well when the cutting line is close to the edge of the workpiece. As the distance increases, however, it becomes difficult to keep the short fence of the guide flush with the edge. One simple solution is to extend the length of the fence by drilling two holes through it and screwing on a 10-inch-long strip of ¾-inch plywood, as shown at right. Chamfer the leading edge of the strip to help it slide along the workpiece more smoothly.

SANDERS

There are three main types of portable power sanders available to woodworkers. The belt sander shown in the anatomy illustration below is the workhorse sanding tool in most shops. It can be used to remove waste wood quickly and perform more delicate smoothing tasks. It will flatten out uneven or slightly misaligned surfaces, making quick work of minor assembly errors or dents. But the belt sander can also be a tricky tool to operate because of its tendency to round over edges and create depressions. One key is to keep the sander flat on the workpiece throughout the operation. Another is to always keep the sander moving on the surface so as to remove stock evenly. Finally, always try to align the sanding belt with the wood grain. When this is impossible—such as when two boards are joined with the grain of the pieces at 90 degrees—smooth the boards in two steps. First, smooth one of them with the grain, sanding part of the other board against the grain at the same time.

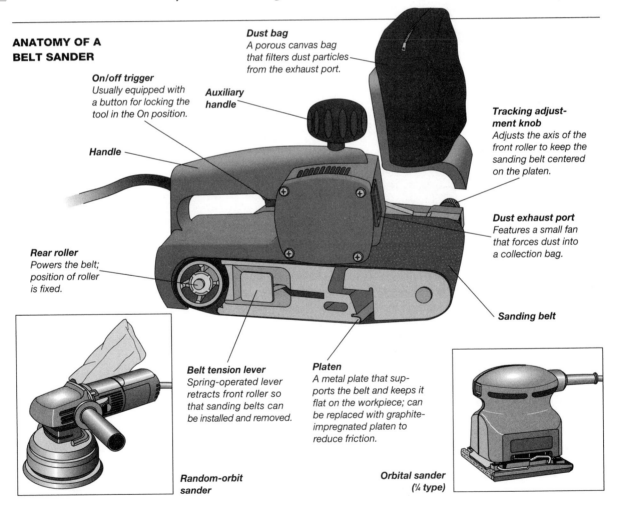

**ANATOMY OF A
BELT SANDER**

Dust bag
A porous canvas bag that filters dust particles from the exhaust port.

On/off trigger
Usually equipped with a button for locking the tool in the On position.

Auxiliary handle

Tracking adjustment knob
Adjusts the axis of the front roller to keep the sanding belt centered on the platen.

Handle

Rear roller
Powers the belt; position of roller is fixed.

Dust exhaust port
Features a small fan that forces dust into a collection bag.

Sanding belt

Belt tension lever
Spring-operated lever retracts front roller so that sanding belts can be installed and removed.

Platen
A metal plate that supports the belt and keeps it flat on the workpiece; can be replaced with graphite-impregnated platen to reduce friction.

Random-orbit sander

**Orbital sander
(¼ type)**

Then smooth the second board with the grain, this time avoiding the first board.

The two other sanders are the orbital sander and the random-orbit sander shown on page 128. The orbital sander comes in two basic sizes, known as ¼ and ½ sanders, so-called because they accept either one-quarter or one-half of a standard sheet of sandpaper. Although both sanders have similar orbits per minute, the ¼ type can be operated with one hand and is ideal for working in tight spaces, such as sanding the insides of drawers. The ¼ sander is less expensive than the ½ sander. Because it is used with two hands, the ½ sander offers more control over large surfaces.

The random-orbit sander is a popular choice for final sanding because it leaves no scratches or swirl marks, and because it removes stock quickly, making it a practical alternative to the belt sander for this purpose. The eccentric motion of this sander, as described below, is created by an off-center bearing that transmits the power from the motor to the sanding pad.

SANDING ACCESSORIES

Lamb's wool buffing pad
Used for buffing and polishing. Works best on random-orbit sander; ties over sanding pad.

Hook-and-loop sanding discs
Fastens to backing pad of sander using hook-and-loop fasteners.

Pressure sensitive adhesive (PSA) sanding discs
Self-adhesive backing holds disc to the backing pad of sander.

Contour sanding pad
Attaches to the sander in place of the standard backup pad; its flexible rubber construction is handy for sanding contoured surfaces.

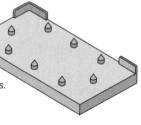

Hole-punching plate
Used to punch holes in sandpaper for sanders with built-in dust collection systems.

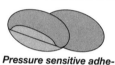

Sponge applicator pad
For applying paste wax and buffing lacquer finishes; fastens to sander backup pad using hook-and-loop method.

Most of the accessories shown above can be used on both orbital and random-orbit sanders. Sanding discs can be fastened to a sander in a couple of different ways. Hook-and-loop discs have several advantages over PSA discs. Although more expensive, they are removable and reusable. They are also firmer and stiffer—a plus on contoured surfaces. PSA discs are prone to contamination and cannot be reused.

ORBITAL ACTIONS

Different sanders sand in different ways. On belt sanders, the rotation of the belt causes the abrasives to cut in a straight line. Because of this cutting action, it is important to keep the sander aligned with the grain of the surface being sanded. The sanding pad of an orbital sander moves in a circular motion at up to 12,000 orbits per minute. Random-orbit sanders also produce a high-speed circular motion, but the pad simultaneously oscillates from side to side, which tends to eliminate scratch marks on the surface of the workpiece. Still, as a final step, it is a good idea to lightly hand-sand the surface with the grain.

SANDERS

CHOOSING THE BEST SANDING GRIT

The abrasives used for sandpaper vary from extra coarse to very fine. For most sanding jobs, use a series of successively finer grits: 40 to 60 grit to level a surface or remove imperfections; 80 to 120 grit to begin the smoothing process and obliterate the scratches left by coarser grits; grits in the 150- to 180-range for preparing wood surfaces for staining. The chart at right groups grits by their typical uses.

GRIT	USES
40-60	Preliminary surfacing of rough stock; leveling surfaces. Removing deep scratches and surface imperfections.
80-120	Smoothing surfaces; removing light scratches and torn wood fibers.
150-180	Final preparation of wood before staining and finishing
220-240	Sanding heavy-bodied sealers and leveling raised grain.
280-320	Removing dust spots and bubbles between coats of finish.
360-600	Fine sanding to alter luster and remove surface blemishes.

READING SANDPAPER LABELS

As the sample label (*below, right*) shows, the information printed on the back of sandpaper sheets and sanding belts and discs is often sparse and rather cryptic, but it can be useful. The absence of any labeling generally indicates low quality, poor durability, and questionable uniformity of grit. Manufacturers of quality abrasives generally trademark their products, specify the grit, and identify both the type of abrasive and the thickness of the backing.

Sandpaper sheets and sanding belts and discs are made of abrasives such as garnet, aluminum oxide, and silicon carbide. Both garnet and aluminum oxide are very durable; the former is rela-tively inexpensive, while the latter cuts quickly. Silicon carbide is sharp, but brittle. Abrasives with heavier backing generally hold up better when mounted to soft pads. A designates the lightest backing weight; E is the heaviest, although it is nor-mally used for commercial work. Sandpapers are avail-able in either open coat or closed coat. Open-coat sand-papers have abrasives that are spaced farther apart and tend not to clog quickly. They are suitable for working with softwoods. Closed-coat sand-papers have abrasives that are more closely packed and are best suited for working with hardwoods.

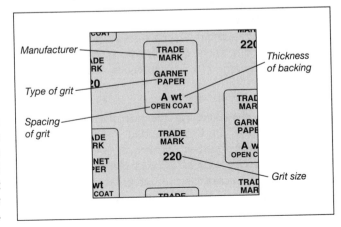

Belt sanders are ideal for smoothing broad surfaces, such as the face of a panel. To prevent the sander from driving the workpiece back toward you—particularly if you are using a coarse-grit belt—clamp a stop rail [1] slightly thinner than the panel along the back end. Then set the sander flat on the panel along one edge and turn it on. Keeping the sanding belt in alignment with the grain, allow the tool to creep forward to the opposite end

of the panel, then draw it back so that its return path overlaps about one-half of the first pass. Continue this process of overlapping passes (represented by the faint line in the illustration). Avoid tipping the sander so that the platen is not flat on the surface, or allowing it to remain stationary in one spot. In leveling exceptionally rough surfaces, it is better to make multiple passes than to slow down the sander's rate of travel and try to smooth the surface all at

once. Periodically stop and check the surface for level by sliding a straightedge, on edge, across it. Points where light reflects beneath the straightedge indicate unevenness.

To secure a circular workpiece for smoothing, use a V-notched stop block [2]. Cut the stop block from stock that is slightly thinner than the workpiece. To prevent the workpiece from spinning as the sander approaches the sides, glue strips of sandpaper to the edges of the V-notch.

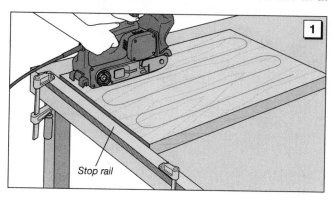

1

Stop rail

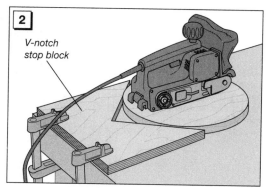

2

V-notch
stop block

*QUICK*TIP

Gang sanding

Sanding the edges of several boards at the same time offers several benefits. First, it is quicker. It also provides a wider and more stable surface for the sander, resulting in flatter edges and sharper corners on each of the workpieces. A third benefit is that the boards will be dimensionally uniform. Clamp the boards together near their ends, then secure the clamps to a work surface. Be sure to keep the sander level to avoid rounding the edges.

PLATE JOINER

Developed in postwar Europe, the plate joiner has only recently become popular in North America. The tool is equipped with a high-speed cutter wheel that plunges from a slot at the front of the tool and cuts arc-shaped slots in mating workpieces. Thin wafers of compressed wood are then inserted with glue in the slots. The biscuits swell as they absorb moisture from the adhesive, creating a solid joint.

ANATOMY OF A PLATE JOINER

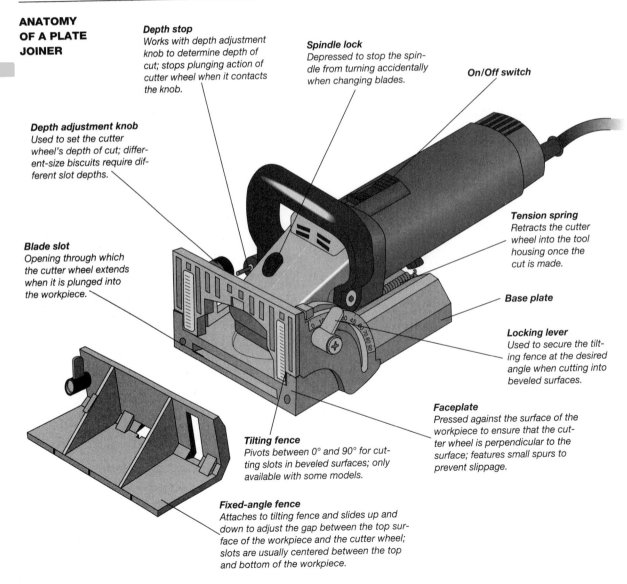

Depth stop
Works with depth adjustment knob to determine depth of cut; stops plunging action of cutter wheel when it contacts the knob.

Spindle lock
Depressed to stop the spindle from turning accidentally when changing blades.

On/Off switch

Depth adjustment knob
Used to set the cutter wheel's depth of cut; different-size biscuits require different slot depths.

Tension spring
Retracts the cutter wheel into the tool housing once the cut is made.

Blade slot
Opening through which the cutter wheel extends when it is plunged into the workpiece.

Base plate

Locking lever
Used to secure the tilting fence at the desired angle when cutting into beveled surfaces.

Faceplate
Pressed against the surface of the workpiece to ensure that the cutter wheel is perpendicular to the surface; features small spurs to prevent slippage.

Tilting fence
Pivots between 0° and 90° for cutting slots in beveled surfaces; only available with some models.

Fixed-angle fence
Attaches to tilting fence and slides up and down to adjust the gap between the top surface of the workpiece and the cutter wheel; slots are usually centered between the top and bottom of the workpiece.

Although some purists frown on the use of plate (or biscuit) joinery, its advantages are undeniable. Plate joints are much easier to make than spline or dowel joints. Like splines, biscuits offer ample gluing area to hold a joint, and like dowels, they are concealed. As a result, biscuits are highly effective in strengthening a wide range of joints. Several plate joints are illustrated on pages 258 and 260.

As a relatively specialized tool, the plate joiner has a limited variety of accessories. Metal and plastic biscuits are available for industrial applications, but for woodworking, you will normally use standard compressed wood biscuits in one of three sizes, shown at right.

On some joiners, the standard cutter wheel can be replaced by a wood-trimming blade that converts the tool into a mini-power saw for cutting grooves and trimming stock. The special glue applicator makes glue-up a much smoother operation.

PLATE JOINER ACCESSORIES

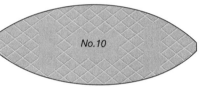
No.0

No.10

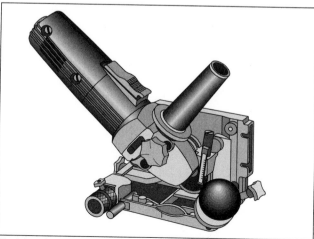
No.20

Wood biscuits
Made of compressed cross-grain beech; range in length from 1¹⁵⁄₁₆ to 2³⁄₁₆ inches. Available in three standard sizes: 0, 10, and 20; for strength, use the largest biscuit that will fit the joint.

Wood-trimming blade
An accessory blade available with some plate joiners. Used to cut grooves along the edge of panels for mounting tap-on moldings; can be used to trim thin stock up to ¼ inch thick.

Glue applicator
Base holds applicator upside down to keep the tip full of glue; tip of applicator is flat and features two holes, which helps to spread glue evenly along both sides of slots.

Standard cutter wheel
Carbide-tipped blade for cutting biscuit slots.

The jointer/spliner shown above can do more than cut recesses for biscuits. It also functions as a groove-cutting device, simplifying an otherwise time-consuming procedure.

PLATE JOINER

USING THE PLATE JOINER: REINFORCING BUTT JOINTS

Plate joinery is generally used to reinforce butt joints. Common applications include assembling frames and carcases, and as shown on this page, edge-gluing boards into a panel. The first step is to mark slot location lines 1 on the workpieces. When gluing up a panel, start by arranging the boards so their top surfaces will form a visually appealing composite. If you are using plain-sawn lumber *(page 186)*, it is also a good idea to arrange the boards so the U-shaped end grain of adjacent pieces runs in opposite directions. This will improve the panel's stability and minimize warping when it is exposed to changes in humidity. Once you have a satisfactory lay-

Slot location mark

out, lightly mark a triangle on the face of the panel to help you rearrange the boards after cutting the slots. Mark the slot locations by drawing short perpendicular lines across the seams, as shown.

Space the marks 6 to 8 inches apart. Stay clear of knots or other defects that might break out as the biscuits absorb glue and swell. In addition, do not locate any biscuits closer than 3 or 4 inches from the ends of the boards to allow room for fasteners or joinery, or for trimming the panel later.

Cutting slots with the plate joiner is relatively straightforward. Adjust the joiner's fence to center the slots in the edges of the boards. If the biscuits are too close to either face, their shapes may become visible on the panel when you later thickness plane or sand the stock. Also adjust the depth of cut to accommodate the size of biscuit you will use. To cut each slot 2, hold the board firm-

ly on a work surface and butt the plate joiner's faceplate against the edge of the stock. Align the slot center indicator on the faceplate with the slot location mark on the board, and push the tool forward to plunge the cutter wheel into the stock.

Once you have cut all of the slots, spread glue along adjoining edges of the boards and on both sides of the slots. Insert one biscuit for each pair of mating slots and clamp the panel together 3. Because the biscuits are made of compressed wood, they will begin to swell as soon as they are exposed to the glue; it is important to work quickly. Lay out your bar clamps ahead of time. To keep

the clamps from tipping over, cut notches in wood blocks and set the clamps in them. Before tightening the clamps, insert wood pads between the jaws of the clamps and the edges of the panel to prevent marring your stock. Space the clamps at 12- to 18-inch inter-

vals, alternating between the top and bottom of the panel. Tighten the clamps evenly until a thin bead of glue squeezes out of the joints. Once the adhesive has cured, scrape away the excess glue and sand the panel.

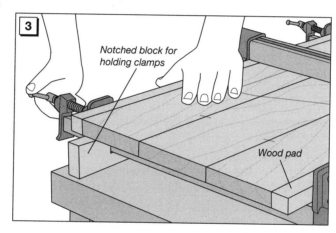

Notched block for holding clamps

Wood pad

---

*QUICK*TIP

Cutting slots into beveled surfaces

Biscuit joints are especially good at reinforcing edge miter joints. If your plate joiner is not equipped with a tilting fence, you can make a simple jig to get the job done. Rip a strip of wood at the same angle as the bevel, cut it to length, and screw it to the bottom of the fence with the beveled edge facing down. Adjust the fence to locate the slot closer to the inside corner of the joint; this will ensure that the cutter wheel does not plunge through the outside face of the workpiece. To cut the slot, butt the plate joiner faceplate against the beveled surface of the workpiece and the jig against its top face.

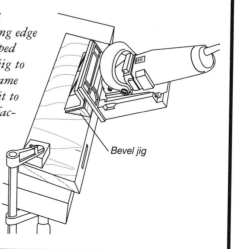

Bevel jig

PORTABLE PLANER

Although many woodworkers prefer the feel of a hand plane, the portable planer is exceptionally handy for tasks such as fitting doors or leveling tabletops. The two tools use entirely different cutting actions. The portable planer removes waste by lifting a series of chips; the hand plane shears off a continuous curl. The resulting surface reflects this difference: The power planer leaves a series of depressions across the grain while the hand plane shears wood smooth. As a result, surfaces that have been power-planed generally require light scraping or sanding before staining.

ANATOMY OF A PORTABLE PLANER

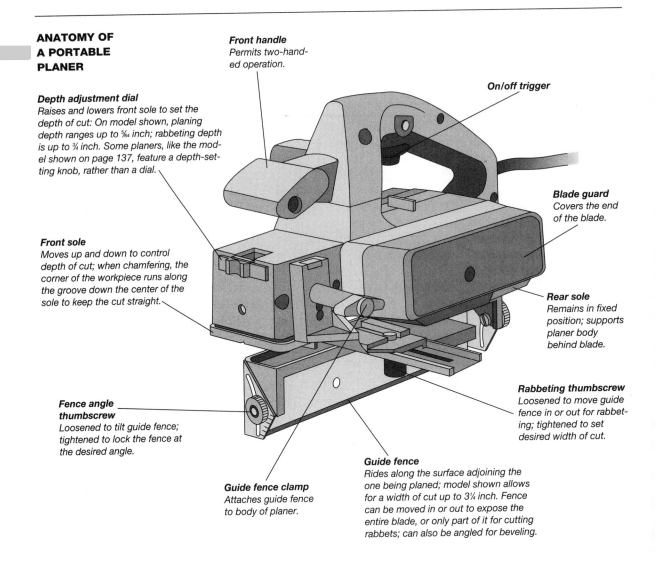

Front handle
Permits two-handed operation.

On/off trigger

Depth adjustment dial
Raises and lowers front sole to set the depth of cut: On model shown, planing depth ranges up to ⁵⁄₆₄ inch; rabbeting depth is up to ¾ inch. Some planers, like the model shown on page 137, feature a depth-setting knob, rather than a dial.

Blade guard
Covers the end of the blade.

Front sole
Moves up and down to control depth of cut; when chamfering, the corner of the workpiece runs along the groove down the center of the sole to keep the cut straight.

Rear sole
Remains in fixed position; supports planer body behind blade.

Rabbeting thumbscrew
Loosened to move guide fence in or out for rabbeting; tightened to set desired width of cut.

Fence angle thumbscrew
Loosened to tilt guide fence; tightened to lock the fence at the desired angle.

Guide fence clamp
Attaches guide fence to body of planer.

Guide fence
Rides along the surface adjoining the one being planed; model shown allows for a width of cut up to 3¼ inch. Fence can be moved in or out to expose the entire blade, or only part of it for cutting rabbets; can also be angled for beveling.

In some ways, using a power-er planer is like using a hand plane: You must keep the sole of the tool flat on the surface for the entire pass. Turn on the tool with the sole clear of the workpiece. Then set the front sole flat on the stock. As you move the tool forward, shift the pressure slowly to the back sole until the entire length of the sole is resting flush on the work-piece 1. Guide the planer with both hands; grip the main handle with one hand and press down on the aux-iliary handle with the other. Some models, like the one shown at right, feature a thumb rest, rather than an auxiliary handle, on the front sole. Keep the planer steady at all times; do not allow it to rock from side to side. Maintain a wide stance with your toes pointing roughly in the direction of trav-el. To minimize tearout at the

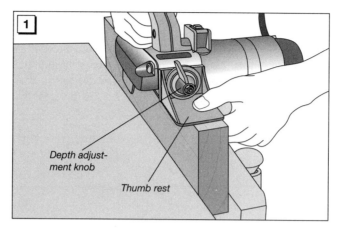

Depth adjust-ment knob

Thumb rest

end of the cut, slow the rate of feed or use a wood block, as shown below.

Creating bevels with the portable planer can be chal-lenging, since the weight of the tool and the vibration it produces make it harder to manage than a hand plane. Start by adjusting the guide fence 2 to the required angle. Hold the fence firmly against the side of the workpiece while you make the pass.

Guide fence

QUICKTIP

Preventing tearout

The high-speed cutting action of a power planer works well on end grain. As with a hand plane, however, it is a good idea to reduce the depth of cut and make several passes to reach your final depth. The most serious problem when planing end grain is tearout as the blade approaches the end of the cut. To remedy this, clamp a wood block against the far edge of the workpiece as shown at right. Be sure the top of the block is level with the end of the workpiece.

PORTABLE PLANER

The guide fence 3 that comes with most power planers provides a convenient way to cut rabbets. Depending on how it is adjusted, the fence limits the amount of the sole that contacts the workpiece. On the model shown in the illustration, the shaft of the guide slides through the body of the planer so that you can set the fence for the desired rabbet width. A lock knob on the front of the tool secures the fence in place. The depth of the rabbet is controlled by the number of passes you make.

If your planer does not have an adjustable fence, you can improvise by attaching an L-shaped wood guide 4 to the sole of the planer. Some planers have holes in the back sole for this purpose. Otherwise, you will have to drill holes into the sole. Cut slots in the guide for the screws so that you can vary the cutting width by sliding the guide across the sole. Another alternative for planers with a fixed fence is to screw a wood block of the appropriate thickness to the fence to set the desired width of cut 5.

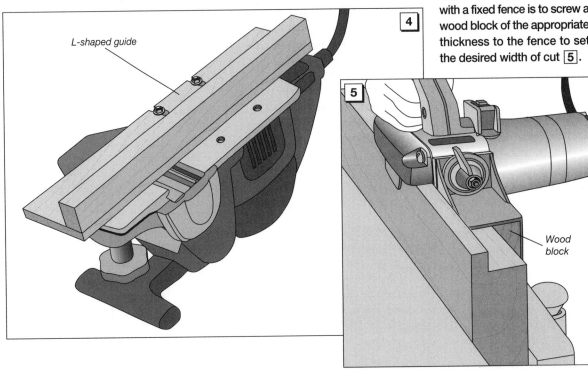

Lock knob

Guide
fence

3

L-shaped guide

4

Wood
block

5

STATIONARY POWER TOOLS

While it is possible to build furniture with nothing but hand tools and portable power tools, few woodworkers today ever attempt it. Imagine ripping an 8-foot-long plank of 8/4 hardwood with a handsaw or circular saw, or jointing it with a hand plane, and you have an idea of the vital role played by stationary machines. The question for most woodworkers is not whether they need stationary tools, but which ones they need.

If you have deep pockets and a large workshop, the answer is simple: Buy one of each. If budget considerations or space limitations come into play, however, you will have to temper desire with reality. The choice depends partly on what type of work you do. If, for example, you buy rough lumber, you will at least need a jointer, a planer, and a table saw. The standard procedure for preparing rough stock is to joint a face and then an edge, giving you adjoining surfaces that are perpendicular to each other. Next, rip the second edge parallel to the jointed edge. Finally, plane the stock to thickness. If you buy your stock surfaced and expect to spend most of your time making chairs, for example, you probably need no more than a lathe, a few hand tools, and perhaps a band saw.

Each of the stationary power tools presented in this chapter has strengths and weaknesses. In the case of the table saw (*page 140*) and the radial arm saw (*page 148*), there is some overlap. Either tool can, in a pinch, take the place of the other, but the table saw excels at ripping, while the radial arm saw works best when crosscutting.

The drill press (*page 158*), shaper (*page 168*), and belt/disc sander (*page 173*) have unique capabilities, but portable tools with accessories can do the same jobs. A table-mounted router, for example, can do much of the work of a shaper—with less power and a smaller range of cutters at its disposal.

This chapter approaches stationary power tools by examining the range of choices and weighing their pros and cons. Each machine is presented with a brief description of how it works and how it is set up to perform the tasks it does best.

TABLE SAW

Opinions vary as to whether the table saw or the radial arm saw represents the best stationary saw for woodworking. Both tools have unique advantages. The table saw is convenient and simple to use, and it cuts accurately. Since it has fewer moving parts than the radial arm saw, the table saw is easier to adjust and holds alignment well. Another advantage is that its table can serve as a work surface when the tool is not in use. The radial arm saw (*page 148*), on the other hand, is best at crosscutting, and can be positioned against a wall if space is at a premium in your shop.

If you plan to buy a table saw, there are several things to consider, including blade capacity, horsepower, table size, weight, and price. Models that feature a 10-inch-blade capacity and 1½- to 3-horsepower motors are generally adequate for home shop woodworking. A large and heavy cast-iron table-top provides both durability and stability and minimizes vibration. You should also look for a rugged and well-designed rip fence that is easy to align; or plan on upgrading the fence that comes with the saw. There are numerous after-market fences that are more precise and convenient to use than the standard rip fence that comes with most saws. Other additions to consider include table extensions, a mobile stand with lock casters, and commercial jigs, like those shown on page 141. A variety of shop-made jigs for the table saw are described in the Jigs and Shop Helpers chapter (*page 387*).

If budget and shop space are limited, consider a portable bench-top saw. Despite their small size, some models feature a 10-inch-blade capacity and can perform most of the functions of a full-size machine. They are easily carried around the shop by one person. A bench-top saw can be placed on a workbench, or built in so that its table is level with the bench top, providing a large work surface.

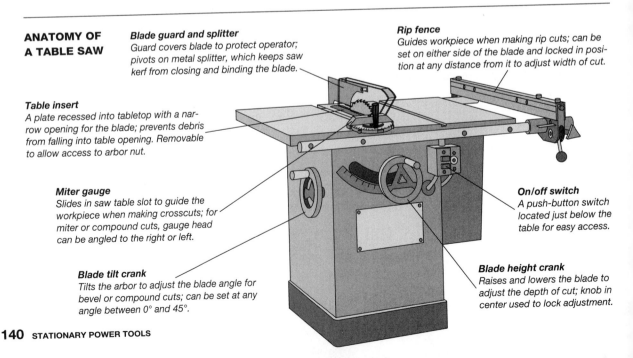

ANATOMY OF A TABLE SAW

Blade guard and splitter
Guard covers blade to protect operator; pivots on metal splitter, which keeps saw kerf from closing and binding the blade.

Rip fence
Guides workpiece when making rip cuts; can be set on either side of the blade and locked in position at any distance from it to adjust width of cut.

Table insert
A plate recessed into tabletop with a narrow opening for the blade; prevents debris from falling into table opening. Removable to allow access to arbor nut.

Miter gauge
Slides in saw table slot to guide the workpiece when making crosscuts; for miter or compound cuts, gauge head can be angled to the right or left.

On/off switch
A push-button switch located just below the table for easy access.

Blade tilt crank
Tilts the arbor to adjust the blade angle for bevel or compound cuts; can be set at any angle between 0° and 45°.

Blade height crank
Raises and lowers the blade to adjust the depth of cut; knob in center used to lock adjustment.

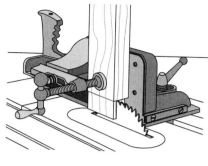

Tenoning jig
Holds stock upright to cut tenon cheeks and open mortises. Features a metal runner that slides in saw's miter slot; slides sideways to set thickness of tenons and mortises.

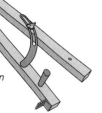

Taper jig
For making taper cuts; taper angle is adjustable. One arm of jig rides along rip fence; workpiece butts against other arm. Can be used on radial arm saw.

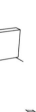
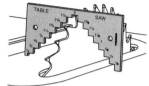

Pyramid gauge
Used to adjust cutting height of blade; model shown is graduated in ¼-inch increments or steps.

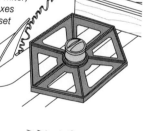

Blade stabilizers
Large steel washers mounted on the arbor on each side of the blade; help prevent vibration for smoother cuts. Can be used on radial arm saw.

Interchangeable table inserts
Used instead of standard insert. Opening in dado head insert (top) is wider than standard insert; molding head insert (bottom) is wider still, but shorter.

Multi-angle gauge
Used to quickly set angle of miter gauge or blade for miter, bevel, or compound cuts when making frames or boxes with 4, 5, 6, 8, or 12 sides. Set face up as shown to set miter gauge angle; placed on edge to adjust blade angle. Can be used with radial arm saw.

Stop rod
Used for repeat crosscuts; attaches to miter gauge to hold end of workpiece a predetermined distance from blade.

Anti-kickback hold-downs
Wheels hold workpieces flat on saw table and tight against fence; models with one-way wheels also prevent kickback. Can also be installed on radial arm saw table.

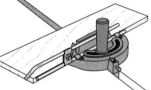

Roller stand
Supports long workpieces when making rip cuts; adjustable height allows roller to be positioned slightly below level of tabletop. Can be used with radial arm saw.

QUICKTIP

A miter gauge extension fence
Crosscutting long boards on the table saw can be difficult because the face of the miter gauge is too short to provide adequate support. For additional stability, attach a board as an extension fence to the gauge, as shown at right. Most miter gauges provide mounting holes for screws.

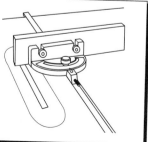

TABLE SAW

No matter how good your table saw is, the quality of the cuts it makes is no better than the saw blades you use. Over the past 25 years, the design of blades and the materials used in their manufacture have undergone considerable change. As shown on page 143, woodworkers now have a range of blades to choose from for specific applications, including combination blades, plywood and paneling blades, and hollow-ground planer blades. Specialty cutters, such as dado heads and molding heads, both examined on page 144, expand the versatility of the table saw.

Perhaps the most significant development in blade technology has been the introduction of blades with carbide teeth. Composed of tungsten-carbide, these teeth are brazed onto the blade. Their diamond-like hardness can extend the interval between sharpenings by as much as 50 times. Although more expensive and more difficult to sharpen than conventional high-speed steel blades, their convenience and durability have made them a popular choice among woodworkers.

Despite these technological advancements, blade selection and maintenance are still important considerations. As shown below, factors such as the hook angle, set, spacing, and number of teeth all contribute to a blade's performance. In addition, blades should be kept clean; use mineral spirits or a commercial gum remover to wipe off pitch and gum deposits. Check your blades regularly for damage; do not use a blade if it is cracked or warped, or has damaged teeth.

ANATOMY OF A BLADE

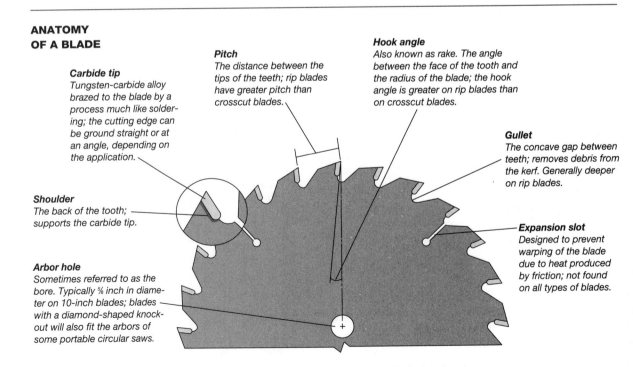

Carbide tip
Tungsten-carbide alloy brazed to the blade by a process much like soldering; the cutting edge can be ground straight or at an angle, depending on the application.

Shoulder
The back of the tooth; supports the carbide tip.

Arbor hole
Sometimes referred to as the bore. Typically ⅝ inch in diameter on 10-inch blades; blades with a diamond-shaped knockout will also fit the arbors of some portable circular saws.

Pitch
The distance between the tips of the teeth; rip blades have greater pitch than crosscut blades.

Hook angle
Also known as rake. The angle between the face of the tooth and the radius of the blade; the hook angle is greater on rip blades than on crosscut blades.

Gullet
The concave gap between teeth; removes debris from the kerf. Generally deeper on rip blades.

Expansion slot
Designed to prevent warping of the blade due to heat produced by friction; not found on all types of blades.

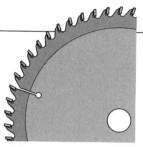
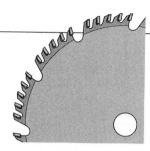

Rip
Features flat-ground teeth, wide pitch, deep gullets, and a pronounced hook angle for fast and relatively rough cutting. Example shown is carbide-tipped.

Crosscut
Alternate top bevel teeth slice wood fibers and minimize fraying; has more teeth than rip blade to produce smoother cuts. Example shown is carbide-tipped.

Combination blade
For ripping or crosscutting; although does not produce as smooth a cut as crosscut blade, this blade makes frequent blade changes unnecessary. Example shown is carbide-tipped.

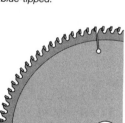

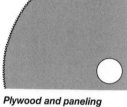

Cutoff
For making smooth crosscuts; has even more teeth than crosscut blade. Example shown is carbide-tipped.

Smooth-cut trim
A high-speed steel blade with no set for making smooth cuts; center of blade is ground thinner than teeth to reduce binding in cut.

Hollow-ground planer
For making smooth finishing cuts in fine furniture work; body of blade is thin and teeth are not set, which minimizes binding. Example shown is high-speed steel.

Plywood and paneling
Produces the smoothest cut in plywood, but requires frequent sharpening. Example shown is high-speed steel.

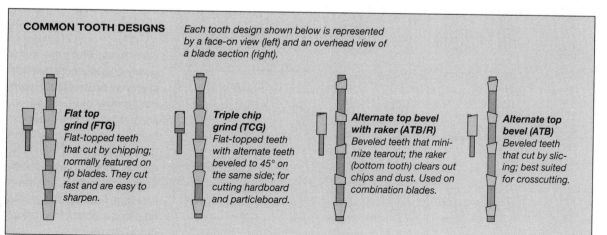

COMMON TOOTH DESIGNS   Each tooth design shown below is represented by a face-on view (left) and an overhead view of a blade section (right).

Flat top grind (FTG)
Flat-topped teeth that cut by chipping; normally featured on rip blades. They cut fast and are easy to sharpen.

Triple chip grind (TCG)
Flat-topped teeth with alternate teeth beveled to 45° on the same side; for cutting hardboard and particleboard.

Alternate top bevel with raker (ATB/R)
Beveled teeth that minimize tearout; the raker (bottom tooth) clears out chips and dust. Used on combination blades.

Alternate top bevel (ATB)
Beveled teeth that cut by slicing; best suited for crosscutting.

Illustrations Courtesy Freud Canada

TABLE SAW

DADO HEADS AND BLADES

A dado head or blade enables a table saw to cut dadoes and rabbets up to 1 inch wide in a single pass. Refer to page 267 for instructions on using this accessory to cut a rabbet; for a dado, see page 269.

Blade

Chipper

Hub

Stack-type dado head
Consists of two outer blades that sandwich a variable number of chippers and spacers; width of dado can typically range from ¼ inch with only outer blades installed, up to 1 inch with chippers and shims.

Wobble-type dado blade
Blade is mounted on hubs that can be adjusted to set width of dado; blade literally wobbles on hubs. Requires a slow rate-of-feed for smooth cuts.

MOLDING HEADS AND KNIVES

Illustrations of molding knives and profiles courtesy Richards Engineering Co.

Equipped with a molding head, the table saw can cut a variety of profiles in wood—ideal for making molding or trim. A molding head is a solid metal wheel you can install on the arbor like a blade. The head is slotted to accept three identical cutters, each held in place by a setscrew.

Make several passes to reach your final depth, increasing the cutting height no more than ⅟₁₆ to ⅛ inch between each pass. Feed the stock slowly and at a constant rate to prevent burning and tearout. For narrow molding strips, first cut the desired profile on the edge of a wide board and then rip it to width. Similarly, do not mold boards shorter than 12 inches. For short molding, first cut the profile on a longer board, then crosscut to length.

Molding head

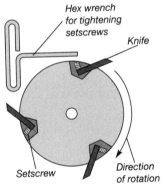

Hex wrench for tightening setscrews

Knife

Setscrew

Direction of rotation

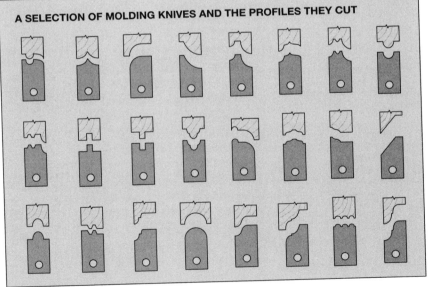

A SELECTION OF MOLDING KNIVES AND THE PROFILES THEY CUT

Aligning your table saw properly is crucial to blade life, the precision of your work, and safety. Test and adjust the saw's alignment

To test miter gauge-to-blade alignment 2, place the gauge at the front of the saw and butt the face of a board against the fence and the

owner's manual. To test the rip fence, check that it is parallel to the miter slot.

Check the accuracy of your adjustments as shown in the illustration 3. First, crosscut a board face down *(top)*. Then turn over the cut-off and press the cut ends together *(middle)*. Any gap indicates that the blade is not at 90 degrees to the table; the gap represents twice the error. Test the cut again, this time with the board on edge *(bottom)*. Again, any gap between the two pieces will represent double the error between the blade and the miter gauge.

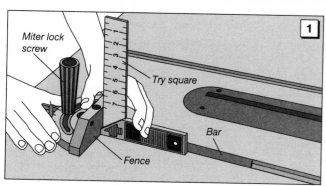

Miter lock screw

Try square

Bar

Fence

1

whenever you change blades. The procedure involves checking the relationships between four components—the miter gauge, the blade, the saw table, and the rip fence. Check the miter gauge first. Start by using a try square to verify that the gauge fence is perpendicular to the edge of the bar. If not, loosen the miter lock screw, adjust the fence, and tighten. Insert the gauge in its slot to check whether the gauge fence is square to the saw table 1. If not, take the gauge to a machine shop and have the fence milled flat. Next, check whether the blade is square to the table. Raise the blade, remove the table insert, and use a combination square. Turn the blade angle crank to square the blade.

2

end against one blade tooth. Holding the board against the fence, rotate the blade so that the same tooth is toward the back of the saw and slide the gauge so that the board again aligns with the chosen tooth. If a gap appears between the board and the blade tooth, or the tooth pushes the board sideways, repeat with a different blade. If you get the same result, align the table following the instructions in your

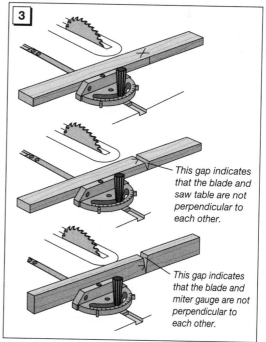

3

This gap indicates that the blade and saw table are not perpendicular to each other.

This gap indicates that the blade and miter gauge are not perpendicular to each other.

TABLE SAW

**FOUR CUTS
WITH THE
TABLE SAW**

Any cut on the table saw must be guided by the rip fence, the miter gauge, or a jig. Use the rip fence for ripping, the miter gauge for crosscuts, and a jig for repetitive cuts, or for unwieldy or small workpieces. To keep a board against the fence while ripping narrow strips from it, for exam-

above the blade to keep the workpiece flat on the table; clamp another to the table. For added stability, brace the second featherboard with a support board clamped to the table. Also, shim the featherboard so that it presses against the middle of the board and keeps it stable. Since the

location. Start the pass from the front of the table, as shown. Halfway through the cut, move to the other side of the table and pull the stock past the blade. Turn the board around and make a second pass to finish the cut.

One useful accessory for the table saw is the taper jig 3. You can use it to make a diagonal cut across the face of a workpiece. The taper jig consists of two bars hinged at one end. Spread the bars apart to the required angle and fix them in place by tightening the wing nuts on the locking brace. Seat the workpiece against the bar with the workstop, making sure the end is butted against the stop. Align the cutting mark on the workpiece with the blade and position the rip fence against the other bar of the jig. Feed

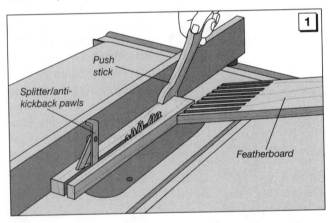

Push stick

Splitter/anti-kickback pawls

Featherboard

ple, clamp a featherboard 1 to the table just in front of the blade. As the trailing end of the board approaches the blade, feed it with a push stick to keep your hands a safe distance from the blade. Refer to pages 406 and 407 for instructions on making push sticks and featherboards.

If you are using the table saw to resaw wide stock, you have to make the cut in two passes. Attach a wide board to the rip fence as an auxiliary fence 2. Use two featherboards for this cut: Clamp one to the fence directly

blade is hidden during this cut, mark two lines on the table insert indicating the blade's

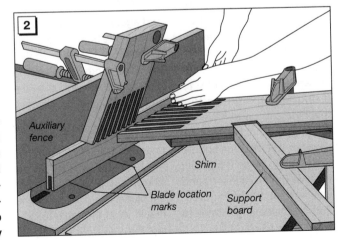

Auxiliary fence

Shim

Blade location marks

Support board

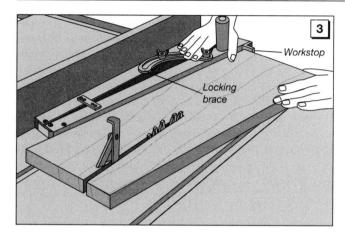

3

Workstop

Locking brace

workpiece against the fence with its leading end raised above the dado head as shown. Holding the stock firmly against the stop block, pivot it down onto the blade. Once the workpiece rests flat on the table, push it forward until the trailing marks are aligned. Immediately pivot the trailing end of the board clear of the dado head.

the workpiece and jig along the fence, as shown. A shop-made taper jig is shown on page 391.

You can also cut stopped grooves on the table saw. Mark the beginning and end of the groove ④ on the outside face of the workpiece. Mark its location and width on the board's leading end. Install a dado head on the saw, adjusting its width to

that of the groove. Mark blade cutting lines on the table insert. To position the rip fence, align the groove width marks with the dado head and butt the fence against the stock. Clamp a block to the rip fence so that the forward marks on the workpiece and table insert align with the board butted against the block at the start of the cut. Turn on the saw and hold the

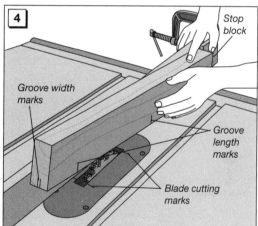

4

Stop block

Groove width marks

Groove length marks

Blade cutting marks

QUICKTIP

Repeat crosscuts

Sawing several boards to exactly the same length is a common task in woodworking. Provided the pieces are not too long, you can speed up the process and guarantee precision using a miter gauge extension fence and a stop block. Screw the extension fence to your miter gauge and mark a cutting line on the fence, measuring from the blade. Clamp a stop block to the extension fence, aligning one end with the cutting mark. To make the cuts, butt the workpiece against the stop block and extension fence, and feed the stock with the miter gauge.

RADIAL ARM SAW

Owners of radial arm saws generally appreciate their convenience in performing crosscuts, dadoes, and miters. Because the blade is pulled into the stock, which remains stationary on the table, the radial arm saw excels at crosscutting long boards. Also, the blade cuts from above, giving the operator a better view of the cutting edge. This makes some operations, such as cutting stopped dadoes, easier.

The major drawback of the radial arm saw is that all crosscuts are climbing cuts, which tend to self-feed, adding an element of danger to the operation. In addition, the saw is complicated to set up and realign; and it requires frequent realignment. Choosing between the table saw and radial arm saw should rest on the intended use. Ideally, the well-equipped workshop would include both machines. A few useful radial arm saw accessories are shown on page 149. All of the blades shown on page 143, as well as the dado and molding head (*page 144*) and some of the items on page 141, can be used on the radial arm saw.

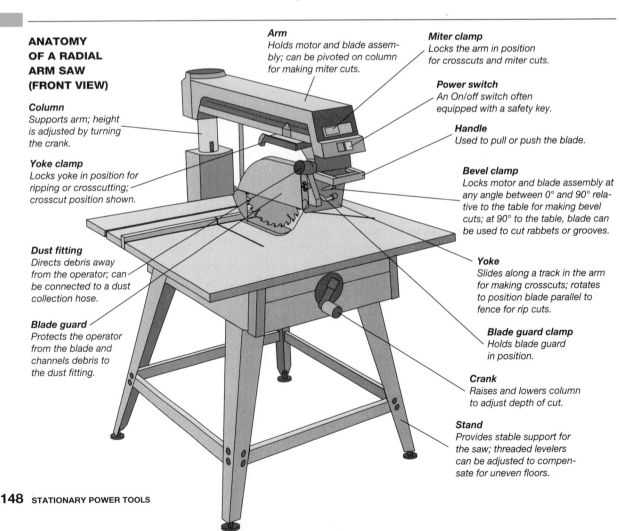

ANATOMY OF A RADIAL ARM SAW (FRONT VIEW)

Column
Supports arm; height is adjusted by turning the crank.

Yoke clamp
Locks yoke in position for ripping or crosscutting; crosscut position shown.

Dust fitting
Directs debris away from the operator; can be connected to a dust collection hose.

Blade guard
Protects the operator from the blade and channels debris to the dust fitting.

Arm
Holds motor and blade assembly; can be pivoted on column for making miter cuts.

Miter clamp
Locks the arm in position for crosscuts and miter cuts.

Power switch
An On/off switch often equipped with a safety key.

Handle
Used to pull or push the blade.

Bevel clamp
Locks motor and blade assembly at any angle between 0° and 90° relative to the table for making bevel cuts; at 90° to the table, blade can be used to cut rabbets or grooves.

Yoke
Slides along a track in the arm for making crosscuts; rotates to position blade parallel to fence for rip cuts.

Blade guard clamp
Holds blade guard in position.

Crank
Raises and lowers column to adjust depth of cut.

Stand
Provides stable support for the saw; threaded levelers can be adjusted to compensate for uneven floors.

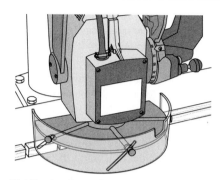

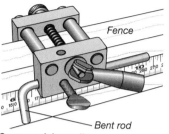

Fence

Bent rod

Commercial stop jig
Clamps to saw fence; bent rod can be adjusted to act as a stop for repeat cuts.

Molding head guard
Functions like a standard blade guard, protecting the operator from a molding head or blade in the horizontal position.

Collet chuck
Attaches to accessory shaft on saw motor for holding attachments.

Bore adapter
Fits onto the saw's arbor to reduce the bore to ½ inch, enabling the saw to be used with accessories with ½-inch shanks.

RADIAL ARM SAW ACCESSORIES

Sanding drum
A 3-inch-diameter rubber drum that mounts to accessory shaft on saw motor. Accepts sanding sleeves of various grits; useful for sanding concave surfaces.

Sanding disc
Attached like a saw blade. Available in several diameters; accepts self-adhesive sanding discs (page 129).

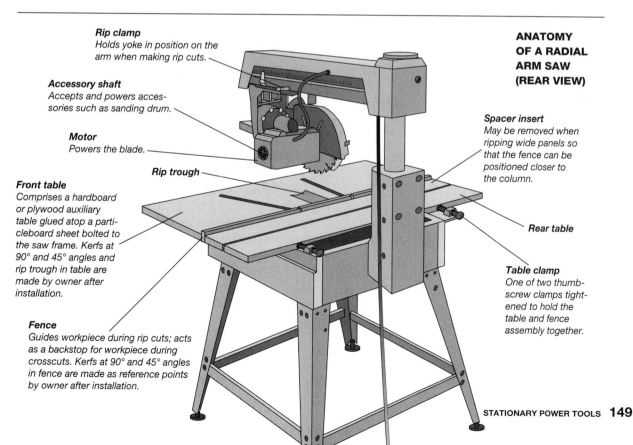

Rip clamp
Holds yoke in position on the arm when making rip cuts.

Accessory shaft
Accepts and powers accessories such as sanding drum.

Motor
Powers the blade.

Rip trough

Front table
Comprises a hardboard or plywood auxiliary table glued atop a particleboard sheet bolted to the saw frame. Kerfs at 90° and 45° angles and rip trough in table are made by owner after installation.

Fence
Guides workpiece during rip cuts; acts as a backstop for workpiece during crosscuts. Kerfs at 90° and 45° angles in fence are made as reference points by owner after installation.

ANATOMY OF A RADIAL ARM SAW (REAR VIEW)

Spacer insert
May be removed when ripping wide panels so that the fence can be positioned closer to the column.

Rear table

Table clamp
One of two thumbscrew clamps tightened to hold the table and fence assembly together.

RADIAL ARM SAW

SETTING UP THE RADIAL ARM SAW

To keep a radial arm saw cutting accurately, you must maintain proper tension on the miter, yoke, and bevel clamps. The procedures for adjusting these clamps

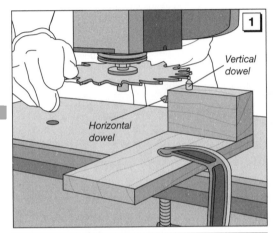

Vertical dowel

Horizontal dowel

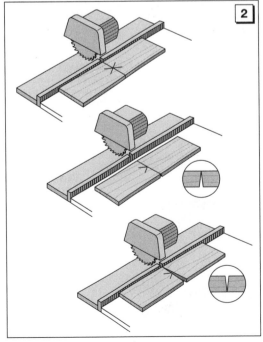

depend on the model of saw; consult your owner's manual for detailed instructions. However, the methods for diagnosing problems apply to virtually all saws.

To check the miter clamp, rotate the arm of the saw to any position other than the 45- or 90-degree setting. Lock the clamp and then try to push the arm out of position. There should be no play. To test the yoke clamp, rotate the yoke to a setting between the crosscut and rip cut positions, lock it in place, and then attempt to turn it. Again, there should be no play. Test the bevel clamp by rotating the motor, locking it in a position between 45 and 90 degrees, and checking it for play. Also test the tension between the column and the column base: Turn the crank while resting your free hand on the top of the arm. The arm should not bounce or vibrate when you stop turning the crank.

Another potential problem is "blade heel," the term used to indicate that the blade is not rotating perpendicular to the table when in the vertical position, or parallel to the table in the horizontal position. Blade heel will cause the saw to make rough cuts with wide kerfs. Test for blade heel with the blade in both

the horizontal and vertical positions, using the simple jig shown in the illustration ⬚1. To make the jig, insert two sharpened dowels into adjoining sides of a small wood block. Then screw the block to a board and clamp the board to the saw table, as shown. Unplug the saw, remove the blade guard, and rotate the motor assembly so the blade is parallel to the table. Lower the blade until the tip of a tooth just touches the vertical dowel, then spin the blade backwards, listening intently to the pinging sound it makes. Next, slide the yoke along the arm and repeat the test on another part of the blade. The sound should be identical. Rotate the motor assembly so that the blade is at 90 degrees to the table and repeat the sound tests with the jig's horizontal dowel. If the saw fails either sound test, adjust the motor mount, as described in your owner's manual.

Check the accuracy of your adjustments as shown in the illustration ⬚2. Crosscut a board face down (top). Then turn the cutoff over and press the cut ends together. Any gap between the two when viewed from the edges (middle) or the top (bottom) indicates that the saw needs further adjustment.

To make a crosscut with the radial arm saw, pull the yoke toward you while holding the stock against the fence. Since the blade cuts into the workpiece from above, you have a good view of the cut. And because the blade spins down and back toward both the table and fence, it tends to hold the workpiece in place. With long boards, use a roller stand like the one shown on page 141 to support the portion extending off the table.

This visibility and stability make the saw well suited to precision cuts, such as miters. To set up for a miter cut, pivot the arm of the saw to the 45-degree position and butt the stock against the fence, aligning your cutting mark just inside the 45-degree angle kerf $\boxed{1}$ in the fence. For repeat cuts, as when making picture frames, clamp a stop block to the fence as shown.

To make rip cuts on the radial arm saw, pivot the yoke so the blade is parallel to the fence. Set the width of cut by positioning the yoke at the appropriate point on its track and locking it in place with the rip clamp. The yoke can be rotated so that the motor is between the blade and the column, or on the other side

of the blade. Always feed the stock against the rotation of the blade $\boxed{2}$. Although the saw permits good visibility of ripping operations, the blade tends to lift up the stock and send debris back toward the operator. This contrasts with the table saw's configuration, which tends to pull the workpiece down on the table and channel debris out through the table insert. To minimize the inconveniences of ripping on the radial arm saw, adjust the blade guard $\boxed{3}$ to capture debris and help keep the stock on the table. Also lower the splitter assembly to minimize kickback. To make a wide rip cut, such as in a panel, pivot the yoke to position the blade outside the motor. Butt the edge of the workpiece against the fence as you feed it slowly into the blade, as shown. Most saws are set up for a maximum cut of 24 inches. For a wider cut, reposition the

fence. As shown on page 149, the fence is usually set up between the front table and spacer insert. To move it, loosen the table clamps and reposition the fence between the insert and rear table, or even behind the rear table. In the latter case, place the insert between the fence and the column to prevent the fence from bowing during the cut.

USING THE RADIAL ARM SAW: MITER CUTS AND RIPPING

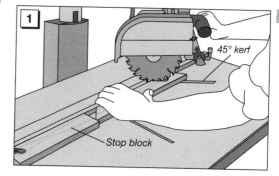
45° kerf

Stop block

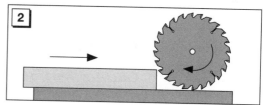
Splitter

Blade guard

RADIAL ARM SAW

USING THE RADIAL ARM SAW: CUTTING GROOVES

The radial arm saw can cut grooves in the edge of a workpiece. For grooves wider than the thickness of a rip blade, install a dado head on the saw. Remove the standard blade guard and replace it with a molding head guard, as shown below. This guard enables the dado head to be lowered close to the table. Also remove the standard fence and insert a notched fence in its place. Make the notch long enough to clear the guard, and a lip that will support the workpiece. Then use the bevel clamp to release the motor assembly and tilt the assembly down so the dado head is parallel to the saw table. To adjust the depth of cut, slide the yoke along its track behind the fence. The dado head should protrude from the fence by an amount equal to the desired groove depth. Clamp a featherboard to the table in line with the dado head to minimize kickback and ensure the depth of cut is uniform. Brace the featherboard with a support board, also clamped to the table. Start feeding the board by hand, as shown, but complete the pass with a push stick.

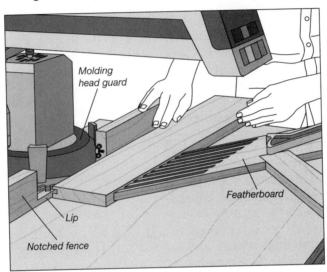

Molding head guard

Featherboard

Lip

Notched fence

QUICKTIP

Cutting short stock

Crosscut a short workpiece on the radial arm saw safely by anchoring it to the fence and table with a toggle clamp—instead of holding it with your hand. Fasten the clamp to an auxiliary fence that is wider than the standard fence. Then install the fence between the front table and the table spacer, making sure that the clamp will not be in the way of the blade. Set your workpiece against the fence, then tighten the clamp, protecting the stock with a wood pad. Do not overtighten; this may lift the fence out of its slot.

BAND SAW

The band saw is the stationary machine of choice for making curved cuts in thick stock and for resawing. With the 6-inch depth of cut typical of most saws, most resawing operations can be done easily. The thin blade wastes less wood than the table saw or radial arm saw. Many band saw cuts can be made freehand so that relatively few accessories are required.

Band saws are sold according to their throat width—the distance between the blade and the column that supports the machine's upper wheel. A 14-inch saw is a good choice for most shops. Another factor to keep in mind is horsepower. A ½-horsepower motor is adequate for most jobs, but if you expect to do a lot of resawing, consider spending the extra money for a ¾-horsepower machine.

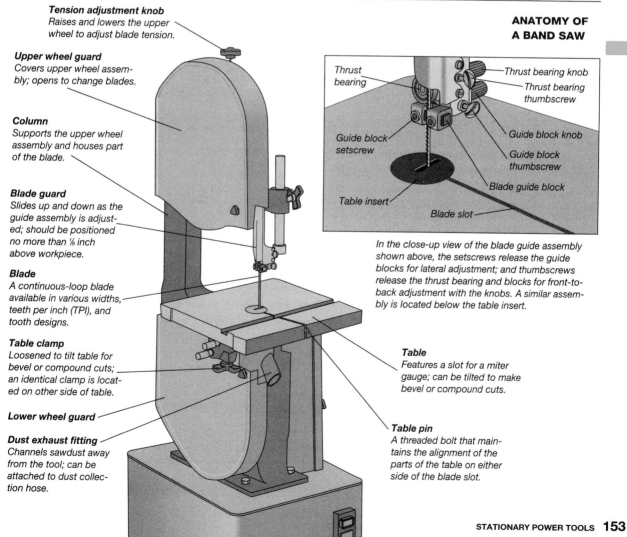

Tension adjustment knob
Raises and lowers the upper wheel to adjust blade tension.

Upper wheel guard
Covers upper wheel assembly; opens to change blades.

Column
Supports the upper wheel assembly and houses part of the blade.

Blade guard
Slides up and down as the guide assembly is adjusted; should be positioned no more than ⅛ inch above workpiece.

Blade
A continuous-loop blade available in various widths, teeth per inch (TPI), and tooth designs.

Table clamp
Loosened to tilt table for bevel or compound cuts; an identical clamp is located on other side of table.

Lower wheel guard

Dust exhaust fitting
Channels sawdust away from the tool; can be attached to dust collection hose.

ANATOMY OF A BAND SAW

Thrust bearing

Thrust bearing knob

Thrust bearing thumbscrew

Guide block setscrew

Guide block knob

Guide block thumbscrew

Blade guide block

Table insert

Blade slot

In the close-up view of the blade guide assembly shown above, the setscrews release the guide blocks for lateral adjustment; and thumbscrews release the thrust bearing and blocks for front-to-back adjustment with the knobs. A similar assembly is located below the table insert.

Table
Features a slot for a miter gauge; can be tilted to make bevel or compound cuts.

Table pin
A threaded bolt that maintains the alignment of the parts of the table on either side of the blade slot.

BAND SAW

BAND SAW BLADES

Band saw performance depends to a great extent on the width of the blade. The wider the blade, the better it will track for straight cuts, and the more resistant it will be to flexing in thick stock. But as shown below, the wider the blade, the less able it is to cut a tight curve. A ½-inch-wide blade, for example, can only cut a 3-inch-radius circle; a ⅛-inch-wide blade, on the other hand, can cut a curve as tight as 3/16 inch.

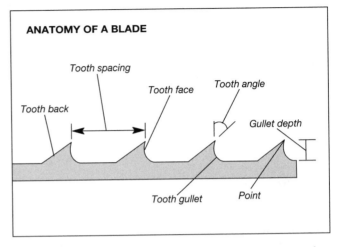

ANATOMY OF A BLADE

Tooth spacing

Tooth face

Tooth angle

Tooth back

Gullet depth

Tooth gullet

Point

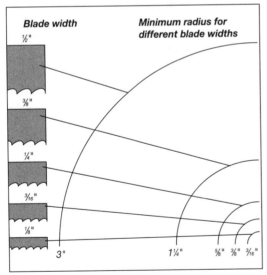

Blade width

Minimum radius for different blade widths

½"

⅜"

¼"

3/16"

⅛"

3"

1¼"

⅝" ⅜" 3/16"

Illustration courtesy
Simonds Industries

The design of the blade teeth is another key factor. The fine, closely spaced teeth of a standard-tooth blade *(far right)* cut smoothly and perform well in thin, dense material. Widely spaced teeth with a slight rake, as in the saber-tooth design, are good for ripping thick stock. For resawing wide boards, a skip-tooth blade is ideal. The extended spacing between the teeth enables the gullets to carry away debris efficiently.

Because band saw blades are flexible, they rely on tension for their rigidity. To minimize binding, band saw teeth are normally set. Some blades feature "every-tooth" set (ETS) *(below)* in which every other tooth is set in the same direction. Blades with less set, like regular-set blades, leave a smoother cut, but they tend to bind more easily.

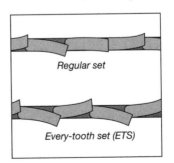

Regular set

Every-tooth set (ETS)

TOOTH STYLES

Standard tooth
All-purpose blade; features a 0° rake angle and full, well-rounded gullets.

Saber tooth
Deep, rounded gullets and 10° rake angle permit faster feeding.

Skip tooth
For soft, gummy materials; features a 0° rake angle and large, open gullets. The flat gullet bottoms act as chip breakers.

Illustration courtesy
Simonds Industries

Adjust your band saw every time you change blades. Start with the blade tracking. Loosen all the guide blocks and thrust bearings and position them away from the blade. Open the wheel covers and check that the blade is centered on both wheels by turning the upper wheel by hand. If the blade is not tracking in the center of the wheel, adjust the tilt knob on the back of the upper wheel guard until the blade is tracking properly. Then tension the blade by tightening the tension adjustment knob. To check the tension, raise the upper guide assembly and try to deflect the blade by hand. The blade should move about ¼ inch. Do not overtighten the blade; this can lead to blade failure.

Adjust the guide assemblies next. Although only the upper assembly is visible at right, there is a similar one below the table. Adjust them both, starting with the upper assembly. First, advance the thrust bearing until it contacts the blade, then back it off slightly and lock it in place by tightening its thumbscrew. To adjust the guide blocks, loosen their setscrews and squeeze the blocks together until they almost contact the blade. Tighten the setscrews. Some woodworkers use a dollar bill to adjust the bearings and guide blocks: a bill folded twice (four thicknesses) between the bearing and blade, and a single thickness between

each guide block and the blade. Next, loosen the guide block thumbscrew and adjust the knob behind the guide assembly so that the front edge of the blocks are just behind the blade gullets. Tighten the thumbscrew.

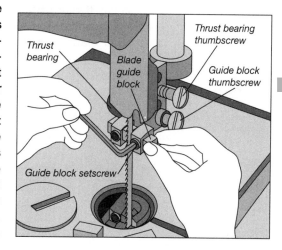

Thrust bearing

Blade guide block

Guide block setscrew

Thrust bearing thumbscrew

Guide block thumbscrew

QUICK*TIP*

Blade storage

It is frequently necessary to change band saw blades; but storing them can pose a problem. To make them more compact, band saw blades can be folded as shown at right. Hold the blade out away from your body, positioning the right thumb up and the left thumb down. Simultaneously twist the right hand forward and down and the left hand forward and up. The blade will contort to compress itself into three concentric coils. Use a twist tie to hold the rings together.

1   2   3

4   5

Illustrations courtesy Delta International Machinery Corp.

BAND SAW

USING THE BAND SAW

Because the band saw blade is flexible, it is relatively sensitive to both rate of feed and side pressure. It is important not to force the machine. As described on page 154, the width of the blade limits how tight a curve you can cut. If your pattern calls for sharper turns, install a narrower blade or make

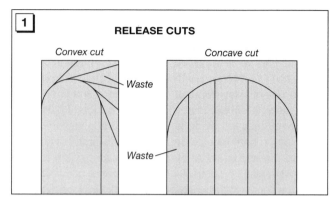

Illustration courtesy Delta International Machinery Corp.

release cuts ① through the waste. For a convex cut, start following the cutting line. To keep the blade from binding, veer off line and make a straight cut through the waste to the end of the board. Then continue along the curve, making a release cut when necessary. For a concave cut, start by sawing a series of straight kerfs through the waste from the board end to the cutting line. Then cut the curve; waste pieces will detach

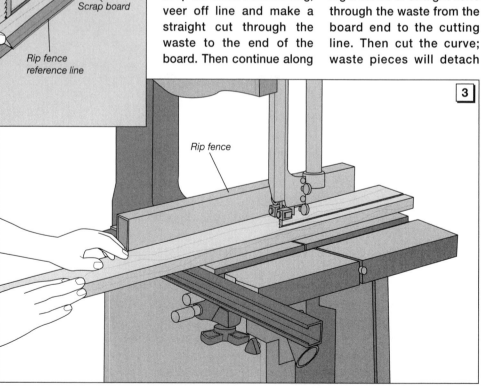

from the board as the blade reaches the release cuts. For any cut on the band saw, feed the workpiece with both hands, pivoting it on the table to cut contours.

Straight cuts on the band saw are complicated by the problem of blade lead. This refers to the tendency of the blade to drift off line, particularly during long rip cuts. You need to compensate for blade lead when positioning the rip fence. To determine where to set up the fence, mark a straight line on a scrap board that is parallel to an edge. Then start a rip cut in the board, keeping the blade on the marked line. About halfway into the cut, turn off the saw. With the blade still in the kerf, mark a line on the saw table along the edge of the board ⎡2⎤. This line represents the blade lead. If you

align the fence parallel with this reference line, your rip cuts will be straight ⎡3⎤.

If you are resawing on the band saw, use a shop-made

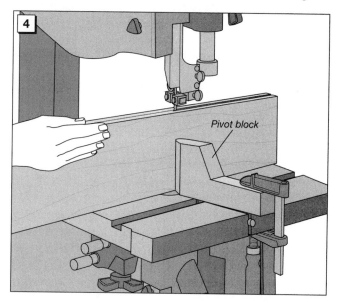

Pivot block

pivot block ⎡4⎤ to help guide the cut. To make the block, cut a board into an L shape

and round one end. The jig will serve as a pivot point as you feed the stock, enabling you to shift the trailing end of the stock to the left or right to

compensate for blade drift. Feed the board with both hands. About halfway through the cut, move to the back of the table with the saw running and pull the stock past the blade.

To make a bevel cut on the band saw, tilt the table and lock it at the desired angle. Screw a board to the miter gauge as an extension fence ⎡5⎤ and feed the workpiece with the gauge. The fence will help you keep the stock square to the blade.

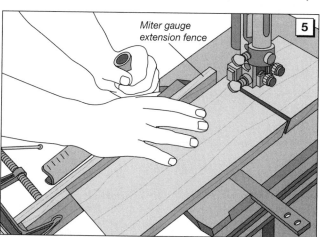

Miter gauge extension fence

DRILL PRESS

Like the portable drill, the drill press owes its popularity to its great versatility. The machine accepts a complete spectrum of drills and bits; you can use any of the bits illustrated in the Drill section *(page 115)*, in addition to those shown on page 159. With the accessories shown, you can also easily convert the drill press into a rotary rasp or rosette cutter. Another useful accessory, the mortising attachment *(page 275)*, enables the machine to drill rectangular mortises. An undeniable benefit of the drill press is that it performs these functions with outstanding precision and control while taking up very little floor space.

The versatility of any one model depends to some degree on its features. Capabilities vary considerably from model to model. Drill presses are sized according to twice the distance between the column and the chuck. Home shop machines are available in the 11- to 16-inch range and are equipped with ¼- to ¾-horsepower motors. A 15-inch tool powered by a ½-horsepower motor is a good choice for the typical woodworker. Look for a machine with a tilting table, a quill stroke of at least 4 inches, smooth feed lever action, variable speeds, and a deep throat between the quill and the column.

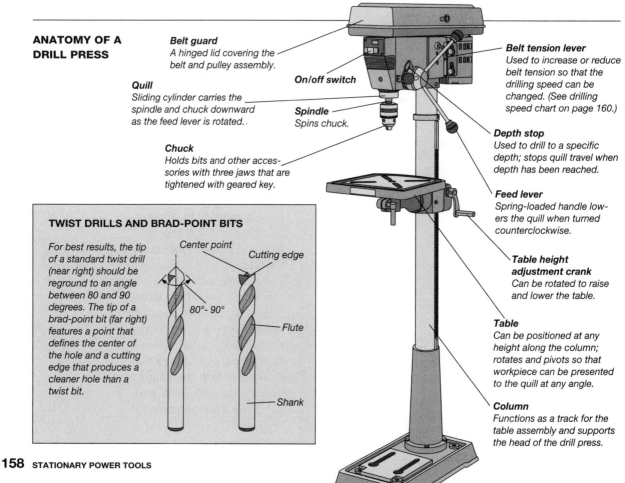

ANATOMY OF A DRILL PRESS

Belt guard
A hinged lid covering the belt and pulley assembly.

Quill
Sliding cylinder carries the spindle and chuck downward as the feed lever is rotated.

On/off switch

Spindle
Spins chuck.

Chuck
Holds bits and other accessories with three jaws that are tightened with geared key.

Belt tension lever
Used to increase or reduce belt tension so that the drilling speed can be changed. (See drilling speed chart on page 160.)

Depth stop
Used to drill to a specific depth; stops quill travel when depth has been reached.

Feed lever
Spring-loaded handle lowers the quill when turned counterclockwise.

Table height adjustment crank
Can be rotated to raise and lower the table.

Table
Can be positioned at any height along the column; rotates and pivots so that workpiece can be presented to the quill at any angle.

Column
Functions as a track for the table assembly and supports the head of the drill press.

TWIST DRILLS AND BRAD-POINT BITS

For best results, the tip of a standard twist drill (near right) should be reground to an angle between 80 and 90 degrees. The tip of a brad-point bit (far right) features a point that defines the center of the hole and a cutting edge that produces a cleaner hole than a twist bit.

Center point

Cutting edge

80°- 90°

Flute

Shank

Spur bit
Bores holes with minimum chipping or splintering; performs well in plywood and veneered surfaces.

Forstner bit
Drills extremely clean, flat-bottomed holes; bit is guided by cutting edges around circumference. Often used to enlarge existing holes.

Countersink bit
Bores cone-shaped holes to seat screw-heads or chamfer the rim of existing holes.

Rotary rasps
Converts drill press into a shaping tool; available in various profiles, including (from top to bottom) cone, drum, and cylinder.

Dowel and plug cutter
Bores into end grain to produce dowels and plugs; can also be used for cutting round tenons.

Adjustable bit
Bores holes ranging from ⅝ inch to 1¾ inches in diameter; set-screw in bit locks cutter in place.

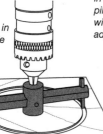

Plug cutter
Used to cut wood plugs for covering counter-bored screw heads; allows plugs to be cut from scraps of stock matching the workpiece.

Drill press clamp
Lever-type clamp can be bolted to drill press table; rotates to hold down stock at any point on table.

Hole saw
Cuts large holes; twist drill in center functions as a pilot. Models are available with fixed-diameter or adjustable blades.

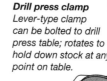

Circle cutter
For cutting large holes in thin material; adjustable cutter arm may be set for diameters ranging from 1⁹⁄₁₆ to 8⅛ inches.

Drill press vise
Secures small or irregularly shaped workpieces on table; jig base can be clamped to table.

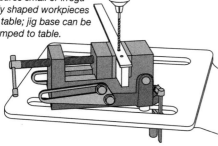

Planer head
Smoothes surfaces and chamfers edges; can also be used on the radial arm saw.

Wheel and rosette cutter
Used to cut concentric molded patterns in the face of stock; interchangeable cutters can be used to produce different patterns.

DRILL PRESS

SETTING UP THE DRILL PRESS

Setting up the drill press involves selecting the appropriate spindle speed for the bit being used, adjusting the drilling depth properly, and securing the workpiece to the table. Also make sure that the table is perpendicular to the quill. Install a steel shaft or a dowel in the chuck and use a try square to check whether the table and shaft or dowel are at 90 degrees to each other. If not, align the table following the instructions in your owner's manual.

As shown in the chart below, the suggested spindle speed (in rpm) for drilling depends on the bit diameter and the material being drilled. In general, the larger the bit, the slower the speed. On most drill presses, spindle speed is adjusted by shifting the location of the belt on the pulleys under the guard at the top of the machine's head. Again, consult your owner's manual for instructions on matching belt positions with the appropriate rpm.

Adjusting drilling depth depends on your model of drill press. Many models, like the one shown on page 158, have a depth stop that limits quill travel.

SUGGESTED DRILLING SPEEDS (IN RPM)

Chart information courtesy Delta International Machinery Corp.

DRILL BIT DIAMETER	SOFTWOOD	HARDWOOD
$1/16"$	3000	3000
$3/32"$	3000	3000
$1/8"$	3000	3000
$5/32"$	3000	3000
$3/16"$	3000	3000
$7/32"$	3000	3000
$1/4"$	3000	3000
$9/32"$	2180	2180
$5/16"$	2180	2180

DRILL BIT DIAMETER	SOFTWOOD	HARDWOOD
$11/32"$	2180	2180
$3/8"$	2180	2180
$13/32"$	2180	2180
$7/16"$	2180	2180
$15/32"$	2180	2180
$1/2"$	2180	1820
$9/16"$	2180	1820
$5/8"$	1820	1820

For most operations on the drill press, hold the workpiece firmly with one hand while depressing the feed lever with the other 1. If you the workpiece in the jig. Clamp the base to the drill press table so that the bit is centered on the edge of the workpiece. Bore the pocket holes using two bits: A wide one for recessing the screw heads, and a smaller one to clear the screw shaft.

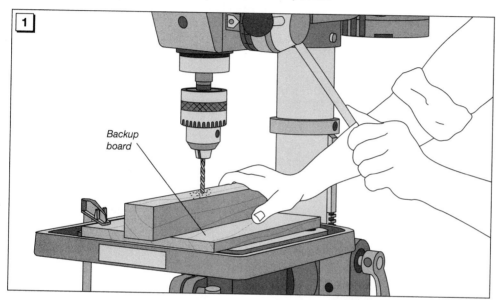

1

Backup board

are working with a small workpiece, clamp it to the table. To minimize tearout as the bit exits the workpiece, clamp a backup board between the stock and the table.

Pocket holes are often used to join rails to the underside of a tabletop. To bore pocket holes, use a jig 2. Make the jig by screwing two boards together into an L-shaped cradle. Set the cradle in wedged brackets so that the longer side of the cradle is angled back at about 15 degrees. Attach the brackets to a base and seat

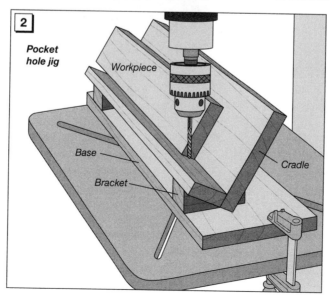

2

Pocket hole jig

Workpiece

Base

Bracket

Cradle

JOINTER

The jointer is the only stationary tool capable of quickly and reliably truing up stock. Whether you are laying out a project, or edge-gluing boards together to form a tabletop, the jointer will enable you to make the edges and faces of boards straight, square, and flat. It can also be used to salvage stock with cups, twists, bows, crooked edges, and uneven surfaces. And as shown on page 319, you can taper a leg on the jointer.

If you do not already own a jointer, buying a combination jointer/planer, like the one shown on page 178, can be an economical choice. Since woodworkers count on a jointer for precision, be sure to choose a model that is ruggedly built. Its adjustable parts, like the fence and infeed table, should fit well and hold settings accurately. Although most models come with standard steel knives, carbide replacements are a good option. Carbide knives do not need to be sharpened as often. Considering the time required to correctly install and adjust jointer knives, this is an undeniable benefit.

ANATOMY OF A JOINTER

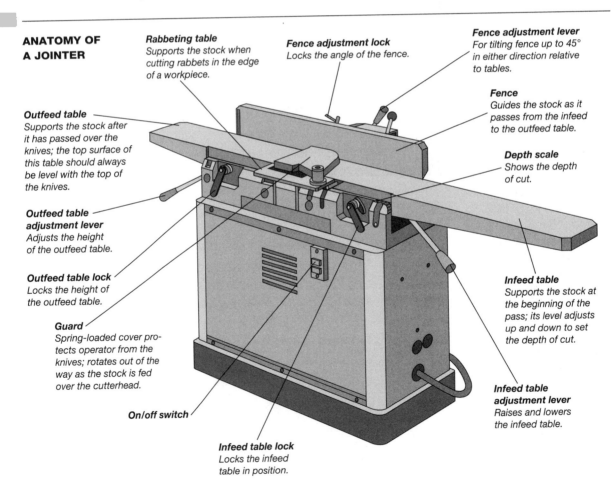

Rabbeting table
Supports the stock when cutting rabbets in the edge of a workpiece.

Fence adjustment lock
Locks the angle of the fence.

Fence adjustment lever
For tilting fence up to 45° in either direction relative to tables.

Fence
Guides the stock as it passes from the infeed to the outfeed table.

Outfeed table
Supports the stock after it has passed over the knives; the top surface of this table should always be level with the top of the knives.

Depth scale
Shows the depth of cut.

Outfeed table adjustment lever
Adjusts the height of the outfeed table.

Outfeed table lock
Locks the height of the outfeed table.

Guard
Spring-loaded cover protects operator from the knives; rotates out of the way as the stock is fed over the cutterhead.

Infeed table
Supports the stock at the beginning of the pass; its level adjusts up and down to set the depth of cut.

On/off switch

Infeed table adjustment lever
Raises and lowers the infeed table.

Infeed table lock
Locks the infeed table in position.

Jointing accurately depends on the precise alignment of the three knives and the outfeed table. Set the outfeed table ①so that its top surface is precisely aligned with the tip of the knives at the top of their rotation. Adjust the infeed table slightly below this level to set the cutting depth, typically $\frac{1}{16}$ to $\frac{1}{8}$ inch.

The knives must be removed from the cutterhead for sharpening. It is a good idea to have an extra set of knives on hand so that you can replace all three knives one at a time. Installing them accurately is critically important to the jointer's performance. The knives must all be set at exactly the same height in the cutterhead. Commercial knife-setting jigs ② can help to take the guesswork out of this procedure. To use the magnetic model shown, set it on the outfeed table and align one of the reference lines on the jig directly above the knife at its highest point. The jig will hold the knife at the correct height as you tighten the screws securing it to the cutterhead.

The knives are held in place by retaining wedges ③, which are anchored to the cutterhead by lock screws. The design of jointer cutterheads varies from model to model; consult your owner's manual for detailed instructions on knife installation.

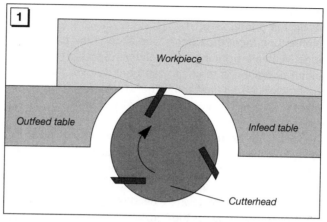

Workpiece

Outfeed table

Infeed table

Cutterhead

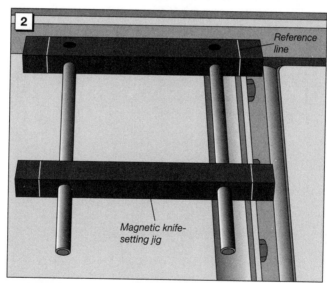

Reference line

Magnetic knife-setting jig

3 *Jointer cutterhead*

Knife jack screw

Blade wedge lock screw

Blade retaining wedge with chipbreaker

Knife

JOINTER

USING THE JOINTER

To prepare rough lumber on the jointer, start by jointing one face, then one edge. A basic principle of jointer operation is to keep the stock flush against the tables and the fence throughout each pass. When jointing a board face, protect your hands from the cutterhead by using push blocks ☐1 to feed the workpiece slowly across the tables. Apply slight downward pressure to keep the board down on the tables and lateral pressure to keep it flush against the fence. As an alternative to the commercial push blocks shown, you can fashion your own *(page 406)*. The shop-made push block features a lip along its back end to ride over the end of the stock, which can help control kickback.

To joint the edge of a board ☐2, use one hand to press the stock against the fence and the other to keep the edge flush against the tables. Use a hand-over-hand technique to maintain uniform pressure on the board throughout the operation, shifting the downward pressure from the infeed table to the outfeed table.

While the jointer is most often used to smooth and square rough stock, it can also be used to straighten the edges of crooked boards ☐3. Start by straightening out the concave edge on the jointer. Pass the high spot at one end of the board across the jointer as many times as needed. In the example shown, two passes *(cuts 1 and 2)* are sufficient to flatten the edge. Then turn the board around and joint the high spot near the other end *(cuts 3 and 4)*. This technique is similar to jointing an entire edge, except

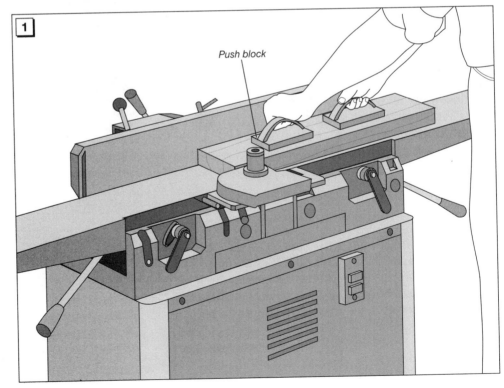

Push block

that you hold the leading edge of the board about 1 inch above the tables at the beginning of the pass 4. Feed the board across the tables with one hand and hold its face against the fence with the other. Once the board is about halfway across the tables, lower the leading end to the outfeed table and continue feeding the board. The knives will cut into the high spot at the board's trailing end.

Once the high spots at both ends are evened out, make a final pass across the jointer *(cut 5)* to square the edge. Rip the convex edge of the board on the table saw, creating two straight, parallel edges.

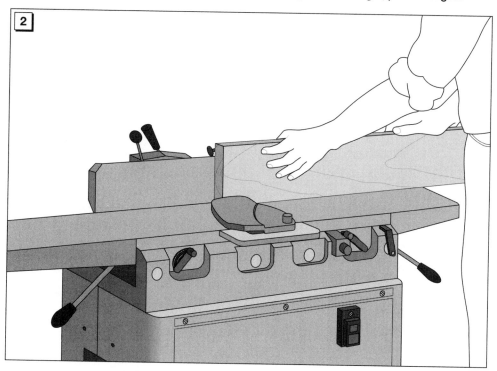

2

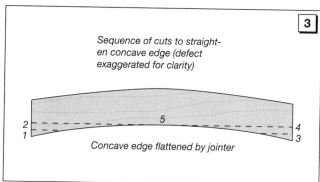

3

Sequence of cuts to straighten concave edge (defect exaggerated for clarity)

Concave edge flattened by jointer

4

PLANER

The thickness planer is a relatively specialized woodworking tool that until recently was seldom found in home workshops. However, increasing lumber prices and the availability of low-cost bench-top planers have increased their popularity. Planers are used to reduce the thickness of stock uniformly and surface the faces of rough boards. You can even use the planer to convert crating and used lumber into serviceable cabinet stock, helping you to realize savings that can recoup the cost of the machine.

As shown in the diagram below, planers feature power rollers that feed the stock across the tool's table, while rotating knives in the cutterhead above the workpiece chip away an even layer of waste.

Planers vary according to their capacity (the maximum board width they will accommodate), horsepower, and rate of feed. Wider, more powerful planers are exceptionally handy for surfacing edge-glued panels. The slower the rate of feed, the smoother the planed surface will be. In general, full-size planers with 15- to 20-inch capacities cost at least twice as much as bench-top machines with 10- to 12-inch capacities.

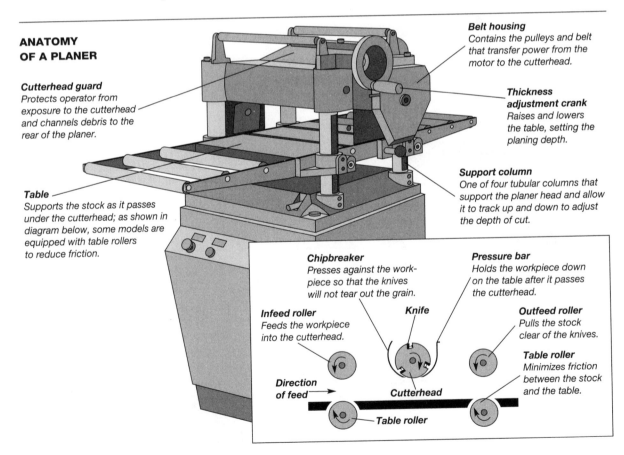

ANATOMY OF A PLANER

Belt housing
Contains the pulleys and belt that transfer power from the motor to the cutterhead.

Cutterhead guard
Protects operator from exposure to the cutterhead and channels debris to the rear of the planer.

Thickness adjustment crank
Raises and lowers the table, setting the planing depth.

Support column
One of four tubular columns that support the planer head and allow it to track up and down to adjust the depth of cut.

Table
Supports the stock as it passes under the cutterhead; as shown in diagram below, some models are equipped with table rollers to reduce friction.

Chipbreaker
Presses against the workpiece so that the knives will not tear out the grain.

Pressure bar
Holds the workpiece down on the table after it passes the cutterhead.

Infeed roller
Feeds the workpiece into the cutterhead.

Knife

Outfeed roller
Pulls the stock clear of the knives.

Table roller
Minimizes friction between the stock and the table.

Direction of feed

Cutterhead

Table roller

The number of knives in a planer cutterhead varies from model to model. Newer 12-inch bench-top machines generally have two knives; larger planers often have three. As with the jointer, installing and aligning the knives in the cutterhead is the most challenging adjustment. Typically, planers come with a small tool or template to assist in this procedure; your owner's manual will explain how to use it. The planer's other assemblies seldom need adjustment.

To use the planer, adjust the thickness adjustment crank to set the depth of cut. Although most planers are capable of removing up to $\frac{1}{8}$ inch of stock in a single pass, they perform best when the depth of cut is $\frac{1}{16}$ inch or less. If your machine

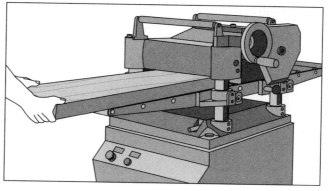

offers a variable speed feature, choosing a slower rate of feed will yield a smoother surface. As shown above, feed a board into the planer so that it is parallel to the table edges. Hold the board level until the leading end is well beyond the outfeed roller. When the board is midway through the pass, move to the outfeed side of the planer to support the board and keep it level until

the trailing end clears the outfeed roller.

A planer will not flatten a warped board; it will simply make it thinner. This is because the feed rollers press the board flat as it passes under the cutterhead. The best solution is to flatten one face of the warped board on the jointer, then plane the other face. This will yield two parallel and flat surfaces.

QUICKTIP

Planing short stock

Whenever possible, plane your lumber before cutting it into shorter workpieces. Short boards are difficult to plane and tend to come out with chatter marks near the trailing end. If you have to plane a short piece, simplify the task by gluing guide strips along each edge, as shown at right. The strips should extend beyond the ends of the work-piece far enough so that they are under both the infeed and outfeed rollers when the workpiece is in contact with the cutterhead.

SHAPER

Although a table-mounted router can perform many shaping operations, a shaper with a ¾-inch-diameter spindle, like the machine shown below, is a far more capable tool. It provides the power to drive a much broader array of specialized cutters, such as those shown on page 170. The shaper is virtually indispensable in shops that specialize in the production of cabinets and doors. Since it has been used in furniture making for many years, woodworkers involved in repro-duction work often discover that it is the only practical tool for duplicating some decorative profiles that were popular in early 20th-Century pieces.

While the shaper's power, high-speed capacity, and precision are important advantages, these features also make it a dangerous woodworking tool. Never attempt to shape small parts without setting up properly to ensure your hands will remain safely away from the spindle.

ANATOMY OF A SHAPER

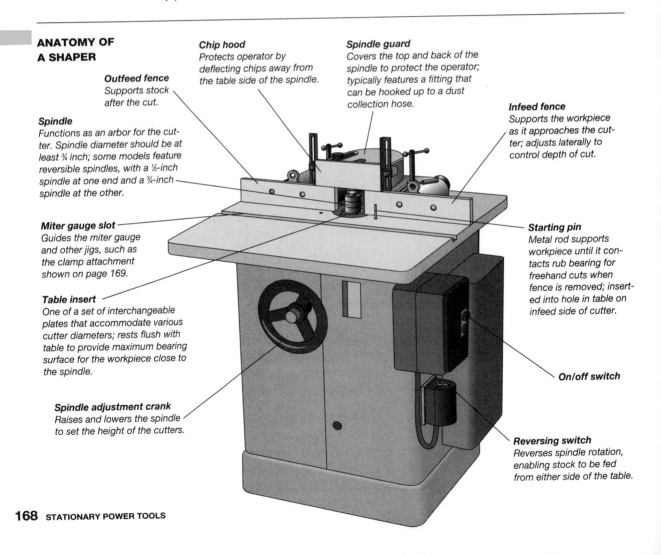

Chip hood
Protects operator by deflecting chips away from the table side of the spindle.

Spindle guard
Covers the top and back of the spindle to protect the operator; typically features a fitting that can be hooked up to a dust collection hose.

Outfeed fence
Supports stock after the cut.

Infeed fence
Supports the workpiece as it approaches the cutter; adjusts laterally to control depth of cut.

Spindle
Functions as an arbor for the cutter. Spindle diameter should be at least ¾ inch; some models feature reversible spindles, with a ½-inch spindle at one end and a ¾-inch spindle at the other.

Miter gauge slot
Guides the miter gauge and other jigs, such as the clamp attachment shown on page 169.

Starting pin
Metal rod supports workpiece until it contacts rub bearing for freehand cuts when fence is removed; inserted into hole in table on infeed side of cutter.

Table insert
One of a set of interchangeable plates that accommodate various cutter diameters; rests flush with table to provide maximum bearing surface for the workpiece close to the spindle.

Spindle adjustment crank
Raises and lowers the spindle to set the height of the cutters.

On/off switch

Reversing switch
Reverses spindle rotation, enabling stock to be fed from either side of the table.

The shaper accessories illustrated on this page are designed to improve the machine's precision or make it safer to use by holding the wood. As illustrated below, shaper accessories vary in size and complexity from simple bushings and spacers to self-powered feeders.

Spindle spacer collars
Slide over the spindle to position the cutter at the desired height.

Bushings
Enable small-diameter spindles to accept large-bore cutters; fit into holes on each side of cutter.

Spindle rub bearings
Slip on the spindle above or below cutter to function as a pilot or bearing surface for workpiece or template.

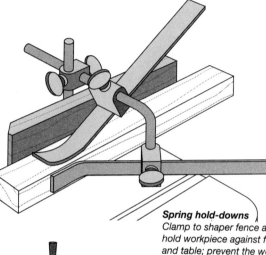

Spring hold-downs
Clamp to shaper fence and hold workpiece against fence and table; prevent the workpiece from kicking away from the cutter. Jig adjusts to accommodate different dimensions of stock.

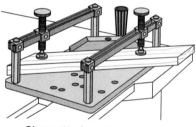

Clamp attachment
Secures workpiece at appropriate angle to cutters and rides in miter gauge slot; like a miter gauge, jig features a feed handle and an adjustable fence.

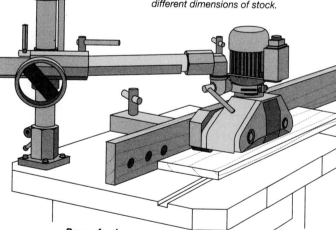

Power feeder
A motorized jig with feed rollers or a belt that draws a workpiece past the cutter at a constant feed rate; adjusts to accommodate fence position and workpiece thickness. Most models feature adjustable speed and tension.

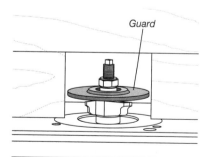

Guard

Ring guard
A plastic spindle-mounted guard designed to protect the operator's hands from the cutter.

SHAPER

**CUTTERS
AND SHAPERS**

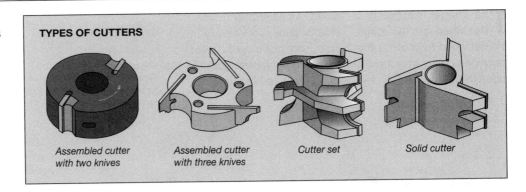

TYPES OF CUTTERS

Assembled cutter
with two knives

Assembled cutter
with three knives

Cutter set

Solid cutter

**A SELECTION
OF SHAPER
KNIVES AND
THE PROFILES
THEY CUT**

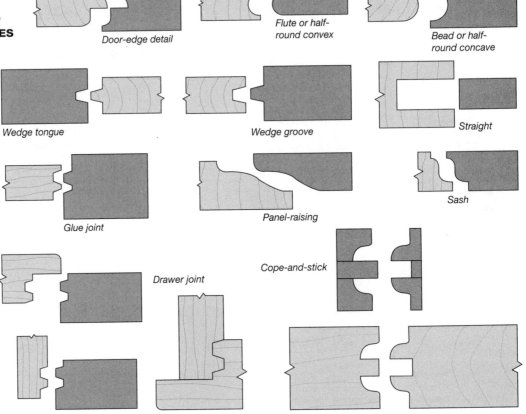

Door-edge detail

Flute or half-
round convex

Bead or half-
round concave

Wedge tongue

Wedge groove

Straight

Glue joint

Panel-raising

Sash

Drawer joint

Cope-and-stick

Illustrations courtesy Delta International Machinery Corp.

The shaper requires little initial alignment, but as shown on page 172, most operations involve extensive setup. One alignment task you should perform periodically is to check the spindle

Correct alignment of the fences depends on the depth of cut and on whether you will be shaping the entire edge of the stock. Position the infeed fence to control the depth of cut. If you are

port the workpiece once the cut is made. If you are shaping only a part of the edge, the fences should align with each other. Be sure the fences are locked in place and the cutter will spin clear of them before turning the shaper on.

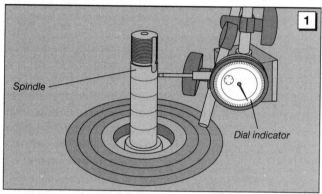

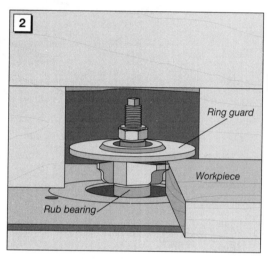

for wobble or runout. Either will affect the quality of cuts, the life of the cutters, and safe operation. Spindle alignment is best tested with a dial indicator ☐1. The type shown is attached to a magnetic base. Position the jig on the shaper table so that the spring-loaded probe of the indicator contacts the spindle. Rotate the spindle by hand; if the dial indicator registers runout exceeding 0.005 inch, have the main bearings replaced.

To adjust the spindle height for a shaping operation, set the workpiece flat on the table ☐2 and raise or lower the cutter until the cutter profile aligns as desired with the edge of the board.

shaping the full edge, as in illustration ☐3, position the outfeed fence in front of the infeed fence so that it will sup-

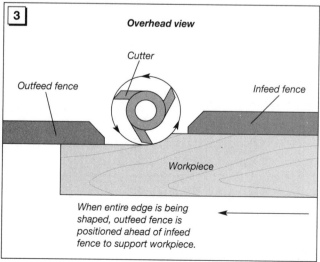

Illustration courtesy Delta International Machinery Corp.

SHAPER

**USING THE
SHAPER**

For a straight cut on the shaper ⟦1⟧, mount a cutter and a guard on the spin-dle, and position the fences. Use three featherboards to press the workpiece flush against the fence and flat on the shaper table: Clamp one featherboard to each fence and another to the table. To protect your hands, feed the stock with a push stick.

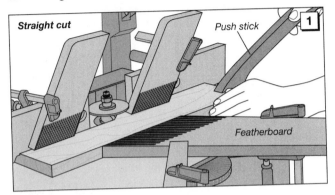

Straight cut **Push stick** ⟦1⟧

Featherboard

For a curved cut shaping only part of an edge ⟦2⟧, clamp the workpiece to a template. Set the spindle height so that enough of the template will be supported by the rub bearing *(left)*. If the spindle is adjusted too high and only a thin sliver of the template rides against the bearing *(right)*, the sliver may break off and jam between the cutter and the bearing.

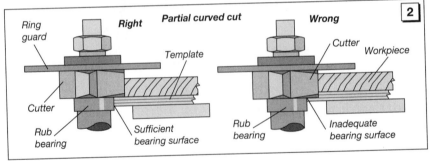

Right **Partial curved cut** **Wrong** ⟦2⟧

Ring guard

Template

Cutter

Workpiece

Cutter

Rub bearing

Sufficient bearing surface

Rub bearing

Inadequate bearing surface

Illustrations courtesy
Delta International
Machinery Corp.

For a curved cut on an entire edge, clamp the work-piece to a template as well ⟦3⟧. The template will ride along the rub bearing as the cutter shapes the workpiece. Cut one edge of the template to the desired profile and cut the workpiece slightly over-size. Screw wood blocks to the template to support the workpiece and screw toggle clamps to the blocks to secure the workpiece to the template. Insert the starting pin in its hole. As you begin feeding the template, brace it against the pin. Once the template is in contact with both the pin and the rub bearing, slowly swing it away from the pin while keeping it in contact with the bearing.

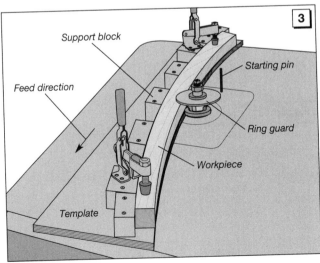

Support block

Feed direction

Starting pin

Ring guard

Workpiece

Template

⟦3⟧

BELT/DISC SANDER

The main advantages of the stationary belt/disc sander are convenience and precise control of otherwise labor-intensive and difficult sanding procedures. The ¾-horsepower model shown below features a 9-inch disc and a 6 x 48-inch belt. The removable table is slotted to accept a miter gauge and will tilt to any angle up to 45 degrees. The belt assembly can be set to the horizontal position, as shown, or to the vertical position.

Belt/disc sanders are available in various sizes. While larger models have more capacity, they require larger and more costly belts and discs. They also occupy more shop space and consume more electricity.

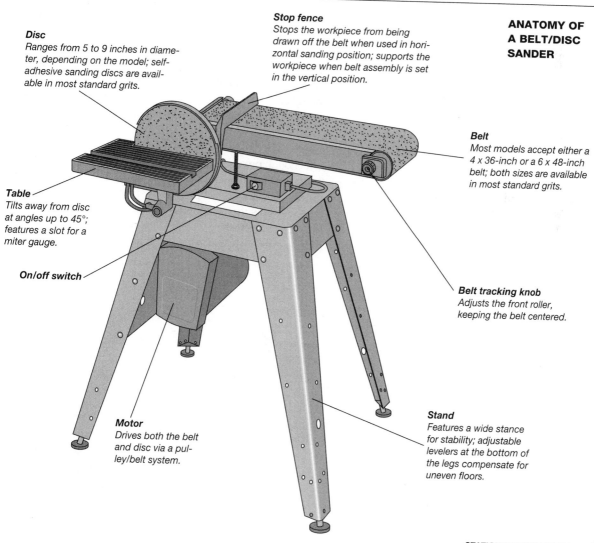

ANATOMY OF A BELT/DISC SANDER

Disc
Ranges from 5 to 9 inches in diameter, depending on the model; self-adhesive sanding discs are available in most standard grits.

Stop fence
Stops the workpiece from being drawn off the belt when used in horizontal sanding position; supports the workpiece when belt assembly is set in the vertical position.

Belt
Most models accept either a 4 x 36-inch or a 6 x 48-inch belt; both sizes are available in most standard grits.

Table
Tilts away from disc at angles up to 45°; features a slot for a miter gauge.

On/off switch

Belt tracking knob
Adjusts the front roller, keeping the belt centered.

Motor
Drives both the belt and disc via a pulley/belt system.

Stand
Features a wide stance for stability; adjustable levelers at the bottom of the legs compensate for uneven floors.

BELT/DISC SANDER

SETTING UP
AND USING
THE SANDER

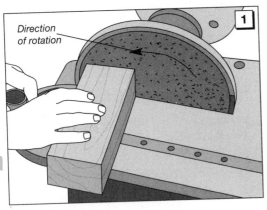

Direction of rotation

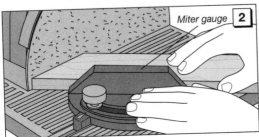

Miter gauge

The controls on belt/disc sanders vary by model, but adjusting the tool is relatively straightforward. Replace a sanding disc by peeling off the old self-adhesive disc and pressing on the new one. To replace the sanding belt, release the tension, remove the old belt, and slide the new one over the back and front rollers. Then tension the belt, turn on the sander, and adjust the tracking knob until the belt remains centered on the rollers.

When operating the sander, it is important to let the machine do the work. Apply just enough pressure to keep the workpiece in contact with the abrasive. Excessive pressure will slow the rotation of the disc or belt and actually reduce cutting action. Move the workpiece from side to side across the abrasive. This will give you a smoother surface and extend the life of the disc or belt.

In general, use the sanding disc to smooth ends, and the sanding belt for edges, faces, or contoured surfaces. When disc-sanding, position the workpiece on the left-hand side of the disc 1. This draws the stock down onto the table and makes it easier to hold it perpendicular to the disc. To sand mitered or beveled surfaces, guide the workpiece into the disc with the miter gauge adjusted to the appropriate angle 2.

To sand a contoured surface 3, such as a cabriole leg, hold the stock freehand against the front roller.

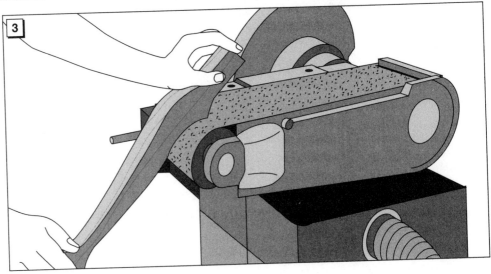

BENCH GRINDER

The grinder's principal purpose in the woodworking shop is as a sharpening tool for chisel and plane blades, bits, and turning and carving tools. While some woodworkers prefer hand sharpening stones and strops for sharpening tools, advocates of the grinder find it a more precise—and rapid—alternative for restoring the bevel on chipped or worn tools.

Most bench grinders mount two wheels: For woodworking, use a medium or fine grinding wheel for squaring and sharpening, and a cloth wheel with compound for pol-ishing. A machine with a ¼- to ½-horsepower motor is adequate. For safety, a grinder should feature eye shields, wheel guards, and adjustable tool rests. The model illustrated below comes with a stand. Bench-top grinders can be bolted to a work surface.

When sharpening with the grinder, good results depend on the type of grinding wheel you use. For most operations, a wheel coded A80H8V will serve you well. The illustration below explains how to decipher grinding wheel codes.

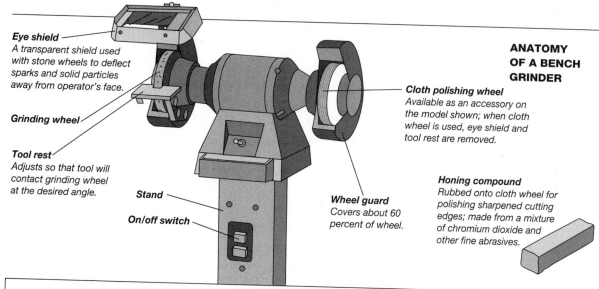

Eye shield
A transparent shield used with stone wheels to deflect sparks and solid particles away from operator's face.

Grinding wheel

Tool rest
Adjusts so that tool will contact grinding wheel at the desired angle.

Stand

On/off switch

ANATOMY OF A BENCH GRINDER

Cloth polishing wheel
Available as an accessory on the model shown; when cloth wheel is used, eye shield and tool rest are removed.

Honing compound
Rubbed onto cloth wheel for polishing sharpened cutting edges; made from a mixture of chromium dioxide and other fine abrasives.

Wheel guard
Covers about 60 percent of wheel.

DECIPHERING THE CODE ON GRINDER WHEELS

7"x 1/2"x 1-1/4"
A80-H8V

Abrasive type
A means that the wheel is made of an aluminum oxide; other aluminum oxides are RA (Ruby), WA (White), and SA (Special). Silicon carbides are divided into C (Regular) and GC (Refined). Combinations are also available.

Grit size
80 is a medium grit. Coarse ranges from 12 to 36, Medium from 46 to 120, Fine from 150 to 280, and Very Fine from 320 to 600.

Hardness
H is a soft stone; ranges are: Soft (E to I), Medium (J to M), Hard (N to R), and Very Hard (S to Z).

Structure
A number that ranges from 23 (open structure) to 5 (the densest structure); standard structure is 8.

Bond type
Denotes how particles that make up the wheel are held together. V stands for vitrification, a process that uses heat fusion.

Courtesy Unicorn Abrasives of Canada Ltd.

BENCH GRINDER

SETTING UP AND USING THE GRINDER

The grinder requires few adjustments. However, grinding wheels eventually get clogged with metal and its edges may become out-of-square. To remedy these problems, dress the wheel. This will true and square it and expose fresh abrasive particles. Two types of wheel dressers are available: Star-wheel and diamond-tipped dressers. A diamond-tipped model is shown in the illustration 1. To use the dresser, hold it in both hands as shown with the tip set on the tool rest. With the tip clear of the wheel, turn on the grinder and slowly move the tip toward the wheel. Once the dresser contacts the wheel, gently slide it back and forth across the wheel.

To restore the correct bevel angle on a plane blade, you

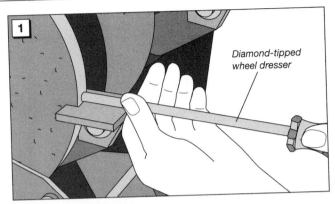

Diamond-tipped wheel dresser

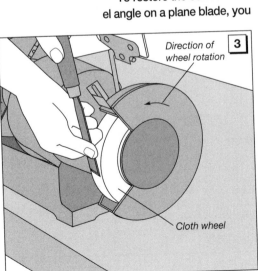

Grinding jig

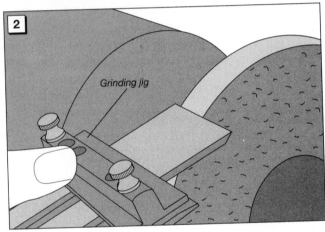

Direction of wheel rotation

Cloth wheel

can use a commercial grinding jig 2. Install the blade bevel down in the jig; the jig will keep the blade tip square to the wheel and present the blade at an angle of 25 to 30 degrees to the wheel. Hold the jig on the tool rest and advance the blade toward the wheel. Pressing lightly, slide the blade side to side across the wheel. If you need to make several passes, lift the tool away from the wheel after one or two passes to allow it to cool.

To polish a chisel or plane blade's bevel after sharpening, use the grinder's cloth wheel. Charge the wheel with honing compound, then holding the tool almost vertically, press the bevel flat against the lower half of the wheel. Move the blade slowly from side to side until the bevel is polished. To remove the burr that forms as a result of sharpening, polish the other side of the blade 3.

OTHER STATIONARY TOOLS

Choosing the best combination of power tools for a shop is a subjective process. Every woodworker has a personal list of indispensable machines. Consider your individual needs before making a purchase. If, for example, you are considering a radial arm saw for its crosscutting capability, a power miter saw, like the one shown below, may satisfy your needs—for much less money. Similarly, if you do not have the budget or the space for a full complement of stationary tools, a combination machine *(page 178)* may solve your problem.

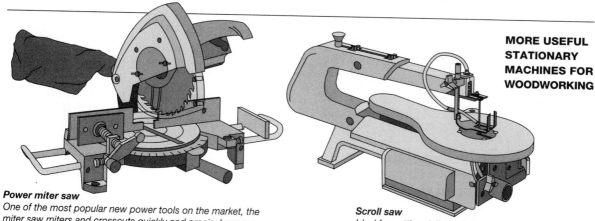

MORE USEFUL STATIONARY MACHINES FOR WOODWORKING

Power miter saw
One of the most popular new power tools on the market, the miter saw miters and crosscuts quickly and precisely; some models can cut compound miters. Most models can be adjusted to cut right and left miters up to 45°. The workpiece is held against the table and back fence, and the cut is made by lowering the motor/blade assembly down toward the table.

Scroll saw
Ideal for cutting delicate fretwork patterns; negotiates the tight curves often encountered in making wooden toys and knick-knacks. The blade can be detached and fed through a starter hole for making inside cuts; the blade's up-and-down cycle is similar to the saber saw's, except that the scroll saw cuts on the down stroke. The large throat capacity is an important feature since wide clearance is often needed when rotating a workpiece on the table.

Lathe
Although not required for all woodworking projects, the lathe has unique capabilities that no other power tool can provide. Turning is a craft in itself; the lathe is indispensable to woodworkers who make spindle-type furniture parts, decorative turnings, and bowls.

OTHER STATIONARY TOOLS

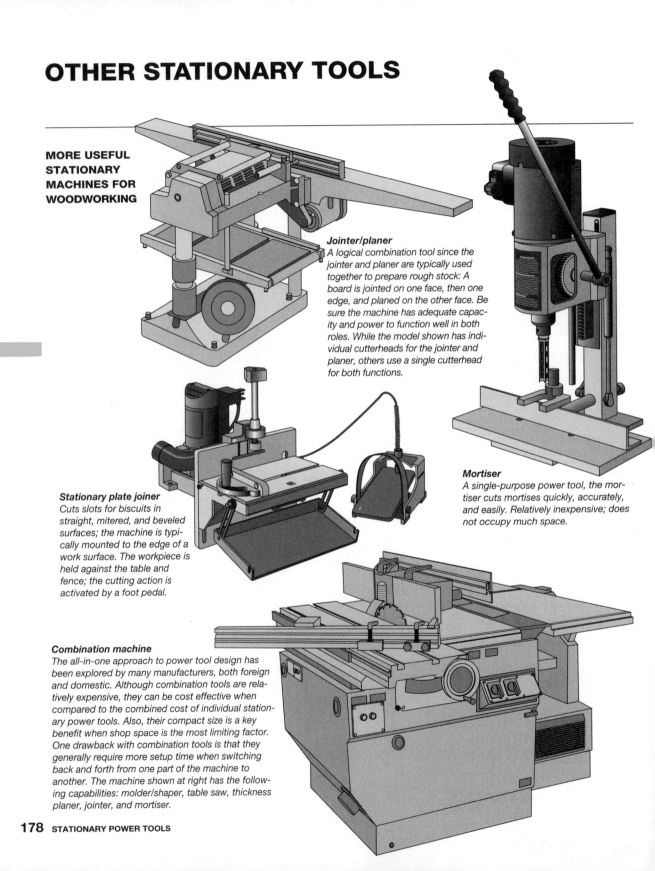

**MORE USEFUL
STATIONARY
MACHINES FOR
WOODWORKING**

Jointer/planer
*A logical combination tool since the
jointer and planer are typically used
together to prepare rough stock: A
board is jointed on one face, then one
edge, and planed on the other face. Be
sure the machine has adequate capacity and power to function well in both
roles. While the model shown has individual cutterheads for the jointer and
planer, others use a single cutterhead
for both functions.*

Stationary plate joiner
*Cuts slots for biscuits in
straight, mitered, and beveled
surfaces; the machine is typically mounted to the edge of a
work surface. The workpiece is
held against the table and
fence; the cutting action is
activated by a foot pedal.*

Mortiser
*A single-purpose power tool, the mor-
tiser cuts mortises quickly, accurately,
and easily. Relatively inexpensive; does
not occupy much space.*

Combination machine
*The all-in-one approach to power tool design has
been explored by many manufacturers, both foreign
and domestic. Although combination tools are relatively expensive, they can be cost effective when
compared to the combined cost of individual stationary power tools. Also, their compact size is a key
benefit when shop space is the most limiting factor.
One drawback with combination tools is that they
generally require more setup time when switching
back and forth from one part of the machine to
another. The machine shown at right has the following capabilities: molder/shaper, table saw, thickness
planer, jointer, and mortiser.*

LUMBER AND VENEER

Understanding wood is perhaps the greatest of woodworking's many unique challenges. Because wood is an organic material, virtually no two pieces of it are identical. Add to that the fact that at least 100,000 plant species produce wood, and you have some idea of the tremendous diversity of the material: From jet black ebony to stark white holly, from feather-light balsa to lignum vitae, a wood so heavy that a cubic foot of it may weigh more than 70 pounds.

A color photo gallery of more than 60 popular cabinet woods starts on page 208. The chapter also explains how living plants produce woody tissue; how softwoods differ from hardwoods; and how both are processed into lumber, veneer, and a broad array of other building materials.

Wood is perhaps the most subtly complex of all craft materials. Selecting the best species

and grade for a project depends on a host of factors, not least of which is the fact that wood is hygroscopic: As explained on page 206, it swells or shrinks as the humidity level in its environment changes. Pages 242 and 243 describe how the shape of a piece of wood changes when its moisture content changes, and how the change in shape depends on both the species of the wood and what part of the log the piece of wood came from.

Not all the rewards of woodworking are to be found in a successfully completed project. The pleasant scent of many woods makes them a pleasure to work with, but the complex chemistry of others, which contributes to both color and scent, has its darker side. As discussed on page 185, many woods are potentially toxic, and woodworkers must take commonsense precautions to protect themselves against them.

THE NATURE OF WOOD

To understand why each of the more than 100,000 wood species in the world has its own unique qualities and working properties, you have to look at what goes on at the microscopic level. For it is here that the character of a wood is determined. Although wood is an organic material, only a very small fraction of the billions of cells in a "living" tree are actually alive. As shown in the illustration below, living tissue forms the cambium layer. As the cells of this layer divide, phloem is produced on the outer side, while xylem, or sapwood, is laid down along the cambium's inner surface.

In temperate climates, the arrival of spring causes an explosion of growth, producing a band of large, thin-walled wood cells called earlywood. As the season progresses, however, the cambium begins to produce what is called latewood. The rate of growth slows and the wood cells formed at this time are smaller in diameter and develop thicker walls. For most species, the arrival of winter brings about a period of dormancy marked by the annual rings, which are clearly visible on the end grain. With each succeeding season, the cambium lays down a new layer of woody tissue, expanding the diameter of the tree and causing older layers of bark to crack and break away. As growth continues, contact between the cambium and the interior of the trunk is maintained through rays that extend out horizontally from the pith like the spokes of a wheel.

For the first few years after its formation, the sapwood helps to conduct water and nutrients from the roots to the leaves. Eventually, though, the innermost bands of sapwood become imbedded by succeeding layers and no longer participate in the growth process. The tree then begins to use this dormant, heartwood tissue for storage, transferring extractives inward along the rays and depositing them in the cell cavities. These extractives help the tree ward off decay organisms. They eventually polymerize and form pigments, giving the heartwood of various species such as walnut and cherry their attractive rich color.

Virtually all commercially important timbers fall into one of two categories: softwoods or hardwoods. These terms can be misleading: Some softwoods are physically heavier and harder than some hardwoods. Douglas-fir,

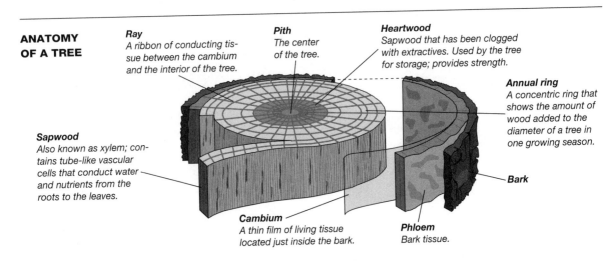

ANATOMY OF A TREE

Ray
A ribbon of conducting tissue between the cambium and the interior of the tree.

Pith
The center of the tree.

Heartwood
Sapwood that has been clogged with extractives. Used by the tree for storage; provides strength.

Annual ring
A concentric ring that shows the amount of wood added to the diameter of a tree in one growing season.

Sapwood
Also known as xylem; contains tube-like vascular cells that conduct water and nutrients from the roots to the leaves.

Cambium
A thin film of living tissue located just inside the bark.

Phloem
Bark tissue.

Bark

for example, the world's most plentiful species of softwood, is actually almost four times as dense as balsa, the world's softest and lightest commercially important hardwood. The term softwood is used to designate woods produced by gymnosperm species, primarily needle-bearing conifers such as pine, spruce, and fir. The hardwoods, or angiosperms, are represented by the broad-leafed flowering trees.

The anatomical structure of softwoods is less complex than that of hardwoods. Under magnification, as shown below, the end grain of a softwood reveals annual rings intersected by rays. The vertical, vascular tissue consists of tube-like cells called tracheids; the earlywood and latewood can be differentiated by the thickness of the cell walls. In some softwood species, such as pine, spruce, and Douglas-fir, resin canals appear in the form of large, round gaps between the tracheids. At first glance, these resin canals look like the vessel pores in hardwoods, but they are far less plentiful, randomly located, and are not surrounded by a cell wall of their own.

The magnified end grain of hardwoods reveals a more complex anatomy. The annual rings, rays, and tracheids are far more varied in structure. The rays are often wider or of varying widths, and the tracheids, called fiber cells in hardwoods, have much heavier walls. While the softwoods rely exclusively on tracheid cells to carry fluids, the hardwoods contain much larger tube-like vessels to perform this function. The locations of the vessels form unique patterns in various hardwood species and help in wood identification.

These differences may sound inconsequential, but it is precisely because of these variations that hardwoods and softwoods are different. For example, hardwoods are generally stronger than softwoods because their tracheid walls are heavier. Also, the anatomical complexity of hardwoods accounts for their typically more interesting figure. Or, the large pores or vessels in some hardwoods, like oak, explain why a filler is required to create a smooth surface for finishing.

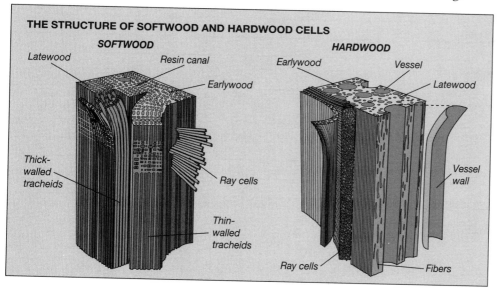

THE STRUCTURE OF SOFTWOOD AND HARDWOOD CELLS

SOFTWOOD

Latewood
Resin canal
Earlywood
Thick-walled tracheids
Ray cells
Thin-walled tracheids

HARDWOOD

Earlywood
Vessel
Latewood
Vessel wall
Ray cells
Fibers

PROPERTIES OF WOOD

PHYSICAL PROPERTIES OF COMMON DOMESTIC WOODS

TYPE	DENSITY soft (1) to hard (5)	TEXTURE fine (1) to coarse (5)	BENDABILITY flexible (F), brittle (B), stiff (S)	COMPRESSION STRENGTH weak (1) to strong (5)	SHOCK RESISTANCE low (1) to high (5)	DECAY RESISTANCE low (1) to high (5)	AVAILABILITY lumber (L) veneer (V)	COST low (1) to high (5)
Ash, white	3	4	F	3	5	1	L, V	2
Aspen	2	2	F	2	2	1	L, V	1
Basswood	1	1	F	1	1	1	L	2
Beech, American	3	3	S	3	3	3	L	2
Birch, yellow	4	1	S	4	5	2	L, V	2
Butternut	2	3	B	3	2	2	L, V	3
Cedar, aromatic	3	1	B	3	3	5	L, V	3
Cedar, Western red	1	2	B	1	1	5	L	3
Cherry, American	3	1	S	3	3	4	L, V	3
Douglas-fir	3	3	S	3	3	3	L, V	2
Elm, American	3	3	F	3	3	1	L	1
Hickory	5	3	F	5	5	2	L	2
Maple, hard	5	1	S	5	5	1	L, V	2
Oak, red	4	5	S	4	3	2	L, V	3
Oak, white	5	5	F	5	4	5	L, V	2
Pecan	4	3	F	5	5	2	L	4
Pine, Eastern white	2	2	S	2	2	3	L,V	2
Pine, Southern yellow	3	2	S	3	4	3	L	1
Poplar, yellow	2	1	S	2	3	2	L, V	1
Redwood	1	3	B	1	1	5	L	3
Spruce, sitka	2	2	F	2	2	2	L	3
Sycamore	4	3	S	4	4	2	L, V	2
Walnut, black	3	3	F	3	5	4	L, V	4

WORKING PROPERTIES OF COMMON DOMESTIC WOODS

TYPE	PLANING	SANDING	DRILLING	TURNING	GLUING	FASTENING*
Ash, white	Average	Good	Good	Average	Average	Average
Aspen	Good	Fair	Fair	Fair	Average	Average
Basswood	Good	Excellent	Excellent	Fair	Excellent	Good
Beech, American	Excellent	Good	Excellent	Average	Excellent	Good
Birch, yellow	Good	Poor	Good	Excellent	Good	Good
Butternut	Excellent	Poor	Good	Average	Good	Good
Cedar, aromatic	Fair	Average	Average	Good	Fair	Poor
Cedar, Western red	Fair	Fair	Fair	Average	Good	Fair
Cherry, American	Excellent	Good	Good	Good	Good	Good
Douglas-fir	Average	Average	Average	Average	Good	Average
Elm, American	Poor	Fair	Fair	Average	Good	Good
Hickory	Average	Good	Good	Good	Good	Average
Maple, hard	Good	Excellent	Good	Excellent	Good	Good
Oak, red	Average	Good	Fair	Average	Average	Average
Oak, white	Average	Good	Fair	Good	Average	Average
Pecan	Average	Good	Good	Good	Average	Average
Pine, Eastern white	Good	Good	Good	Good	Good	Good
Pine, Southern yellow	Average	Average	Average	Fair	Average	Fair
Poplar, yellow	Good	Good	Good	Good	Good	Excellent
Redwood	Excellent	Good	Good	Good	Excellent	Fair
Spruce, sitka	Good	Average	Average	Average	Good	Average
Sycamore	Average	Good	Fair	Average	Average	Good
Walnut, black	Good	Good	Good	Good	Average	Good

*Includes holding power and splitting resistance

PROPERTIES OF WOOD

FINISHING PROPERTIES OF COMMON DOMESTIC WOODS

TYPE	GRAIN Open (O) Closed (C)	FILLER (needed to flatten surface)	STAIN	RECOMMENDED FINISHES		
				Topcoat	Penetrating oil	Paint
Alder, red	C	No	Optional	Yes	Yes	Yes
Ash, white	O	Yes	Optional	Yes	Yes	No
Aspen	C	No	Optional	Yes	Yes	Yes
Basswood	C	No	No	Yes	Yes	Yes
Beech, American	C	No	Optional	Yes	Yes	No
Birch, yellow	C	No	Optional	Yes	Yes	No
Butternut	O	Yes	Optional	Yes	Yes	No
Cedar, aromatic	C	No	No	No	No	Yes
Cedar, Western red	C	No	Optional	Yes	Yes	Yes
Cherry, American	C	No	Optional	Yes	Yes	No
Douglas-fir	C	No	No	Yes	Yes	No
Elm, American	O	Yes	Optional	Yes	Yes	No
Hickory	O	Yes	Optional	Yes	Yes	No
Maple, hard	C	No	Optional	Yes	Yes	No
Oak, red and white	O	Yes	Optional	Yes	Yes	No
Pecan	O	Yes	Optional	Yes	Yes	No
Pine, Eastern white	C	No	Optional	Yes	Yes	Yes
Pine, Southern yellow	C	No	No	Yes	Yes	No
Poplar, yellow	C	No	Optional	Yes	Yes	Yes
Spruce, sitka	C	No	Optional	Yes	Yes	No
Sycamore	C	No	Optional	Yes	Yes	No
Walnut, black	O	Yes	No	Yes	Yes	No

Most woods, domestic and foreign, are known to be toxic to some degree. The effect usually results from prolonged or heavy exposure to fine particles of dust or volatiles given off by the wood. Eventually these allergens cause some individuals to develop a sensitivity to a particular species or even related species they have not previously worked with, but which have a similar chemical makeup. Domestic woods like redwood, oak, and Western red cedar can cause respiratory problems, while other native species, including Douglas-fir and sitka spruce, have been known to affect the skin. Woods like beech and walnut, and imports such as lauan, lacewood (silky-oak), African mahogany, and rosewood, result in both types of problem with some woodworkers. Respiratory problems can range from rhinitis and coughing to bronchial asthma and bronchitis. Skin disorders can include itching, dermatitis, and skin blistering.

One way to minimize the risks of working with toxic woods is to protect yourself from inhaling or contacting all wood dust. Install a dust collection system in your shop (page 50). A couple of other tips: Wear a respirator or a National Institute of Occupational Safety and Health–approved "toxic dust" mask when cutting or machining stock; also ensure there is good ventilation in your shop. And, since dust clings to the perspiration on bare skin, try to work in cool temperatures. But the soundest approach is: If a particular species causes a noticeable allergic reaction, don't use it.

Working with pressure-treated lumber

Among the most toxic of wood products is pressure-treated lumber. Of the three major types of treating agents used, creosote, pentachlorophenol (penta), and inorganic arsenical, the first two should not be used indoors at all. If you are working with pressure-treated wood, saw and machine your stock out-of-doors. Wear safety glasses and a dust mask or approved respirator, long sleeves and pants, and vinyl-coated gloves that are impervious to chemicals. Wash yourself thoroughly as soon as you finish work. Furniture made with pressure-treated lumber should be coated with a urethane, epoxy, or shellac sealer before it is used. Do not use pressure-treated wood in countertops or cutting boards.

MILLING WOOD

CONVERTING LOGS INTO LUMBER

Converting logs to lumber might seem to be a simple task of pushing the logs through a saw. In reality, the sawyer's job requires considerable skill and the ability to make quick and often very subjective decisions. How a log is cut will determine both the quantity and quality of the lumber it yields.

There are three basic methods of sawing logs; each has advantages and disadvantages. The simplest method is the through-and-through cut; here the log is sawn repeatedly without changing its orientation to the blade. As shown in the illustration at right, this method produces relatively wide boards, but very little select-grade lumber. This is because knots and defects are more plentiful near the center of a log and most of the boards resulting from through-and-through cutting include a portion of the interior heartwood. (See page 192 for more information on lumber grading.)

To maximize the number of select-grade boards, the plain-sawn method is generally preferred. In this method, the log is rotated 90° after each pass through the saw. The resulting lumber is not as wide as with through-and-through cutting, but the outside boards will contain the least possible number of

knots. As shown in the drawing on page 187, the growth rings will be approximately parallel to the board faces.

The third method of cutting, called quarter-sawing, is time-consuming and somewhat wasteful, but it yields lumber

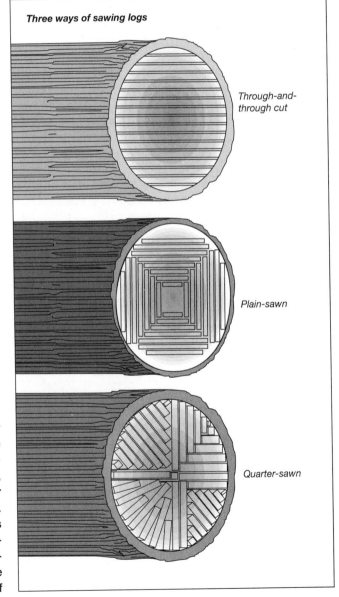

Three ways of sawing logs

Through-and-through cut

Plain-sawn

Quarter-sawn

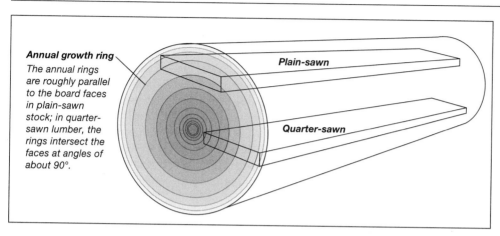

Annual growth ring
The annual rings are roughly parallel to the board faces in plain-sawn stock; in quarter-sawn lumber, the rings intersect the faces at angles of about 90°.

Plain-sawn

Quarter-sawn

that is structurally sound and far more stable than the two other techniques. Using one of several techniques, the log is first quartered and then ripped so that the maximum number of boards will have radially oriented grain. In other words, the annual rings on most of the stock run perpendicular to the face of the board. In some species, such as oak, sycamore, and lacewood,

quarter-sawing exposes the rays in cross section and enhances the wood's figure. Quarter-sawn lumber has other advantages: It resists cupping and warping, and experiences less movement due to changes in moisture. This is because wood shrinks more than twice as much along the annual rings as it does across them. Loss of moisture in a quarter-sawn board may cause its

thickness to contract slightly more than in plain-sawn boards, but the more noticeable shrinkage in the width of the board will be only one-half as much. For example, a plain-sawn piece of green sugar maple 10 inches wide may lose as much as ¾ inch in width as it dries, while a similar-sized quarter-sawn board of the same species will shrink less than ½ inch in width.

PLAIN-SAWN

- Figure patterns resulting from the annual rings and some other types of figure are brought out more conspicuously.
- Round or oval knots affect the surface appearance and strength less than spike-shaped knots found in some quarter-sawn boards.
- Shakes and pitch pockets extend through fewer boards.
- Shrinks and swells less in thickness.
- Costs less because it is easier to manufacture.

QUARTER-SAWN

- Lumber shrinks and swells less in width.
- Wood twists and cups less; checks and splits less common in seasoning and in use.
- Wears more evenly.
- Types of figure due to pronounced rays, interlocked grain, and wavy grain are brought out more conspicuously.
- Holds paint better in some species.

ADVANTAGES OF PLAIN-SAWN AND QUARTER-SAWN LUMBER
Courtesy Wood Handbook: Forest Products Laboratory, United States Department of Agriculture

BUYING WOOD

SELECTING
AND ORDER-
ING LUMBER

With the rising cost of lumber, decisions regarding what to order and how to go about it should be made with care. The best way to start is with a carefully drafted cutting list *(page 191)*. The list will provide the quantities and sizes of the pieces required for the project. These can then be converted into equivalent board feet *(page 189)*. In most cabinetmaking projects, desired widths are less critical than necessary lengths because edge-gluing several boards together is a practical way to establish the final width of many elements. If the project consists of mostly short lengths, the less expensive lower grades normally prove to be most economical; in many species, lower-grade boards also provide the most attractively figured material.

When using these grades, allow an extra 20 to 40 percent for waste.

Once these decisions are made, a written order can be prepared. Since the order must be interpreted by your lumber dealer, it should be drafted in the terminology of the trade and absolutely precise as to what is needed. The order should specify the quantity, sizes, grades, and kinds of wood, plus any unique processing or milling requirements. (Grades are explained in more detail starting on page 192.) If buying a softwood from a retail dealer who only stocks surfaced lumber, you can normally omit milling instructions. For example, if you were buying a supply of 60 board feet of Select-grade pine, the order might read: 12 pcs. 1 x 6 - 10' sel. pine. Orders for cabinet

hardwoods generally require more detailed specifications. For example, to make your instructions clear, a comparable 60-board-foot order of white oak might read: 12 pcs. 1 x 6 - 10' FAS, KD white oak surfaced S2S - 3/4 net. This would tell the dealer that you want 12 pieces of 1 x 6 white oak, each 10 feet long. FAS refers to Firsts-and-Seconds grade; KD means that the wood should be kiln-dried. The remaining part of the order specifies that the wood should be surfaced on both sides to a final thickness of ¾ inch.

While softwoods are normally kiln-dried and surfaced at the mill, it is not uncommon to find hardwoods sold in random widths, either air-dried or kiln-dried and either surfaced or left rough. Many cabinetmakers prefer to buy hardwoods unsurfaced and

---

Lumber buying tips

- *Determine whether plain-sawn or quarter-sawn lumber (page 186) is more appropriate for your project: Remember that they have different shrinkage ratios.*
- *Hardwoods are usually sold in random sizes, and all species may not be available in wide boards: Order accordingly.*
- *Keep a copy of your cutting list (page 191), after giving the original to the lumber dealer.*

- *Inspect boards before buying them, if possible, rejecting any with unworkable defects. (See page 196 for a chart on wood defects.)*
- *Make sure that your lumber is stacked properly (page 241) to prevent warping.*
- *When chosing lumber, keep in mind where each piece will end up. If you are buying surfaced lumber to be made into an edge-glued panel, check that the pieces to be joined have an attractive look when placed side by side.*

then plane the stock to precise thicknesses as it is used. If you want the dealer to surface your wood, you must say so in the order and specify the net thickness required.

For fine cabinet work, where the character and figure of the wood is of vital importance, there is no substitute for visiting the lumberyard and personally picking out the stock board by board. Cultivating a friendly working relationship with your lumber dealer is an important aspect of woodworking. Since wood is an organic material, not every board will be perfect, but then not every piece in a project demands perfection. Over the long run, knowing when to ask your dealer for special consideration and when to take a serviceable but less marketable board out of the pile, can generate goodwill that will pay dividends.

The term "board foot" defines a volume of lumber equal to 144 cubic inches. It is usually described as a piece of wood 1 inch thick by 12 inches wide and 12 inches long. To calculate the board footage in a piece of wood, simply multiply its thickness by its width and then its length—each in inches—and then divide the total by 144. For example, to determine the number of board feet in a 6-foot-long 2 x 4, the calculation would be as follows: 2 x 4 x 72, divided by 144 = 4 board feet. If the length of the board can be expressed in feet (with no inches left over), you can simplify the formula by leaving the length in feet and then dividing by 12 instead of 144. In the above example (a 6-foot-long 2 x 4), the calculation would be 2 x 4 x 6, divided by 12 = 4 board feet. The illustration at right shows other examples. (Also see the chart on page 190.) The one remaining point to keep in mind is that board footage is always calculated using the lumber's *nominal* rather than actual dimension. (See pages 193 and 195 for rough/surfaced and nominal/actual-size charts.) So a softwood 2 x 4, for example, is calculated as though it were actually 2 inches by 4 inches, rather than its real size of 1½ inches by 3½ inches.

CALCULATING BOARD FEET

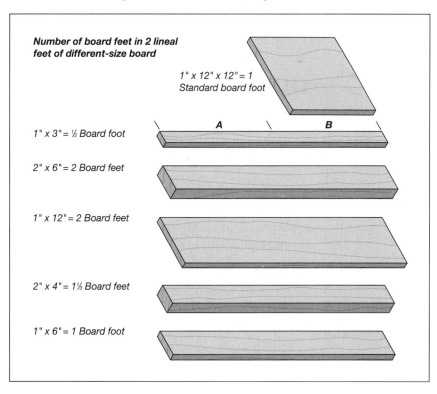

Number of board feet in 2 lineal feet of different-size board

1" x 12" x 12" = 1 Standard board foot

A   B

1" x 3" = ½ Board foot

2" x 6" = 2 Board feet

1" x 12" = 2 Board feet

2" x 4" = 1½ Board feet

1" x 6" = 1 Board foot

BUYING WOOD

BOARD FOOT EQUIVALENTS

The chart at right provides a convenient reference for converting commonly available lengths of standard-size lumber to their board-foot equivalents. With a little experience, translating lineal feet into board feet is not difficult. Given that 1 lineal foot of 1 x 12 equals 1 board foot, a 1 x 6 must be twice as long to contain the same volume of wood, while a 1 x 3 must be four times as long. Similarly, a 2 x 6 contains twice the volume of a 1 x 6 of equal length, and therefore 1 lineal foot of 2 x 6 represents 1 board foot. Board footage is always figured using the lumber's "nominal" dimensions.

DIMENSIONS IN INCHES	LENGTH IN FEET				
	6'	8'	10'	12'	14'
1 x 2	1	1 1/3	1 2/3	2	2 1/3
1 x 3	1 1/2	2	2 1/2	3	3 1/2
1 x 4	2	2 2/3	3 1/3	4	4 2/3
1 x 6	3	4	5	6	7
1 x 8	4	5 1/3	6 2/3	8	9 1/3
1 x 10	5	6 2/3	8 1/2	10	11 2/3
1 x 12	6	8	10	12	14
2 x 2	2	2 2/3	3 1/3	4	4 2/3
2 x 4	4	5 1/3	6 2/3	8	9 1/3
2 x 6	6	8	10	12	14
2 x 8	8	10 2/3	13 1/3	16	18 2/3
2 x 10	10	13 1/2	16 2/3	20	23 1/3
2 x 12	12	16	20	24	28

QUICKTIP

Examining lumber for warp

Twisted boards can sometimes prove difficult to spot. A couple of shop-made winding sticks will help you solve the problem. Cut two narrow sticks to a length about twice the width of the board to be examined. Place the board on sawhorses or a flat work surface. Then place the winding sticks across the ends of the board, perpendicular to the edges. Sight across the tops of the winding sticks to check for twist. If the tops of the sticks are not aligned, the board is warped.

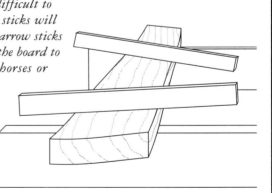

A cutting list (or materials list) is a written summary of what is needed to complete a given project. This list should include the quantity of each part, a brief notation of its function in the project (such as shelves or top/bottom), and its size. It should also identify hardware, fasteners, finishes, and other shop supplies the project will require. For cabinetmakers building products to be sold, a well-constructed cutting list is invaluable in helping to arrive at a price for the finished piece. But even for the amateur woodworker, a complete list means fewer unscheduled trips to the lumberyard and hardware store.

The illustration at right shows how a sketch of a piece of furniture—here, a small bookcase—can be used to develop a cutting list. Once you know the size of the parts and how many of each part you need, list the sizes of standard lumber that will be required to produce each of them. Then convert these amounts into board feet using nominal measures. This last column of the cutting list should contain the information required to draft the lumber order. It is wise to purchase more than the project's minimum requirements to allow for flexibility in grain selection and to cover the occasional mistake. This is especially important if you are working with hardwoods, such as walnut and cherry, that can vary in color from shipment to shipment.

DRAFTING A CUTTING LIST

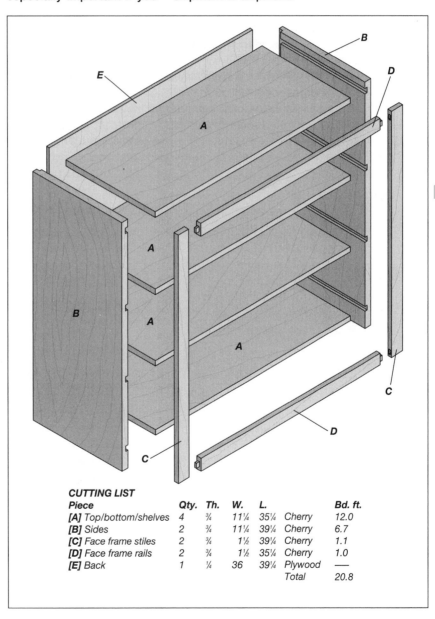

CUTTING LIST

Piece	Qty.	Th.	W.	L.		Bd. ft.
[A] Top/bottom/shelves	4	¾	11¼	35¼	Cherry	12.0
[B] Sides	2	¾	11¼	39¼	Cherry	6.7
[C] Face frame stiles	2	¾	1½	39¼	Cherry	1.1
[D] Face frame rails	2	¾	1½	35¼	Cherry	1.0
[E] Back	1	¼	36	39¼	Plywood	—
					Total	20.8

LUMBER GRADES

Like the sawyer, the lumber grader needs a good eye and the ability to make fast, accurate judgments. Armed with no more than experience and a specialized measuring stick with a hooked end called a lumber rule, the grader sorts through boards at the rate of three or four a minute, segregating them into as many as six or seven separate grades. The task is made more difficult

Based on rules set by the National Hardwood Lumber Association (NHLA), each grade requires that a given percentage of a board be usable if cut into pieces of a certain minimum width and length. The higher the grade, the higher the usable percentage must be and the larger the size of the cuttings, as shown in the chart on the following page. Although there are technically eight distinct

divisions are seldom seen at the retail level. Generally, the spread in prices between the various grades makes it highly advantageous to buy the lowest grade that will yield large enough cuttings for a given project. It is not unusual for the highest grades of lumber to be as much as three times as expensive as the lowest.

With projects that require only a few large pieces and a multitude of smaller ones, experienced woodworkers buy the absolute minimum necessary in the higher grade and rely on lower grades for the smaller parts. If only one side of a board will show in the finished project, Select grade lumber is as serviceable as FAS. Also, since lumber is graded at its full, "rough" thickness, a project that requires thinner stock, say ⅝ inch net, can also use Select grade stock. The superficial, one-sided defects in the Select grade can often be planed off, yielding lumber equal in quality to the FAS grade. The lower grades also have their benefits. As they contain more knots and the grain around knots is more contoured, they generally yield more attractively figured wood. Also, in some species, lower grade lumber often has a darker, richer color, because it is cut near the center of the log.

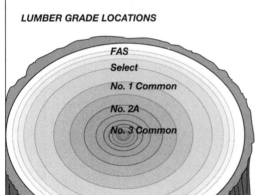

LUMBER GRADE LOCATIONS

FAS

Select

No. 1 Common

No. 2A

No. 3 Common

The closer a board comes from the center of a tree, the poorer the quality of lumber. Central heartwood is prone to splitting and is used mostly in the manufacture of crates and pallets.

No. 2A and No. 3 Common stock comes mostly from logs 12 inches in diameter or smaller; FAS and Select lumber is generally harvested from bigger trees.

when grading hardwoods because a board's grade is not based on its overall quality, but rather on the size and quantity of clear cuttings it will yield. Because most hardwood is used for making cabinets and furniture, the boards are usually machined into smaller pieces and the grading standards reflect this reality. Each cutting must be clear on one face and at least structurally sound on the other.

grades of hardwood, they are normally marketed in groups. For example, the top two grades are usually combined and sold as Firsts and Seconds (FAS) or they may be combined with the next lower grade, Select, and marketed as "Select & Better." At the other end of the spectrum, the Number 3 Common grade can be divided into two quality levels: No. 3A and No. 3B, but these highly specialized sub-

GRADE	MINIMUM LENGTH (feet)	MINIMUM WIDTH (inches)	% OF CLEAR WOOD IN BOARD	MINIMUM SIZE OF CLEAR CUTTINGS	NUMBER OF CLEAR CUTTINGS
FAS (First and Seconds)	8 (6 for walnut)	6 (5 for walnut)	83 1/3	3" x 7' or 4" x 5'	1–4
SELECT or FAS one face	6	4	83 1/3	3" x 7' or 4" x 5'	1–4
NO. 1 COMMON	4	3	66 2/3–83 1/3	4" x 2' or 3" x 3'	1–5
NO. 2 A (Utility)	4	3	50–66 2/3	3" x 2'	1-7
NO. 3 COMMON	4	3	25–33 1/3	3" x 2'	NO LIMIT

Chart courtesy National Hardwood Lumber Association

As shown in the chart above, hardwood lumber grades emphasize the size of clear cuttings that each board will yield, rather than its strength or the number and size of defects it incorporates. For example, to qualify as top-grade (FAS) lumber, no board may be shorter than 8 feet long or narrower than 6 inches. At least 83 1/3 percent of the board must be usable as clear cuttings and no cutting can be smaller than 3 inches by 7 feet or 4 inches by 5 feet long. Only four of the cuttings may be counted in calculating the 83 1/3 percent yield requirement. Lower grades allow boards as short as 4 feet and more cuttings of progressively smaller size. Some species, such as walnut, are in such high demand that grading practices are relaxed somewhat and shorter lengths are permissible in the highest grade.

Most hardwoods are surfaced on only two sides (S2S); the standard net thicknesses do not always correspond to their softwood equivalents (page 195). For example, a 1-inch-thick hardwood board is referred to as 4/4 stock and is surfaced S2S to a net thickness of 13/16 inch. See the chart below for other standard hardwood thicknesses.

STANDARD THICKNESSES FOR ROUGH AND SURFACED (S2S) HARDWOOD LUMBER IN INCHES

ROUGH	SURFACED	ROUGH	SURFACED
3/8	3/16	1 1/2	1 5/16
1/2	5/16	2	1 3/4
5/8	7/16	3	2 3/4
3/4	9/16	4	3 3/4
1	13/16	5	4 3/4
1 1/4	1 1/16	6	5 3/4

Chart courtesy National Hardwood Lumber Association

LUMBER GRADES

Since most softwood lumber is used in the construction industry, softwood grading rules are substantially different from those used for grading hardwoods. The rules governing softwood species generally used for framing, such as Douglas-fir, emphasize the wood's structural properties. The rules for species such as Eastern white pine, which are commonly used for trim, place more emphasis on the wood's appearance. In both cases, however, the board's overall quality is taken into consideration. Unlike hardwoods, the grades for softwoods are based on the number, location, and size of defects rather than the board's potential for clear cuttings. This is because most softwood boards are used as-is and are seldom machined other than being trimmed to length.

The most commonly used softwoods in woodworking are the softer white pines, including Eastern white pine, Western white (Idaho) pine, and sugar pine. Since the entire board is considered in establishing its grade, a board must be nearly perfect to qualify as select. As a result, the price of select grades of pine are as high or even higher than many species of top-grade hardwoods. The corresponding advantage for cabinetmakers in this "whole-board" grading approach is that the lower grades of pine are very economical and often yield a high proportion of clear cuttings. The chart below lists appearance grades for softwood lumber.

The white pines make excellent cabinet wood, but they require some special care. In processing pine for the construction trade, the mills generally only kiln dry it to between 12 and 15 percent moisture content (MC). This level is low enough to prevent decay, but the boards may still contain considerable drying stress. For cabinetmaking purposes, it is better to have the wood kiln dried to a moisture content of 7 to 8 percent.

SOFTWOOD LUMBER APPEARANCE GRADES

GRADES	CHARACTERISTICS	FLAWS	AVAILABILITY	COST
SELECT B AND BTR (Supreme)	Highest quality and clear appearance	Minor blemishes and defects	Limited	Expensive
C SELECT (Choice)	High quality	Small blemishes and defects	Scarce	Expensive
D SELECT (Quality)	Good quality	Blemishes and defects more pronounced	Common	Moderate
SUPERIOR FINISH	Highest quality of finish-grade lumber	Minor blemishes and defects	Rare	Expensive
PRIME FINISH	High quality	A few blemishes and defects	Rare	Expensive
NO. 1 COMMON (Colonial)	Lower quality; knotty appearance	May have small, tight knots	Limited quantity and size ranges	Moderate
NO. 2 COMMON (Sterling)	Lower quality; knotty appearance	Larger, coarser blemishes and defects	Common	Moderate

NOMINAL (in inches)	ACTUAL (in inches; surfaced dry)	NOMINAL (in inches)	ACTUAL (in inches; surfaced dry)	
1 x 2	3/4 x 1 1/2	2 x 4	1 1/2 x 3 1/2	**NOMINAL AND ACTUAL SOFTWOOD LUMBER SIZES**
1 x 3	3/4 x 2 1/2	2 x 6	1 1/2 x 5 1/2	
1 x 4	3/4 x 3 1/2	2 x 8	1 1/2 x 7 1/4	
1 x 6	3/4 x 5 1/2	2 x 10	1 1/2 x 9 1/4	
1 x 8	3/4 x 7 1/4	2 x 12	1 1/2 x 11 1/4	
1 x 10	3/4 x 9 1/4	4 x 4	3 1/2 x 3 1/2	
1 x 12	3/4 x 11 1/4	4 x 6	3 1/2 x 5 1/2	
2 x 2	1 1/2 x 1 1/2	6 x 6	5 1/2 x 5 1/2	

DECODING A GRADE STAMP

Most cabinet-grade hardwoods and softwoods are not stamped, since the indelible inks used with grading stamps would mar the appearance of the wood. However, most construction-grade lumber is stamped; it is a helpful skill to be able to interpret the information it contains. The American Lumber Standards Committee provides guidelines for softwood grading rules, but the rules are administered by trade associations. These regional associations each have their own stamps, but in general they include the logo of the association whose rules were used to grade the lumber, the identification number of the mill that processed the board, the board's grade, the species or group of species, and the wood's moisture content at the time it was surfaced. The illustration below shows a typical stamp for Eastern white pine.

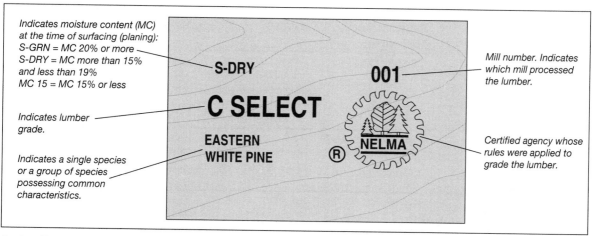

Indicates moisture content (MC) at the time of surfacing (planing):
S-GRN = MC 20% or more
S-DRY = MC more than 15% and less than 19%
MC 15 = MC 15% or less

Indicates lumber grade.

Indicates a single species or a group of species possessing common characteristics.

Mill number. Indicates which mill processed the lumber.

Certified agency whose rules were applied to grade the lumber.

S-DRY
C SELECT
EASTERN WHITE PINE
001
NELMA

Courtesy Northeastern Lumber Manufacturers Association

WOOD DEFECTS

Although wood is by nature seldom perfect for all applications, not all defects are equally important. For example, cupped boards are not a serious handicap if they are to be ripped into narrow strips, and bowed or crooked boards pose little difficulty when cut into short pieces.

While defects such as checks and splits seriously weaken the strength of a board, others can actually enhance the beauty and character of the finished project. These include tight knots, irregular grain, and fungus stain. In fact, some abnormal features in wood, such as bird's-eye, fiddleback, interlocked (ribbon-striped) grain, and spalted figure, are so desirable that you have to pay a premium to acquire them.

In general, most defects tend to reduce the value of lumber and make it more difficult to work with or less reliable once in use. A large proportion of defects relate to growing conditions and the physical anatomy of the tree. Trees have branches and branches produce knots. Similarly, boards cut from the outer sections of the log may have bark along the edges. The cellular structure and chemical makeup of various species cause certain defects too. For example, the difference between tangential and radial shrinkage in some species is so great that the wood tends to warp and check as it dries. (Information on wood shrinkage begins on page 242.) Also, some species produce natural compounds that make them highly durable and resistant to decay organisms, while others succumb to blue stain or dry rot very easily.

Regardless of species, all trees will produce abnormal wood tissue called reaction wood when conditions demand that they change their direction of growth. The resulting wood features compressed growth rings and a dull, silvery color. All trees will occasionally produce gum or resin pockets to help heal wounds caused by insects, fires, or other natural disasters. The following chart summarizes some of the most common defects, and how to deal with them.

WOOD DEFECTS: CAUSES AND SOLUTIONS

TYPE OF DEFECT	RECOGNIZABLE FEATURES	CAUSES	EFFECTS	SOLUTIONS
Knot, dead or loose	A dark ring encircling a whorl.	A dead branch that has not been integrated into the surrounding tissue.	Mars appearance and may weaken wood.	Should be cut out.
Knot, tight	A whorl integrated with surrounding tissue.	A live branch that was enveloped by wood tissue as the tree's girth increased.	Does not adversely affect stock.	May be removed for appearance.
Gum	Accumulations on the face or in pockets below the surface.	Fire, insect attack, or other injury to tree.	Bleeds through most finishes.	Should be cut off, or scraped out and filled.

TYPE OF DEFECT	RECOGNIZABLE FEATURES	CAUSES	EFFECTS	SOLUTIONS
Crook	Warping along the edge from one end to the other; common on stock in which the edge is near the pith.	Incorrect seasoning, or presence of reaction wood.	Stock difficult to work.	High spots can be cut away on table saw or jointer, or cut into shorter boards.
Cup	Warping across the face from one edge to the other; most often found on plain-sawn lumber.	Drying one board face at a more rapid rate than the other.	Stock difficult to work.	Allow both faces to dry to same moisture content; rip into narrow boards on band saw, or remove high spots on jointer.
Bow	A curve along the face from one end to the other.	Improper storage, or presence of reaction wood.	Stock is difficult to cut.	Cut into shorter boards, or remove high spots on jointer.
Twist	Irregular warping that causes opposite corners to be out of alignment; common on stock with irregular grain or reaction wood.	Growing conditions; uneven drying.	Stock difficult to work.	Cut into shorter boards, or remove high spots on jointer.
Checks or splits	Breaks along the grain, usually at board ends.	Rapid drying.	Affect strength and appearance.	Should be cut off.
Ring check or ring shank	Ruptures in the wood along annual growth rings.	Improper drying or damage during harvesting.	Affects strength, and appearance, if stain is applied.	Stock can be used, but not where appearance is important.
Wormholes	Small holes in the wood.	Insects boring through the wood.	Can be used to simulate "wormy chestnut."	Cut off; if used for "wormy chestnut" effect, ensure stock is kiln-dried and insects are dead.
Blue stain	Discoloration on the surface of the wood; common in woods like sycamore, pine, and holly.	Molds that flourish in warm, moist, or poorly ventilated areas; improper drying.	Mars appearance and may weaken wood.	Cut off; on pine, can be concealed with a dark stain.

WOOD DEFECTS

One of the most common defects in lumber is warp. The term includes any distortion in a board's surface, such as cup, crook, bow, and twist, which are shown on page 197. Each term defines the direction of the distortion. A cup, for example, twists edge to edge along the face, while a bow is an end-to-end curve along the face. Although improper storage can cause boards to warp, the primary cause is natural shrinkage stress. As wood dries, it does not shrink uniformly in all three dimensions. Although the amount of shrinkage varies by species, most woods shrink less than one-half as much radially (across the annual rings) as they do tangentially (roughly parallel to the rings).

The chart below indicates the different warping tendencies of some common woods. A comparison between this chart and the wood shrinkage chart on page 242 reveals an obvious connection between high shrinkage and the tendency to warp, but the relationship between the two is not absolute. For example, the shrinkage data on elm would indicate that it should be a fairly stable wood, but it is not. This is because elm commonly contains interlocked grain that adds to its drying stress. Another example is basswood. Its high rate of shrinkage would suggest that it should warp. In fact, basswood's cell walls are so thin that it is able to absorb stress without severe distortion.

WARPING TENDENCIES OF COMMON DOMESTIC WOODS

SPECIES	LOW	INTER-MEDIATE	HIGH
Alder	X		
Ash, white		X	
Aspen	X		
Basswood		X	
Beech			X
Birch, yellow		X	
Butternut	X		
Catalpa	X		
Cedar, aromatic			X
Cedar, Western red	X		
Cherry	X		
Douglas-fir		X	
Elm, American			X

SPECIES	LOW	INTER-MEDIATE	HIGH
Hemlock			X
Hickory		X	
Maple, hard		X	
Oak, red		X	
Oak, white		X	
Pecan			X
Pine, ponderosa	X		
Pine, Southern yellow			X
Pine, white	X		
Redwood	X		
Spruce	X		
Sycamore			X
Walnut	X		

lywood has been used as a building material for more than 100 years—and with good reason. Since the sheets are made of layers of veneer with alternating grain direction, plywood is extremely stable; it shrinks and swells almost imperceptibly in response to changes in humidity. It is also economical and convenient to use. Since scarce woods are normally only used for the thin face veneers, plywood panels are less expensive than solid-stock, and their use places less demand on dwindling reserves of rare species.

Most plywoods are produced in 4 x 8-foot panels, more than ample for nearly all furniture-making. But wider and longer sheets are available for special applications. Also, plywoods are made from either hardwoods or softwoods, or combinations of the two

where high-quality hardwood face veneers are bonded to softwood core stock.

A variety of hardwoods and softwoods are used to make plywood for interior paneling, cabinets, and furniture. Although the core stock may be of any species, plywood is identified by the species used for its face veneer.

Since back and face veneers are critical to the overall bending strength of plywood, you should consider two factors when ordering plywood: the wood species used and the particular requirements for your furniture project. So, for example, if you are using plywood for shelves, strength and not visual appeal is the overriding factor. You would use a plywood made of a stronger veneer than you would if you were using the plywood for a cabinet door, where appearance is more important.

Five-ply veneer core construction
Face veneer
Core
Back veneer
Crossbands

Three-ply medium density fiberboard core construction
Face
Core
Back veneer

Multi-ply veneer core construction
Face veneer
Core
Back veneer
Crossbands

TYPICAL PLYWOOD CONSTRUCTION
Illustrations courtesy Hardwood Plywood & Veneer Association

Five-ply lumber core construction
Face veneer
Core
Crossbands
Back veneer

Three-ply particleboard construction
Face veneer
Core
Back veneer

Five-ply construction with banding or railing
Face veneer
Banding
Crossbands
Core
Back veneer

PLYWOOD

CHARACTERIS-
TICS OF VARI-
OUS PLYWOOD
TYPES
Chart courtesy
Architectural
Woodwork
Institute
and Hardwood
Plywood & Veneer
Association

PANEL TYPE	APPEARANCE OF EDGE	FLATNESS	SURFACE UNIFORMITY	DIMENSIONAL STABILITY	SCREW-HOLD-ING ABILITY	BENDING STRENGTH	AVAILABILITY
Medium density particleboard core	Good	Excellent	Excellent	Fair	Fair	Good	Common
Medium density fiberboard core	Excellent	Excellent	Excellent	Fair	Good	Good	Common
Hardwood veneer core	Good	Fair	Good	Excellent	Excellent	Excellent	Common
Softwood veneer core	Good	Fair	Fair	Excellent	Excellent	Excellent	Common
Lumber core	Good	Good	Good	Good	Excellent	Excellent	Limited
Standard hardboard core	Excellent	Excellent	Excellent	Fair	Good	Good	Common
Tempered hardboard core	Good	Excellent	Good	Good	Good	Good	Limited

PLYWOOD: GRADES, CORES, AND COSTS

The grade of a plywood panel is a primary concern when the appearance of the panel outweighs its structural specifications. As shown on page 201, softwood plywoods are graded using letter designations to describe the quality of both the face and back veneers. Hardwood plywoods use a combined letter and number grading system, with the face veneer described by a letter as in softwood grading, and a number to describe the back veneer. The higher the grade of plywood the smaller the maximum diameter of knotholes and other "voids." Aside from the grades of its veneers, plywood can have any one of a multitude of core constructions. Some of the more common types are illustrated on page 199. The chart above rates the different core constructions in terms of appearance, working characteristics, and availability.

Plywood ranges in thickness from ⅛ inch (hardwood only) to 1⅛ inch, in ⅛-inch increments. The more commonly available panels are from ¼ inch to ¾ inch in thickness. In recent years, however, imported plywoods manufactured to metric standards have become increasingly popular, such as finely veneered Baltic-birch panels from northern Europe. This relatively high-quality plywood is designed for construction and industrial uses, but is equally suited to many woodworking applications.

Prices vary widely for plywood. In general, softwood plywood is cheaper than hardwood plywood, which can cost $100 a sheet and more, depending on the core stock. Unlike solid stock, plywood does not increase in price according to thickness. A sheet of hardwood plywood ¾ inch thick is often only slightly more expensive than ¼-inch plywood.

PLYWOOD GRADES

GRADES	CHARACTERISTICS AND USES
N	An all-heartwood or all-sapwood select, natural-finish veneer; features a smooth surface. Free of open defects; has no more than six wood-only repairs per 4 x 8 panel, made parallel to the grain, and well matched for grain and color.
A	A smooth and paintable veneer; may be used for a natural finish. Has no more than 18 neatly made repairs, made parallel to the grain.
B	A solid-surface veneer; may have shims, circular repair plugs, and tight knots up to 1 inch across the grain. May also have minor splits.
C-PLUGGED	An improved C-grade veneer with splits limited to $1/8$ inch wide and knotholes and borer holes limited to $1/4$ x $1/2$ inch; may have some broken grain and synthetic (non-wood) repairs.
C	Has tight knots to $1 1/2$ inches in diameter; also has knotholes up to 1 inch across the grain. May have synthetic (non-wood) or wood repairs, splits, and sanding defects that do not impair strength.
D	Has knots and knotholes up to $2 1/2$ inch wide across the grain; may have limited splits. Limited to interior applications.

HARDWOOD PLYWOOD VENEER GRADES

Chart courtesy Hardwood Plywood & Veneer Association

FACE GRADES	CHARACTERISTICS AND USES
AA	Highest quality face grade for high-end uses, such as architectural paneling, doors, cabinets, and furniture.
A	Uniform; has few natural defects. Used in cabinets and furniture.
B	Has a few natural defects.
C, D, AND E	Sound surface; allow color variations, knots and repairs. Used where a more natural appearance is desired.
Specialty	Nonstandard appearance characteristics, subject to agreement between individual buyer and seller as in factory-finished wall paneling.
BACK GRADES	
1	Made of sapwood; may contain mineral streaks. Can have up to 16 tight knots with a maximum diameter of $3/8$ inch; has no ruptured grain.
2	Made of sapwood; may contain mineral streaks. Can have up to 16 tight knots with a maximum diameter of $3/4$ inch; may have slightly ruptured grain.
3	Made of sapwood; may contain mineral streaks. Can have an unlimited number of tight knots up to $1/2$ inch in diameter; can have up to 16 tight knots with a maximum diameter of $1 1/2$ inches; may have ruptured grain up to 1 inch in height.
4	Made of sapwood; may contain mineral streaks. Can have an unlimited number of tight knots; may have ruptured grain.

PLYWOOD GRADES

UNDERSTAND-ING SOFTWOOD PLYWOOD GRADING STAMPS

As shown at right, grading stamps for softwood plywood appear on the back *(top)* or edge *(bottom)* of the sheets. The stamp indicates the association whose rules were applied in grading the panel (in this case, the APA, or American Plywood Association). For sanded plywood, a two-letter grade for the face and back veneers will usual-

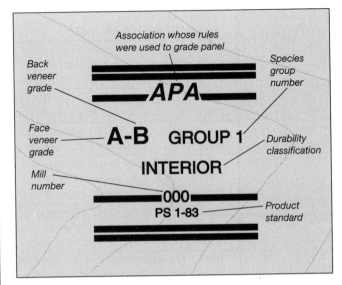

Courtesy American Plywood Association

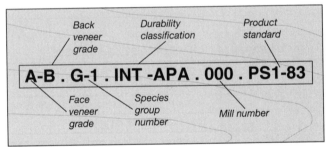

---

ly appear in large type; the first letter refers to the face veneer and the second to the back veneer. Also in the stamp will be a reference to the species group used to manufacture the plywood (in this case, Group 1); this provides an indication of the strength of the panel. (There are five groups, with Group 1 comprising the strongest woods and Group 5 the weakest.) Stamps also indi-

cate the durability classification of the plies used (interior); the association code number of the mill where the panel was manufactured; and the product standard the panel meets. Because grade stamps mar the surface of plywood, they are seldom used on hardwood panels. These panels generally carry an abbreviated edge-stamp designating the grade of the face and back veneers.

Ordering plywood

Provide your supplier with the following information when ordering plywood:

1. *Number of panels*
2. *Type of plywood (i.e. interior or exterior)*
3. *Number of plies*
4. *Thickness of face veneer and of panels*
5. *Width*
6. *Length*
7. *Species of face ply and whether light, medium, or dark color*
8. *Grade of face ply and matching requirements*
9. *Grade of back ply*
10. *Grade of lumber core and type of banding (if required)*
11. *Type and grade of particleboard core (if required)*
12. *Type of medium density fiberboard and hardboard core (if required)*
13. *Type of special core (if required)*
14. *Whether you require solid core*

Courtesy Hardwood Plywood & Veneer Association

PARTICLEBOARD AND FIBERBOARD

Until the development of particleboard in the late 1930s, sawdust, shavings, and other sawmill by-products were burned as residue. The development of formaldehyde resins as bonding agents allowed these once-wasted materials to be reconstituted into usable wood-based products. To make particleboard, wood chips, shavings, and sawdust are milled to a uniform size, combined with resins, and formed in a press. Heat and pressure are used to create panels of any desired thickness. By altering the heat, pressure, and size of particles, various densities of particleboard can be produced. While the softer forms have working characteristics comparable to ordinary wood, denser forms provide very hard, abrasion-resistant surfaces that require carbide-tipped blades and bits to cut and shape. A comparable product, marketed as waferboard, employs larger shavings, but the resulting surface's unevenness has limitations in some of the typical applications where particleboard excels.

Particleboard's ingredients—particularly formaldehyde—pose some hazards for the woodworker. Whenever you generate dust during cutting or other machining operations, be sure to wear a government-approved dust mask.

In cabinetmaking, particleboard is commonly used as underlayment for plastic laminates in kitchen countertops and bathroom vanities. In many roles, particleboard has its limitations. Since it is made of wood particles, it shares wood's sensitivity to changes in humidity, which may cause it to shrink and swell. Furthermore, particleboard is relatively brittle. When exposed to repeated stress, fasteners tend to tear out. In shelving applications, where it must bear heavy loads across long spans or over long periods of time, particleboard can sag. Sound shelf design *(page 8)* and proper fastening techniques *(page 304)* can overcome this problem.

(page 8) ... *(page 304)*

TYPES OF PARTICLEBOARD

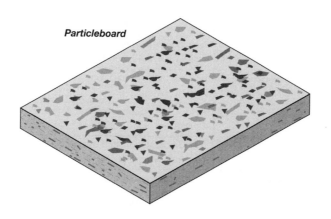

Particleboard

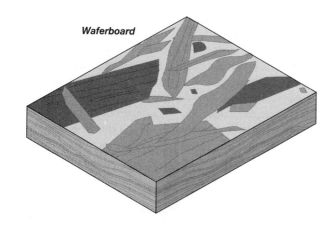

Waferboard

PARTICLEBOARD AND FIBERBOARD

TYPE	CHARACTERISTICS	USES
Unfinished core	Includes materials with different densities and properties.	Laminated components, casework, doors, paneling, furniture.
Veneered	Core stock covered with wood veneer; ready to use.	Furniture, panels, wainscotting, carcase dividers.
Overlaid	Has a thin layer of material such as plastic laminate bonded to core stock.	Countertops, paneling, furniture, cabinetwork, doors.
Filled	Made of material that has undergone surface filling and sanding.	For projects that will be painted.
Undercoated or primed	Has a painted base coat applied by the manufacturer.	For projects that will be painted.

FIBERBOARD

Like particleboard, fiberboard is made of sawmill residue and resins. But both the manufacturing process and the working characteristics of the final product are substantially different. While particleboard contains finely milled particles of wood, fiberboard is made by first cooking the wood chips and breaking them down into fine cellulose fibers in much the same way that paper is made. These fibers are then mixed with resin binders and heat-pressed into panels. By altering the type and quantity of the resins, fiberboard can be produced in various densities. They range from medium density fiberboard—used for plywood core stock, exterior siding, and paneling —to high-density hardboard, which is most frequently used for the backs of cabinets and for making templates and patterns.

Hardboard—also known as Masonite™—is generally sold in two forms: tempered and standard. Tempered hardboard is subject to a longer drying and pressing time during its manufacture. The result is a denser, less porous material.

Fiberboard panels are most commonly available in 4 x 8 sheets in either ⅛-inch or ¼-inch thicknesses. The randomly oriented, interlocked fibers of fiberboard make it far less brittle than particleboard, giving fasteners much greater holding power. The denser hardboard is also exceptionally stable when exposed to changes in humidity.

Fiberboard's smooth surface makes it readily paintable, but the random orientation of its fibers generally requires that an undercoat or a heavy-bodied sealer be used to prevent the panel from soaking up too much paint. Special pre-sealed and sanded panels designed to be easier to paint are available and are used in many industrial and construction applications. Depending on density, fiberboard accepts most woodworking adhesives. However, because of its extreme flexibility, it must be supported by the more rigid components in a project. Like particleboard, fiberboard is abrasive, and carbide-tipped blades and bits are recommended, especially when working with the higher-density hardboards.

The relative costs of particleboard and fiberboard depend on the density of the material. Since fiberboard is denser, it is generally about 25 percent more costly than a sheet of particleboard of comparable size. Both particleboard and fiberboard are less expensive than either softwood or hardwood plywood.

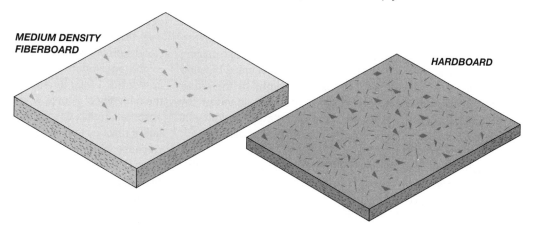

MEDIUM DENSITY FIBERBOARD

HARDBOARD

WORKING CHARACTERISTICS	PARTICLEBOARD	MEDIUM DENSITY FIBERBOARD	HARDBOARD Standard	Tempered
Bending	Fair	Fair	Good	Excellent
Drilling	Good	Excellent	Good	Excellent
Laminating	Good	Excellent	Good	Excellent
Nailing	Good	Good	Good	Good
Painting	Fair (unfilled); Good (filled)	Good (unfilled); Excellent (filled)	Fair	Excellent
Routing	Fair	Excellent	Fair	Excellent
Sanding	Good	Excellent	Fair	Excellent
Sawing	Good	Excellent	Fair	Excellent
Screw-holding	Good	Excellent	Good	Good
Shaping	Good	Excellent	Fair	Excellent

WORKING CHARACTERISTICS OF MANUFACTURED BOARDS

MOISTURE IN WOOD

Like the human body, a living tree is made up largely of water. Not only are its cell walls fully saturated, but the cell cavities contain what is called free moisture. Once a log is cut into lumber and exposed to the atmosphere, this free moisture is given up until there is no water left in the cell cavities. The wood tissue is now said to be at its fiber saturation point (FSP). The only water left in the wood is stored in the cell walls. Until this point is reached, the board's dimensions remain unchanged.

With most wood species, the FSP is reached when the moisture content of the wood drops to slightly below 30 percent. The moisture content is the amount of water in a piece of wood compared to its water-free weight. So, for example, if a 40-pound block of wood weighs only 30 pounds when it is completely dry, then the moisture content of the original piece of wood is the weight of the water —10 pounds—divided by the wood's dry weight—30 pounds, or 33⅓ percent.

Once a piece of wood drops below its FSP, a further loss of moisture content will cause the wood to shrink. Each species of wood is affected differently. (See the chart on page 242.) Although different wood-drying methods are aimed at reducing moisture content in a controlled fashion, moisture content is always changing. For every atmospheric humidity level, there is a corresponding wood moisture content known as the equilibrium moisture content or EMC. Whenever the humidity changes, wood absorbs or releases moisture until it reaches the new EMC. Because warm air can carry more moisture than cold air, the average moisture content of wood tends to be higher in the summer than in the win-

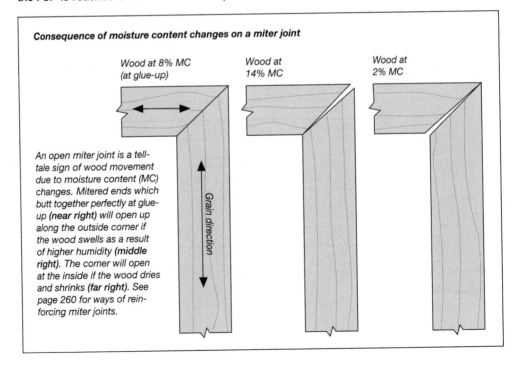

Consequence of moisture content changes on a miter joint

Wood at 8% MC (at glue-up)

Wood at 14% MC

Wood at 2% MC

Grain direction

An open miter joint is a telltale sign of wood movement due to moisture content (MC) changes. Mitered ends which butt together perfectly at glue-up (*near right*) will open up along the outside corner if the wood swells as a result of higher humidity (*middle right*). The corner will open at the inside if the wood dries and shrinks (*far right*). See page 260 for ways of reinforcing miter joints.

ter, but the long-term average will be greater in humid climates than in arid ones. For example, the moisture content of wood in the midwestern and northeastern United States will experience wide seasonal fluctuations, averaging about 12 percent. In the more humid southeast, it will remain relatively stable at around 15 percent.

What does this mean for the furniture you build? As shown in the illustration of a miter joint on page 206, wood shrinkage or swelling due to moisture content changes can weaken and even force a joint apart. One safeguard is to work with wood that is rough-ly at its EMC for the environment in which it will be used. For most cabinetmaking projects, the moisture content should be 10 percent or less. If it is higher, let the wood continue to dry. A wood's moisture content can be measured using a commercial moisture meter; one model is shown below. To be certain the sample is representative, press the prongs of the meter into the face halfway through the board's thickness. Avoid taking a reading near the end of the board or in any defects, such as knots, pith, or gum pockets.

The vast majority of woodworkers attempt to avoid problems related to moisture content by buying only kiln-dried lumber, which is typically dried to 8 percent moisture content. As a rule, this approach works, but it is not an absolute solution. Even kiln-dried lumber, if improperly stored, can absorb enough moisture to make it unsuitable for cabinet work. Since you have no control over how lumber has been stored before you buy it, try to purchase your lumber in advance of when it will be used and store it for several weeks, either in the shop, attic, or in the room where the furniture will be used.

QUICKTIP

Measuring moisture content in thick stock

The metal pins on most commercial resistance-type moisture meters are about 1 inch long. Ideally, these pins should extend at least halfway through a board's thickness to ensure a proper reading. For stock thicker than 2 inches, this can pose a problem. One solution is to drive two nails into the stock until the nail tips reach the halfway point. Then simply touch the meter pins to the nail heads to take the reading.

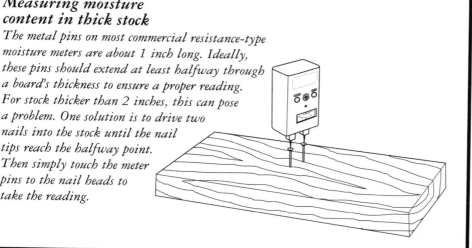

WOOD GALLERY

One of the great pleasures of woodworking, and also one of its marvelous complexities, is the wealth of different woods that are available. At one time, craftsmen were limited to the few dozen species that grew in their area. However, by the 17th Century, a trickle of exotic timbers began to enter into the Western woodworking tradition. Today, that trickle has turned into a flood. Upwards of 100,000 plant species produce woody tissue, and the majority of those that attain tree size are used for lumber.

This biological diversity accounts for the availability of literally thousands of unique timbers, but how these timbers are processed also affects the appearance of the lumber. As shown opposite, some species, like white oak, yield remarkably different cabinet woods based on how the boards are cut from the log. While plain-sawn, or tangentially cut, samples expose the wood's flowing, ring-porous figure (**A**), quarter-sawn (radially cut) boards have an entirely different character (**B**). Oak's large rays, which show as only flecks on the plain-sawn board, explode into lustrous bands when the wood is quarter-sawn. See page 186 for more on cutting and milling lumber; page 245 offers information on veneer cutting methods.

Some woods, like sapele, have interlocked grain, where alternating bands of fibrous tissue are aligned in different directions. When these woods are quarter-sawn, they display a ribbon figure (**C**) made up of alternating lustrous and dull stripes. Rarer still, abnormal tissue in species like maple produces the famous bird's-eye figure (**D**) when flat-sawn (rotary-sliced), and yet another, totally different curly figure (**E**) when quarter-sawn.

A wood's appearance can also be affected by where the lumber or veneer is cut from a tree. Sawn from the stump, maple reveals the unique butt figure (**F**). The feathery grain found where branches fork from a tree is revealed in crotchwood, as in amburana (**G**). Many species occasionally produce contorted tissue called burls. While the grain in burl makes this wood difficult to work and structurally frail, it is much prized for decorative veneers (**H**).

Some vividly pigmented woods, such as Brazilian rosewood, reveal a sharp contrast between heartwood and sapwood (**I**). The pigments in rosewood develop very slowly, and only very old and somewhat decrepit specimens of this endangered species possess vividly colored heartwood. With most cabinet woods, the sapwood is not used and defects of any kind are meticulously avoided, but there are exceptions. The lower grades of white pine, for example, provide a cabinet wood that is decidedly different from clear pine, simply because its dark, reddish brown knots lend a special character to rustic furniture (**J**).

The gallery of color photos following on pages 210 to 240 presents a representative sample of some of the world's most important timbers. Hardwoods are listed first, followed by softwoods, in alphabetical order according to their most commonly used names. While some fine woods have necessarily been left out, an important objective of this directory is to survey the magnificent diversity of wood as a craft medium. Each species is described with respect to its characteristics, special properties, common uses, relative cost, source, weight, and current availability. Because a wood's working characteristics and strength relate closely to its weight, this property is expressed in terms of its air-dried weight per board foot. This is a function of the wood's specific gravity: its dry weight relative to the weight of an equal volume of water.

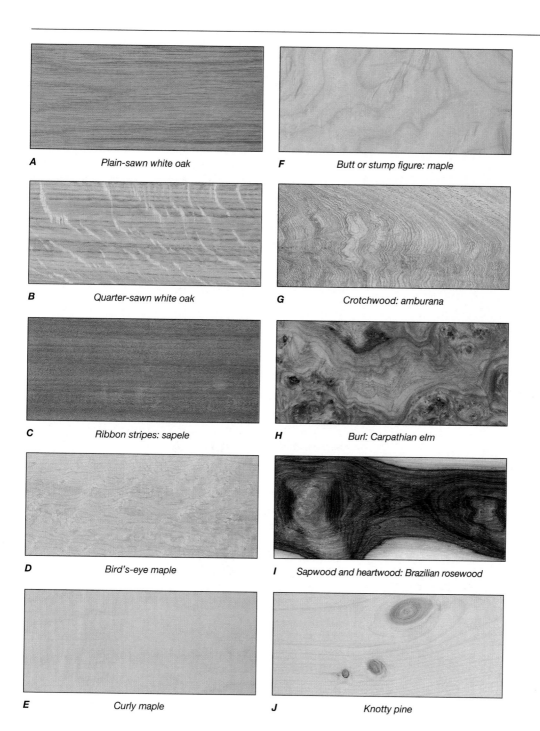

A   *Plain-sawn white oak*

B   *Quarter-sawn white oak*

C   *Ribbon stripes: sapele*

D   *Bird's-eye maple*

E   *Curly maple*

F   *Butt or stump figure: maple*

G   *Crotchwood: amburana*

H   *Burl: Carpathian elm*

I   *Sapwood and heartwood: Brazilian rosewood*

J   *Knotty pine*

HARDWOODS

AFRORMOSIA

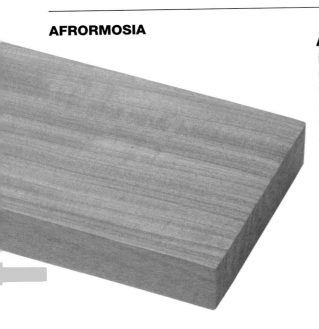

A fine-textured yellowish brown timber with excellent weathering properties, afrormosia is similar in appearance to teak, but slightly stronger, heavier, and harder. Lacking teak's oily nature, afrormosia accepts adhesives and finishes without difficulty. The wood is easily worked with hand tools, but interlocked grain may cause tearout when planing. Fasteners containing iron should be avoided, since ferrous compounds cause the wood to turn black. The fine dust of this species is known to cause eye irritation and respiratory difficulties, so good ventilation is important. As a teak substitute, afrormosia is popular in boat building, especially for decking, due to its high abrasion resistance.

COMMON USES: Boat building, furniture, cabinetmaking, flooring, decorative veneer.
COST: Expensive.
ORIGIN: West Central Africa, Ghana, Ivory Coast.
OTHER NAMES: Kokrodua, assamela, devil's tree, red bark.
BOTANICAL NAME: *Pericopsis elata (Afrormosia elata).*
WEIGHT: 3.6 pounds per board foot.
STATUS: Becoming scarce due to high demand and limited native range.

AGBA

A gba resembles pale mahogany in color and figure, but it is softer and somewhat finer-textured. The tree attains a massive size, up to 200 feet tall and 8 feet in diameter; it is an ideal species for lumber production. Aside from its high gum content, which tends to clog blades and cause finishes to occasionally bubble up, agba has excellent working properties and is quite stable in use. It also has good weathering characteristics, but is a little too soft and fragile for heavy construction.

COMMON USES: Light construction, millwork, plywood core stock, boat building, furniture.
COST: Inexpensive to moderate.
ORIGIN: Tropical West Africa.
OTHER NAMES: Achi, egba, tola branca.
BOTANICAL NAME: *Gossweilerodendron balsamiferum.*
WEIGHT: 2.5 pounds per board foot.
STATUS: Becoming scarce.

A light pinkish brown in color, alder has a faint but pleasant figure. The wood is soft and easy to work. It also accepts fasteners with little risk of splitting. Adhesives and finishes adhere well, but uneven patches may occur when dark stains are used. Alder has extremely poor weathering properties and should not be used for exterior projects. In interior applications where it may be exposed to high humidity, such as kitchen and bathroom cabinets, a moisture-resistant varnish top coat is advisable.

ALDER

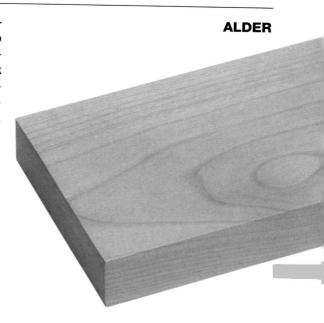

COMMON USES: Cabinetmaking, plywood veneers, turning, paneling, carving.
COST: Inexpensive.
ORIGIN: North American west coast from central California to Alaska.
OTHER NAMES: Red alder, western alder.
BOTANICAL NAME: *Alnus rubra*.
WEIGHT: 2.2 pounds per board foot.
STATUS: Plentiful; responds well to forest management and grows quickly.

W hite ash is a cream-colored ring-porous wood with a very showy figure. Much used in mass-produced mixed-wood furniture during the late 1800s, ash is an excellent, inexpensive cabinet wood. Although lighter in color than either white or red oak, white ash heartwood often displays grayish brown streaks. The closely related black ash, *Fraxinus nigra*, is a slightly softer wood with a warm tan color. While white ash is strong and very elastic, both white and black ash are excellent woods for steam bending. Because the earlywood contains large pores, fillers are required to achieve a smooth surface, but ash accepts adhesives and finishes very well. It should not be used for exterior projects.

ASH, WHITE

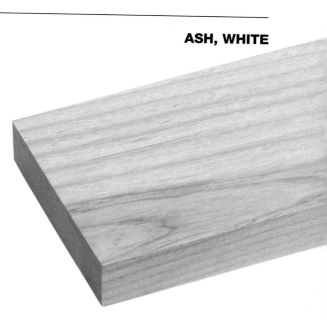

COMMON USES: Tool handles, baseball bats, furniture (steam-bent components), cooperage, paneling, decorative veneers.
COST: Inexpensive.
ORIGIN: Eastern North America west to the Great Plains.
OTHER NAMES: American ash.
BOTANICAL NAME: *Fraxinus americana*.
WEIGHT: 3.1 pounds per board foot.
STATUS: Plentiful.

HARDWOODS

ASPEN

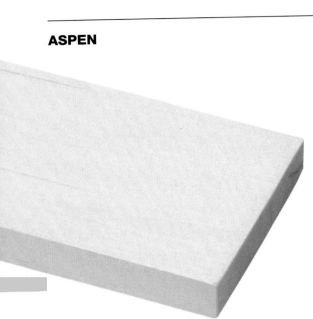

Aspen is a fine-textured, light-colored wood with little color variation between sapwood and heartwood. Streaks may appear around knots, but otherwise aspen is bland in color and very modestly figured. Almost as soft as white pine, it is easy to work, shapes well, and accepts fasteners without splitting. Reaction wood may cause staining problems, resulting in a patchy or blotchy appearance. Aspen is a poor choice for exterior use, but it can serve as a lightweight substitute for maple or birch in interior cabinetmaking applications.

COMMON USES: Interior paneling, plywood core stock veneers, furniture, turning, carving.

COST: Very inexpensive.

ORIGIN: Temperate North America, from Nova Scotia to Alaska and south through the Rocky Mountains to northern Mexico.

OTHER NAMES: Popple, quaking aspen, bigtooth aspen.

BOTANICAL NAMES: *Populus tremuloides and Populus grandidentata.*

WEIGHT: 2.1 pounds per board foot.

STATUS: One of the most plentiful hardwoods in North America and one of the first species to grow back after logging.

BALSA

Balsa is the softest and lightest commercially important timber in the world. Although too weak for structural parts in cabinets or furniture, it has an extremely high strength-to-weight ratio, making it ideal for model-airplane building. Its very fine, uniform texture and thin-walled cells make it easy to carve and sand while leaving a surface that is smooth enough for painting. Balsa is also an extremely buoyant wood which resists absorbing liquids. It is one of the few timbers whose sapwood is commercially more valuable than the heartwood.

COMMON USES: Modelmaking, carving.

COST: Moderate.

ORIGIN: Tropical America, from the West Indies and southern Mexico south to Brazil.

OTHER NAMES: Corcho, gatillo, pung, lana, tami.

BOTANICAL NAME: *Ochroma pyramidale.*

WEIGHT: 0.5 to 1.2 pounds per board foot.

STATUS: Supplies are adequate and sustainable. Most balsa wood is plantation grown. Given ideal growing conditions, it will attain harvestable size in only five to ten years.

Extremely fine-textured, soft and creamy white in color, basswood ranks as one of the world's most popular carving woods. Because of its high shrinkage, the large (4- to 6-inch-thick) flitches preferred by carvers are difficult to season without checking. Once dry, however, basswood is relatively stable and so uniform in texture that it will hold sharp details when shaped with carving tools, files, and abrasives. Basswood is an acceptable species for secondary furniture parts such as divider panels and drawer sides.

COMMON USES: Carving, veneer substrate, plywood core stock, kitchen utensils, decorative turning, secondary furniture parts.

COST: Moderate as lumber; expensive in carving blocks.

ORIGIN: Northeastern United States and southeastern Canada.

OTHER NAMES: American linden, American lime tree, bee tree.

BOTANICAL NAME: *Tilia americana.*

WEIGHT: 2 pounds per board foot.

STATUS: Plentiful.

BASSWOOD

Bayo is relatively new on the North American market and touted as one of the "sustainable yield" timbers that are being harvested with minimum impact on their native rain forests. Bayo has excellent working qualities. Its fine texture and density make it a reasonably good substitute for boxwood. Its stunning color, with warm pink and yellow streaks highlighting a soft tan, maple-like background, give it an added advantage. Because of its extreme density, pilot holes are required when installing fasteners and blades must be frequently sharpened.

COMMON USES: Flooring, furniture, paneling, turning.

COST: Moderate.

ORIGIN: Central America and northern South America.

OTHER NAMES: Araracanga, volador, alcarreto, copachi.

BOTANICAL NAME: Species of *Aspidosperma.*

WEIGHT: 4.5 to 5.3 pounds per board foot.

STATUS: Relatively plentiful, but not all species consistently produce the vividly colored wood prized for cabinetmaking.

BAYO

HARDWOODS

BEECH, AMERICAN

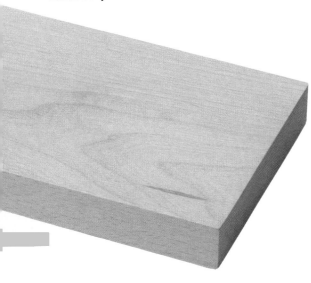

Belonging to the same family as the oaks, beech prominently features small but abundant dark rays. Unlike the oaks, however, beech is diffuse-porous with a moderately fine texture and can be finished to a smooth surface without fillers. Beech requires considerable physical effort to work with hand tools, but it planes and shapes more predictably than most oaks. Also, the orderly pattern produced by the rays gives quarter-sawn beech a very interesting figure. European beech, while similar in appearance, is softer and slightly finer in texture.

COMMON USES: Turning, kitchenware, flooring, veneer, cabinetmaking.

COST: Moderate to low.

ORIGIN: Eastern North America, from Texas to southern Ontario.

OTHER NAME: Beech.

BOTANICAL NAME: *Fagus grandifolia.*

WEIGHT: 3.6 pounds per board foot.

STATUS: Plentiful.

BIRCH, YELLOW

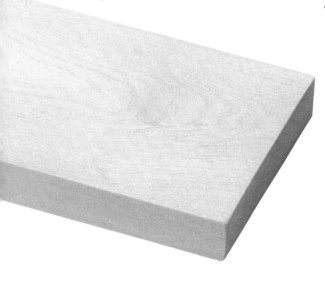

Although the popular image of birch is that of a tree with papery, chalk-white bark, this is not the primary species used for producing lumber. Most lumber and veneer are cut from yellow birch and sweet birch. While the wood of paper birch is yellowish white, relatively soft, and sometimes used for inexpensive turnings, the wood of yellow birch and sweet birch is finer-textured, hard, and a very light grayish white. Birch has similar figure, appearance, and working characteristics to maple. Few hardwoods with comparable density and strength are as easy to finish as birch.

COMMON USES: Interior trim, paneling, plywood veneers, cabinetry, furniture.

COST: Moderate.

ORIGIN: Eastern North America, from northern Georgia to Quebec and west to Minnesota.

OTHER NAME: Sweet birch.

BOTANICAL NAMES: *Betula Allegheniensis* and *Betula lenta.*

WEIGHT: 3.5 to 3.7 pounds per board foot.

STATUS: Moderately plentiful, but high-quality veneer logs are becoming scarce.

Various species of *Cordia* are plentiful and widespread, but the wood varies so much in weight, texture, and appearance that it is difficult to characterize. The highest quality bocote resembles African zebrawood with sharply defined, swirled streaks of black and yellow grain. The wood is hard and moderately fine-textured, with a waxy feel and relatively high surface luster. It polishes extremely well, is very durable, and requires no protective sealer. Bocote is somewhat difficult to cut and shape with hand tools because of its high density.

BOCOTE

COMMON USES: Decorative veneer, furniture, flooring, turning, gunstocks.

COST: Moderate to expensive with the most highly figured lumber selling at a substantial premium.

ORIGIN: Throughout tropical America.

OTHER NAMES: Canalete, loro negro, cordia.

BOTANICAL NAME: Species of *Cordia*.

WEIGHT: 4 to 5.4 pounds per board foot.

STATUS: Supplies are adequate.

A fine-textured wood with a warm reddish color and vivid purple highlights, bubinga is stunningly attractive and often used as a rosewood substitute. Highly figured logs are harvested to produce a distinctive veneer marketed as Kevazingo. Bubinga has good working properties, but like rosewood, it is becoming so scarce that it is prohibitively expensive for use as solid stock in furniture. The species that produce bubinga are large rain forest trees capable of growing taller than 150 feet, with trunks up to 6 feet in diameter. Demand for this nearly ideal cabinet wood has outpaced its rate of recovery.

BUBINGA

COMMON USES: Fine furniture, veneers, inlay work, decorative turning.

COST: Expensive.

ORIGIN: Rain forest regions of equatorial Africa.

OTHER NAMES: Essingang, ovang, waka, African rosewood.

BOTANICAL NAME: Species of *Guibourtia*.

WEIGHT: 4.2 to 5 pounds per board foot.

STATUS: Becoming scarce because of high demand.

HARDWOODS

BUTTERNUT

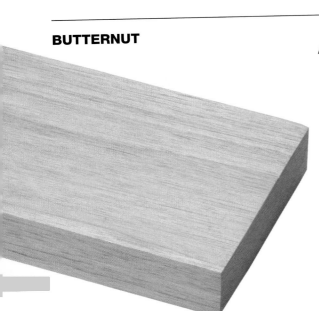

As a close relative of walnut, butternut has a comparably attractive figure, but is coarser in texture, much softer, and light brown. Too soft for chairs, tables, and other types of furniture subject to constant abuse, butternut has traditionally been limited to more delicate projects such as clock cases, display shelves, turnings, and carvings. Although easy to cut and shape, it is more difficult to sand and finish than black walnut. Sandpaper tends to tear the grain, leaving the surface woolly. The wood's coarse texture requires multiple coats of varnish to seal the pores.

COMMON USES: Cabinetry, furniture, carving, veneer.
COST: Moderate, but increasing.
ORIGIN: Northeastern United States and southeastern Canada.
OTHER NAME: White walnut.
BOTANICAL NAME: *Juglans cinerea.*
WEIGHT: 2.1 pounds per board foot.
STATUS: Endangered because of the butternut canker blight.

CATALPA

A soft ring-porous wood with a flamboyant ash-like figure and grayish tan color, catalpa can be distinguished from black ash by its strong creosote-like odor. It is easy to cut, shape, and plane, but care must be taken when sanding it to prevent the porous earlywood from tearing out. Catalpa shrinks very little and ranks with genuine mahogany as one of the most stable woods in the world. Because of its stability and exceptionally attractive figure, it is a popular turning and carving wood.

COMMON USES: Cabinetry, turning, carving.
COST: Inexpensive, but difficult to buy through retail channels.
ORIGIN: Midwestern United States.
OTHER NAMES: Northern catalpa, catawba, Indian cigar tree.
BOTANICAL NAME: *Catalpa speciosa.*
WEIGHT: 2.3 to 2.6 pounds per board foot.
STATUS: Supply is limited because of the sporadic range of the species.

Various species of *Sickingia* have been on the market for years, but chactacote has recently come into vogue as one of the new sustainable-yield species. The wood itself has a fine texture and working characteristics comparable to hard maple, except it is vivid red and occasionally highlighted with bright yellow streaks. Unfortunately, the color fades, so an ultraviolet blocking varnish is recommended to stop the wood's natural patina-forming process. Otherwise, chactacote eventually turns a rich, amber brown, which is still attractive, if somewhat less stunning.

COMMON USES: Cabinetry, furniture, turning, carving.
COST: Moderate.
ORIGIN: Central America.
OTHER NAMES: Sickingia, rosita, palo colorado, quina.
BOTANICAL NAME: *Sickingia salvadorensis*.
WEIGHT: 3.3 to 3.8 pounds per board foot.
STATUS: This species is relatively plentiful, but the tree is small and does not yield large timbers.

American black cherry is one of the most popular cabinet woods in the world. It is a fine-textured, relatively soft, diffuse-porous wood, with a beautiful, warm pink color and outstanding stability. Its working characteristics are nearly ideal, except that the wood's high gum content causes router and shaper bits to leave burn marks if the cutters are dull or the rate of feed is not kept constant. Cherry ages with amazing grace, developing a rich, translucent patina that continues to darken over decades.

COMMON USES: Cabinetry, furniture, interior trim, turning, carving, decorative veneer.
COST: Moderate.
ORIGIN: Eastern North America and sporadically at high elevations south through the mountains of Mexico.
OTHER NAMES: American black cherry, rum cherry, wild cherry.
BOTANICAL NAME: *Prunus serotina*.
WEIGHT: 2.8 pounds per board foot.
STATUS: Supply is adequate but subject to fluctuations in demand as furniture styles change.

HARDWOODS

CHESTNUT

Virtually all American chestnut on the market today comes from resawn timbers salvaged from old barns and other buildings. Until this species was exterminated by blight, it was one of the most valuable of all North American timbers. Light, easy to split, and exceptionally durable, it served as a raw material for a host of industrial and construction applications. Although somewhat too soft and brittle to be a primary cabinet wood, its orange tan color and subtle figure lend charm to clock cases, picture frames, and spice cabinets.

COMMON USES: Fence posts and rails, coffins, paneling, interior trim, loose cooperage, cabinetry, furniture.
COST: Expensive and increasingly difficult to find.
ORIGIN: Eastern United States and extreme southeastern Canada.
OTHER NAMES: American chestnut, sweet chestnut.
BOTANICAL NAME: *Castanea dentata*.
WEIGHT: 2.5 pounds per board foot.
STATUS: Extinct as a source of commercial timber.

EBONY

Ebony trees seldom exceed 50 feet in height and about 18 inches in diameter. Only the heartwood is jet black and it seldom exceeds 10 to 12 inches in diameter. The wide sapwood is yellowish white. As a result, ebony is only available in small billets and generally sells by the pound rather than by the board foot. Prized for its jet black color and extremely fine texture, it has become so scarce that many woodworkers have turned to dyed holly or pearwood as a substitute. True ebony is hard and heavy, but very consistent in texture. The fine dust can cause skin rash and respiratory problems.

COMMON USES: Turning, carving, inlay, marquetry, piano keys and parts for other musical instruments, jewelry, knife handles.
COST: Very expensive.
ORIGIN: Sri Lanka, India, Africa.
OTHER NAMES: Ceylon ebony, East Indian ebony, African ebony.
BOTANICAL NAME: Species of *Diospyros*.
WEIGHT: 5 to 5.4 pounds per board foot.
STATUS: Rare. Large and high-quality supplies are very limited.

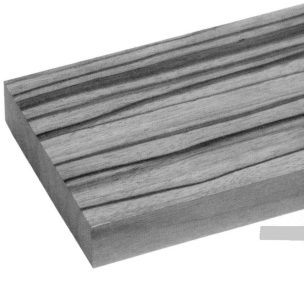

Like true ebony, macassar ebony is cut from numerous species of *Diospyros*. The term macassar is used to distinguish ebony with marbled figure and variegated amber and black stripes. Depending upon species and growing conditions, the wood may vary in texture from medium fine to very fine and from hard to very hard. The softest of the macassar ebonies are comparable in working characteristics to hickory, except that the wood is brittle, fracturing into powdery sawdust that can be irritating to the nose and skin.

COMMON USES: Inlaying, carving, turning, decorative veneers.
COST: Very expensive.
ORIGIN: Southeast Asia, Celebes, Borneo.
OTHER NAMES: Marblewood, coromandel, calamander.
BOTANICAL NAME: Species of *Diospyros*.
WEIGHT: 4.2 to 5.8 pounds per board foot.
STATUS: Scarce.

ELM

Elm is a ring-porous, creamy-white wood comparable in weight to cherry. Once plentiful, it is becoming rare because of Dutch elm disease, introduced into North America in the 1920s. Although fairly soft and very attractively figured, elm can be difficult to work because of its interlocked grain, which tends to tear out when planed. Also, elm is prone to warping. Given its rather light weight, it is a very tough wood. Its ability to withstand shock made it highly prized in the 19th Century for the ribbing in wooden war ships. Elm accepts fasteners without splitting and takes finishes very well, but gives off a rancid odor when cut, shaped, and sanded.

COMMON USES: Paneling, decorative veneers, boat building, cabinetry, furniture.
COST: Inexpensive, but becoming difficult to find.
ORIGIN: Eastern United States and southern Canada.
OTHER NAMES: American elm, gray elm, water elm.
BOTANICAL NAME: *Ulmus americana*.
WEIGHT: 2.7 pounds per board foot.
STATUS: Scarce because of blight.

HARDWOODS

GONCALO ALVES

Goncalo alves grows over a broad range. These various regions produce woods with different textures and densities. However, compared to familiar North American hardwoods, all goncalo alves lumber is very hard. Although physically demanding to work with hand tools, it polishes to a natural, smooth finish. The wood's figure is highly variable. It ranges from quite plain to a marble-like figure composed of chocolate-brown, gold, and sometimes rust-red swirls. It is one of the most attractive and unusual cabinet woods in the world. A member of the same family as poison sumac, goncalo alves is known to cause serious skin irritation for some individuals.

COMMON USES: Furniture, decorative veneer, carving, turning, knife handles, gunstocks.

COST: Expensive.

ORIGIN: Southern Mexico south to Brazil.

OTHER NAMES: Guarita, gateado, palo de cera.

BOTANICAL NAME: *Astronium graveolens*.

WEIGHT: 4.6 to 5.4 pounds per board foot.

STATUS: Plentiful, but highly figured logs are scarce.

HICKORY

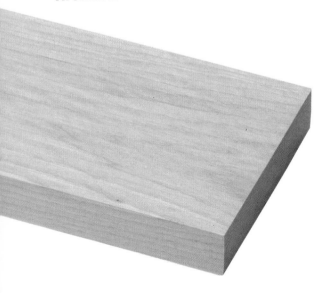

Although a member of the walnut family, which is found worldwide, the hickory genus *(Carya)* is exclusively North American. The dozen or so species in the genus are divided into two distinct cabinet woods: Hickory and pecan. Hickory is the harder, stronger, and lighter-colored of the two, but all species in the genus produce tough, very elastic woods prized worldwide for making hammer handles. For this purpose, the wood from fast-grown saplings with straight, wide annual rings is preferred. For cabinetmaking, the darker-colored heartwood of old growth trees provides more interesting figure. Hickory's density makes the wood difficult to work with hand tools.

COMMON USES: Tool handles, sports equipment, furniture, plywood veneer.

COST: Inexpensive to moderate.

ORIGIN: Eastern North America.

OTHER NAMES: Shagbark, shellbark, mockernut, pignut.

BOTANICAL NAME: Species of *Carya*.

WEIGHT: 3.7 to 4.3 pounds per board foot.

STATUS: Plentiful.

HOLLY

A very fine-textured, dense wood with minimum figure, holly is prized for the clarity of its pure white sapwood and heartwood. Since it has little resistance to decay organisms, it must be carefully seasoned to avoid blue staining. (See page 196 for more on blue stain and other wood defects.) A similar species, *Ilex aquifolium*, which is native to Europe, has been a part of the Western woodworking tradition for centuries. Holly's high rate of shrinkage makes it extremely unstable, but it is normally used in such small pieces that this shortcoming is manageable.

COMMON USES: Inlay, carving, turning, marquetry.
COST: Expensive.
ORIGIN: Southeastern United States, from central Texas to Massachusetts.
OTHER NAME: American holly.
BOTANICAL NAME: *Ilex opaca.*
WEIGHT: 3.8 pounds per board foot.
STATUS: Supplies are adequate.

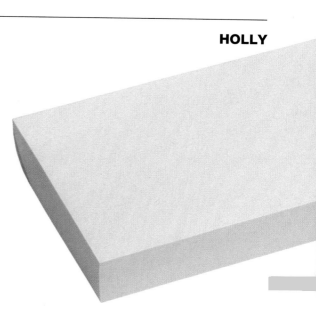

IROKO

Comparable in density to hard maple, but substantially coarser in texture, iroko varies in color from yellowish brown to a warm chocolate brown. Interlocked grain gives the wood an attractive ribbon figure when quarter-sawn. Iroko is exceptionally durable and recognized as an acceptable substitute for teak in boat building and other exterior applications. The wood works well and is very stable, but it contains chlorophorin, a sensitizing compound that may cause respiratory allergic reactions in some individuals.

COMMON USES: Boat building, flooring, furniture, veneer.
COST: Moderate but increasing.
ORIGIN: West Central Africa.
OTHER NAMES: Semli, odoum, rokko, oroko, kambala.
BOTANICAL NAMES: *Chlorophora excelsa* and *Chorophora regia.*
WEIGHT: 3.6 pounds per board foot.
STATUS: Becoming scarce as a result of increasing demand for iroko as a teak substitute.

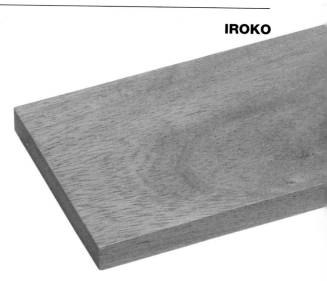

HARDWOODS

JARRAH

This dark red wood is hard, heavy, and coarse-textured. Because of its outstanding weathering characteristics and great strength, jarrah has long been popular for heavy construction applications. However, its attractive color and bold, coarse figure also make it an interesting, though challenging-to-work cabinet wood. Jarrah tends to fray when crosscut, leaving needle-sharp splinters, and is highly susceptible to checking. Pilot holes are required for fasteners, but adhesives and finishes adhere without difficulty. Fillers are required to achieve a smooth surface.

COMMON USES: Exterior decking, interior flooring, furniture.
COST: Moderate.
ORIGIN: Southwestern Australia.
OTHER NAME: Red ironwood.
BOTANICAL NAME: *Eucalyptus marginata.*
WEIGHT: 4.5 pounds per board foot.
STATUS: Supplies are adequate, but its increasing popularity as a durable species for exterior decking has increased demand.

KENTUCKY COFFEETREE

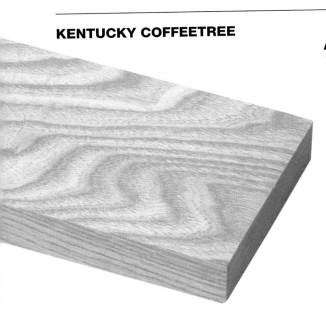

A reddish tan-colored wood with an attractive mahogany-like figure, coffeetree is about as dense as black walnut. With a low rate of shrinkage, green to oven-dry, it is relatively stable. The wood also holds fasteners well, cuts and shapes with little difficulty, and accepts adhesives and finishes very well. Throughout much of its range, this species seldom grows larger than a shrub, but given ideal growing conditions, it can attain 100 feet in height and 3 feet in diameter. Kentucky coffeetree is one of North America's most underutilized cabinet woods. It is difficult to find at most retail outlets, but it is well worth the effort.

COMMON USES: Turning, furniture, carving.
COST: Inexpensive, but difficult to find.
ORIGIN: Midwestern United States.
OTHER NAME: Coffee bean tree.
BOTANICAL NAME: *Gymnocladus dioicus.*
WEIGHT: 3.4 pounds per board foot.
STATUS: Moderately plentiful.

C ut from species in two separate genera native to Australia, the woods are nearly identical. Both have extremely lustrous and showy rays. When quarter-sawn or quarter-sliced into veneer, the rays produce an orderly, woven pattern. The wood has excellent working properties in virtually all respects except for its potential toxicity. Both the foliage and the wood contain a sensitizing phenol which affects some individuals like poison ivy.

COMMON USES: Decorative veneer, inlaying, marquetry, furniture, turning.

COST: Moderate to expensive with top-quality veneers selling at a premium.

ORIGIN: Australia and warm, arid regions throughout the world.

OTHER NAMES: Silky-oak, selena, grevillea.

BOTANICAL NAMES: *Cardwellia sublimis* and *Grevillea robusta*.

WEIGHT: 2.9 pounds per board foot.

STATUS: Supplies are adequate and sustainable.

LACEWOOD

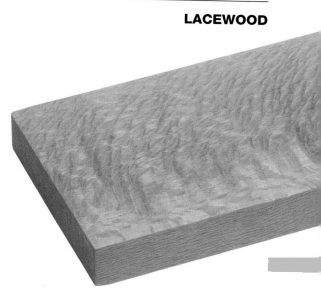

T he various lauans are so varied in terms of color, texture, and density that they are grouped and sold on the basis of these characteristics rather than by species. The softest of the light red lauans is comparable in weight to basswood, while the hardest and heaviest is about as dense as white oak. Although often referred to as "Philippine mahogany," because their color and figure can resemble genuine mahogany, lauans all lack mahogany's renowned stability and most have a much coarser texture. The lauans account for a larger percentage of the world's plywood production than any other hardwood.

COMMON USES: Plywood veneer, interior trim, cabinetry, furniture, heavy construction, flooring, paneling.

COST: Inexpensive to moderate.

ORIGIN: Southeast Asia, Philippines, Malaysia, Indonesia.

OTHER NAMES: Philippine mahogany, meranti, balau.

BOTANICAL NAME: Species of *Shorea*.

WEIGHT: 2.1 to 4.4 pounds per board foot.

STATUS: Plentiful, but rapidly declining.

LAUAN

HARDWOODS

LIGNUM VITAE

Lignum vitae is the heaviest of all commercially important timbers. Even when oven-dried, this wood is too heavy to float in water. The wood is grayish green, very fine-textured, oily, and exceedingly hard. Because of its great strength, durability and self-lubricating properties, it is a valuable industrial commodity that is becoming increasingly scarce. Lignum vitae trees grow extremely slowly and take centuries to reach full maturity.

COMMON USES: Turning, mallet heads, hand plane soles.
COST: Very expensive.
ORIGIN: West Indies, Central and South America.
OTHER NAMES: Guayacan, palo santo.
BOTANICAL NAME: *Guaiacum officinale.*
WEIGHT: 6.8 pounds per board foot.
STATUS: Supplies are critically scarce.

LOCUST

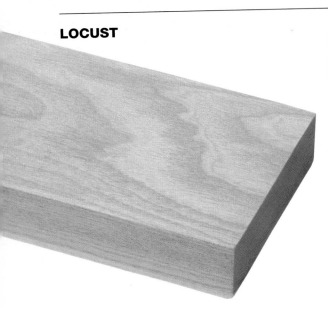

Hard, heavy, and extremely strong, locust ranks with hickory as one of the toughest woods native to North America. Although not as elastic as hickory, it is substantially more stable and much more durable. The wood ranges in color from creamy white to vivid yellow. Because of its extreme density, pilot holes are required for fasteners, but locust works well. During the 19th Century it was a favorite species for mallet heads and the pegs used to fasten posts and beams together.

COMMON USES: Turing, furniture.
ORIGIN: Midwestern United States.
COST: Inexpensive.
OTHER NAME: Black locust.
BOTANICAL NAME: *Robinia pseudoacacia.*
WEIGHT: 4.2 pounds per board foot.
STATUS: Plentiful.

MAHOGANY, SOUTH AMERICAN

Arguably the world's best all-around cabinet wood, mahogany is often used as the standard to which other hardwoods are compared. It is the most stable of the world's major timbers, though its color and density can vary widely as a result of growing conditions. The name mahogany is believed to be of American Indian origin, and properly includes woods of the *Swietenia* genus. African mahogany, belonging to the genus *Khaya*, is also an exceptionally fine cabinet wood and a member of the broader mahogany family.

COMMON USES: Fine furniture, cabinetry, decorative veneers, turning, carving, model making.

COST: Moderate.

ORIGIN: Central and South America from Mexico to Brazil.

OTHER NAMES: American mahogany, Honduras mahogany, caoba.

BOTANICAL NAME: *Swietenia macrophylla*.

WEIGHT: 2.5 to 4.3 pounds per board foot.

STATUS: Rapidly becoming scarce.

MAPLE, HARD

The woods of sugar maple and black maple are nearly identical. Both are regarded as "hard" maple by the lumber trade. Hard maple is strong, fine-textured, and light creamy tan. It turns well, resists abrasion, and polishes to a smooth natural finish. While ordinary maple lumber has a very subtle figure, maple also produces bird's-eye, fiddleback (tiger stripe), and quilted figures. The irregular grain direction in these special figures tends to tear out; they require extreme care when planing and shaping.

COMMON USES: Turning, decorative veneer, flooring, interior trim, cabinetry, plywood, furniture.

COST: Moderate, but figures such as bird's-eye and fiddleback sell at a premium.

ORIGIN: Eastern United States and southeastern Canada.

OTHER NAMES: Hard maple, sugar maple, black maple, rock maple.

BOTANICAL NAMES: *Acer saccharum* and *Acer nigrum*.

WEIGHT: 3.2 pounds per board foot.

STATUS: Plentiful except for bird's-eye and fiddleback.

HARDWOODS

MESQUITE

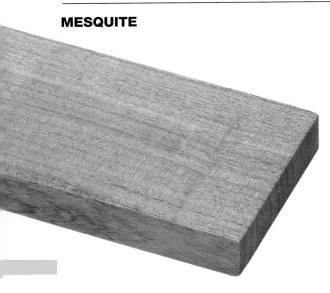

As a scrub tree that seldom grows higher than 50 feet, mesquite does not yield lumber in the conventional sense. This is unfortunate, because the wood is extremely attractive and would make a good substitute for the now scarce Hawaiian koa, to which it is closely related. Mesquite is reddish brown, moderately coarse-textured, hard, heavy, and strong. It turns exceptionally well and, if properly seasoned, it has relatively good stability. The wood is enjoyable to work because of its pleasant scent. Mesquite has a low natural luster, but a coat of varnish brings out hidden highlights.

COMMON USES: Turning, carving, cabinetry, flooring.
COST: Inexpensive, but difficult to find at retail outlets.
ORIGIN: Southwestern United States, Mexico, Central and South America.
OTHER NAMES: Screwbean, algaroba, tornillo.
BOTANICAL NAME: *Prosopis juliflora*.
WEIGHT: 4.2 to 4.8 pounds per board foot.
STATUS: Plentiful.

MYRTLE

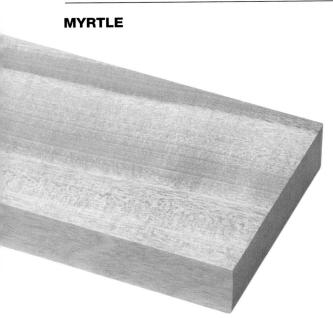

A diffuse-porous wood with a soft, golden hue sometimes displaying pink or purple highlights, myrtle is comparable in density to black walnut. It has good working characteristics but is perhaps most prized for its burl and mottled veneers. As a member of the laurel family *(Lauraceae)*, like sassafras, it has a pleasant scent. The tree is usually small and poorly shaped for lumber production, but it can attain a height of 80 feet and diameters of up to about 3 feet.

COMMON USES: Decorative veneers, furniture, cabinetry.
COST: Moderate for ordinary lumber, but burl is expensive.
ORIGIN: West coast of North America from extreme northern Baja to central Oregon.
OTHER NAMES: Oregon myrtle, California laurel, pepperwood, spice tree.
BOTANICAL NAME: *Umbellularia californica*.
WEIGHT: 2.9 pounds per board foot.
STATUS: Supplies are adequate.

A bout 50 species of oak are native to North America, but the lumber trade separates them into only two groups: red oak and white oak. Most of the oak now used is red oak, a ring-porous wood with a loud figure and dark ray flecks. The wood's overall color is pinkish tan. The heartwood may be streaked with dark brown stains or edged by pinkish yellow sapwood. Oak is coarse-textured and requires a filler for a smooth finish, but its other working properties are good. Its high tannin content gives the wood a harsh scent. Fasteners containing iron should be avoided, since tannin reacts with iron, turning the surrounding wood black.

OAK, RED

COMMON USES: Trim, cabinetry, plywood, furniture.
COST: Moderate.
ORIGIN: Eastern United States and southeastern Canada.
OTHER NAMES: Northern red oak, gray oak, pin oak, black oak, scarlet oak.
BOTANICAL NAME: Species of *Quercus* (*Quercus rubra*).
WEIGHT: 3.2 pounds per board foot.
STATUS: Plentiful.

W hite oak is stronger, harder, and more durable than red oak. The primary species used for lumber production is Eastern white oak, but midwestern bur oak is also a major species. The rays in white oak are generally larger and lighter in color than those in red oak, and when the wood is quarter-sawn they yield a wild and lustrous figure sometimes referred to as silvered oak. White oak owes its superior decay resistance to the fact that the pores are clogged with tyloses, which hold out moisture. For this same reason, white oak can be used for tight cooperage, such as wine barrels, while red oak is too porous to hold liquids.

OAK, WHITE

COMMON USES: Cabinetry, flooring, interior trim, plywood, boat building, tight cooperage (wine barrels), furniture.
COST: Moderate.
ORIGIN: United States and Canada.
OTHER NAMES: Swamp oak, chestnut oak, bur oak, overcup oak.
BOTANICAL NAME: Species of *Quercus* (*Quercus alba*).
WEIGHT: 3.7 pounds per board foot.
STATUS: Plentiful.

HARDWOODS

OLIVEWOOD

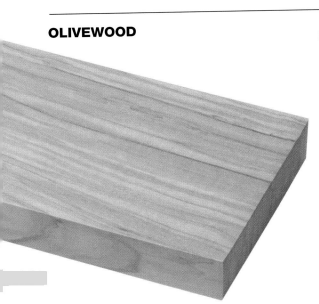

Grown primarily for its fruit and oil, the olive tree is too small to be a major source of timber, but its wood has long been prized for carving and turning. Olivewood has a very uniform and smooth texture, and will hold fine details without chipping. Its color is light golden tan with darker brown swirls. The figure of the wood has considerable character and it is pleasant to work with because of its mild fragrant scent. Woodworkers with access to olive orchards can forage for the wood; it is difficult to find through commercial sources.

COMMON USES: Inlay, turning, carving, marquetry.

COST: Very expensive and difficult to find through commercial hardwood channels.

ORIGIN: Southern Europe, Middle East, coastal North Africa, California, Australia.

OTHER NAME: Olive.

BOTANICAL NAME: *Olea europea*.

WEIGHT: 4.2 to 4.6 pounds per board foot.

STATUS: Supply is sustainable.

OSAGE ORANGE

Extremely hard, heavy and very elastic, osage orange is best known for its vivid yellow color. A small scrub tree originally native to Louisiana, Texas, and Arkansas, it was widely planted throughout the midwestern United States in the 19th Century by farmers who used it as a hedgerow to restrain livestock. The pigment that gives the wood its yellow color is water soluble and was once popular as a fabric dye. The wood is relatively unstable and difficult to work. It is extremely durable, but loses its vivid color when left exposed. Although varnish helps to retard the wood's patina-developing process, it eventually turns amber brown.

COMMON USES: Turning, marquetry, hunting bows (American Indian).

COST: Moderately expensive.

ORIGIN: Midwestern United States.

OTHER NAMES: Bois d'arc, bodark.

BOTANICAL NAME: *Maclura pomifera*.

WEIGHT: 4.4 pounds per board foot.

STATUS: Relatively scarce.

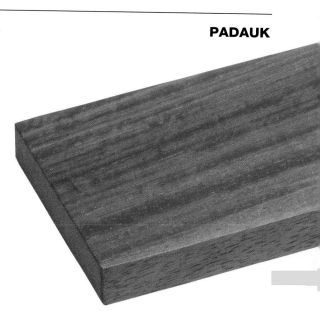

PADAUK

Padauk comes from two closely related species, one native to the Andaman Islands off the east coast of India and the other from the rain forests of equatorial Africa. Both are coarse-textured, heavy, strong timbers and vivid red in color. The Andaman variety is very rare and therefore difficult to buy. African padauk is usually slightly softer, coarser-textured, and less figured, but with very attractive purple highlights. African padauk experiences color change with exposure. Both varieties often have interlocked grain that tends to tear out when planed. Otherwise, their working characteristics are good.

COMMON USES: Turning, carving, flooring, decorative veneer, inlay, marquetry, furniture.
COST: Moderate to expensive.
ORIGIN: Andaman Islands and west central Africa.
OTHER NAMES: Vermilion, andaman redwood, ngula.
BOTANICAL NAMES: *Pterocarpus dalbergioides* and *Pterocarpus soyauxii*.
WEIGHT: 3.5 to 4.2 pounds per board foot.
STATUS: Andaman padauk is very rare; the African variety is becoming scarce.

PECAN

Pecan belongs to the hickory genus, *Carya*. The same species that produces commercial pecan nuts yields the wood traditionally used in French Provincial furniture of American origin. It is a darker, cinnamon-tan and softer than most other hickories. The softest of the pecan hickories is nutmeg hickory, an exceptionally fine cabinet wood. However, it is seldom marketed separately. The wood of bitternut hickory, a northern species, is also sold as pecan, but it is generally harder and lighter in color than any of the southern pecans. Pecan wood is difficult to work with hand tools, but it machines well.

COMMON USES: Furniture, veneer, turning, tool handles.
COST: Moderate.
ORIGIN: Midwestern United States.
OTHER NAMES: Sweet pecan, bitter pecan, bitternut hickory, nutmeg hickory.
BOTANICAL NAME: Species of *Carya*.
WEIGHT: 3.2 to 3.7 pounds per board foot.
STATUS: Supplies are adequate but quality is highly variable.

HARDWOODS

POPLAR, YELLOW

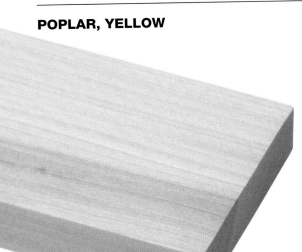

Yellow poplar is a diffuse-porous, fine-textured wood with stark white sapwood and olive drab heartwood, sometimes streaked with black or chocolate-brown stains. The tree grows quickly and can reach heights of up to 200 feet, making it an outstanding timber species. The wood is soft, easily worked, and relatively stable. It accepts fasteners without splitting and makes an excellent secondary wood for drawer sides and internal parts. Yellow poplar accepts stains, varnish, and other clear finishes well.

COMMON USES: Cabinetmaking, interior trim, furniture, plywood veneers.

COST: Inexpensive.

ORIGIN: Eastern United States.

OTHER NAMES: American whitewood (sapwood), tulip poplar, tuliptree.

BOTANICAL NAME: *Liriodendron tulipifera*.

WEIGHT: 2.5 pounds per board foot.

STATUS: Plentiful.

PURPLEHEART

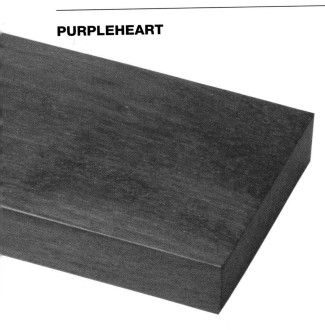

One of the most vividly colored woods in the world, purpleheart is produced by more than a dozen species. Although always some shade of purple, the vessel flecks may range from white to black in color. Usually brittle and somewhat stringy, it can be difficult to work with. Freshly cut surfaces tend to be lighter in color, but soon darken with exposure. Although a sealing coat of varnish will retard the wood's patina-building process, the vivid purple color changes to a warm amber brown over time. Purpleheart is very durable and a good choice for exterior projects.

COMMON USES: Turning, inlay, marquetry, decorative veneer, flooring, pool cues, boat building, furniture.

COST: Moderate.

ORIGIN: Central and South America, from southern Mexico to Brazil.

OTHER NAMES: Palo morado, amaranth, nazareno, pau roxo, violetwood.

BOTANICAL NAME: Species of *Peltogyne*.

WEIGHT: 4.2 to 5.5 pounds per board foot.

STATUS: Relatively plentiful.

The widespread rosewood genus *Dalbergia* produces more than a dozen timbers. All rank among the world's most attractive and prized woods, including kingwood, cocobolo, and tulipwood. Brazilian rosewood *(see photo, page 209)* is now so rare that its export is prohibited. Indonesian rosewood, a slightly coarser-textured and less-figured wood, is available in limited quantities. Most rosewoods are hard, with marble-like figure and a soft, oily luster. They machine very well and give off an aromatic scent, but the dust is irritating and can be toxic.

COMMON USES: Cabinetry, decorative veneer, turning, inlay, marquetry, musical instruments.
COST: Very expensive.
ORIGIN: Tropical America, India, Southeast Asia.
OTHER NAMES: Brazilian rosewood, Honduras rosewood, Indonesian rosewood.
BOTANICAL NAME: Species of *Dalbergia*.
WEIGHT: 3.9 to 5.3 pounds per board foot.
STATUS: Very rare; several species now endangered.

ROSEWOOD, INDONESIAN

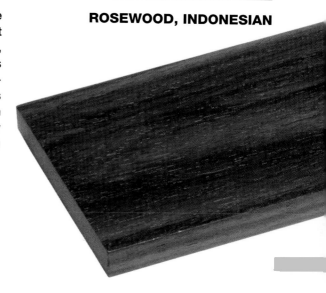

Although sassafras looks like black ash, and the two are frequently sold together as "mixed hardwoods," they may be easily distinguished on the basis of weight and scent. Sassafras is much softer and lighter in weight than black ash, and its spicy aroma is both pleasant and unmistakable. Sassafras is easy to work, but very prone to splitting and checking. It is too soft and brittle for many of the furniture applications in which ash excels, such as bentwood chairs and tables, but it is far superior to ash in exterior applications. Its durability and buoyancy make it popular in boat building.

COMMON USES: Furniture, turning, carving, musical instruments.
COST: Inexpensive.
ORIGIN: Eastern United States.
OTHER NAMES: Red sassafras, cinnamon wood.
BOTANICAL NAME: *Sassafras albidum*.
WEIGHT: 2.7 pounds per board foot.
STATUS: Supplies are adequate but limited; the tree achieves timber size only in ideal growing conditions.

SASSAFRAS

HARDWOODS

SATINWOOD

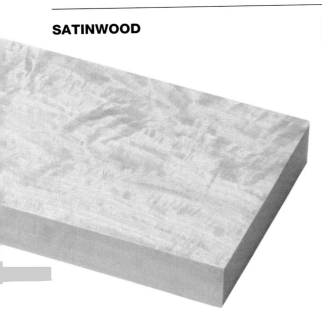

Fine-textured, highly lustrous, and extremely hard, satinwood generally has interlocked grain and produces attractive veneers. The golden yellow wood refracts light in such a way that it sparkles with jewel-like translucence. Because satinwood is rare, it is usually used in veneer form, although several unrelated species with similar color and texture are also marketed as satinwood and are reasonably good substitutes. Satinwood is dense and therefore difficult to work with hand tools, but it machines well and gives off a fragrant scent when heated by the friction of abrasives or high-speed cutters.

COMMON USES: Veneer, turning, inlay, furniture.
COST: Expensive.
ORIGIN: Southern India and Sri Lanka.
OTHER NAMES: Ceylon satinwood, East Indian satinwood, billu.
BOTANICAL NAME: *Chloroxylon swietenia*.
WEIGHT: 5.1 pounds per board foot.
STATUS: Very scarce.

SWEETGUM

About as dense and hard as cherry, the heartwood of sweetgum—called red gum in the lumber trade—is a dull grayish pink or warm brown. Fine-textured and rather bland in figure, this wood is frequently used in commercial furniture making. It can be stained to resemble other woods and used for inconspicuous parts or for the framing in upholstered pieces. As a primary wood, it is more popular in Europe where it is referred to as silver walnut. Although the wood works well and accepts adhesives and finishes without difficulty, it experiences high shrinkage and is prone to cupping and twisting.

COMMON USES: Furniture parts, trim, cabinetry, plywood.
COST: Inexpensive.
ORIGIN: Eastern United States, from Florida to New Jersey and west to Texas.
OTHER NAMES: Red gum, star gum, silver walnut (Europe).
BOTANICAL NAME: *Liquidambar styraciflua*.
WEIGHT: 2.6 pounds per board foot.
STATUS: Plentiful.

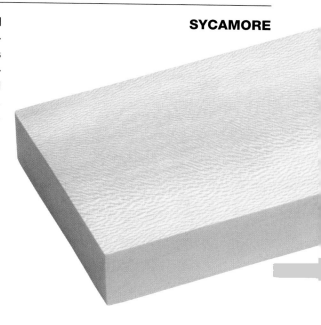

SYCAMORE

Sycamore is a diffuse-porous, moderately fine-textured wood with a light grayish yellow color. Its figure is dominated by plentiful and very lustrous ray flecks. Although its rays are somewhat smaller than those of lacewood (silky-oak), the two woods have a similar quarter-sawn figure and both produce stunning quarter-sliced veneer. Sycamore is extremely hard to split. Its relatively high volumetric shrinkage makes it a little unstable, but it works well. It is available in wide, thick planks.

COMMON USES: Decorative veneer, inlay, turning, furniture.
COST: Inexpensive
ORIGIN: Eastern United States and extreme southern Ontario.
OTHER NAMES: Buttonwood, American planetree, water beech.
BOTANICAL NAME: *Platanus occidentalis.*
WEIGHT: 2.6 pounds per board foot.
STATUS: Plentiful.

TEAK

Golden brown in color, relatively coarse-textured and noticeably oily to the touch, teak is one of the world's most durable woods. Long a favorite species for shipbuilding and decking, it has been so heavily logged that it is now scarce in the wild. Fortunately, it responds well to plantation management and is now being grown commercially both in southeast Asia and tropical America. About as dense as red oak, teak wood is not difficult to work, but its high oil content causes problems with adhesives and finishes, and its high silica content makes it very hard on planer knives. It has a pleasant aromatic scent, but the dust can cause allergic reactions, primarily skin rash.

COMMON USES: Boat building, veneer, cabinetry, furniture, turning, carving, flooring.
COST: Expensive.
ORIGIN: Native to southeastern Asia; now grown on plantations elsewhere in the tropics.
OTHER NAMES: Eyun, sagwan.
BOTANICAL NAME: *Tectona grandis.*
WEIGHT: 3.3 pounds per board foot.
STATUS: Scarce.

HARDWOODS

TULIPWOOD

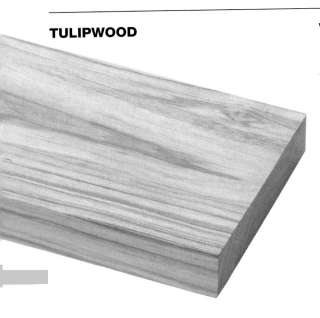

Very fine-textured and hard, tulipwood is the lightest-colored wood in the rosewood genus. A creamy yellow with beautiful, coral-pink swirls at its best, it is easy to mistake for fine marble. Like Brazilian rosewood, it is now extremely scarce and will undoubtedly remain so. This species is a small, slow-growing tree and only very old specimens yield vividly pigmented wood. Like other rosewoods, tulipwood has a pleasant, floral scent, but it can be toxic. Although excessive exposure to the dust presents the greatest risk, some individuals experience a reaction by merely touching the wood.

COMMON USES: Decorative veneer, turning, inlay, marquetry, fine furniture.
COST: Very expensive.
ORIGIN: Brazil.
OTHER NAMES: Pinkwood, jacaranda rosa, pau de fuso.
BOTANICAL NAME: *Dalbergia frutescens*.
WEIGHT: 5.4 pounds per board foot.
STATUS: Rare.

WALNUT, BLACK

One of the world's most prized cabinet woods, walnut has excellent working properties. Dark chocolate brown, occasionally with magenta or purple highlights, the characteristic color of walnut is so popular that many less attractive cabinet woods are stained to imitate it. Walnut's ability to absorb shock and its beautiful figure make it an outstanding choice for high-quality gun stocks. The wood contains a complex compound, juglone, which has antiseptic, sedative, and laxative properties. Many woodworkers find walnut's strong odor pleasant. Decorative walnut veneers, such as stump, crotch, and burl, are exceptionally popular and correspondingly expensive.

COMMON USES: Furniture, cabinetry, carving, turning, decorative veneers, musical instruments, inlay, marquetry.
COST: Moderately expensive.
ORIGIN: Eastern United States and southeastern Canada.
OTHER NAMES: American walnut.
BOTANICAL NAME: *Juglans nigra*.
WEIGHT: 2.9 pounds per board foot.
STATUS: Supplies are adequate.

Hard, and very coarse-textured, wenge's greatest virtue is its stunning black and brown color. Although it produces beautiful veneer, wenge is difficult to slice and therefore quite expensive. Wenge has high resistance to shock and is relatively elastic, making it a good wood for hammer handles. It is also very durable and stable. Unfortunately, it is so fibrous and tough that it is difficult to cut and shape.

COMMON USES: Decorative veneer, furniture, tool handles, flooring.
COST: Moderately expensive.
ORIGIN: Equatorial Africa.
OTHER NAMES: Awong, panga panga, mpande.
BOTANICAL NAME: Species of *Milletia*.
WEIGHT: 4.2 to 5 pounds per board foot.
STATUS: Becoming scarce.

WENGE

About as soft as white pine, black willow is easy to work with hand tools. Because of its fine texture, it will hold sharp details when shaped and carved. Although classed as a diffuse-porous wood, its earlywood pores are large enough to give it a subtle but interesting figure, and its light pinkish tan color is very attractive. The tree tends to grow in a gnarly fashion and consequently the lumber is not usually available in long lengths. However, it is a good, inexpensive utility wood for small projects. A fast grower, black willow often contains reaction wood that may cause it to warp, check, and accept stains unevenly.

COMMON USES: Furniture, carving, turning.
COST: Inexpensive.
ORIGIN: Extreme southeastern Canada, eastern United States and north-central Mexico.
OTHER NAMES: Willow, native willow.
BOTANICAL NAME: *Salix nigra*.
WEIGHT: 2.2 pounds per board foot.
STATUS: Plentiful.

WILLOW, BLACK

HARDWOODS

ZEBRAWOOD

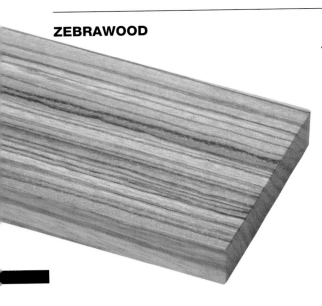

A golden yellow wood with jet-black stripes, zebrawood makes stunningly attractive veneer. Hard and moderately coarse-textured, the wood is difficult to work and its interlocked grain tends to tear out when planed. Its high rate of shrinkage causes serious drying stress and it can be somewhat unpredictable in use. Because zebrawood is becoming more scarce, wood from the tree's enlarged lower trunk—called a buttress—occasionally ends up being sold. Lumber containing buttress wood is usually softer, extremely unstable, and tends to fracture, producing fine checks across the grain.

COMMON USES: Decorative veneers, inlay, turning, furniture, tool handles.

COST: Expensive.

ORIGIN: West central Africa.

OTHER NAMES: Zibrano, zingana.

BOTANICAL NAME: *Microberlinia brazzavillensis*.

WEIGHT: 4.4 pounds per board foot.

STATUS: Scarce.

ZIRICOTE

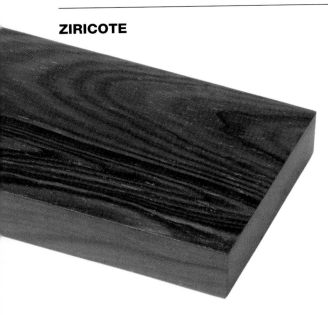

Many woods of the *Cordia* genus vary from soft to hard and from fine- to coarse-textured. Most are rather bland in appearance and used primarily in rough construction within their native ranges. However, a few species are extremely attractive and produce high-quality cabinet woods, such as bocote and ziricote. Ziricote is similar to bocote in most respects except for color. While bocote displays a strong golden yellow color with black marbling, ziricote is dark brown with black marbling, giving it a more subdued figure. Although hard, ziricote has reasonably good working characteristics and finishes exceptionally well.

COMMON USES: Furniture, flooring, turning, decorative veneer.

COST: Expensive.

ORIGIN: Central and South America.

OTHER NAMES: Cordia, siricote.

BOTANICAL NAME: *Cordia dodecandra*.

WEIGHT: 4.0 to 5.4 pounds per board foot.

STATUS: There is an adequate supply of the timber.

BALDCYPRESS

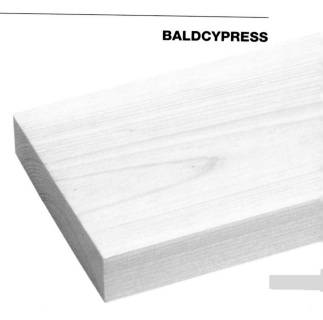

A member of the same family as redwood, baldcypress is an ancient species which was once widespread in North America and Europe. The wood is warm tan in color with a satiny luster and an oily feel. The heartwood of older trees is exceptionally durable and is often used for boat building. The sapwood and the heartwood of young, second-growth timber is less durable. Baldcypress works well and is substantially stronger than its redwood cousin. It grows slowly, and good-quality old-growth timber is becoming difficult to find.

COMMON USES: Construction, paneling, vats, fence posts, boat building, millwork, outdoor furniture.

COST: Moderate.

ORIGIN: Southeastern coastal United States and Mississippi basin as far north as southern Illinois.

OTHER NAMES: Pondcypress, red cypress, yellow cypress, gulf cypress.

BOTANICAL NAME: *Taxodium distichum*.

WEIGHT: 2.7 pounds per board foot.

STATUS: Old-growth timber is becoming scarce.

CEDAR, AROMATIC

This fine-textured, reddish-brown wood is much prized for making blanket chests and wardrobes because of its aromatic scent. The wood shapes and carves very well, but it is exceptionally brittle and often splits when nailed. Its volatile oils interfere with turpentine-based finishes, preventing them from curing. Being a rather small, slow-growing tree, most aromatic cedar contains a multitude of small knots and even the heartwood may contain random patches of yellowish white sapwood. Although in most woods these features would be considered defects, they give aromatic cedar a certain rustic charm.

COMMON USES: Furniture (chests and wardrobes), closet lining, carving, fence posts, flooring, pencils.

COST: Moderate.

ORIGIN: Eastern United States and southeastern Ontario.

OTHER NAMES: Eastern red cedar, juniper.

BOTANICAL NAME: *Juniperus virginiana*.

WEIGHT: 2.7 pounds per board foot.

STATUS: Supplies are adequate, but large, old-growth trees are becoming scarce.

SOFTWOODS

CEDAR, WESTERN RED

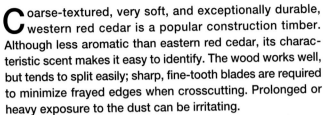

Coarse-textured, very soft, and exceptionally durable, western red cedar is a popular construction timber. Although less aromatic than eastern red cedar, its characteristic scent makes it easy to identify. The wood works well, but tends to split easily; sharp, fine-tooth blades are required to minimize frayed edges when crosscutting. Prolonged or heavy exposure to the dust can be irritating.

COMMON USES: Decking, siding, interior paneling, lawn furniture, millwork, dugout canoes (American Indian).
COST: Inexpensive.
ORIGIN: West coast of North America from northern California to Alaska and sporadically in moist habitats in the northern Rocky Mountains.
OTHER NAMES: Canoe cedar, giant arborvitae.
BOTANICAL NAME: *Thuja plicata.*
WEIGHT: 1.9 pounds per board foot.
STATUS: Supplies are presently adequate, but this species cannot sustain the current rate of harvest.

DOUGLAS-FIR

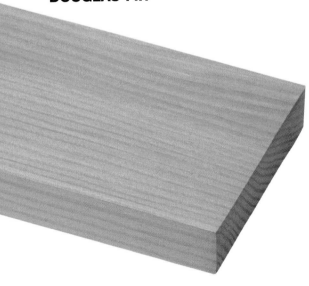

Douglas-fir is a resinous member of the pine family *(Pinaceae),* but not a true fir. Usually thought of as a construction timber, a role in which it excels, Douglas-fir has many characteristics that also make it a respectable cabinet wood. It is relatively hard and strong for a softwood, and it has a pleasant orange-brown color and an attractive linear grain pattern when quarter-sawn. The wood works well, but it contains an irritant so that even minor wounds caused by Douglas-fir splinters are painful and slow to heal.

COMMON USES: Heavy construction, flooring, plywood, siding, paneling, furniture, boat building.
COST: Inexpensive to moderate.
ORIGIN: Northwestern United States and southwestern Canada, south through the Rocky Mountains to northern Mexico.
OTHER NAMES: Oregon pine, red fir, Douglas spruce, douglasie.
BOTANICAL NAME: *Pseudotsuga menziesii.*
WEIGHT: 2.8 pounds per board foot.
STATUS: Very plentiful, but logging restrictions are constricting the supply.

In the lumber trade, southern yellow pine refers to woods of more than half a dozen separate species. Although there are noticeable differences in their weight, they are similar in appearance, possessing a racy figure, coarse texture, and high resin content. A natural source of turpentine, they also have a strong resinous scent. Although they have been used for centuries in southern country-style furniture, they are better known as construction timbers.

PINE, SOUTHERN YELLOW

COMMON USES: Construction, decking, construction plywood, flooring, shipbuilding, rustic furniture.
COST: Inexpensive.
ORIGIN: Southeastern United States and now also plantation-grown in South America.
OTHER NAMES: Loblolly, longleaf, shortleaf, slash and Virginia pines.
BOTANICAL NAME: Species of *Pinus*.
WEIGHT: 2.6 to 3.6 pounds per board foot.
STATUS: Very plentiful.

Three North American species account for virtually all white pine lumber: Western white pine, Eastern white pine, and sugar pine. Eastern white pine was used in primitive, country-style furniture in New England during the American colonial period. Western white pine, often marketed as Idaho white pine (IWP), is almost identical to the eastern species. Sugar pine has very large resin canals that mark its figure with fine dark lines. All these pines have excellent working characteristics, but they are so soft that furniture made with them needs heavier panels and stouter framework.

PINE, WHITE

COMMON USES: Interior trim, cabinetry, millwork, furniture, carving, model making.
COST: Inexpensive to moderate.
ORIGIN: United States, Canada, Mexico.
OTHER NAMES: Idaho white pine, Western white pine, Northern pine, sugar pine, Eastern white pine.
BOTANICAL NAME: Species of *Pinus*.
WEIGHT: 2.1 pounds per board foot.
STATUS: Supplies are adequate.

SOFTWOODS

REDWOOD

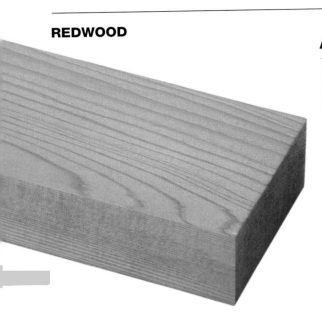

Although not as massive as its close cousin, giant sequoia, redwood is the tallest tree in the world. The wood is fine-textured and deep reddish brown. Because of its great durability, it has been a popular choice for exterior siding, decking, and lawn furniture, but most of the remaining virgin stands of this species are now protected. Although redwood regenerates quickly, the lumber obtained from immature second-growth trees is lighter in color, with wider annual rings, and is far less durable. As this second-growth timber matures, redwood will likely become more available in the 21st Century.

COMMON USES: Siding, decking, millwork, exterior furniture.
COST: Moderate.
ORIGIN: Coastal California and southwestern Oregon.
OTHER NAMES: Coast redwood, California redwood.
BOTANICAL NAME: *Sequoia sempervirens*.
WEIGHT: 2.2 pounds per board foot.
STATUS: Remaining virgin stands of this species are now protected so that old-growth redwood lumber is scarce.

SPRUCE

Spruce dominates the boreal forests of Canada, northern Europe, and Siberia. In this harsh, cold environment, trees rarely grow to great size, but along part of the Pacific coast of North America, sitka spruce reaches heights of more than 200 feet. Spruce wood is yellowish white, occasionally with reddish orange streaks in the heartwood. It has a very high strength-to-weight ratio and similar working characteristics to pine. Its unique resonance properties make it ideal for sound boards in stringed and keyboard musical instruments.

COMMON USES: Millwork, boat building, musical instruments.
COST: Inexpensive.
ORIGIN: Temperate and boreal forest of North America with similar species plentiful in both Europe and Asia.
OTHER NAMES: Black spruce, red spruce, white spruce, Engelmann spruce, sitka spruce.
BOTANICAL NAME: Species of *Picea*.
WEIGHT: 2.2 pounds per board foot.
STATUS: Very plentiful.

DRYING WOOD

The aim of kiln drying and air drying is to reduce the moisture content of wood to a level in balance with the environment in which the wood will be used. This level is roughly 12 to 15 percent. Since wood seeks this Equilibrium Moisture Content (EMC) anyway, it would seem immaterial which method is used. In reality, though, there can be substantial differences between kiln-dried and air-dried lumber. Aside from reducing the time required to season wood, the kiln drying process has other advantages. Because temperature and moisture conditions within a kiln can be closely controlled, accurate kiln schedules can be followed for different wood species. Also, the relatively high temperatures used in kiln drying make it possible to relieve some of the drying stress in lumber.

Air-dried lumber has its advantages too. While more time-consuming, the process is less costly. It also has a lesser effect on the color of some species. Learning to air dry lumber offers the woodworker both economy and variety.

The air drying process is relatively simple. Once your green boards are cut, stack them in what is called a drying pile, as shown at right. Set up the pile above the ground on a platform of concrete blocks and 4 x 4s so that air circulates around all the surfaces of each board. The boards should be spaced about 1 inch apart in each layer and the layers separated with spacers, called stickers. Use dried wood for stickers to avoid staining your stock. The stickers should be of uniform thickness, laid down across the boards at about 2-foot intervals, and positioned directly above the stickers in the previous layer. This arrangement allows the stickers to bear the weight of the pile without distorting the still relatively pliable green boards. To protect the pile from precipitation and to force the boards flat while they dry, set a sheet of plywood on top of the last row of stickers and weight it down with stones or cement blocks. To minimize end checking, coat the end grain of each board with a sealer.

A small quantity of lumber earmarked for a specific room of a home can be air dried in an inconspicuous spot in the room. Depending upon climate, most species of 1-inch-thick lumber can be adequately seasoned in less than a year. Both kiln-dried and air-dried lumber should be brought into the shop well in advance of when it will be used to allow it to adjust to interior humidity conditions.

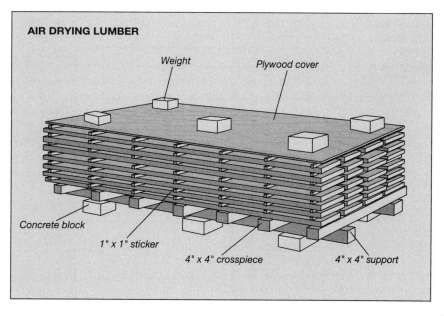

AIR DRYING LUMBER

Weight

Plywood cover

Concrete block

1" x 1" sticker

4" x 4" crosspiece

4" x 4" support

WOOD SHRINKAGE

WOOD SHRINKAGE

Wood shrinkage varies greatly from one species to another both in terms of the overall amount of shrinkage and also in the difference between radial and tangential shrinkage. On average, most woods shrink about 12 to 14 percent in overall volume as they dry from their "green" state (any moisture content above their fiber saturation point) down to "oven-dry" (0 percent moisture content). However, it is the difference between a wood's radial shrinkage (across the annual rings) and its tangential shrinkage (parallel to the rings) that causes it to distort or warp. As shown in the chart below, most woods tend to shrink about twice as much tangentially as they do radially. But virtually no shrinkage occurs longitudinally (along the grain). Keep in mind that these percentages represent the average maximum shrinkage potential from green to oven-dry wood. Since the normal moisture content of cabinet wood at the time it is used ranges between 8 and 12 percent, the actual shrinkage values will amount to perhaps two-thirds of what is indicated in the chart.

The illustration at left depicts how a typical board (in this case, a 1 x 12 plank of maple) would shrink across its width as it dries from its FSP down to 0 percent moisture.

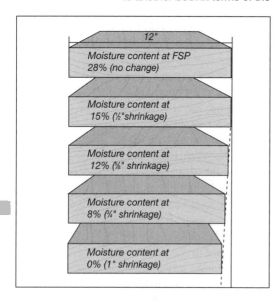

SHRINKAGE VALUES OF SELECTED WOOD SPECIES

SPECIES	TANGEN-TIAL (%)	RADIAL (%)	SPECIES	TANGEN-TIAL (%)	RADIAL (%)
Ash, white	7.8	4.9	Mahogany, Honduras	4.1	3.0
Basswood, American	9.3	6.6	Maple, sugar	9.9	4.8
Beech, American	11.9	5.5	Oak, Northern red	8.6	4.0
Butternut	6.4	3.4	Oak, white	10.5	5.6
Cedar, Western red	5.0	2.4	Pine, Eastern white	6.1	2.1
Cherry, black	7.1	3.7	Pine, ponderosa	6.2	3.9
Douglas-fir	7.5	4.8	Sycamore, American	8.4	5.0
Elm, American	9.5	4.2	Teak	5.8	2.5
Hickory, shagbark	10.5	7.0	Walnut, black	7.8	5.5

As illustrated at right, a typical flat-sawn board with the annual rings running roughly parallel to its faces will experience far more shrinkage across its width than it will in thickness or length. Since boards are normally much wider than they are thick, the loss in width is more noticeable and usually of greater concern to the woodworker.

The illustration below demonstrates how a board's original location in the log will have a bearing on how it shrinks. Flat-sawn boards, aside from experiencing greater shrinkage in width, tend to cup, with the edges lifting outward away from the heartwood side of the board. Quarter-sawn boards, whose annual rings generally run perpendicular to the faces, will shrink the least in width and, more importantly, do not have a tendency to cup. Square pieces, such as 2 x 2 and 4 x 4 stock, may distort and become out-of-square if they are cut with their annual rings running diagonally from corner to corner.

DIRECTION OF WOOD SHRINKAGE

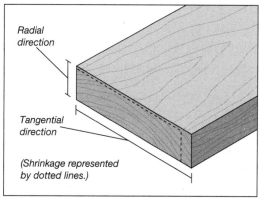

Radial direction

Tangential direction

(Shrinkage represented by dotted lines.)

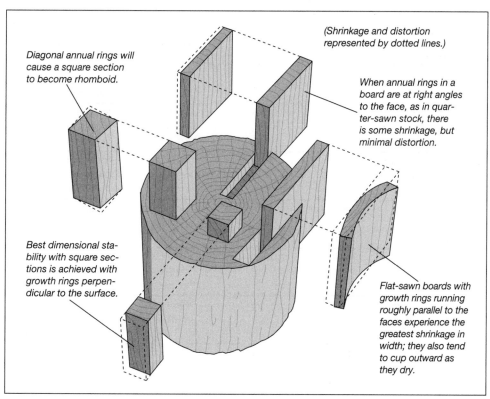

(Shrinkage and distortion represented by dotted lines.)

Diagonal annual rings will cause a square section to become rhomboid.

When annual rings in a board are at right angles to the face, as in quarter-sawn stock, there is some shrinkage, but minimal distortion.

Best dimensional stability with square sections is achieved with growth rings perpendicular to the surface.

Flat-sawn boards with growth rings running roughly parallel to the faces experience the greatest shrinkage in width; they also tend to cup outward as they dry.

VENEERS

The use of thin sheets of rare woods to cover furniture made of less attractive but more plentiful species dates back at least to the time of ancient Egypt. Veneering has undeniable benefits as a means of conserving precious woods and creating glamorous furniture at a fraction of the cost of using solid stock. But if economy were veneer's only virtue, it is unlikely it would feature so prominently in the tombs of pharaohs and the palaces of Europe's wealthiest monarchs. The truth is, the greatest advantage of using veneer is that it expands the artistic potential of woodworking and makes decorative effects possible that cannot be achieved with solid stock.

Because of its flexibility, veneer can be used to carry a wood's figure around a curved surface. Without veneer, the intricate patterns achieved through inlaying and marquetry would be virtually impossible. In fact, because of their brittle nature, some highly figured forms of wood, such as burl, would be structurally unusable in tabletops and other load-bearing parts of furniture. The chart below offers only a sampling of some of the world's most popular and attractive veneers.

COMMON DECORATIVE VENEERS

TYPE	APPEARANCE AND FIGURE	AVAILABLE CUTS	SOURCE	SUPPLY AND PRICE RANGE	WORKING CHARACTERISTICS
Black walnut	Light gray-brown to dark purple-brown; wavy figure.	Crotch, butt, flat-cut, quarter-cut, burl.	North America.	Plentiful; moderate to costly.	Medium-textured; variable working properties; accepts finish well.
Carpathian elm	Brick-red or greenish brown to light tan; burl figure.	Burl.	Europe.	Moderate; very costly.	Medium-textured; moderately hard to work; accepts finish well.
Lacewood	Silvery pink to reddish brown; fleck figure.	Flat-cut.	Australia.	Moderate; costly.	Medium-textured; simple to work; accepts finish well.
Mahogany	Light pink to reddish brown; striped and fiddleback figures.	Quarter-cut, flat-cut, crotch, butt.	Central and South America.	Moderate; moderate to costly.	Coarse-textured; simple to work; accepts finish well.
Maple	Creamy white sapwood with tan heartwood; curly and bird's-eye figure.	Quarter-cut, flat-cut, rotary, burl.	North America.	Plentiful; moderate to costly.	Fine-textured; hard to work; accepts finish well.
Oak, white	Golden brown to yellowish green; mottled and burl figures.	Quarter-cut, flat-cut, burl, rotary.	North America.	Plentiful; moderate.	Coarse-textured; moderately hard to work; filler recommended.
Pearwood	Rosy cream; straight-grained figure, sometimes curly.	Quarter-cut, flat-cut.	Europe.	Rare; costly.	Fine-textured; simple to work; accepts finish well.

COMMON DECORATIVE VENEERS

TYPE	APPEARANCE AND FIGURE	AVAILABLE CUTS	SOURCE	SUPPLY AND PRICE RANGE	WORKING CHARACTERISTICS
Purpleheart	Deep purple with light gray sapwood; striped figure.	Quarter-cut, flat-cut.	Central and South America.	Plentiful; costly.	Coarse-textured; difficult to work; accepts finish well.
Zebrawood	Cream background with dark brown lines; striped figure.	Quarter-cut.	Africa.	Rare; costly.	Medium-textured; moderately hard to work; accepts finish well.

Modern veneers range in thickness from about ⅛ inch to less than ¼₀ inch. Although economizing on scarce woods accounts for the thinner veneers, the texture and figure of various species place limits on what is feasible. Coarse-textured and ring-porous woods require greater thickness.

As shown in the illustration below *(right)*, there are various methods of cutting veneer from logs. Each one accentuates certain features of the wood's figure. Rotary cutting, where the log is soaked and then peeled on a huge lathe, represents the fastest and most efficient means of producing veneer. High-quality logs suited to this method are in great demand. Flat-slicing yields a figure comparable to flat-sawn, tangentially cut lumber; this method may also be used to cut crotch and butt veneers. Quarter-slicing produces a figure comparable to quarter-sawn, radially cut lumber and is used to highlight the vivid rays in such woods as white oak and lacewood, or to expose the ribbon figure of woods with interlocked grain such as mahogany. Half-round-slicing accents the figure of most burls.

VENEER CUTTING METHODS

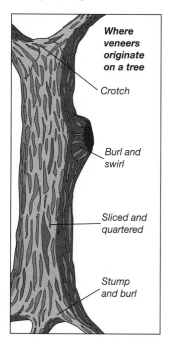

Where veneers originate on a tree

Crotch

Burl and swirl

Sliced and quartered

Stump and burl

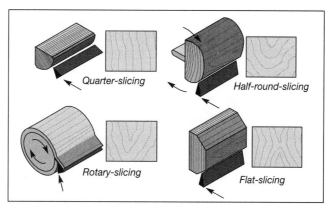

Quarter-slicing

Half-round-slicing

Rotary-slicing

Flat-slicing

VENEERS

TYPE	DIMENSIONS	SOME AVAILABLE SPECIES
Burl	Irregular dimensions; sheet sizes vary from 8" x 10" to 36" x 54"; average sheet size 12" x 24".	Carpathian elm, English oak, madrone, myrtle, olive ash, redwood, thuya, walnut.
Butt and stump	Irregular dimensions; sheet sizes vary from 10" x 36" to 18" x 54"; average sheet size 12" x 36".	Maple, walnut.
Crotch	Length from 18" to 54"; width from 10" to 24"; average sheet size 12" x 36".	Amburana, mahogany, walnut.
Flat-sliced	Length 3' to 6'; width from 4" to 24".	Ash, Brazilian rosewood, cherry, maple, oak, teak.
Quarter-sliced	Length 3' to 6'; width from 4" to 12".	Avodiré, mahogany, oak, lacewood, sapele, satinwood, zebrawood.
Rotary-sliced	Length up to 12'; width 8" to 48".	Bubinga, Douglas-fir, masur birch, lauan.

**MATCHING
VENEER**

Working with veneer can be as much an art form as carving, sculpting, or painting. The species and types of veneer available provide the woodworker with a broad range of colors, textures, and patterns. The natural figures of some species are spectacular enough to make them decorative by themselves. For example, the marbled figure of rosewood, the vivid contrasts in quarter-sliced white oak, or the orderly stripes of ribbon-grain mahogany can be stunning when used as one-piece veneers. However, even less flamboyant veneers can be matched to create attractive patterns and symmetrical designs. Since veneers are not always available in large sizes, pattern-matching techniques make it possible to cover bigger surfaces with the beautifully intricate figure of rare and special cuts such as burl, crotch, and bird's-eye. Some of the more commonly used matching patterns are illustrated below. Also, differences between the color, texture, and figure of various veneers can be employed in decorative banding, inlays, and marquetry to create high-contrast designs.

VENEER MATCHING PATTERNS

Four-way center and butt   Checkerboard match   Slip match   Book match   Diamond match   Reverse-diamond match   Herringbone

APPLYING VENEER

The art of veneering has evolved over the centuries with the advent of more precisely cut veneers, better glues, optional substrate materials, and special tools. In ancient times, solid wood was the only substrate available. Veneer had to be sawed by hand and then bonded to the substrate using heated, animal-hide glues with very short tack times and questionable holding power. Because veneers were heavy and uneven, surfaces had to be built up and then laboriously scraped down and rubbed out to achieve the final finish.

While veneers still need to be trimmed and glued down, both tasks can now be achieved much more easily. Today's thin, precisely cut veneers, more patient adhesives (*page 326*), and very stable substrate materials, such as plywood, particleboard, and fiberboard, allow the woodworker to concentrate more on the esthetics of achieving balanced patterns and tight seams. Contact adhesives specifically for gluing down veneers are available as are self-adhesive veneers. And although veneering tools like the veneer saw, hand roller, and veneer hammer have changed little since antiquity, high-speed laminate trimmer bits for the router and edging jigs for use on the shaper take much of the drudgery and uncertainty out of the more mechanical aspects of cutting, matching, and edging veneers.

COMMON VENEERING TOOLS

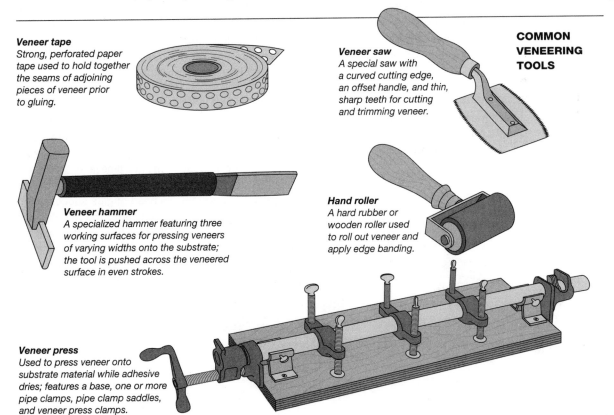

Veneer tape
Strong, perforated paper tape used to hold together the seams of adjoining pieces of veneer prior to gluing.

Veneer saw
A special saw with a curved cutting edge, an offset handle, and thin, sharp teeth for cutting and trimming veneer.

Veneer hammer
A specialized hammer featuring three working surfaces for pressing veneers of varying widths onto the substrate; the tool is pushed across the veneered surface in even strokes.

Hand roller
A hard rubber or wooden roller used to roll out veneer and apply edge banding.

Veneer press
Used to press veneer onto substrate material while adhesive dries; features a base, one or more pipe clamps, pipe clamp saddles, and veneer press clamps.

APPLYING VENEER

PREPARING VENEER FOR GLUING

To veneer a substrate panel, begin by gluing strips of veneer onto the panel's edges. The strips should overhang the edges by about ½ inch. Clamp the veneer in place—three-way clamps *(page 331)* work well. Once the glue has cured, trim the excess with a veneer saw or a router with a piloted trimmer bit. Next, veneer the faces of the panel. If your veneer is too small to cover the entire substrate, you will have to join pieces of veneer together. The trick is to make sure that adjoining pieces are perfectly square so they butt against each other seamlessly. The simplest way to

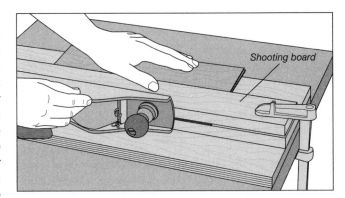

Shooting board

do this is to set up a shooting board like the one shown above. Sandwich the veneer between two parallel hardwood strips and then clamp the assembly down on top of a third board that is wide enough to accommodate a hand plane resting on its side. Press down on the top strip to ensure that the veneer is pinched tight as the plane is run along the edge. Several sheets of veneer can be trimmed at the same time. Then join the pieces edge to edge with veneer tape.

SECURING VENEER IN PLACE WITH A VENEER PRESS

Spread a thin layer of glue on one face of the substrate panel and place the veneer on top. (If you used veneer tape, make sure the tape is facing up.) Place this assembly face down on the base of a veneer press. Protecting the upper face of the substrate with wood pads, tighten the press clamps one at a time *(left)*; start at the center and work outward until a bead of glue squeezes out from under the panel. Once the glue has cured, repeat the procedure on the other face. Then trim the excess flush with the edge of the substrate.

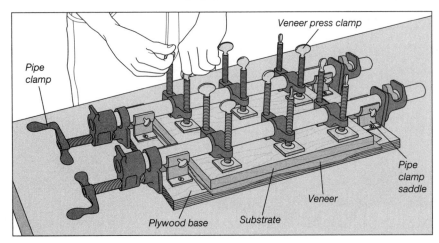

Veneer press clamp

Pipe clamp

Pipe clamp saddle

Veneer

Plywood base

Substrate

ENCYCLOPEDIA OF JOINERY

This chapter surveys the most common joints used in cabinetmaking—from the basic butt joint to the classic dovetail. For the practicing woodworker, the choice of joints for any given project can be bewildering. Seasoned cabinetmakers narrow down the options by considering the strength, usefulness, appearance, and ease of construction of different joints.

For starters, the joints you select must be strong enough to withstand the stresses to which they will be subjected. The four basic types of stress that joints undergo in a piece of furniture are illustrated on page 254. And as explained on pages 250 and 251, not all joints are created equal. Some are inherently weak, and should only be used if they are reinforced. Others are strong and reliable, because of the shapes of the pieces or the glue bond between them.

Another factor to consider is a joint's function. Most joints have been developed to fulfill a particular purpose. Whether it has to support a shelf in a bookcase or connect a drawer front to the sides, the joint you choose has to be appropriate for the task at hand.

The chart on pages 252 and 253 describes the relative strength, advantages and disadvantages, and typical applications of various joints.

Choosing a joint on the basis of appearance and ease of construction is more subjective. A drawer built with hand-cut dovetails (page 282), for example, may be sturdier and more visually appealing than one assembled with drawer lock joints (page 269), but the latter option is easier to produce and sufficiently strong for most applications. On the other hand, dovetails cut with a router and jig (page 285) may not look as good as hand-crafted joints, but they are equally strong and can be made in a fraction of the time.

Throughout this chapter, you will find step-by-step descriptions of how to fashion many joints. Tips and summary charts provide guidelines on the most appropriate jigs and tools to use to simplify their construction.

Although in many respects joinery is a subjective art, the chapter will help you weigh the advantages and disadvantages of many joints.

JOINT STRENGTH

The strength of a joint can come from glue, from the shape of the joint, or from fasteners. In the simplest case, gluing two pieces edge to edge results in a strong joint. End grain glues poorly, however, so you can-not rely entirely on glue to join the end of a board to the edge of another. One way to solve the problem is to shape the parts so the long grain glues to long grain, as in the lap joint *(page 264)*.

WHERE JOINTS DERIVE THEIR STRENGTH

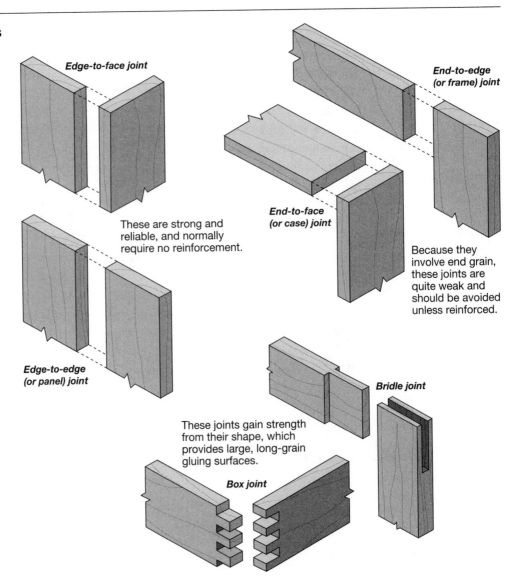

Edge-to-face joint

End-to-edge (or frame) joint

These are strong and reliable, and normally require no reinforcement.

End-to-face (or case) joint

Edge-to-edge (or panel) joint

Because they involve end grain, these joints are quite weak and should be avoided unless reinforced.

Bridle joint

These joints gain strength from their shape, which provides large, long-grain gluing surfaces.

Box joint

If the parts are shaped to interlock, the joint will have mechanical strength in addition to glue strength. The mortise-and-tenon is one example. The dovetail joint is another. Joints that lack both glue strength and mechanical strength can be salvaged by fasteners. Dado *(page 268)* and rabbet *(page 266)* joints usually rely on fasteners, like screws or dowels, for additional strength. Splines are another common way to reinforce a joint.

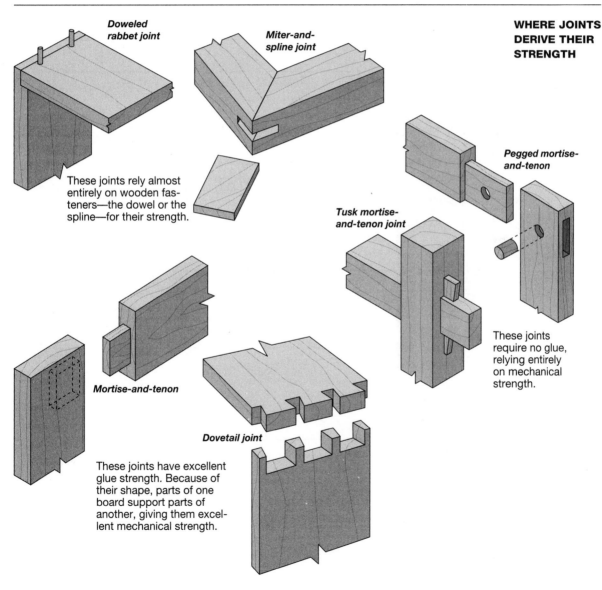

WHERE JOINTS DERIVE THEIR STRENGTH

Doweled rabbet joint

Miter-and-spline joint

These joints rely almost entirely on wooden fasteners—the dowel or the spline—for their strength.

Pegged mortise-and-tenon

Tusk mortise-and-tenon joint

These joints require no glue, relying entirely on mechanical strength.

Mortise-and-tenon

Dovetail joint

These joints have excellent glue strength. Because of their shape, parts of one board support parts of another, giving them excellent mechanical strength.

JOINT STRENGTH

DIRECTIONS OF MECHANICAL STRENGTH	PROVIDES GOOD GLUING SURFACES	AIDS ALIGNMENT	ADVANTAGES	DISADVANTAGES	TYPICAL USES
End-butt	No	No	Requires no special shaping.	Useless unless fasteners like nails, screws, dowels, or plates (biscuits) are added.	Building construction.
Rabbet	No	Somewhat	Very easy to cut; adds some mechanical strength.	Useless unless fasteners like nails, screws, dowels, or plates (biscuits) are added.	Joining cabinet backs to carcases.
Dado	No	Yes	Easy to cut; strong as shelf support.	Usually requires additional fasteners.	Supporting shelf ends.
Miter	No	No	Provides clean appearance.	Difficult to assemble and clamp; usually requires additional fasteners.	Assembling box corners and picture frames.
Box	Yes	Yes	Easy to cut for strength provided.	Utilitarian appearance; jig required to make easily.	Assembling boxes.
Dovetail	Yes	Yes	Adds great strength; craftsmanlike appearance.	Time-consuming to make; jig required to make easily.	Assembling drawer, box, and chest corners.

DIRECTIONS OF MECHANICAL STRENGTH	PROVIDES GOOD GLUING SURFACES	AIDS ALIGNMENT	ADVANTAGES	DISADVAN- TAGES	TYPICAL USES	STRENGTHS AND USES OF SOME COMMON JOINTS
Edge-butt	Yes	No	Requires no special shaping.	Difficult to keep aligned during assembly.	Making wide panels from narrow boards.	
Tongue-and-groove	Yes	Yes	Aligns edges well; unglued, permits expansion and contraction.	Requires special cutters to make efficiently.	Flooring; rustic-looking doors.	
Lap	Yes	Somewhat	Easy to cut; glues well.	Unattractive from edges.	Assembling frame corners.	
Bridle	Yes	Yes	Fairly easy to cut; glues very well.	Unattractive from edges.	Assembling frame corners.	
Mortise-and-tenon	Yes	Yes	Adds great strength.	Time-consuming to make.	Assembling frame corners and joining legs to aprons.	

JOINT STRENGTH

FOUR KINDS OF STRESS

Woodworkers refer to four kinds of stress: tension, compression, shear, and racking, as shown at right. The mechanical resistance of a variety of joints to these stresses is shown on pages 252 and 253. When choosing a joint, consider the anticipated stress, the mechanical resistance of the joint to the stress, and the quality and area of the gluing surfaces.

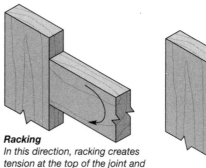

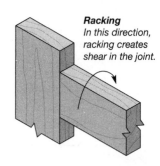

Racking
In this direction, racking creates shear in the joint.

Racking
In this direction, racking creates tension at the top of the joint and compression at the bottom.

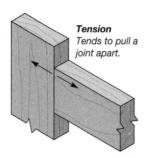

Tension
Tends to pull a joint apart.

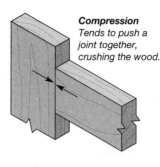

Compression
Tends to push a joint together, crushing the wood.

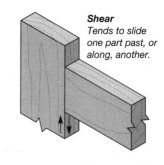

Shear
Tends to slide one part past, or along, another.

ORIENTING GRAIN

Wood movement can affect the durability of a joint. In the mortise-and-tenon with flat-saw grain shown *(below, left)*, the tenon workpiece's maximum expansion is in the direction of the mortise's minimum expansion. Similarly, the mortise workpiece's maximum expansion is in the direction of the tenon's minimum expansion. (For more on wood movement, see page 242.) If quarter-sawn stock is used *(below, right)* the movement of one piece more closely matches the movement of the other.

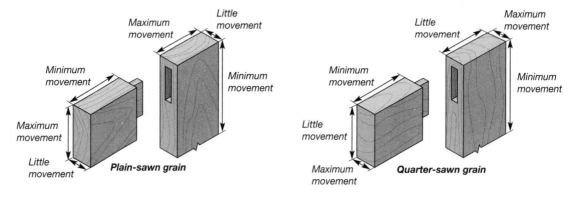

Plain-sawn grain

Maximum movement / Little movement / Minimum movement / Minimum movement / Maximum movement / Little movement

Quarter-sawn grain

Little movement / Maximum movement / Minimum movement / Minimum movement / Little movement / Maximum movement

BUTT JOINTS

The butt joint is the simplest joint of all: One workpiece is simply cut to abut against another. While butt joints that only involve long grain have good gluing strength, those that involve end grain have very little; they require reinforcement.

The simple glued edge-to-edge joint is the most common of the unreinforced butt joints. It is used to make wide boards from narrower stock. The face-to-face joint is used to build up thicker stock from more common sizes. It is useful when massive thicknesses are needed, as in some lathe work or to make a leg blank. The edge-to-face joint is as strong as the edge-to-edge joint, and is often used for attaching face frames to carcases.

The unreinforced end-to-edge joint is very weak, but may be used to join the corners of face frames if the carcase provides adequate strength. Even then, a pair of dowels or a mortise-and-tenon would make a better joint. The end-to-face joint should not be used at all without reinforcement.

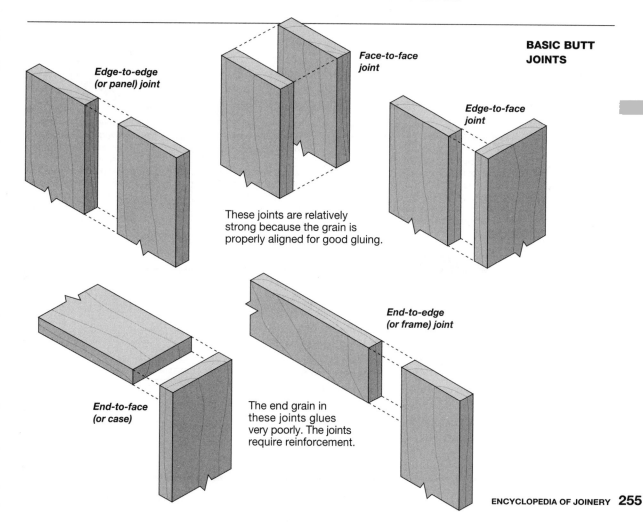

BASIC BUTT JOINTS

Edge-to-edge (or panel) joint

Face-to-face joint

Edge-to-face joint

These joints are relatively strong because the grain is properly aligned for good gluing.

End-to-face (or case)

End-to-edge (or frame) joint

The end grain in these joints glues very poorly. The joints require reinforcement.

DOWEL JOINTS

Dowels strengthen butt joints that would otherwise be weak because the long grain of the dowels is glued to the long grain of one of the boards. When one surface of the joint is entirely end grain, a dowel adds at least some long grain, reinforcing the joint.

As shown in the illustrations below, most joints that depend on dowels for reinforcement involve a compromise. Dowels lend a joint most strength when the dowel hole is drilled into the end of one of the boards so that the grain of the stock and the dowel will run in parallel. However, dowel holes in the face or edge of the mating board are largely end grain. Here, the dowels do not add as much strength.

Dowels are sometimes used to help align edge-to-edge and edge-to-face joints. However, alignment is the only benefit. These joints are sufficiently strong without dowels.

Dowel joints are easy to make. As shown on page 118, using a commercial doweling jig with a drill is the quickest way to bore dowel holes accurately.

COMMON DOWEL JOINTS

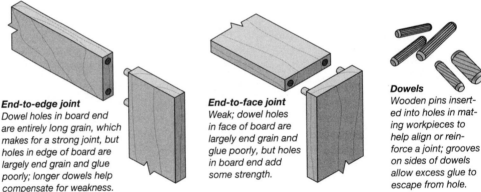

End-to-edge joint
Dowel holes in board end are entirely long grain, which makes for a strong joint, but holes in edge of board are largely end grain and glue poorly; longer dowels help compensate for weakness.

End-to-face joint
Weak; dowel holes in face of board are largely end grain and glue poorly, but holes in board end add some strength.

Dowels
Wooden pins inserted into holes in mating workpieces to help align or reinforce a joint; grooves on sides of dowels allow excess glue to escape from hole.

_QUICK_TIP

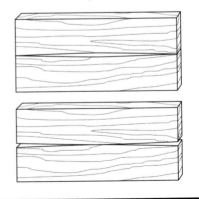

Panel joint basics
Boards that will be edge-glued to form a panel should be cut and jointed as precisely as possible so that mating edges are flat and square. Slightly concave edges (top) are acceptable, but convex edges (bottom) can cause problems. Even though clamping pressure will close minor gaps, convex edges may eventually split apart at the ends as the result of stresses.

SPLINE JOINTS

Splines add even more glue surface to a joint than dowels; as a result, they are stronger. Like dowel joints, they are easy to make. Simply cut or rout matching grooves in the mating boards, cut a spline to fit in the grooves, and glue it in.

In edge-to-face and edge-to-edge spline joints, cut the spline so its grain is parallel to that of the boards being joined. The spline will expand and contract in the same direction as the wood surrounding it. In end-to-edge and end-to-face spline joints, however, parallel grain is not practical. With these joints, use a spline cut from plywood, or a solid-wood spline with diagonal grain. Some cabinetmakers make all their spline joints with plywood or diagonal-grain splines because the spline's wood fibers will be perpendicular to the stress on the joint.

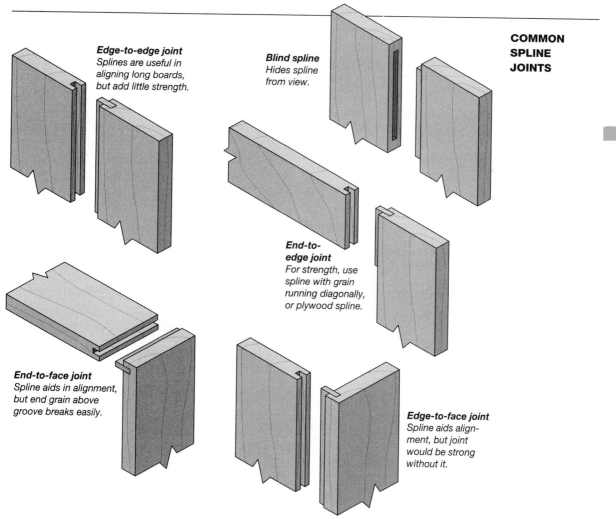

COMMON SPLINE JOINTS

Edge-to-edge joint
Splines are useful in aligning long boards, but add little strength.

Blind spline
Hides spline from view.

End-to-edge joint
For strength, use spline with grain running diagonally, or plywood spline.

End-to-face joint
Spline aids in alignment, but end grain above groove breaks easily.

Edge-to-face joint
Spline aids alignment, but joint would be strong without it.

PLATE JOINTS

P late joints (also called biscuit joints) are extremely easy to lay out and produce. As shown on page 134, a plate joiner cuts slots in the mating boards. Glue is applied to the slots and a compressed-wood biscuit is inserted into each one. The biscuits absorb the glue and swell, ensuring a well-aligned, tight-fitting joint. Since the grain of the biscuits runs diagonally, plate joints are an ideal substitute for spline joints requiring diagonal-grain splines. They also offer a quick way to join carcase panels together.

Because the biscuits are thin, plate joints are not as strong as mortise-and-tenon joints. But they are a good substitute when joining plywood pieces together, since the mortise-and-tenon cannot be used with plywood. To increase the strength of a plate joint in thick stock, you can double or triple the biscuits across the thickness of the mating pieces.

A GALLERY OF PLATE JOINTS

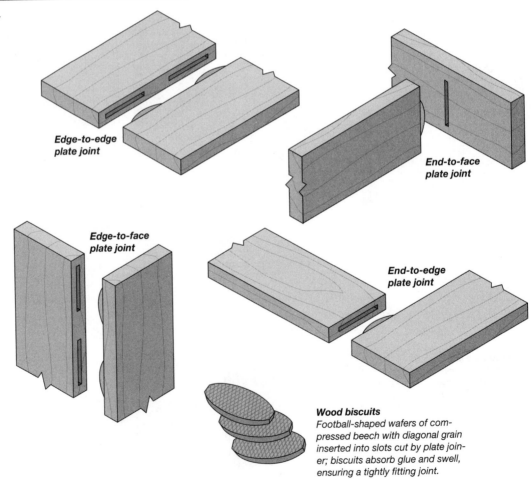

Edge-to-edge plate joint

End-to-face plate joint

Edge-to-face plate joint

End-to-edge plate joint

Wood biscuits
Football-shaped wafers of compressed beech with diagonal grain inserted into slots cut by plate joiner; biscuits absorb glue and swell, ensuring a tightly fitting joint.

MITER JOINTS

Miters create clean joints in which there is only one visible line separating mating pieces. Miter joints offer a way of wrapping moldings around a corner without interrupting the surface profile. Of the unreinforced joints shown below, the edge miter is the strongest because it involves two long-grain surfaces glued together. End and face miters are weak because they involve end grain.

Dowels, splines, and wood biscuits can be used to strengthen miter joints that involve end grain, like the face and end miter. If you are making a miter-and-spline,

make sure the grain runs diagonally across the spline. Refer to page 263 for ways of cutting grooves for splined miter joints.

Miters are quick and easy to cut, but it pays to take the time to set up carefully. If you are cutting miters with a handsaw, use a miter box, as shown on page 75. The best power tool for the job is the radial arm saw, as illustrated on page 151.

The mitered half-lap has the æsthetic benefits of miter joints along with the strength of lap joints—a substantial area of long-grain contact between the mating pieces, allowing the glue to establish a good bond.

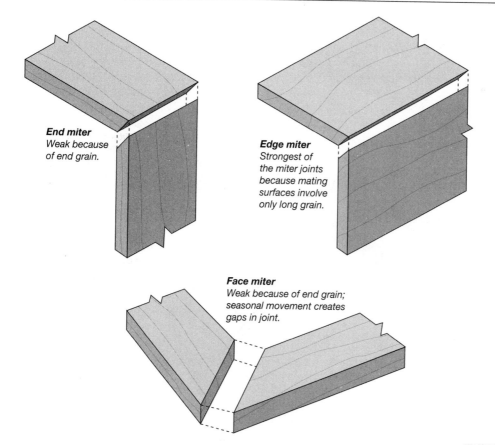

UNREINFORCED MITER JOINTS

End miter
Weak because of end grain.

Edge miter
Strongest of the miter joints because mating surfaces involve only long grain.

Face miter
Weak because of end grain; seasonal movement creates gaps in joint.

MITER JOINTS

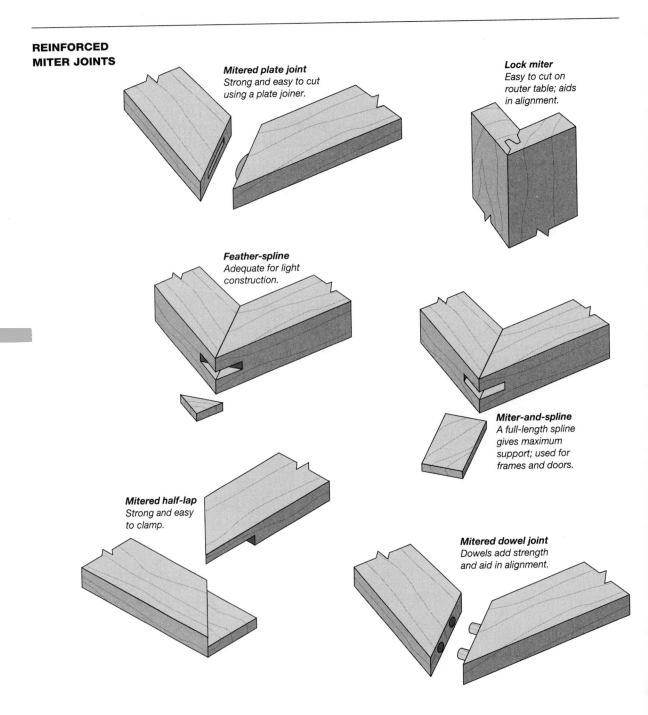

Mitered plate joint
Strong and easy to cut
using a plate joiner.

Lock miter
Easy to cut on
router table; aids
in alignment.

Feather-spline
Adequate for light
construction.

Miter-and-spline
A full-length spline
gives maximum
support; used for
frames and doors.

Mitered half-lap
Strong and easy
to clamp.

Mitered dowel joint
Dowels add strength
and aid in alignment.

One of the disadvantages of unreinforced miter joints involving end grain is their susceptibility to wood movement. The illustrations below show how a face miter can open when adjoining boards swell or contract due to changes in humidity. Use quarter-sawn stock to minimize these problems.

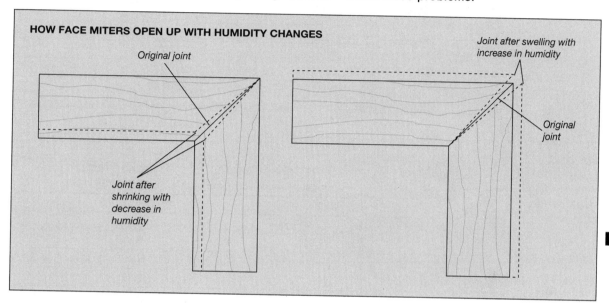

HOW FACE MITERS OPEN UP WITH HUMIDITY CHANGES

Original joint

Joint after swelling with increase in humidity

Original joint

Joint after shrinking with decrease in humidity

QUICKTIP

Positioning a spline

If you are using a spline to reinforce a miter joint, locate the groove closer to the inside corner (right, top). Positioning the spline near the outside corner (right, bottom) will weaken the joint and increase the likelihood that the groove will break through the outside faces of the stock.

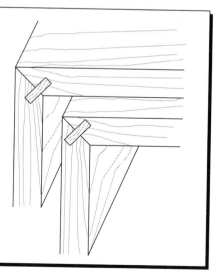

MITER JOINTS

ANGLES FOR CUTTING POLYGONS

NUMBER OF SIDES	MITER GAUGE ANGLE (If gauge reads 90° at center)	MITER GAUGE ANGLE (If gauge reads 0° at center)
3	60°	30°
4	45°	45°
5	36°	54°
6	30°	60°
7	25.7°	64.3°
8	22.5°	67.5°

CUTTING COMPOUND MITERS ON A FOUR-SIDED BOX

SLOPE OF FRAME	MITER GAUGE ANGLE (If gauge reads 90° at center)*	BLADE TILT FROM VERTICAL
85°	86°	44.75°
80°	82.25°	44.25°
75°	78.25°	43.5°
70°	74.5°	42.25°
65°	71°	40.75°
60°	67.5°	39°
55°	64.25°	36.75°
50°	61°	34.5°
45°	58.25°	31.75°
40°	55.5°	29°
35°	53.25°	25.75°
30°	51°	22.5°
25°	49.25°	19°
20°	47.75°	15.5°
15°	46.5°	11.75°
10°	45.75°	7.75°
5°	45.25°	4°

* If miter gauge reads 0° at center, subtract angle in table from 90° to get miter gauge setting.

The miter-and-spline joint is simply a miter joint with a reinforcing strip of wood—the spline—inserted into a groove cut in the adjoining ends of the miter. You can cut the joint using only a table saw, but a table-mounted router with a three-winged slotting bit makes the job easier. First, miter the ends of each workpiece on the table saw. To cut the grooves on the router, begin by aligning the fence over the slotting bit to set the depth of cut. Place one of the workpieces flat on the table and butt it against the bit. Adjust the cutting height so the groove will be centered on the mitered end of the piece. Make a test cut on a piece of scrap stock.

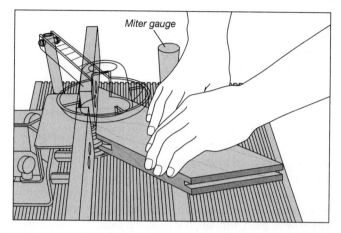

Miter gauge

ROUTING A MITER-AND-SPLINE JOINT

Next, press the mitered end of the workpiece against the fence and swivel the miter gauge until it butts against the workpiece. Turn on the router and groove both ends of each workpiece as shown above. For the splines, cut a strip of wood with diagonal grain or use plywood so that it will slide snugly in the groove, then trim its width to slightly less than the combined depth of the grooves in the two workpieces. Glue the miter together. After the adhesive dries, trim off the excess spline with a sharp chisel.

Cutting the grooves for installing a spline in an edge miter looks complicated because the grooves must be perpendicular to the adjoining mitered edges. Actually, the process for making this joint is quite simple. Tilt the table saw blade to 45° and bevel the edges of both workpieces. Then adjust the blade height to about one-half the thickness of the stock and position the rip fence so that the groove will be closer to the inside corner of the joint. Rip the groove in each workpiece as shown at right. If you need a thicker spline, readjust the fence and depth of cut to widen the groove, or use a dado head. Next, rip the spline stock to a thickness that allows it to slip snugly into the grooves. Then rip the width of the spline so that it is approximately $\frac{1}{32}$ inch narrower than twice the depth of the groove. Apply glue in the grooves of both workpieces and along one of the beveled edges. Insert the spline and clamp the joint together.

CUTTING GROOVES FOR SPLINES

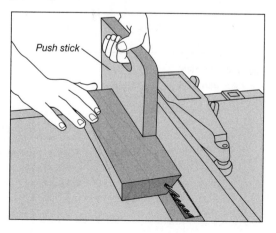

Push stick

LAP JOINTS

Lap joints are much stronger than butt joints because each member provides a substantial area of long-grain surface or "cheek", which enables the glue to establish a good bond. The shoulders cut into both parts of the joint also strongly resist racking stress. Each type of lap joint has its own uses and advantages. The half-blind half-lap hides end grain, while the cross half-lap is often used in drawer cabinet facings where both parts must extend beyond the joint. The T half-lap allows one piece to cap off the other. The dovetailed half-lap achieves the same objective as the T half-lap, but locks the joint, providing maximum resistance to tension stress. The full lap is used to join members that have different thicknesses; it is an easier joint to prepare since only one of the workpieces needs to be channeled. The keyed dovetail half-lap prevents the joining pieces from separating, but it is a tough joint to cut accurately. Both the angled half-lap and the edge half-lap are simply modifications of the cross half-lap, with two members that come together at different angles. Lap joints come in many highly specialized variations, such as the glazing bar half-lap used to connect the muntins in multiple-pane window sashes.

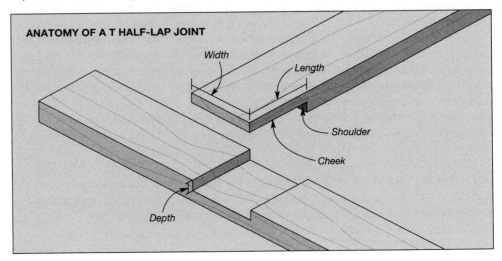

ANATOMY OF A T HALF-LAP JOINT

Width

Length

Shoulder

Cheek

Depth

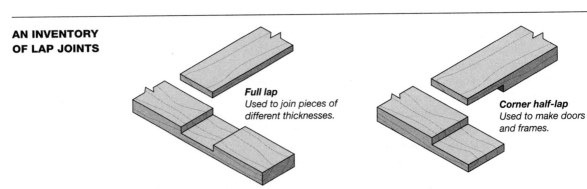

AN INVENTORY OF LAP JOINTS

Full lap
Used to join pieces of different thicknesses.

Corner half-lap
Used to make doors and frames.

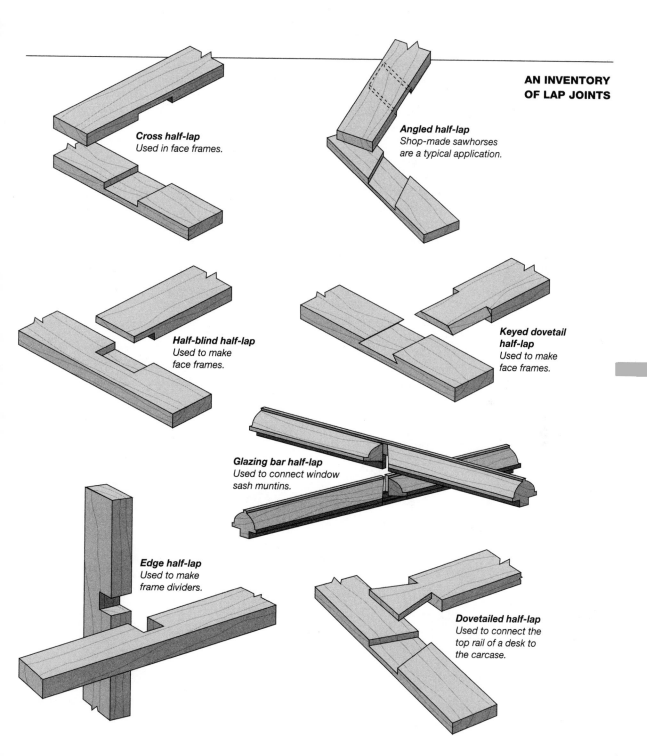

Cross half-lap
Used in face frames.

Angled half-lap
Shop-made sawhorses
are a typical application.

Half-blind half-lap
Used to make
face frames.

**Keyed dovetail
half-lap**
Used to make
face frames.

Glazing bar half-lap
Used to connect window
sash muntins.

Edge half-lap
Used to make
frame dividers.

Dovetailed half-lap
Used to connect the
top rail of a desk to
the carcase.

RABBET JOINTS

In rabbet joints, one or both members are rabbeted—or notched—to hold the mating workpiece. The resulting shoulders provide greater resistance to stress than a simple butt joint. The shiplap joint employs complementary rabbets along the edges of the members and is often used in exterior house siding. As the edge-joined boards expand and contract with changes in their moisture content, the matching rabbets prevent them from separating far enough to create an open gap.

The other rabbet joints shown below are used in carcase and drawer construction. The stopped rabbet joint has two advantages: It conceals the angles of the joint on the front edge and resists shear stress better than a plain rabbet joint. The mitered rabbet is used to hide end grain, but it is a difficult joint to cut and fit. The double rabbet adds an extra measure of strength in resisting racking stress, while the dovetailed rabbet is both attractive and superior to other forms of the joint in coping with tension stress. Even so, many of these joints are quite weak unless reinforced by fasteners, such as dowels, screws, or nails.

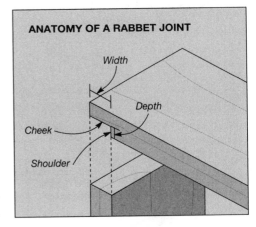

ANATOMY OF A RABBET JOINT

Width

Depth

Cheek

Shoulder

A SELECTION OF RABBET JOINTS

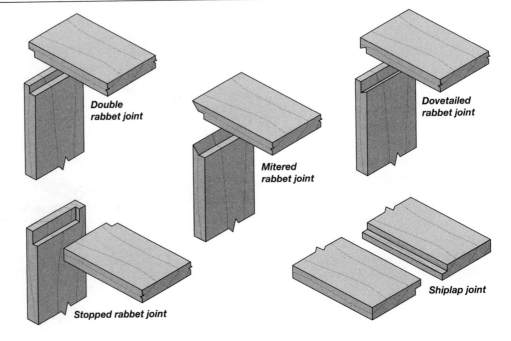

Double rabbet joint

Mitered rabbet joint

Dovetailed rabbet joint

Stopped rabbet joint

Shiplap joint

Cutting a through rabbet on the table saw requires a dado head slightly wider than the desired width of the rabbet. Attach a wooden auxiliary fence to the rip fence. With the saw running, raise the dado head to cut a relief notch in the wooden fence. This notch will house part of the dado head while cutting the rabbet. Position the fence so the exposed part of the dado head will plow out the rabbet. Use featherboards **1** to apply pressure against the fence and the table. If you are rabbeting narrow stock, remember to use a push stick to complete the pass.

A router is also a good tool for cutting rabbets—particularly stopped rabbets because it leaves the least amount of waste to be removed. When many identical stopped rabbets must be cut, the best approach is to mount the tool in a table equipped with an adjustable fence. Set the height of the bit and position the fence for the desired depth and width of cut. Draw a reference mark on the fence at the contact point between the workpiece and the bit **2**. Next, place an end-of-cut mark on the top surface of the workpiece. Turn on the router and feed the workpiece along the fence until the two marks are

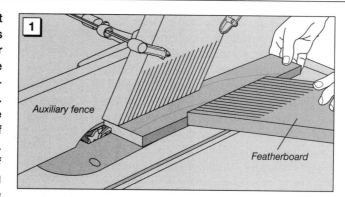

Auxiliary fence

Featherboard

aligned, then pivot the workpiece away from the fence.

To cut a stopped rabbet using a hand-held router, clamp the workpiece to a work surface and mark the point where the rabbet should end. Install a piloted rabbet bit and position the router on top of the workpiece so that the bit rests against the edge of the workpiece and is aligned with the end-of-cut mark. Slide a stop block **3** against the router's base plate and clamp it in place. Rout the rabbet, stopping the cut

Reference mark

End-of-cut mark

when the base plate contacts the stop block, then use a chisel to square the stopped end of the rabbet.

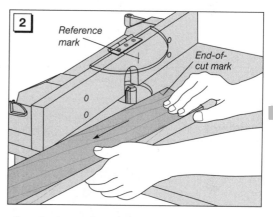

Stop block

End-of-cut mark

DADO JOINTS

The dado is one of the most versatile joints in cabinetmaking. While rabbet joints are used to join the ends or edges of boards, the dado is employed to fit the end of one board into the face of another. In the joint's simplest form, the through dado, the receiving workpiece is channeled to accept the butt end of the other. This is the most common joint for mounting shelves in a bookcase. Other dadoes have more specialized purposes. The stopped dado conceals the joint on the front edge while the blind dado not only conceals it on both edges, but also prevents the shelf from shifting forward or backward. The sliding dovetail and half-dovetail lock the shelf into the dovetail dado and add a decorative touch.

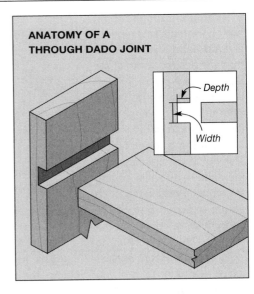

ANATOMY OF A THROUGH DADO JOINT

Depth

Width

A DELUGE OF DADO JOINTS

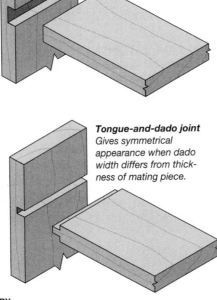

Stopped dado joint
Conceals joint on front edge (back edge shown).

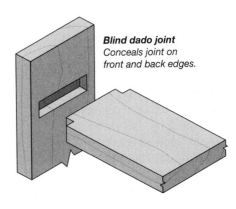

Blind dado joint
Conceals joint on front and back edges.

Tongue-and-dado joint
Gives symmetrical appearance when dado width differs from thickness of mating piece.

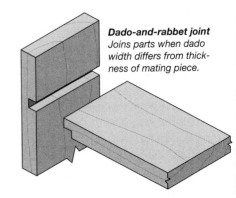

Dado-and-rabbet joint
Joins parts when dado width differs from thickness of mating piece.

Sliding half-dovetail joint
Used to fix shelves in carcases.

Sliding dovetail joint
Locks mating piece into dado. Gives symmetrical appearance; resists racking (see page 112 to cut this joint on a router table).

Drawer lock joint
An easy-to-cut joint that resists tension (see right).

Drawer side

Drawer front

Drawer side
Rout ends of drawer sides on end against fence.

Drawer front
Rout ends of drawer front flat on router table.

Drawer-lock router bit
Used in table-mounted router.

Like rabbet joints, dadoes can be cut with the table saw, radial arm saw, or router. When cutting several through dadoes in a long workpiece, such as a side of a tall bookcase, the radial arm saw is a good choice. The table saw also performs well. With long workpieces, it helps to install a long auxiliary fence on the miter gauge for added control. Mark the location of the dado on the leading edge of each workpiece. Install a dado head and adjust the depth of cut (usually one-third to one-half the thickness of the stock). Align the dado location mark with the dado head and make the cut as shown below.

CUTTING A DADO

Miter gauge extension fence

DADO JOINTS

ROUTING A BLIND DADO

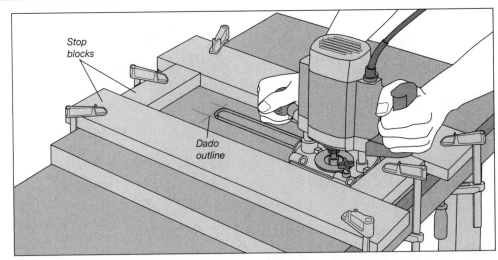

Stop blocks

Dado outline

Cutting blind dadoes is best done using a router and stop blocks. Mark out the dado on your workpiece and clamp it down, positioning the stop blocks to keep the router's travel within the outline. The router bit must be "plunged" into the stock to start the cut. Plunge routers are specifically designed for this. *(See page 102 for more on routers.)* When using a standard router, the bit must be pivoted into the stock. First, pull the router back until its base plate touches one stop block and tip it back so the bit is clear of the stock. Turn on the tool and, holding it firmly in both hands, pivot it forward until the base plate rests flat on the workpiece. Guide the router along the stop blocks until the dado has been cleared. Square up the rounded corners with a chisel and a mallet.

QUICK*TIP*

Reducing tearout
When routing through dadoes or the open end of stopped dadoes, tearout can be a problem where the bit exits the stock. To prevent this, clamp a piece of scrap stock to the edges of the workpiece. The top surfaces of the pieces must be flush. The pressure of the scrap against the edge of the workpiece will minimize splintering.

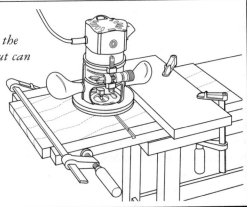

TONGUE-AND-GROOVE JOINTS

Like the shiplap and panel joints, the tongue-and-groove is used to join boards edge to edge—either with or without glue. Normally, the groove is one-third the thickness of the stock and centered along the edge. The tongue should fit snugly, but should not touch the bottom of the groove so that the seam of the joint can be drawn tightly together. The joint can be cut using a router with either a set of tongue-and-groove bits or a slotting cutter for channeling the groove and a straight bit for raising the shoulders on the tongue. The joint can also be cut on the table saw equipped with a dado head.

When used without glue, the tongue-and-groove is a good choice when making a cabinet back out of solid wood. Screws or nails typically hold the boards in place at the ends or along one edge. When the boards shrink in dry weather, the tongues withdraw partially from the grooves, but the boards remain aligned and no through gaps appear. When the humidity rises, the joints tighten up again without pushing the cabinet apart.

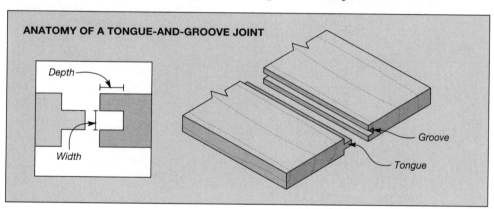

ANATOMY OF A TONGUE-AND-GROOVE JOINT

Depth

Width

Groove

Tongue

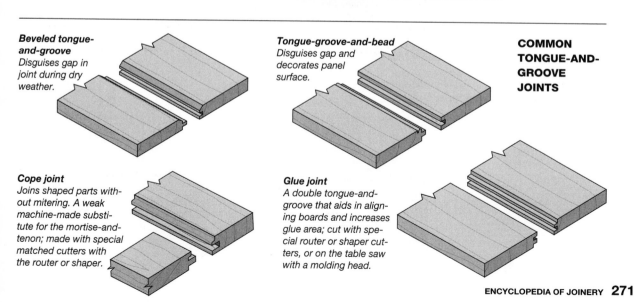

Beveled tongue-and-groove
Disguises gap in joint during dry weather.

Tongue-groove-and-bead
Disguises gap and decorates panel surface.

COMMON TONGUE-AND-GROOVE JOINTS

Cope joint
Joins shaped parts without mitering. A weak machine-made substitute for the mortise-and-tenon; made with special matched cutters with the router or shaper.

Glue joint
A double tongue-and-groove that aids in aligning boards and increases glue area; cut with special router or shaper cutters, or on the table saw with a molding head.

MORTISE-AND-TENON JOINTS

The mortise-and-tenon is one of woodworking's oldest joints. Builders in ancient Egypt relied upon it to fasten wood. Large long-grain gluing surfaces give the joint excellent strength. A pinned or wedged mortise-and-tenon will even function without the aid of adhesives. The basic joint (*shown below*) consists of two elements: the tenon, a projection from the end of one board and a matching slot—the mortise—in the mating piece. The tenon can be square, rectangular, or round in cross section and it may be straight or haunched. It may pass all the way through the mortised member or stop short of the other side to form a blind mortise-and-tenon joint. In addition, the end of the tenon may be kerfed to accept wedges or pinned to lock it in the mortise. An assortment of the most common and useful mortise-and-tenon joints is shown on the following pages.

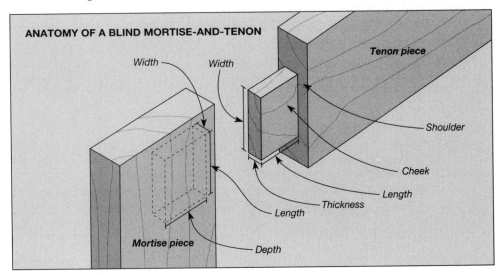

ANATOMY OF A BLIND MORTISE-AND-TENON

Tenon piece

Width   Width

Shoulder

Cheek

Length

Thickness

Length

Mortise piece   Depth

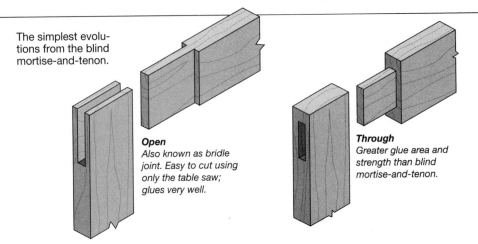

AN ASSORTMENT OF MORTISE-AND-TENONS

The simplest evolutions from the blind mortise-and-tenon.

Open
Also known as bridle joint. Easy to cut using only the table saw; glues very well.

Through
Greater glue area and strength than blind mortise-and-tenon.

Joints used in frame-and-panel construction.

Stub
*Used to join rails to stiles
in light-duty frame-and-
panel doors.*

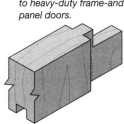

Haunched
*Used to fill the end of the
panel groove in moderate-
to heavy-duty frame-and-
panel doors.*

Mechanically reinforced joints
that do not require glue.

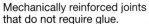

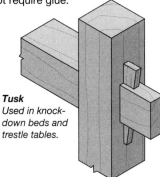

Tusk
*Used in knock-
down beds and
trestle tables.*

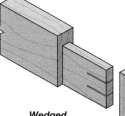

Pegged
*Peg locks tenon
in mortise without
glue; peg shows
on face.*

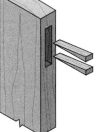

Wedged
*Wedges lock tenon
in mortise without
glue; joinery shows
on edge.*

PROPORTIONING A HAUNCHED TENON

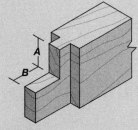

A = B
*Reinforces mortise member
in wedged joints*

A x 3 = B
*Increases gluing surface in glued
joints that are not wedged*

MORTISE-AND-TENON JOINTS

**AN ASSORTMENT
OF MORTISE-
AND-TENONS**

Router-made joints.

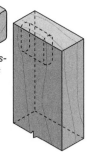

Routed
*Mortises are easy to cut but,
unless jig is used to produce
matching tenons, ends of
mortise must be squared,
or edges of tenon must
be rounded.*

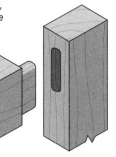

Loose
*Economical when mortis-
es and matching tenons
can be produced easily
and in quantity.*

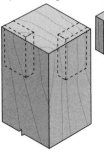

Joints used to attach aprons or rails to table legs.

Barefaced
*Very strong for
joining table
aprons to legs.*

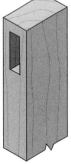

Offset
*Allows longer tenons
when joining table
aprons to legs.*

Twin
*Used to increase long-
grain gluing area and pre-
serve strength in mortise
piece when joining drawer
rail to leg or carcase.*

Joints used in chair construction.

Round
*Used to join chair rails
to legs; allows boring
of angled mortises.*

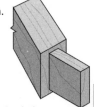

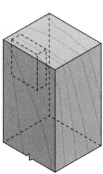

Angled
*Used to join parts
at angles other than
90°, as in chairs or
splayed-leg tables.*

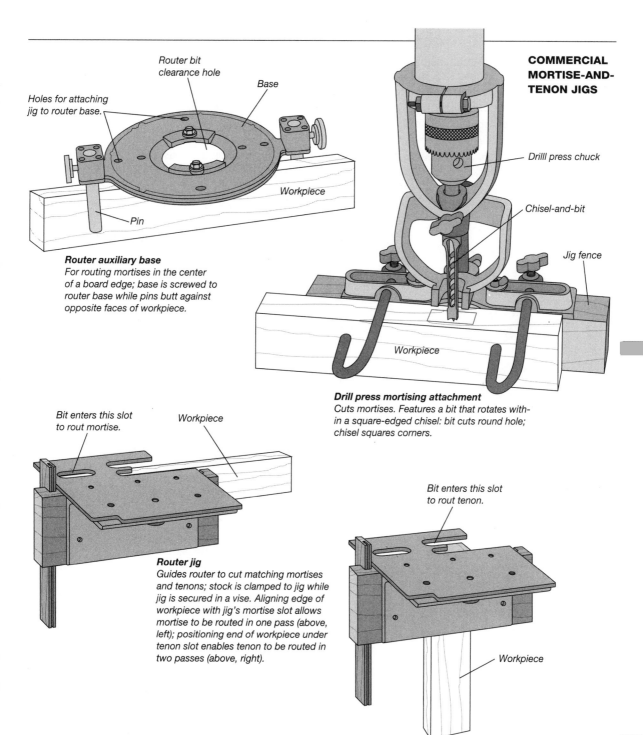

Router bit clearance hole

Base

Holes for attaching jig to router base.

Workpiece

Pin

Drilll press chuck

Chisel-and-bit

Jig fence

Workpiece

Router auxiliary base
For routing mortises in the center of a board edge; base is screwed to router base while pins butt against opposite faces of workpiece.

Drill press mortising attachment
Cuts mortises. Features a bit that rotates within a square-edged chisel: bit cuts round hole; chisel squares corners.

Bit enters this slot to rout mortise.

Workpiece

Bit enters this slot to rout tenon.

Router jig
Guides router to cut matching mortises and tenons; stock is clamped to jig while jig is secured in a vise. Aligning edge of workpiece with jig's mortise slot allows mortise to be routed in one pass (above, left); positioning end of workpiece under tenon slot enables tenon to be routed in two passes (above, right).

Workpiece

MORTISE-AND-TENON JOINTS

CUTTING
A BLIND
MORTISE-
AND-TENON
BY HAND

Although modern power tools are great labor-savers in cutting mortise-and-tenon joints, they are not essential. To cut a blind mortise-and-tenon joint by hand, begin by marking out the tenon. Set a mortise gauge to the length of the tenon and scribe the shoulder line [1] all the way around the workpiece. Next, set the gauge to one-third the thickness of the stock and scribe the tenon thickness on the end and edges of the workpiece as shown. Stop at the shoulder lines. Mark out the width of the tenon the same way. To saw out the tenon, begin by clamping the workpiece vertically in a vise [2]. Saw lay out the mortise on the mating workpiece, scribe two parallel lines along the edge with the mortise gauge still set at one-third the stock thickness. Then use the tenon as a template to outline the length of the mortise. To cut the mortise, first clamp the workpiece to a workbench. Then use a mortising chisel the same width as the mor-

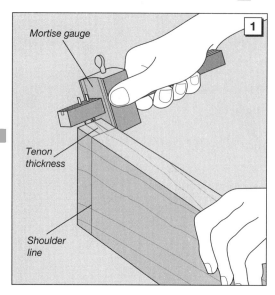

Mortise gauge

Tenon thickness

Shoulder line

1

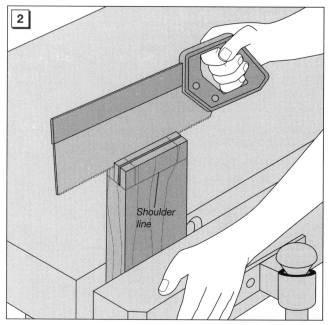

3

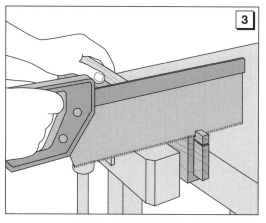

2

Shoulder line

the thickness of the tenon first, down to the shoulder line. Keep the blade on the waste side of the lines. Saw the width of the tenon in the same way. Finally, saw down the shoulder lines to remove the waste [3]. A miter box is useful for long shoulders. To tise to chip out the waste. Hold the chisel perfectly vertical, with its beveled face toward the center of the mortise. With the flat face about ⅛ inch in from the end line of the mortise, use a wooden mallet to drive the blade about ¼ inch into the wood. Move the

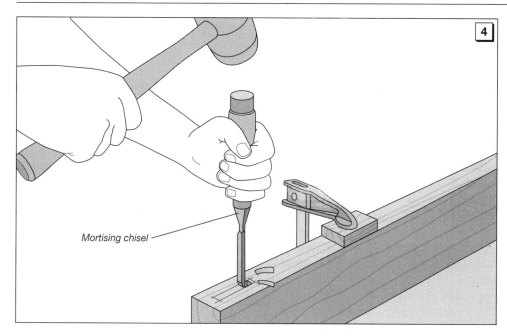

4

Mortising chisel

chisel in about ¼ inch toward the center of the mortise and make another cut 4 . Repeat this process to about the mid-point of the mortise and then lever out the waste with the chisel 5 . With the first layer of chips removed, repeat the process, starting from the other end of the mortise. Continue chiseling and levering out the waste until the mortise is deep enough to accommodate the tenon. To remove the ⅛ inch of waste remaining at each end of the mortise, drive the chisel straight down at the end lines with its beveled face toward the inside of the mortise. Test-fit the joint before glue up.

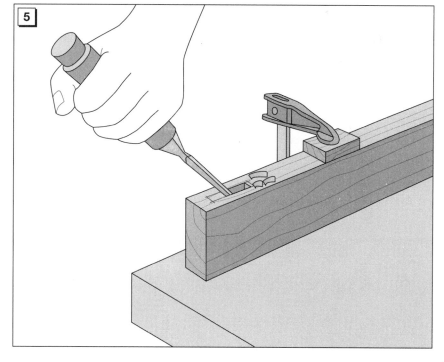

5

MORTISE-AND-TENON JOINTS

MAKING A ROUND TENON

Round tenons are often used to join the legs and rails of chairs. They may be turned on the lathe, but it can be tricky to achieve square shoulders and a tenon of precisely the right diameter. A simpler method is to use the drill press fitted with a dowel cutter. Center the workpiece vertically under the bit and

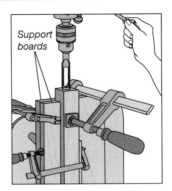

Support boards

clamp it in place with the aid of support boards. Once the tenon is cut to the required length, remove the waste by clamping the workpiece in a vise and cutting the shoulders with a backsaw. The mortise part of the joint is then easy to bore using a bit of the same diameter as the dowel cutter.

CUTTING TENONS ON THE TABLE SAW WITH A JIG

Tenons can be cut on the table saw with the aid of a dado head and a commercial tenoning jig. In the example shown below, twin tenons are being sawn. To lay out the tenons, divide the width of the workpiece into fifths. Clamp the stock end down in the jig and install a dado head the same width as the distance between two of the marks you just made. Set the depth of cut to the desired length of the tenons. Since the twin mortise-and-tenon is usually a blind joint, the tenons should be one-half to two-thirds as long as the thickness of the mortise piece. Adjust the tenoning jig so the first pass will cut the waste in the middle of the workpiece. Next, adjust the jig to cut one outer shoulder. Turn the workpiece around and reclamp it to the jig to cut the remaining shoulder [1]. Once the final shoulder is cut, the tenon piece may be used as a template to mark out the mortises. Chop out the mortises using a chisel and a wooden mallet [2].

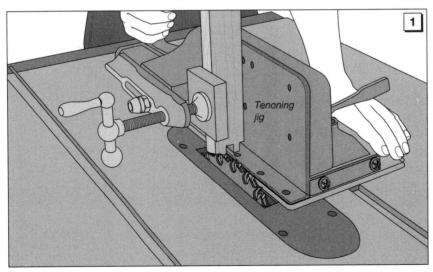

1

Tenoning jig

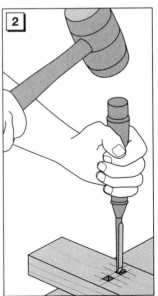

2

You can also cut tenons on the table saw with only a dado head. In the example shown on this page, a haunched tenon is being cut for a haunched mortise-and-tenon joint. In frame-and-panel construction, the haunch fills the grooves at the top and bottom end of the stiles. The joint itself is simply a two-shouldered mortise-and-tenon. When joining stiles and rails to enclose a panel, the tenons are made as thick as the width of the panel groove, often ¼ inch (one-third the thickness of ¾-inch-thick stiles and rails). To cut the tenons on the table saw, install a dado head slightly wider than the length of the tenon. Attach an auxiliary wooden fence to your saw's rip fence and notch it to house a portion of the dado head. This is done by positioning the auxiliary fence over the retracted dado head and slowly raising the blades so that they cut an arc into the wooden fence. Set the cutting height for the tenon cheeks. To cut the cheeks, mark a shoulder line on the leading edge of the workpiece. Then lay the workpiece face down in front of the miter gauge and align it so the outer edge of the dado head is in line with the shoulder mark. Next, butt the auxiliary fence up against the end of the workpiece, turn on the saw, and cut the first tenon cheek. Turn the workpiece over and repeat the pass

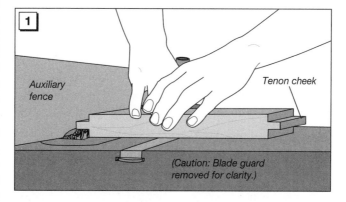

1

Auxiliary fence

Tenon cheek

(Caution: Blade guard removed for clarity.)

to cut the second cheek 1. Once the tenons have been cut on both ends of the tenon pieces, reset the fence for notching the haunch. Adjust the cutting height to the appropriate height for your project. Mark the width of the haunch on the leading face of the tenon, set the workpiece on edge in front of the miter gauge, and align the haunch mark with the dado head. Again, butt the fence against the end of the tenon. Cut the haunches into the tenons at both ends of each work-piece 2.

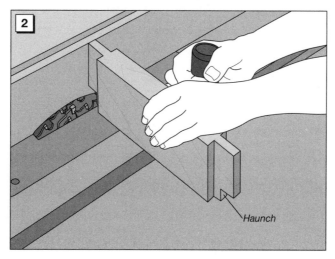

2

Haunch

CUTTING TENONS WITH A DADO HEAD

DOVETAIL JOINTS

The eye-catching dovetail joint is a hallmark of craftsmanship in cabinetmaking. It is also one of the strongest methods of joining two pieces of wood. Its tapered pins and tails interlock to provide outstanding resistance to virtually all types of stress—especially tension. For this reason, it is the preferred joint for connecting the fronts to the sides of drawers. The joint will hold together even if the glue fails.

Shown below are four representative types: the through dovetail, the blind and half-blind, and two examples of decorative dovetails. As with most aspects of joinery, the strength and appearance of the joint depend on the precision with which it is made. The number and spacing of the pins and tails is a matter of personal preference; refer to the illustration at the top of page 281 for information on angling the pins.

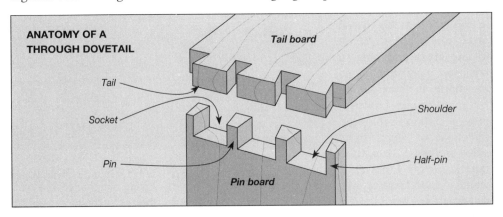

ANATOMY OF A THROUGH DOVETAIL

Tail board

Tail

Socket

Shoulder

Pin

Half-pin

Pin board

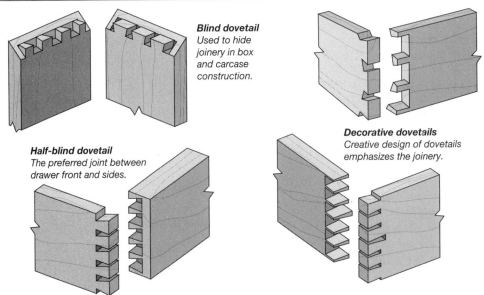

A GALLERY OF DOVETAIL JOINTS

Blind dovetail
Used to hide joinery in box and carcase construction.

Half-blind dovetail
The preferred joint between drawer front and sides.

Decorative dovetails
Creative design of dovetails emphasizes the joinery.

DOVETAIL JOINT PIN ANGLES

There are no precise rules for marking the angles of the pins of a dovetail joint. One rule of thumb is that the slope of the pins in hand-cut joints should be 1 in 6 if you are working with softwood, or 1 in 8 if you are using hardwood; for router-cut dovetails, an angle of 7° to 9° is acceptable with hardwood, or 9° to 14° with softwood. More precision is needed to get a good fit with dovetails at small angles than with dovetails at large angles.

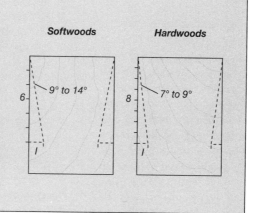

Softwoods

6 — 9° to 14°

Hardwoods

8 — 7° to 9°

COMMERCIAL DOVETAIL JIGS

Interchangeable-template jig
Permits router to cut dovetails with one adjustment; includes guide bushing and router bits. (See page 285 for information on using this jig to cut half-blind dovetails.)

Dovetail square
Used to mark pins at the appropriate angle; 1:6 and 1:8 models available.

Template guides
Used with non-piloted bits and attached to router subbase to maintain uniform distance between cutting edges and template of dovetail jig.

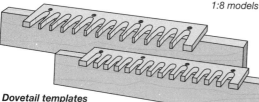

Dovetail templates
Used with router and top-piloted bits to produce through dovetails; consists of one fixed pin template and a fixed tail template, each attached to a backup board. Pin and tail boards are clamped to appropriate jigs with ends butted against fixed template and faces flush against backup boards.

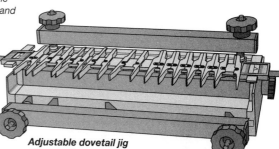

Adjustable dovetail jig
Allows router to cut half-blind and through dovetails with variable and adjustable spacing and width; a single adjustment sets width and spacing of pins and tails. Includes guide bushing and router bits.

DOVETAIL JOINTS

**CUTTING
A THROUGH
DOVETAIL
BY HAND**

Set a marking gauge to the thickness of the tail piece and scribe a shoulder line 1 across both faces of the pin board. Then lay out the pins at the end of the pin board following the sequence shown at right. Using a dovetail square 2, mark half-pins at each edge. Make sure the wide end of the pins is on the inside corner of the joint.

Next, lay out full pins between the half-pins. The number of pins and tails depends on the width of the workpieces, but there is no absolute rule as to their size or spacing. For most

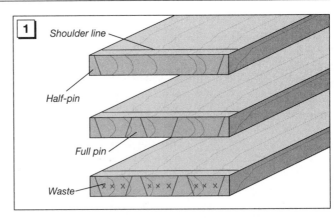

1

Shoulder line

Half-pin

Full pin

Waste

drawers, marking two evenly spaced pins between the half-pins will produce a durable and attractive joint. The width of the widest part of the pins should be roughly the same as the stock's thickness. Outline the pins between the half-pins and mark xs in each waste area as a reminder of what should be removed. Using a try square, extend the pin lines down

to the shoulder lines on the faces of the workpiece. To cut the pins, the ideal tool is a dovetail saw 3. A backsaw works well too. Keep the blade to the waste side of the pin lines and stop sawing at the shoulder line.

To remove the waste between the pins, you can use a coping saw or a band saw. But the traditional method is to chop them out with a mal-

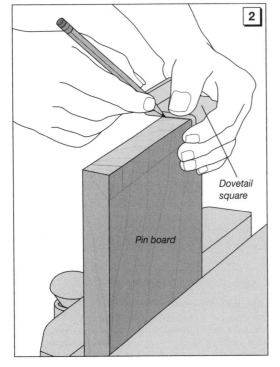

2

Dovetail
square

Pin board

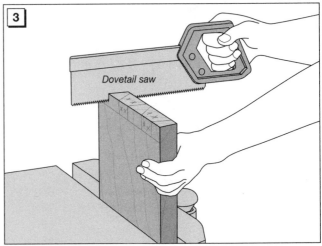

3

Dovetail saw

let and chisel 4 . Place the board on a work surface with the narrow sides of the pins facing up. Next align a guide board along the shoulder line and clamp this setup in place. The chisel blade should be no wider than the narrow side of the waste sections. Hold the chisel perfectly vertical with its flat face flush against the guide board and drive it about ⅛ inch into the waste area. Remove the first chip by tapping the chisel into the end grain. Remove roughly half the thickness of the waste this way, then flip the board over and chop out the other half.

The completed pin board may now be used as a template for laying out the tails. Place the tail board inside face up on the work surface and set the pin board end down on top of it 5 . Align the outer face of the pin board with the end of the tail board. If you are working with long boards, it is easier to clamp the setup in place. Mark the tails using a sharp pencil, then extend the lines over the end of the tail board and down to the shoulder line on the other face using the dovetail square. Now saw the tails the same way you cut the pins. When the tail board is complete,

test-fit the joint and correct any inaccuracies with a sharp chisel before applying the glue for final assembly.

CUTTING A THROUGH DOVETAIL BY HAND

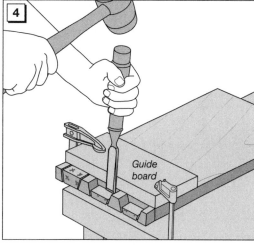

4

Guide board

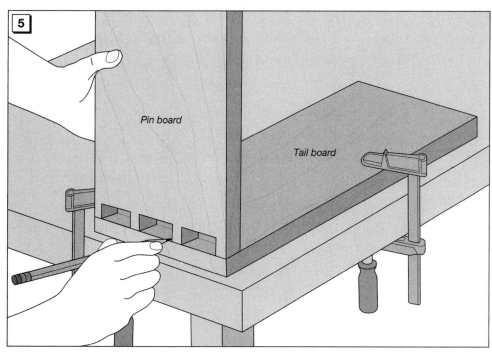

5

Pin board

Tail board

DOVETAIL JOINTS

CUTTING A HALF-BLIND DOVETAIL JOINT

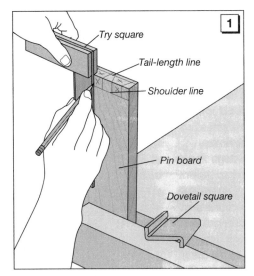

1

Try square
Tail-length line
Shoulder line
Pin board
Dovetail square

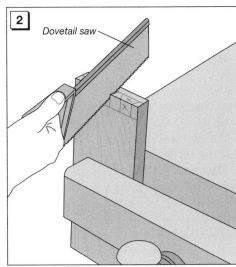

2

Dovetail saw

The half-blind dovetail is the most commonly used joint for fastening drawer fronts to sides. To lay out the joint, begin by scribing a line along the end of the pin member, or drawer front, using a marking gauge. This line represents the length of the tails. The line should be between two-thirds and three-quarters the thickness of the pin piece away from the inside face of the board. Then, with the gauge at the same setting, scribe a shoulder line on the tail piece. Next, adjust the gauge to the thickness of the tail piece, or drawer side, and scribe a shoulder line 1 on the inside face of the pin piece. Mark out the pins on the ends and inside faces of the pin board. Use a dovetail square and try square, following the same spacing guidelines suggested for the through dovetail *(page 282)*. To cut the pins 2, saw diagonally along the waste side of each pin with a dovetail saw. Be certain the kerf stops at the line on the end of the workpiece and the shoulder line on its inside face. Next, place the workpiece inside face up on your drill press table 3. Using a Forstner

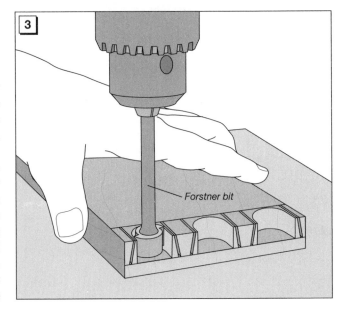

3

Forstner bit

bit no larger than the narrowest part of the waste sections, drill out as much waste as possible; stop when the bit reaches the line on the board end. Finally, clamp the board to a work surface with a guide block 4 aligned with the shoulder line on the face. Pare away the remaining waste with a chisel, tapping the handle with a mallet to cut to the marked lines.

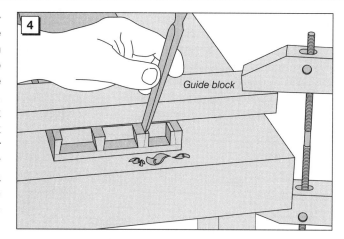

O ne of the easiest and most reliable ways to cut a dovetail is to use one of the many commercial dovetail jigs on the market. Although some cabinetmakers complain that the joints they cut have a mass-produced look and lack the individual appeal of hand-cut dovetails, they guarantee precise results joint after joint. The jig shown at right allows you to cut the pins and tails of a half-blind dovetail joint with a single setup. For this model, the pin and tail pieces are clamped to the jig and the proper template is fixed on top of the boards. Follow the manufacturer's instructions for the correct setup. Install the appropriate bit and template guide in your router, then rout the joint in two passes. First, guide the router in a straight line from right to left along the tail board, removing part of the waste. To finish the job, feed the tool in the opposite direction, moving the bit in and out of the slots between the template's fingers. Keep the template guide in contact with the edges of the fingers throughout the operation.

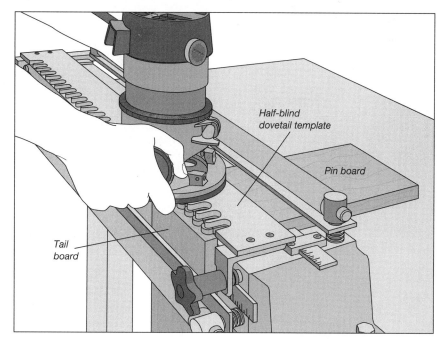

Half-blind dovetail template

Pin board

Tail board

BOX JOINTS

The box joint is similar to the dovetail, but with non-tapered fingers instead of pins and tails. Since the fingers can slide apart in two directions, the box joint does not resist tension as well as the dovetail. Still, the fingers provide plenty of long-grain gluing surface to make this a very sturdy joint.

The greatest advantage of the basic box joint over the dovetail is its ease of construction. As shown on page 287, the joint can be cut with a table saw and a simple jig. Variations of the box joint, such as the half-blind joint and the false box joint, are more complex, but they can all be done by machine.

COMMON BOX JOINTS

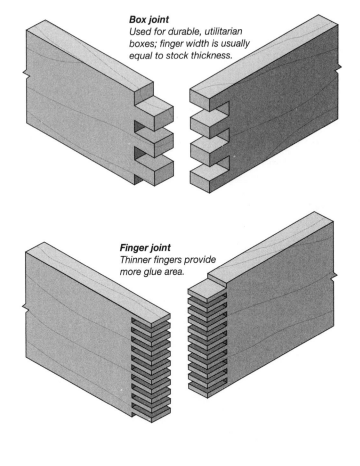

Box joint
Used for durable, utilitarian boxes; finger width is usually equal to stock thickness.

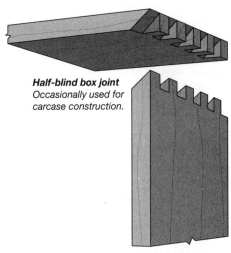

Half-blind box joint
Occasionally used for carcase construction.

Finger joint
Thinner fingers provide more glue area.

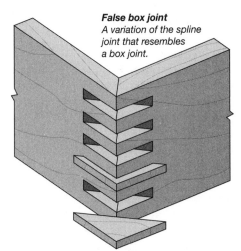

False box joint
A variation of the spline joint that resembles a box joint.

The basic box joint is most easily cut on the table saw, as shown on this page. Install a dado head the same width as the fingers of the joint and adjust the cutting height to the thickness of the stock. Next, prepare a miter gauge extension by cutting two notches [1] in the bottom of a 1 x 4. The space between the notches should be the same as the width of the dado head. Then glue a small wooden block into the first notch to produce a key that protrudes from the extension by slightly more than the thickness of the stock. Mount the extension to the miter gauge with the second notch in line with the dado head. To cut the fingers [2] for the joint, butt one piece end down against the miter

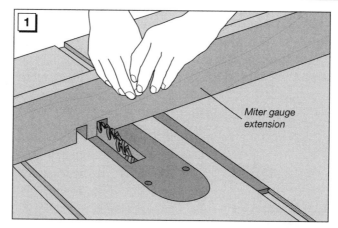

gauge extension. With the edge of the stock flush against the key, make the first pass. Next, move the workpiece over, slipping the notch you just cut down over the key, and make the second pass. Continue this process until all of the notches in the first workpiece have been cut.

Key

Now reverse the board, set the opposite face against the miter gauge extension, and place the first notch you cut over the key. Butt the edge of the mating piece [3] against the first board and make a pass. Continue to notch the second workpiece.

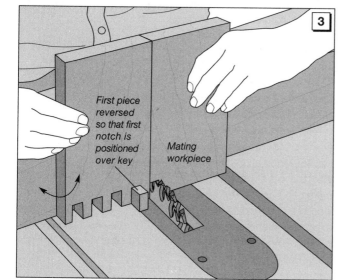

First piece reversed so that first notch is positioned over key

Mating workpiece

RULE JOINT

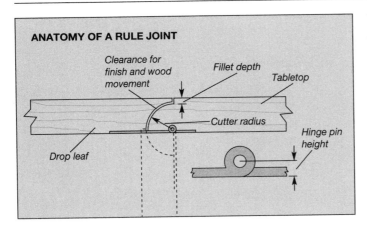

ANATOMY OF A RULE JOINT

Clearance for finish and wood movement

Fillet depth

Tabletop

Cutter radius

Hinge pin height

Drop leaf

Not all joints are designed to be permanently bonded together. The tusk mortise-and-tenon is an example of a joint designed to be rigid while in use, but easy to disassemble. It was commonly used in trestle dinner tables, allowing the table to be knocked down and set out of the way between meals. Another space-saving joint is the rule joint, a decorative joint normally used in drop-leaf tables. It features two hinged pieces that mesh together. The rounded-over edge of the tabletop mates with a cove cut along the edge of the drop leaf.

MAKING A RULE JOINT

Make a rule joint using a router. Start by rounding over the edge of the tabletop and cutting a cove in the edge of the drop leaf. As shown in the illustration above, the most critical requirement is that the center of the hinge pin align with the centers of the round-over arc and the cove arc. The fillet in both pieces must be of the correct depth. To determine the fillet depth, add the radius of either cutter to the height of the hinge pin and subtract your total from the thickness of the top.

To shape the edge of the top, install a piloted round-over bit [1] in your router and make two passes. Hold the pilot against the edge and the router's base plate flat on the workpiece. To cove the drop leaf, use a piloted cove bit the same diameter as the round-over bit. Mount the router in a table [2] and align the fence with the bit's pilot. Again, make two passes. Before the second pass, shape a piece of scrap and test it against the rounded-over edge of the table. The fit must be exact—with some clearance for fin-

ishing materials and wood movement. Once the drop leaf has been coved, place the top and drop leaf face down on a work surface and install the hinges. These must be mortised into place on the underside of the pieces.

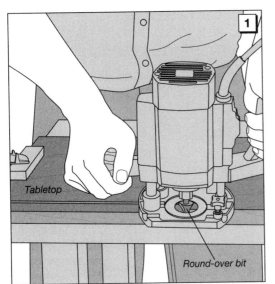

Tabletop

Round-over bit

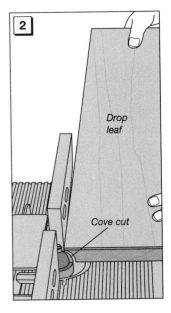

Drop leaf

Cove cut

CABINETMAKING TECHNIQUES

W hile no two pieces of handcrafted furniture are exactly the same, you do not have to reinvent the wheel with every new project. Generations of craftsmen have blazed a well-marked trail, laying down principles and techniques that can be applied to even the most basic projects. This chapter will explore how you can fashion solid and appealing furniture using these time-tested methods and skills.

will highlight the joints that work best in each situation.

Pieces that feature box-like frameworks, or carcases, such as bookcases, chests of drawers, and armoires, are commonly built from either solid wood panels or framed panels. A review of solid wood-panel construction techniques begins on page 296. Building frame-and-panel furniture is examined starting on page 298.

The discussion then shifts to adapting the basic carcase by installing shelves *(page 304)*, tops and bottoms *(page 308)*, drawers *(page 310)*, and doors *(page 316)*. The chapter concludes with a section on legs *(page 318)*. Included are step-by-step instructions on making two popular leg styles—tapered and cabriole legs—and on connecting legs to rails.

Beginning on page 290, the chapter surveys several types of furniture that woodworkers typically build, including bookcases, chests of drawers, tables, chairs, armoires, and beds. The focus is on the structure of the pieces. Although in virtually every instance there are various joinery options for connecting the parts together, the chapter

BOOKCASES

ookcases, such as the one illustrated below, represent the most basic form of solid-panel construction. Rectangular in shape, with two sides, a back, a top, and a bottom enclosing a series of shelves, bookcases are merely partitioned boxes. However, there are several variables to consider when building a bookcase. Foremost is determining the thickness of the stock and the span of the shelves based on the weight they will bear *(page 8)*.

In choosing the joinery for the shelves, consider whether you want adjustable shelves, as shown here, or fixed shelving. A few of the many options are presented beginning on page 304. Shelf support hardware is shown on page 380. Whatever option you select, it must be able to withstand shear *(page 254)*. Fixed shelves can be supported along their span by tacking the back panel to them from behind. If you are designing a bookcase with adjustable shelves, you may need to use thicker stock or stronger building materials (that is, hardwood rather than particleboard), since adjustable shelves are not nailed to the back.

ANATOMY OF A BOOKCASE

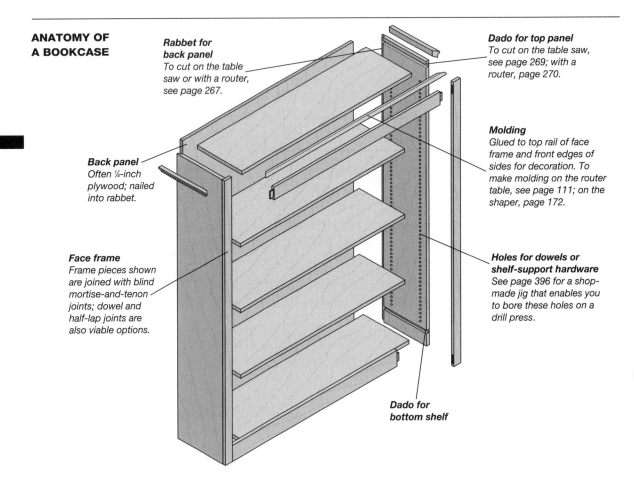

Rabbet for back panel
To cut on the table saw or with a router, see page 267.

Back panel
Often ¼-inch plywood; nailed into rabbet.

Face frame
Frame pieces shown are joined with blind mortise-and-tenon joints; dowel and half-lap joints are also viable options.

Dado for top panel
To cut on the table saw, see page 269; with a router, page 270.

Molding
Glued to top rail of face frame and front edges of sides for decoration. To make molding on the router table, see page 111; on the shaper, page 172.

Holes for dowels or shelf-support hardware
See page 396 for a shop-made jig that enables you to bore these holes on a drill press.

Dado for bottom shelf

CHESTS OF DRAWERS

A chest of drawers can be constructed as a carcase with drawers resting on shelves. However, as shown below, other features are often incorporated for additional strength, convenience, and appearance. The carcase is attached to a base with legs and a separate top overhangs the carcase. Base options are shown on page 297. Since the drawers conceal the interior, the top and base can be fastened to the carcase from the inside with screws. In this example, the carcase top and bottom are joined to the sides with a rabbet-and-dado; other joinery choices are illustrated on page 296.

The drawers are separated by dust frames. Built with frame-and-panel techniques (*page 298*) and joined to the side panels with sliding dovetails, the frames support the drawers and strengthen the carcase, while the panels function as dust barriers. The drawer guides are attached to the dust frames with lap joints. Matching runners will be attached to the drawer bottoms so that the drawers will slide smoothly in their openings. Other drawer-mounting methods are presented on page 313. The drawer openings must be sized to accommodate the expansion and contraction of the drawers as they react to changes in relative humidity.

The carcase must be designed to resist distortion, which might cause binding. Corner blocks lend rigidity and are easy to install.

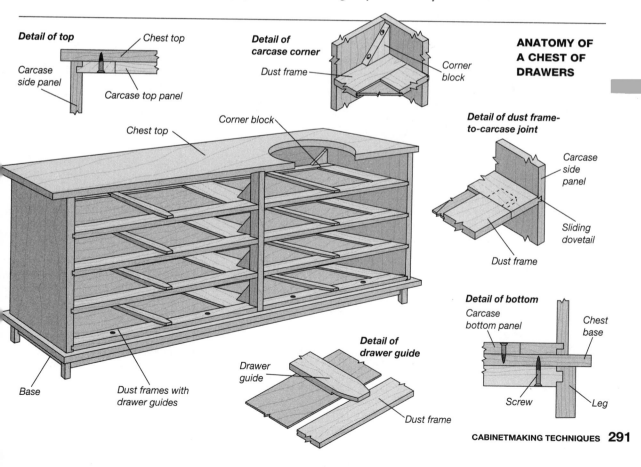

Detail of top
Chest top
Carcase side panel
Carcase top panel

Detail of carcase corner
Dust frame
Corner block

ANATOMY OF A CHEST OF DRAWERS

Chest top
Corner block

Detail of dust frame-to-carcase joint
Carcase side panel
Sliding dovetail
Dust frame

Base
Dust frames with drawer guides

Detail of drawer guide
Drawer guide
Dust frame

Detail of bottom
Carcase bottom panel
Chest base
Screw
Leg

TABLES

Tables are essentially tops supported by legs. To ensure rigidity and avoid having to fasten into the end grain of the legs, tables are built so that the legs are joined to rails, and the rails are attached to the top. The legs can be joined to the rails in several ways, as shown below and on page 323. The most common method is the mortise-and-tenon joint. It provides good long-grain gluing and is resistant to shear, racking, and tension stresses. Other effective options include the dowel joint and commercial brackets that are bolted to the legs and fit into grooves cut in the rails.

While rigidity is crucial in leg-to-rail joinery, the opposite is true in fastening the top to the rails. This connection must be allowed to move so the wood will not split when the top expands or contracts due to humidity changes. Several techniques that will solve this problem are shown on page 309. Since some of these methods require the rails to be prepared in some way, be sure to select your top-fastening option before joining the legs and rails.

ANATOMY OF A TABLE

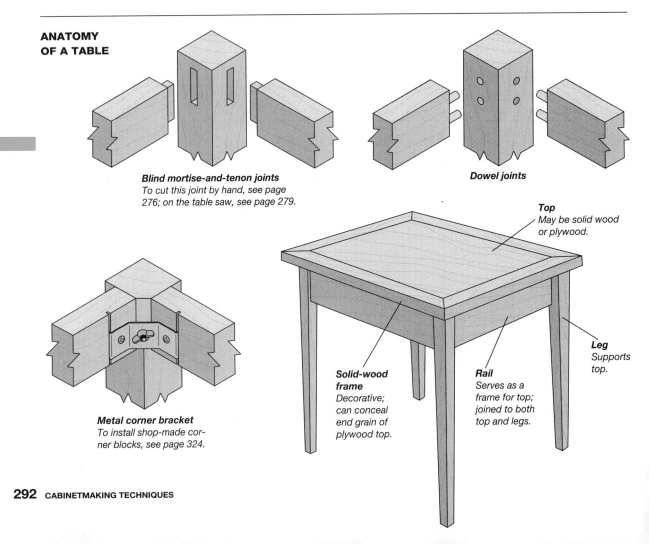

Blind mortise-and-tenon joints
To cut this joint by hand, see page 276; on the table saw, see page 279.

Dowel joints

Metal corner bracket
To install shop-made corner blocks, see page 324.

Top
May be solid wood or plywood.

Leg
Supports top.

Solid-wood frame
Decorative; can conceal end grain of plywood top.

Rail
Serves as a frame for top; joined to both top and legs.

CHAIRS

There are two traditional approaches to chair construction: The platform chair, in which the leg and back assemblies are joined to the seat, and the frame chair, in which the seat is fastened to an independent framework. As shown below, the primary joint in both cases is the mortise-and-tenon. The platform chair uses round mortises and tenons. The frame chair relies on both round and square versions of the joint.

In the typical frame chair, the seat back and the back legs make up one assembly while the front legs and seat frame comprise the other. The seat frame can be adapted to accommodate woven cane or a separate padded and upholstered seat, as shown. In both platform and frame designs, stretchers are commonly used to connect the legs. The stretchers lend rigidity to the chair and help to relieve stress on other joints.

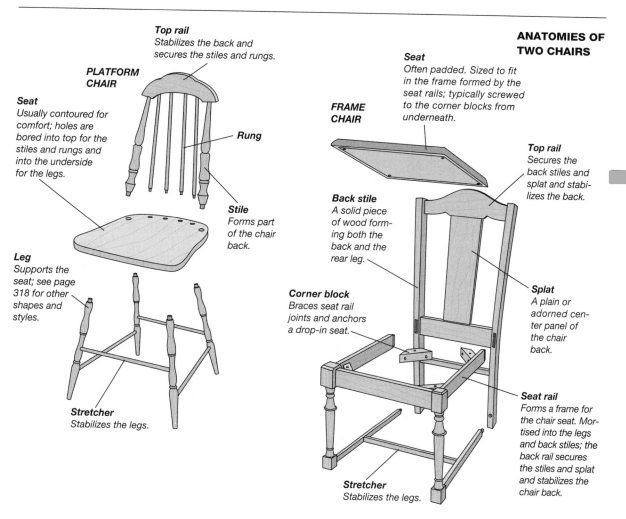

ANATOMIES OF TWO CHAIRS

PLATFORM CHAIR

Top rail
Stabilizes the back and secures the stiles and rungs.

Seat
Usually contoured for comfort; holes are bored into top for the stiles and rungs and into the underside for the legs.

Rung

Stile
Forms part of the chair back.

Leg
Supports the seat; see page 318 for other shapes and styles.

Stretcher
Stabilizes the legs.

FRAME CHAIR

Seat
Often padded. Sized to fit in the frame formed by the seat rails; typically screwed to the corner blocks from underneath.

Top rail
Secures the back stiles and splat and stabilizes the back.

Back stile
A solid piece of wood forming both the back and the rear leg.

Corner block
Braces seat rail joints and anchors a drop-in seat.

Splat
A plain or adorned center panel of the chair back.

Seat rail
Forms a frame for the chair seat. Mortised into the legs and back stiles; the back rail secures the stiles and splat and stabilizes the chair back.

Stretcher
Stabilizes the legs.

ARMOIRES

The armoire shown below is a typical example of frame-and-panel construction (*page 298*) and how it is used to build large storage units. The panels may be raised, as in this example, or flat. Flat panels help to reduce the overall weight of the piece, but raised panels are more decorative. The front, back, and sides of this piece are each frame-and-panel assemblies. Each one features a frame of stiles and rails joined with mortises and tenons. The back and side frames each enclose a panel; the front has doors hinged to the stiles. The doors are also frame-and-panel; other door styles are illustrated on page 316.

Frame-and-panel assemblies are time-consuming to make, but there are definite payoffs: The reduced size of the individual parts enables you to use lower grades of lumber, which can significantly reduce costs. Also, there are structural advantages, especially when building large pieces such as an armoire. Because the panels float in the frames, problems associated with wood expansion and contraction are minimized.

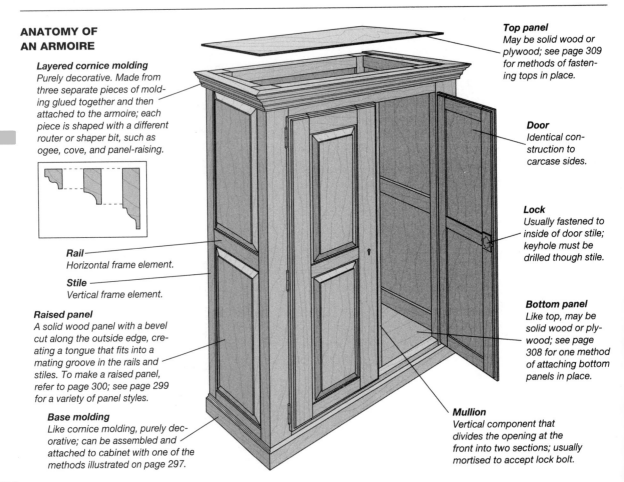

ANATOMY OF AN ARMOIRE

Layered cornice molding
Purely decorative. Made from three separate pieces of molding glued together and then attached to the armoire; each piece is shaped with a different router or shaper bit, such as ogee, cove, and panel-raising.

Rail
Horizontal frame element.

Stile
Vertical frame element.

Raised panel
A solid wood panel with a bevel cut along the outside edge, creating a tongue that fits into a mating groove in the rails and stiles. To make a raised panel, refer to page 300; see page 299 for a variety of panel styles.

Base molding
Like cornice molding, purely decorative; can be assembled and attached to cabinet with one of the methods illustrated on page 297.

Top panel
May be solid wood or plywood; see page 309 for methods of fastening tops in place.

Door
Identical construction to carcase sides.

Lock
Usually fastened to inside of door stile; keyhole must be drilled though stile.

Bottom panel
Like top, may be solid wood or plywood; see page 308 for one method of attaching bottom panels in place.

Mullion
Vertical component that divides the opening at the front into two sections; usually mortised to accept lock bolt.

BEDS

The side rails and posts of beds are commonly connected with knockdown (KD) hardware, or with joinery that can be easily disassembled. None of the options shown below uses glue. The traditional solution is a tusk tenon, which features a wedge to secure the joint. Stub tenons can be used with hex-head bolts to prevent the parts from slipping apart. Knockdown connectors make it possible to connect the posts and rails with simple butt joints. The end rails and headboard can be joined to the posts with permanent joinery, such as a blind mortise-and-tenon.

Most beds consist of two rigidly constructed frames at the head and foot, held in place by the side rails. Cleats screwed and glued along the inside of the rails support the bed slats, which in turn support the box spring and mattress. Despite their size, beds are relatively simple to make.

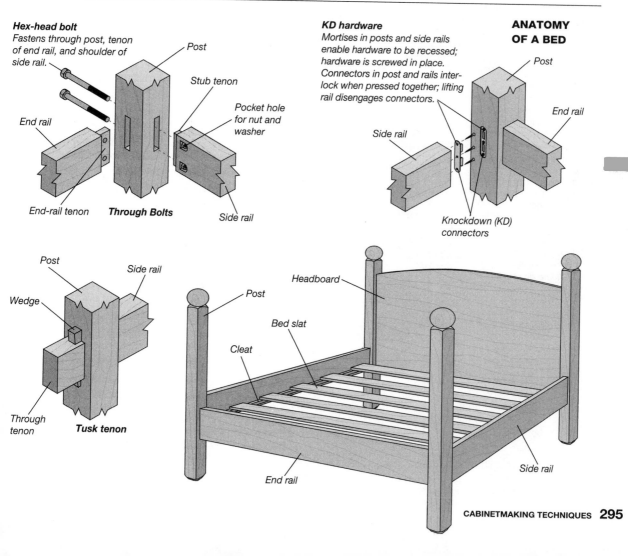

Hex-head bolt
Fastens through post, tenon of end rail, and shoulder of side rail.

Post

Stub tenon

Pocket hole for nut and washer

End rail

End-rail tenon   **Through Bolts**

Side rail

KD hardware
Mortises in posts and side rails enable hardware to be recessed; hardware is screwed in place. Connectors in post and rails interlock when pressed together; lifting rail disengages connectors.

ANATOMY OF A BED

Post

End rail

Side rail

Knockdown (KD) connectors

Post

Side rail

Wedge

Through tenon   **Tusk tenon**

Post

Headboard

Bed slat

Cleat

End rail

Side rail

SOLID-PANEL CONSTRUCTION

Solid-panel carcases are the basis of many types of furniture, including bookcases, chests of drawers, and desks. As shown below, they can be divided vertically or feature shelves, and they can be joined at the corners in various ways, but all solid-panel carcases are essentially four panels attached together to form a box. Some important guidelines apply to all solid-panel carcases. First, make sure the grain of the panels runs in the same direction. This will enable the panels to shrink and swell together; a carcase with the grain of one panel at right angles to

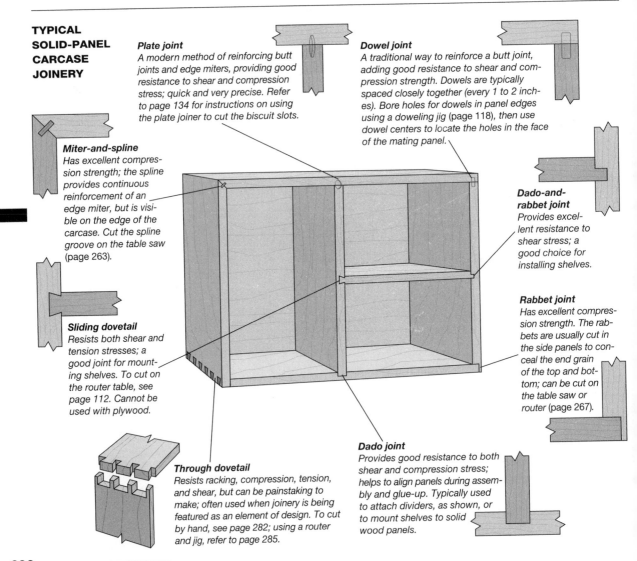

TYPICAL SOLID-PANEL CARCASE JOINERY

Plate joint
A modern method of reinforcing butt joints and edge miters, providing good resistance to shear and compression stress; quick and very precise. Refer to page 134 for instructions on using the plate joiner to cut the biscuit slots.

Dowel joint
A traditional way to reinforce a butt joint, adding good resistance to shear and compression strength. Dowels are typically spaced closely together (every 1 to 2 inches). Bore holes for dowels in panel edges using a doweling jig (page 118), then use dowel centers to locate the holes in the face of the mating panel.

Miter-and-spline
Has excellent compression strength; the spline provides continuous reinforcement of an edge miter, but is visible on the edge of the carcase. Cut the spline groove on the table saw (page 263).

Dado-and-rabbet joint
Provides excellent resistance to shear stress; a good choice for installing shelves.

Sliding dovetail
Resists both shear and tension stresses; a good joint for mounting shelves. To cut on the router table, see page 112. Cannot be used with plywood.

Rabbet joint
Has excellent compression strength. The rabbets are usually cut in the side panels to conceal the end grain of the top and bottom; can be cut on the table saw or router (page 267).

Through dovetail
Resists racking, compression, tension, and shear, but can be painstaking to make; often used when joinery is being featured as an element of design. To cut by hand, see page 282; using a router and jig, refer to page 285.

Dado joint
Provides good resistance to both shear and compression stress; helps to align panels during assembly and glue-up. Typically used to attach dividers, as shown, or to mount shelves to solid wood panels.

another will eventually split as the pieces expand or contract at different rates. Make all four panels the same width and thickness; parallel panels should share equal dimensions.

If you are installing shelves, select a mounting method *(page 304)* before gluing up the carcase. You may need to bore holes or cut dadoes in the side panels. Solid wood panels are generally made up of narrow boards edge-glued together. Arrange the boards to create a pleasing grain pattern and glue them together as explained on page 334.

These two base options are suited to carcases with sides that reach the floor.

BASE OPTIONS

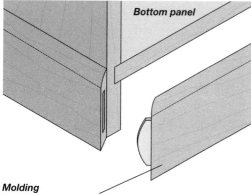

Bottom panel

Molding
Provides a decorative border for the bottom of the carcase; glued to carcase. Joined at corners with reinforced face miters. Miter joints between molding pieces should be reinforced with splines or biscuits; see page 260.

Glue block
Reinforces corner.

Front trim piece
Attached to carcase below bottom panel.

These two base treatments hold a carcase off the floor.

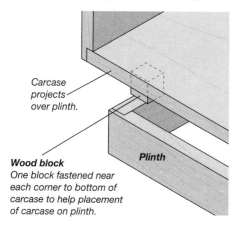

Carcase projects over plinth.

Wood block
One block fastened near each corner to bottom of carcase to help placement of carcase on plinth.

Plinth

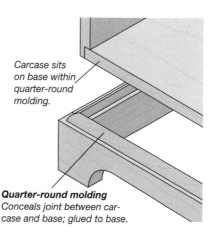

Carcase sits on base within quarter-round molding.

Quarter-round molding
Conceals joint between carcase and base; glued to base.

FRAME-AND-PANEL CONSTRUCTION

In frame-and-panel construction, the frame, made up of stiles and rails, provides the rigidity. The inside edges of the stiles and rails are grooved to house the panel. Although the frame pieces are glued together, the panel is not glued in place. It floats in the grooves so that it is free to expand and contract with changes in humidity. In a cabinet like the one shown below, the sides, front, and back are individual frame-and-panel assemblies. The outside edges of the side stiles are joined to the inside faces of the front and back stiles. To help align the stiles during assembly, you can use biscuits, edge miters-and-splines (*page 263*), or lock miters (*page 260*).

Since the panel is not fastened to the frame, it contributes little to the strength of the assembly. The joints connecting the rails to the

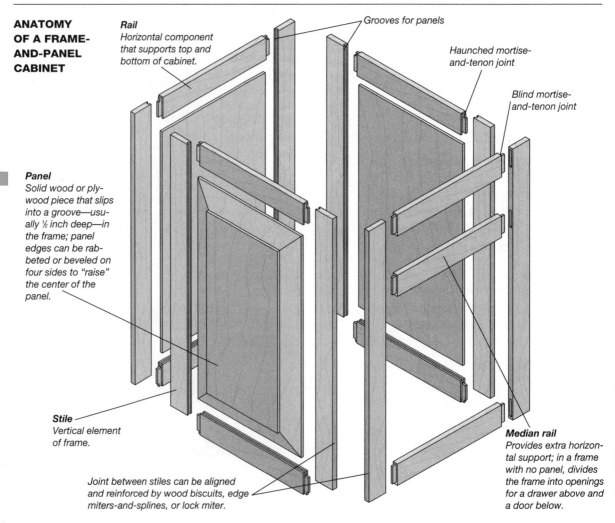

ANATOMY OF A FRAME-AND-PANEL CABINET

Rail
Horizontal component that supports top and bottom of cabinet.

Grooves for panels

Haunched mortise-and-tenon joint

Blind mortise-and-tenon joint

Panel
Solid wood or plywood piece that slips into a groove—usually ½ inch deep—in the frame; panel edges can be rabbeted or beveled on four sides to "raise" the center of the panel.

Stile
Vertical element of frame.

Median rail
Provides extra horizontal support; in a frame with no panel, divides the frame into openings for a drawer above and a door below.

Joint between stiles can be aligned and reinforced by wood biscuits, edge miters-and-splines, or lock miter.

stiles must therefore be able to withstand considerable stress. The traditional joinery choice is the mortise and tenon. On the carcase shown on page 298, the blind version is used for the front assembly; a haunched joint *(page 273)* is used for the sides and back frames of the carcase; the haunch fills the end of the panel grooves.

As illustrated below, frame-and-panel construction offers a wide range of decorative options: The panel may be flat or raised and feature one of many molded bevels. The use of thin plywood flat panels reduces the weight of a finished project and is often the easiest and most economical approach. Raised solid-wood panels, however, lend an appearance of depth and quality to a piece.

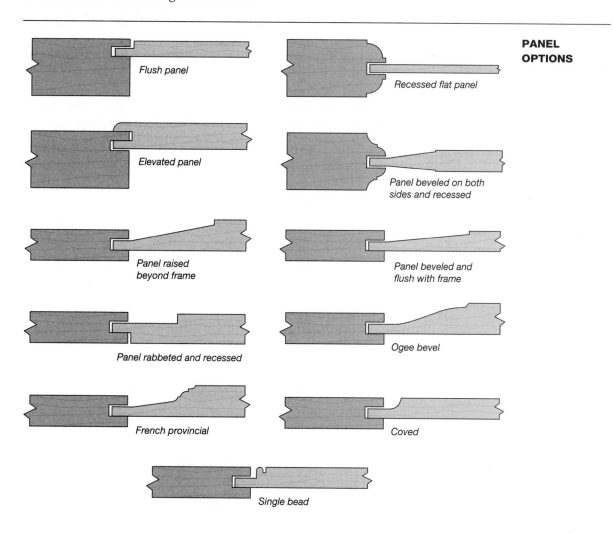

PANEL OPTIONS

Flush panel

Recessed flat panel

Elevated panel

Panel beveled on both sides and recessed

Panel raised beyond frame

Panel beveled and flush with frame

Panel rabbeted and recessed

Ogee bevel

French provincial

Coved

Single bead

FRAME-AND-PANEL CONSTRUCTION

**MAKING A
RAISED PANEL**

There are several effective methods for producing raised panels. One common technique involves using the table saw to bevel the ends and edges of the panel. This method is shown below. To bevel a panel on the table saw, attach a wooden auxiliary fence to the rip fence 1. Because the panel must be fed on end and on edge, the auxiliary fence should be tall enough to prevent the panel from wobbling. Tilt the blade to the desired angle (typically about 7 to 10 degrees). You may have to make fine adjustments to the

blade and fence settings, so make a few passes on a test piece the same thickness as the panel. Holding the workpiece behind the blade, set the cutting height so that the top of the blade just extends beyond the outer face of the panel. Butt the fence up against the panel. To avoid tearout on the panel, cut the ends first; any tearout on the end grain will be trimmed off when the sides are beveled. For additional stability, clamp a guide block to the workpiece so that it will ride along the fence during the pass. Feed the panel with both hands,

keeping them well above the blade. Use one hand to hold the back face of the panel flush against the fence and use the other to push the panel and the guide block forward. Before beveling the sides, test-fit the beveled ends in their frame grooves. The angle of the bevel should prevent the end of the panel from bottoming out in the groove. Ideally, the end of the panel should stop about midway in the groove, providing room for expansion. Adjust the fence or blade settings, if necessary. Once the fit is right, bevel the ends and sides of your panel 2.

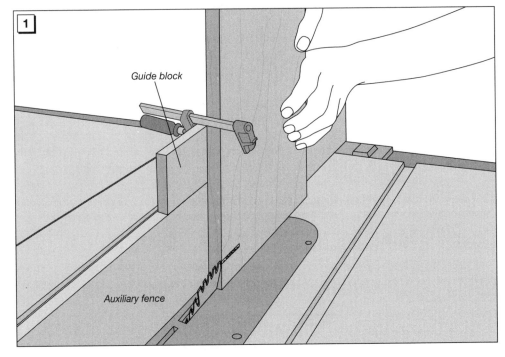

Guide block

Auxiliary fence

2

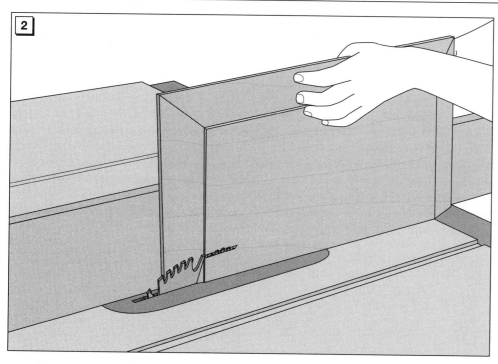

Panels with molded bevels can be cut on the shaper or, as shown in illustration 3, a table-mounted router. Install a piloted panel-raising bit in the router. To produce a smooth, even profile, use a straightedge to align the infeed and outfeed fences with the outer edge of the bit's pilot bearing. Again, to minimize the risk of tearout, rout the ends of the panel first and then the sides. It is best to raise the panel with a series of passes, starting with a cutting depth of about ⅛ inch. Shape all four edges, increase the depth of cut, and repeat the process. To prevent burn marks on the stock, feed the panel at a steady rate, firmly pressing its face down on the table and its edge tight against the fence.

3

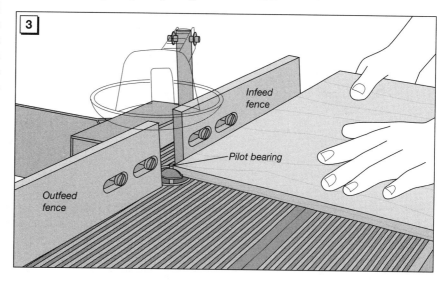

Infeed fence

Pilot bearing

Outfeed fence

EDGE BANDING

Carcases are often made with plywood. In addition to being more economical and easier to build with than solid-wood panels, plywood is more stable when exposed to humidity changes. The major drawback with plywood furniture is the problem of concealing exposed ends and edges. One alternative is to design your pieces with mitered corners and face frames. Edge banding is another practical way of covering exposed ends and edges.

Commercial veneer tape is the simplest solution, but there are some wood species used in plywood face veneers that are not available as veneer tape. The solid-wood edge treatments shown below can be cut from any wood. They offer other important advantages: They resist damage better than veneer tape and can be molded. Solid-wood banding is a good choice for the front edges of plywood shelves. Feathered-lip banding, for example, provides a fine miter-like seam along the upper corner, which makes the banding less obvious than veneer tape. Wider edge treatments, such as the tongue-and-groove or the drop lip, add rigidity to shelves and leave the impression that they are made of heavier stock.

VARIETIES OF SHOP-MADE EDGE BANDING

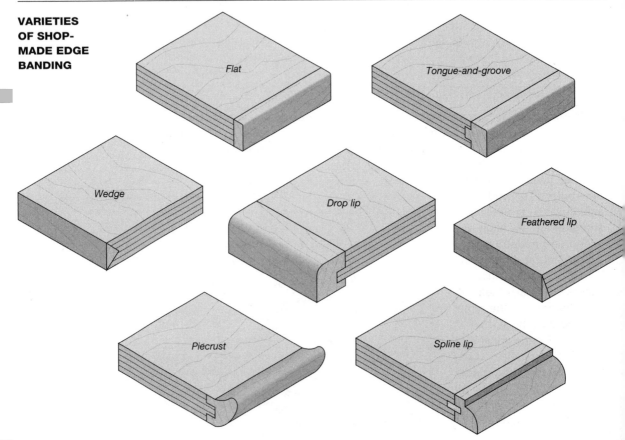

Flat

Tongue-and-groove

Wedge

Drop lip

Feathered lip

Piecrust

Spline lip

Commercial veneer tape is self-adhesive and generally comes in rolls. To install it, cut your panel square and smooth, and apply the tape with a household iron.

To make your own veneer, rip strips from wide boards on the table saw or band saw. Secure the panel in a handscrew, then clamp the handscrew to a work surface to hold the panel upright. Apply the strips with white or yellow glue. Hold the veneer in place with strips of masking tape while the adhesive cures 1. Space the strips 3 to 4 inches apart to apply adequate pressure.

The tongue-and-groove is a good joint for applying wider edge banding to a panel. To cut the joint on the table saw, start by ripping a groove down the middle of the panel's edge. The width of the groove should be about one-third the panel thickness. Outline the tongue on the banding to match the groove in the panel. Feed the banding on edge to cut the sides of the tongue. To cut its shoulders, feed the banding along the fence with a push stick 2. To apply the banding, secure the panel upright, spread glue in the groove and on the tongue, fit the pieces together 3, and use three-way clamps *(page 331)* to hold the joint together.

APPLYING EDGE BANDING

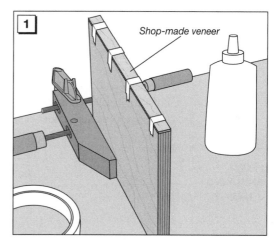

Shop-made veneer

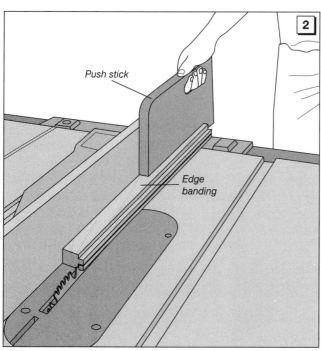

Push stick

Edge banding

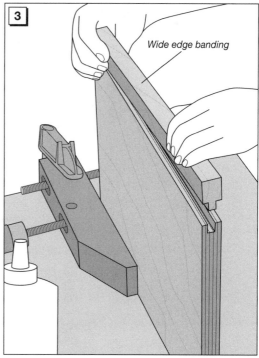

Wide edge banding

SHELVING

Shelving can be either fixed or adjustable. The main advantage of adjustable shelving is that the shelves can be moved after the furniture is assembled. While fixed shelving lacks this flexibility and convenience, it adds to the structural strength of the piece. As shown below, the most common joint for installing fixed shelves is the through dado. The joint is easy to cut with a dado head or router. A variation of the through joint, the stopped dado, enables you to conceal the joinery on the front edge of a bookcase. The sliding dovetail is a decorative variation and is exceptionally strong. Its one drawback is that it is time-consuming to cut *(page 112)* and fit.

All of the adjustable shelving options shown on page 305 are easy to install. In most cases, the hardware is difficult to conceal, but the shop-made method presented on page 306 is almost invisible. Whichever shelf-mounting option you select, be sure to account for the load your shelves will have to bear before designing your piece and sizing your stock *(page 8)*.

**FIXED
SHELVING
JOINERY**

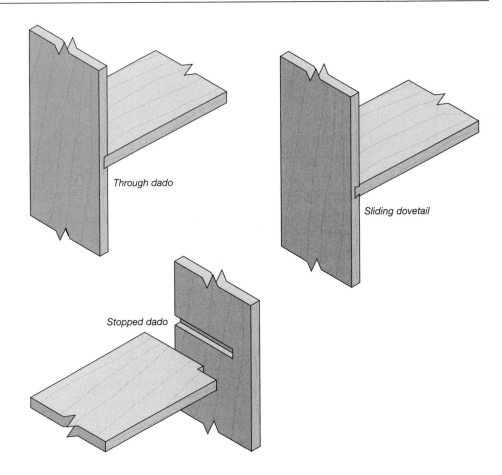

Through dado

Sliding dovetail

Stopped dado

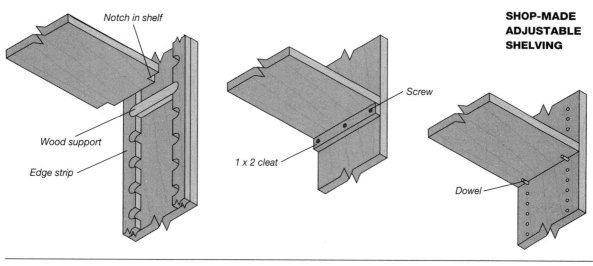

Notch in shelf

Wood support

Edge strip

Screw

1 x 2 cleat

Dowel

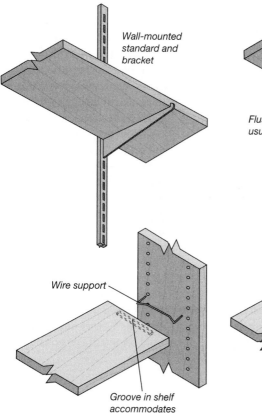

Wall-mounted standard and bracket

Flush clip; usually metal.

Metal pilaster

Wire support

Groove in shelf accommodates wire support

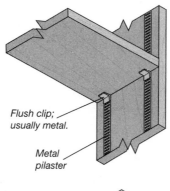

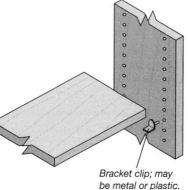

Bracket clip; may be metal or plastic.

Pilaster-type clips

There are various commercial hardware options for holding up shelving. They include spoon-shaped pins, locking pins, and simple metal and plastic clips. There are also several types of clips that will fit into metal pilasters. The pilasters are set into grooves cut in the sides of the carcase.

Spoon-shaped pin support

Locking pin support

SHELVING

ADJUSTABLE SHELVES: HIDDEN SHELF SUPPORTS

The adjustable shelving system shown on this page is easy to install, strong, and relatively inconspicuous. Before gluing up your carcase, bore two parallel rows of holes in the side panels with a brad-point bit. On the drill press, use the jig illustrated on page 396. It will help you space the holes equally and ensure that they are a uniform distance from the edges of the panels. With a drill, you can use a commercial shelf-drilling jig. Clamped to the panel edges, the jig will

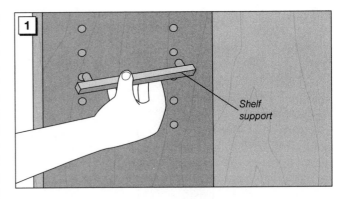

help you align the holes perfectly. Once all the holes are drilled, make the shelf supports from ⅜ x ⅜-inch hardwood strips. To make sure

Shelf support

the dowels in each support line up with the holes in the side panels, insert dowel centers in two of the holes at the same height and press the support in position against the centers. Their pointed ends will punch starting points for drilling the dowel holes. Glue the dowels into the holes in the supports.

Once the carcase is glued up *(page 336)*, position a shelf support 1 in each side panel at every shelf location. To prepare each shelf, position it in the carcase over the supports and draw a line around the supports on the underside of each shelf. Rout a stopped rabbet within the outline *(page 267)* and fit the shelf in place 2. The rabbets not only conceal the supports, they also prevent the shelf from sliding out of position.

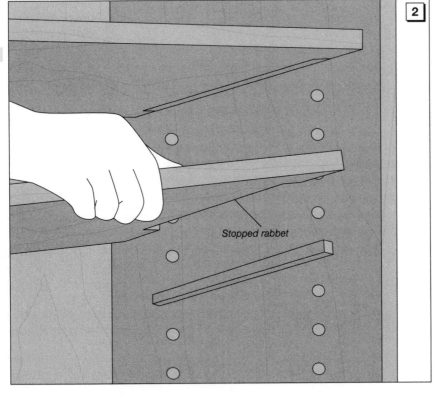

Stopped rabbet

The shelving method shown on page 306 is inappropriate for frame-and-panel furniture because the panels cannot be relied on to support shelves. The system shown here, on the other hand, works well because the shelf supports are held by corner strips anchored to the stiles. Prepare the strips from a board wide enough to yield four of them. Install a dado head 1 on your table saw or radial arm saw, adjusting its width to cut dadoes that will accommodate the shelf supports. Saw a series of dadoes at equal intervals across the board. Then rip the board into four identical strips and screw them to the stiles. Next cut two shelf supports for each shelf. The supports should be thick enough to fit snugly in

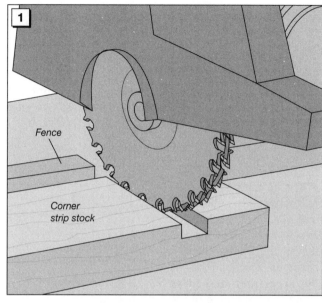

Fence

Corner strip stock

the dadoes and wide enough to extend about ½ inch beyond the edge of the corner strips. This will provide adequate support for the shelves. Trim the supports to fit between the front and back stiles, then install them 2. If you want the shelves to extend from one side panel to the other, notch them to fit around the corner strips.

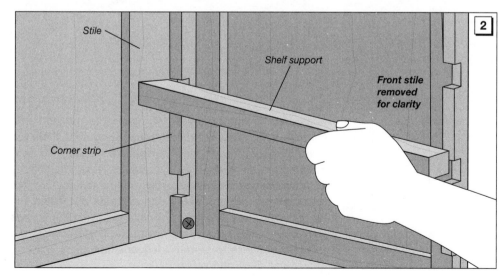

Stile

Shelf support

Front stile removed for clarity

Corner strip

TOPS AND BOTTOMS

In frame-and-panel furniture, a separate top and bottom must be installed after the piece is glued up. To compensate for wood shrinkage and expansion, these components must be fastened in ways that allow the top and bottom to move independently of the frame. This is especially true if you are using a solid-wood, edge-glued top or bottom.

As shown below, bottoms are commonly installed with ledger strips that are fastened to the rails and stiles and the bottom. The clearance holes must be oversize to allow the screws and the bottom to move. Three common methods for installing tops are shown on page 309. Step-by-step instructions are presented for one technique—screws and wood buttons.

INSTALLING A BOTTOM USING LEDGER STRIPS

Cut the bottom panel to fit between the stiles and rails. Then set the cabinet on its side and position the bottom in the frame. Using a pencil, mark location lines on the lower rails and stiles along the underside of the bottom to indicate where the ledger strips should be fastened. Cut four ledger strips from ¾ x ¾-inch hardwood to

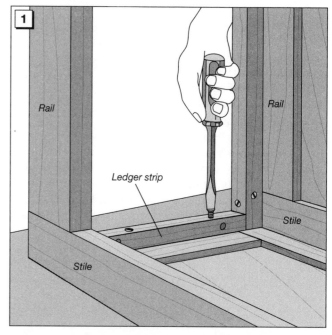

fit around the interior of the cabinet. Drill holes in each strip, boring through one edge for fastening the strip to the frame and through an adjacent edge for screwing the bottom in place. The holes should be slightly larger than the screw shanks to permit movement. Glue and screw

the strips to the rails and stiles [1] so that their top edges are even with the location lines. Next, position the bottom panel against the ledger strips and fasten it in position, driving the screws from the underside of the ledger strips [2].

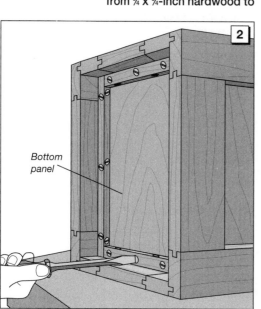

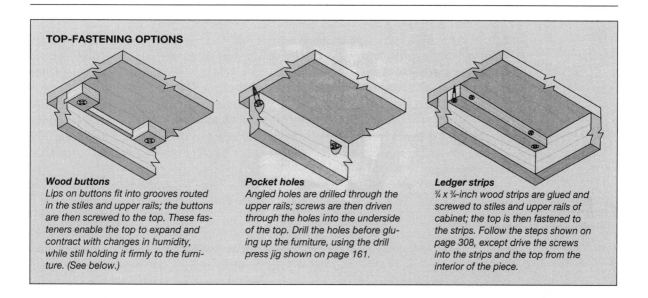

TOP-FASTENING OPTIONS

Wood buttons
Lips on buttons fit into grooves routed in the stiles and upper rails; the buttons are then screwed to the top. These fasteners enable the top to expand and contract with changes in humidity, while still holding it firmly to the furniture. (See below.)

Pocket holes
Angled holes are drilled through the upper rails; screws are then driven through the holes into the underside of the top. Drill the holes before gluing up the furniture, using the drill press jig shown on page 161.

Ledger strips
¾ x ¾-inch wood strips are glued and screwed to stiles and upper rails of cabinet; the top is then fastened to the strips. Follow the steps shown on page 308, except drive the screws into the strips and the top from the interior of the piece.

To accommodate the lips of the wood buttons, cut grooves in the inside face of the stiles and top rails using a router. Install a ¼-inch-wide piloted slotting cutter in the tool and adjust it to rout grooves ½ inch from the top edge of the rails. For each groove, clamp a support board along the outside of the rail. The board will help prevent the router from tipping. As shown at right, keep the router base flat on the rail and the support board, and the pilot bearing flush against the inside of the rail as you feed the tool.

Make all the buttons from a single board of a thickness equal to the gap between the bottom edge of the groove and the top of the rails, less about ¹⁄₁₆ inch. Prepare the buttons so that their grain direction will be perpendicular to the rails they butt against. Cut a rabbet in one end of the board (page 267), leaving a ¼-inch-thick tongue, or lip. This lip will fit into the groove. Then crosscut a strip from the same end about 1¼ inches from the shoulder of the rabbet. Finally, saw 1-inch-wide buttons from the strip and bore a hole through the center of each button slightly larger than the shanks of the screws you will use to fasten the top. Make enough buttons to space them about every 18 to 24 inches around the perimeter of the cabinet.

To install the top, set it face down on a work surface and position the cabinet upside down on top of it. Insert the lips of the buttons into the grooves in the rails with about ¹⁄₁₆ inch of clearance between the end of the lips and the bottom of the grooves. Then screw the buttons to the top, as shown above.

INSTALLING A TOP USING WOOD BUTTONS

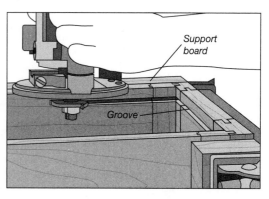

Support board

Groove

DRAWERS

A drawer is merely a box with a front, a back, two sides, and a bottom. However, sizing the parts so that the drawer fits its opening properly, choosing the appropriate joinery to assemble the drawer, and mounting it so that it slides smoothly—all add up to one of the more complex aspects of cabinetmaking.

Drawers are subject to more stress and wear than virtually any other assembly in a cabinet. You must choose a very strong joint to connect the front to the sides. The half-blind dovetail shown on page 311 is the traditional choice for this joint, although the double dado and rabbet can also be used in some situations. A through dado is commonly used for joining the back to the sides. The bottom is usually a plywood panel that fits in a groove in the sides and front (*page 312*). The bottom is also nailed to the back, which is often cut narrower than the front and sides. This enables the bottom to be sized and slid into place after the drawer is glued up.

As shown below, the design of the front can determine how closely a drawer must fit in its opening. Drawers with false or offset fronts can be loosely fitted. A flush-front drawer demands closer tolerances, since any gaps between the drawer and the cabinet are entirely visible. As a rule of thumb, a drawer should both fit precisely and slide in its opening smoothly. Be sure to consider the species of wood and the size of the drawer when determining clearances. Woods that have a high potential for expansion and contraction require more clearance. And slightly wider gaps are less noticeable around large drawers.

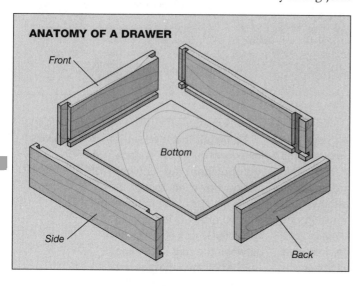

ANATOMY OF A DRAWER

Front

Bottom

Side

Back

DRAWER FRONT DESIGNS

Offset front
A front with a rabbet cut all around the inside face, creating a lip that conceals runners when the drawer is closed. To cut an offset front on the table saw, see page 312.

False front
A separate piece fastened to the drawer front; conceals end grain of drawer sides.

Flush front
Also known as an inset drawer, this front is flush with the front edge of the opening when the drawer is closed.

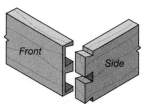

THE STRONGEST DRAWER JOINTS

off

DRAWER JOINTS

Half-blind dovetail
Conceals the end grain of the sides. To cut by hand, see page 284; with a router and jig, see page 285. Used to join the front to the sides.

Through dovetail
The end grain of the sides may be left exposed for decorative purposes or covered with a false drawer front. To cut by hand, see page 282. Can be used at all four corners.

OTHER STRONG JOINTS

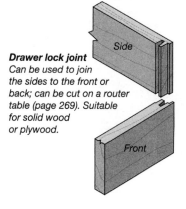

Drawer lock joint
Can be used to join the sides to the front or back; can be cut on a router table (page 269). Suitable for solid wood or plywood.

Double dado
Can be used for joining the sides to the front or back; conceals the end grain of the sides. Only suitable for solid wood.

Sliding dovetail
Used to join back to sides. Only suitable for solid wood; to cut on a router table, see page 112.

AN EASY JOINT FOR LIGHT DUTY

Rabbet
In small drawers, can be used to join the sides to either the front or back if reinforced by nails or screws; the rabbet should be cut in the front to conceal the end grain of the sides. Suitable for solid wood or plywood.

JOINTS FOR JOINING THE SIDES OF A DRAWER TO THE BACK

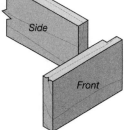

Dado-and-rabbet
A good choice for joining the back to the sides when the sides should not extend beyond the back; suitable for solid wood or plywood.

Through dado
Suitable for solid wood or plywood. To cut on the table saw, see page 269; with a router, page 270.

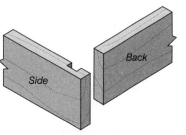

DRAWERS

There are two common methods for preparing a drawer to accept the bottom. Some woodworkers cut the grooves in the front and sides before the drawer is assembled. Others assemble the drawer first and then cut the groove with a router. (In either case, the back is usually made narrower than the front so that its bottom edge is flush with the top of the groove, enabling the bottom to be slipped into place when the drawer is assembled.) The second method is shown at right. Clamp the drawer upside down on a work surface and install a piloted three-wing slotting cutter in your router.

Adjust the bit height to locate the groove about ½ inch from the bottom edge of the drawer. Holding the router base flat on the drawer and the pilot bearing flush against the drawer stock, guide the tool around the drawer, as shown. Use a chisel to square the groove at the corners.

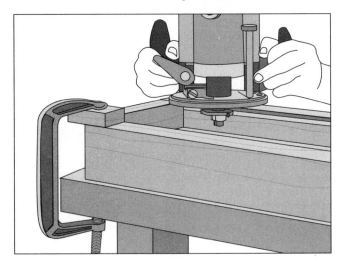

QUICKTIP

Cutting an offset drawer front

Make an offset drawer front by cutting four rabbets in its inside face. This leaves four lips that will extend beyond the drawer opening. For ¾-inch-thick stock, make the thickness of the lips about ⅜ inch. To make the drawer front on the table saw, cut the rabbet shoulders first, creating four intersecting grooves on the inside face. Then cut the rabbet cheeks. Attach a tall auxiliary fence to the rip fence and feed the drawer front on end, with a push stick as shown, and then on edge.

Push stick

Auxiliary fence

BOTTOM-RUN

Drawer slides on rail-and-runner assembly. Rails are usually joined to carcase side panels with mortise-and-tenon joints; runners can be screwed to side panels or one edge of each runner can be rabbeted so the resulting tongue fits into a groove cut in the side panel.

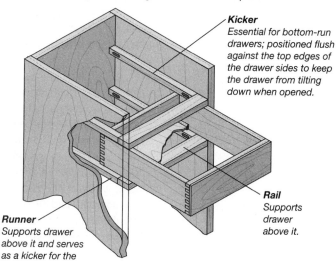

Kicker
Essential for bottom-run drawers; positioned flush against the top edges of the drawer sides to keep the drawer from tilting down when opened.

Runner
Supports drawer above it and serves as a kicker for the drawer below.

Rail
Supports drawer above it.

SIDE-MOUNTED

Wooden slides fastened to carcase side panels run in grooves routed in drawer sides.

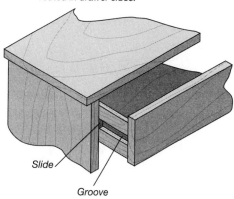

Slide

Groove

COMMERCIAL SLIDE RUNNERS

In two of the examples shown here, matching hardware is attached to drawer sides and sides of cabinet, enabling drawer to slide in and out. In the third example, a guide bracket is fastened to the drawer back; the bracket runs on a guide attached to the front and back of the cabinet.

Metal roller guide

Face frame

Metal roller guide

Metal roller guide

Slide

Runner

Face frame

Attaches to back of cabinet

Guide bracket

DRAWERS

INSTALLING DRAWERS

To ensure drawers fit perfectly in a frame-and-panel piece of furniture, you can fasten corner strips and slides to the stiles as you would to install shelves *(page 307)*. Cut grooves in the drawer sides so that the drawer can be held in place by the slides. Before attaching the corner strips, position the drawer in the cabinet and mark the groove locations on the front and back stiles. Screw the corner strips to the stiles so that the dadoes in the strips align with the groove location marks. To check the fit of the drawer, clamp the corner strips to the back stiles with handscrews as shown at left, slip the drawer slides in the strips, and slide the drawer in place. Check whether the drawer glides smoothly and the drawer front is square to the front of the cabinet when it is closed. If necessary, adjust the location of the corner strips and then screw them in place.

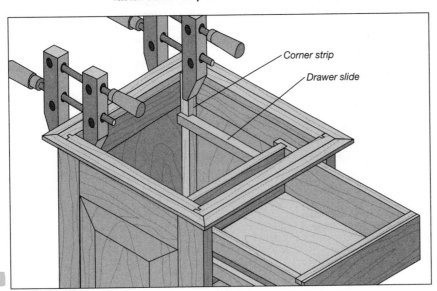

Corner strip

Drawer slide

QUICK*TIP*

Drawer-slide positioning jig

To attach commercial drawer slides to the sides of a drawer, you can use the simple jig shown at right. Make the jig by cutting a wide rabbet in a board at least one-half the length of the drawer sides. Position the jig against the bottom of the drawer and align the drawer slide along the jig's top edge. Mark the screw holes on the drawer side and screw the slide in place. To position the runners inside the cabinet, test-fit the drawer in the carcase and mark the slide locations. Then cut a piece of plywood to fit between the bottom of the carcase and your marked line. Butt the plywood piece against the bottom of the carcase side, set the runner against the top of the plywood, mark the screw holes, and install the runner.

Drawer stops serve two purposes: They prevent drawers from being pushed in too far and from being pulled completely out of a piece of furniture. Unless you want the back of the carcase to act as a stop, a fixed stop like the one shown in illustration 1 can be installed to limit a drawer's inward travel. To make the stop, cut a wood disk and drill an off-center hole through it. Loosely fasten the stop to a side panel near the back of the carcase. Insert the drawer, making sure the front is properly aligned, and rotate the stop until it contacts the drawer. Then tighten the screw, as shown.

The drawer stop shown in illustration 2 will limit a

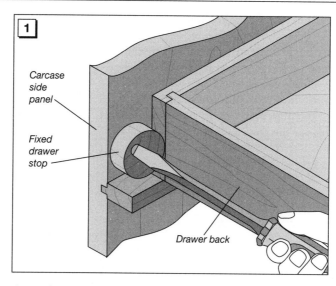

1

Carcase side panel

Fixed drawer stop

Drawer back

drawer's outward travel. Cut the stop so that its width is equal to the thickness of the rail to which it will be attached and round one end. Screw the stop to the inside

of the rail with its long edge parallel to the rail. Insert the drawer about halfway into its opening, then reach up under the rail and rotate the stop 90 degrees, as shown.

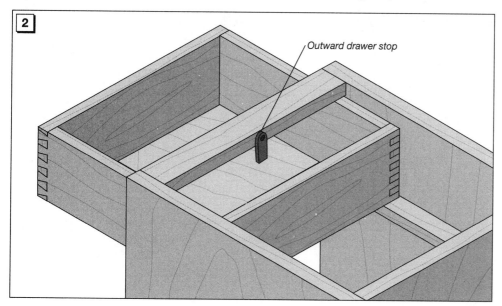

2

Outward drawer stop

DOORS

The type of door you mount on a cabinet depends to some degree on the cabinet's design. Frame-and-panel and glass doors are good choices for reproduction pieces, whereas simple cabinets can be paired with battened or tongue-and-groove doors.

You must also consider how the doors will fit into the piece before building the cabinet. Doors must be fitted with fine tolerances while still allowing enough clearance for wood movement. You also have to make allowances for hardware such as hinges, latches, or locks; purchase your hardware before building the piece. Some elements of its construction, such as the width or thickness of the face frame stiles, may require some advance planning to accept the door and its hardware. Four types of doors and three door-mounting options are illustrated below and on page 317.

ANATOMIES OF DOORS

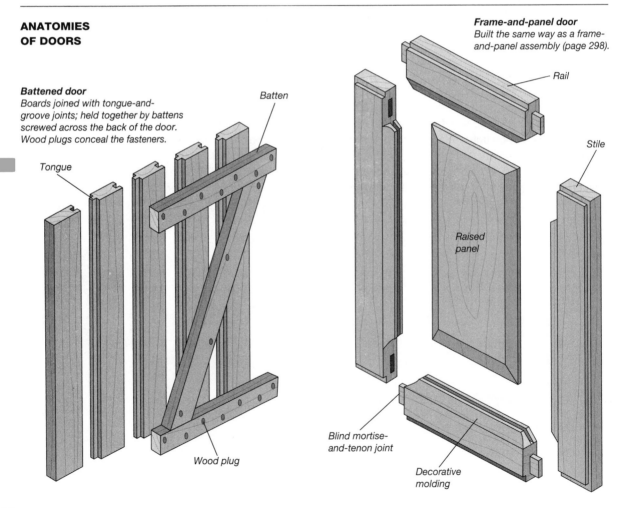

Frame-and-panel door
Built the same way as a frame-and-panel assembly (page 298).

Rail

Stile

Battened door
Boards joined with tongue-and-groove joints; held together by battens screwed across the back of the door. Wood plugs conceal the fasteners.

Batten

Tongue

Raised panel

Wood plug

Blind mortise-and-tenon joint

Decorative molding

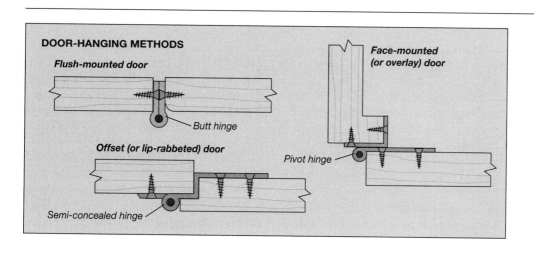

DOOR-HANGING METHODS

Flush-mounted door

Butt hinge

Offset (or lip-rabbeted) door

Semi-concealed hinge

Face-mounted (or overlay) door

Pivot hinge

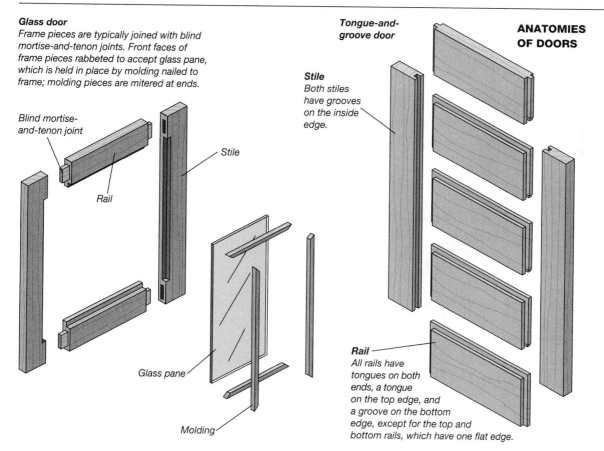

Glass door
Frame pieces are typically joined with blind mortise-and-tenon joints. Front faces of frame pieces rabbeted to accept glass pane, which is held in place by molding nailed to frame; molding pieces are mitered at ends.

Blind mortise-and-tenon joint

Stile

Rail

Glass pane

Molding

Tongue-and-groove door

Stile
Both stiles have grooves on the inside edge.

Rail
All rails have tongues on both ends, a tongue on the top edge, and a groove on the bottom edge, except for the top and bottom rails, which have one flat edge.

ANATOMIES OF DOORS

LEGS

Legs serve the simple purpose of raising the other components of a table, desk, chair, or cabinet to an appropriate level. Since they play a load-bearing role, legs must be both strong and securely joined to the piece. Legs also play an important visual role. The leg types shown below are often thought of as representative of specific styles of furniture. The straight, square leg with its clean and unadorned lines is often used in both modern and Oriental furniture styles. Tapered legs—whether round, square, plain, or fluted—are typical of the neoclassical designs of Hepplewhite and Sheraton. Turned legs appear in styles as diverse as William and Mary and American Country; the decorative contour of the turnings fol-

low definite style patterns. The graceful cabriole leg became a key component of French Rococo furniture and was carried over into the French Provincial and Chippendale styles. The pedestal is actually a complete support assembly consisting of a column with three or more splayed legs. It is a distinctive element of many designs, including those of Sheraton and Duncan Phyfe. It also appears in both Shaker and Golden Oak styles.

For illustrated examples of each of these furniture styles, refer to the Furniture Styles chapter, beginning on page 21. These traditional relationships do not suggest hard and fast rules, however. Leg designs lend themselves to considerable creative freedom.

LEG STYLES

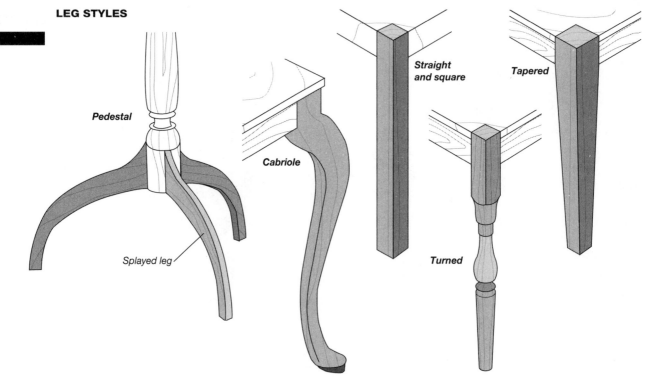

Pedestal

Splayed leg

Cabriole

Straight and square

Tapered

Turned

With a table saw and a taper jig, you can easily cut a taper on two sides of a leg *(page 147)*. When all four sides must be tapered, a jointer will do the job more quickly. Set the jointer's depth of cut at about 1⁄16 inch and, for this operation, remove the guard or install a clamp on the infeed table to hold the guard out of the way. Prepare the leg blank by marking lines on all four sides where the taper should start, then scribe the finished size of the taper on the bottom end using a marking gauge 1. Set the blank on the jointer tables, aligning the taper start line about 1⁄2 inch from the end of the outfeed table 2. Clamp a stop block to the infeed side of the fence flush against the bottom end of the blank. Make the stop block thinner than the leg so that you can use a push stick to feed the blank. Lift the blank off the jointer and turn on the machine. Butt the bottom of the blank against the stop block and lower the blank onto the table. Feed the blank across the tables with a push stick, then repeat the process on the other three sides. Continue to joint all four sides until the taper almost meets the marking gauge lines. Remove the stop block and joint all four sides, beginning with the tapered surface, flat on the infeed table. This will extend the taper up to the start line.

TAPERING A LEG ON THE JOINTER

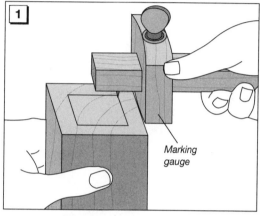

1

Marking gauge

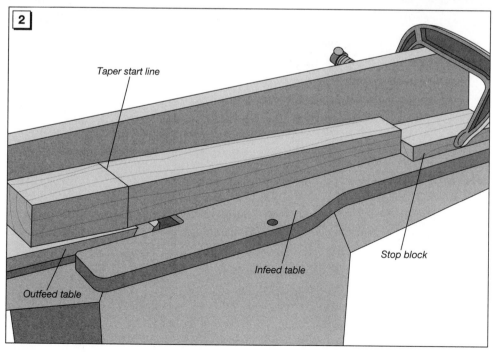

2

Taper start line

Infeed table

Stop block

Outfeed table

LEGS

**MAKING A
CABRIOLE LEG**

To make a cabriole leg, cut a template from hardboard, cardboard, or stiff plastic. Lay out the desired shape on the template, cut it out, and transfer its outline to two adjacent sides of a square leg blank ☐1. You can use a single piece of wood for the blank, or glue up several thinner boards face to face *(page 334)*.

Remove most of the waste from the blank on the band saw. Place the leg blank flat on the saw table with one of the leg outlines facing up. Saw about halfway along one of the cutting lines, then back out of the cut. Turn the blank end for end and saw along the same cutting line from the opposite end. Stop the cut about 1 inch from the first cut, leaving a bridge ☐2 between the two kerfs. Repeat for the remaining cutting lines, leaving a bridge along each one. Then rotate the blank 90 degrees so the second leg outline faces up and cut right through all the cutting lines.

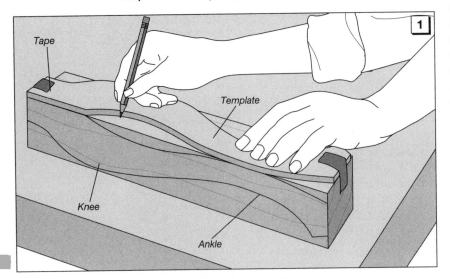

Tape

Template

Knee

Ankle

1

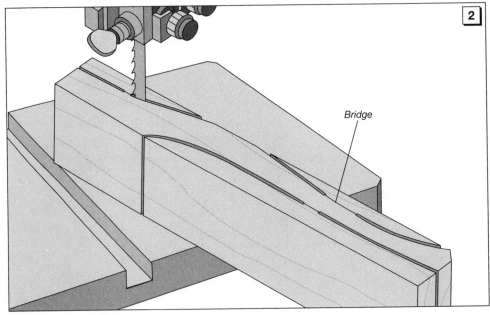

Bridge

2

Rotate the blank again so that the first outline faces up and sever the bridges, cutting away the remaining waste.

To produce the round profile of the leg from the knee to the ankle, chamfer the corners of the blank with a half-round patternmaker's rasp.

by the rasp with a flat mill file and a round file, being careful not to gouge the wood with the edges of the tool, then sand the surface.

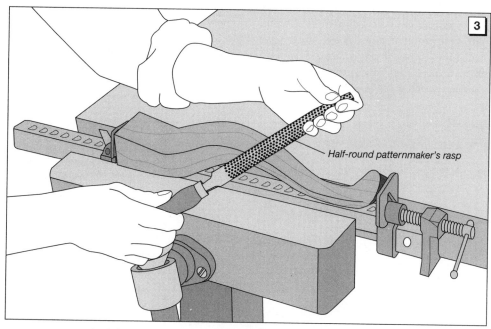

3

Half-round patternmaker's rasp

There are several ways to do the final shaping of the leg, but most woodworkers use spokeshaves, rasps, files, and sandpaper. To make all the sides of the leg easy to reach, secure it lengthwise in a bar clamp and fix the clamp in a bench vise 3 . You can start with a spokeshave *(page 93)* to smooth away the marks left by the band saw. Use a rasp or file to smooth out any spots the spokeshave cannot reach.

Use the rounded side of the rasp on concave surfaces and the flat side on convex surfaces. Continue with the rasp to make the ankle section circular and the section just below the knee square-shaped with rounded corners 4 . Hold the rasp in both hands, one hand on the handle and the other gripping the tip, as shown, and move the tool with a circular motion to shape the curves of the leg. Smooth away the marks left

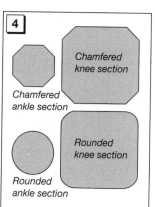

4

Chamfered knee section

Chamfered ankle section

Rounded knee section

Rounded ankle section

LEG-TO-RAIL JOINTS

The joints used to attach legs to rails undergo a great deal of stress. Because you are joining end grain to long grain, you need a strong joinery method. As shown in the illustration of a leg-and-rail assembly below, the traditional choice for connecting legs to rails is the blind mortise-and-tenon joint. One problem you may encounter with smaller legs is that tenons entering a leg from different directions can interfere with each other and weaken the leg. To overcome this problem, you can miter the ends of the tenons, as shown on page 323, or use offset tenons (*page 274*). To attach legs to stretchers, which serve to stabilize the assembly and limit leg movement, dowel joints are adequate.

As shown on page 323, there are other joinery options. Sliding dovetails, for example, are usually used to attach legs to the column in pedestal assemblies. For pieces that need to be disassembled, you can use commercial knockdown hardware or make your own.

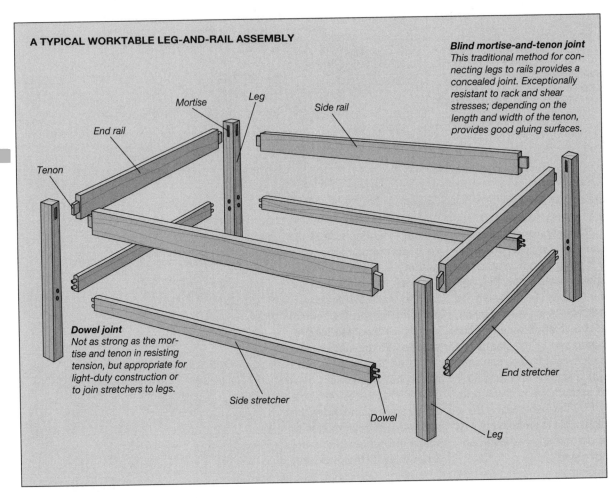

A TYPICAL WORKTABLE LEG-AND-RAIL ASSEMBLY

Mortise

Leg

Side rail

End rail

Tenon

Blind mortise-and-tenon joint
This traditional method for connecting legs to rails provides a concealed joint. Exceptionally resistant to rack and shear stresses; depending on the length and width of the tenon, provides good gluing surfaces.

Dowel joint
Not as strong as the mortise and tenon in resisting tension, but appropriate for light-duty construction or to join stretchers to legs.

Side stretcher

Dowel

End stretcher

Leg

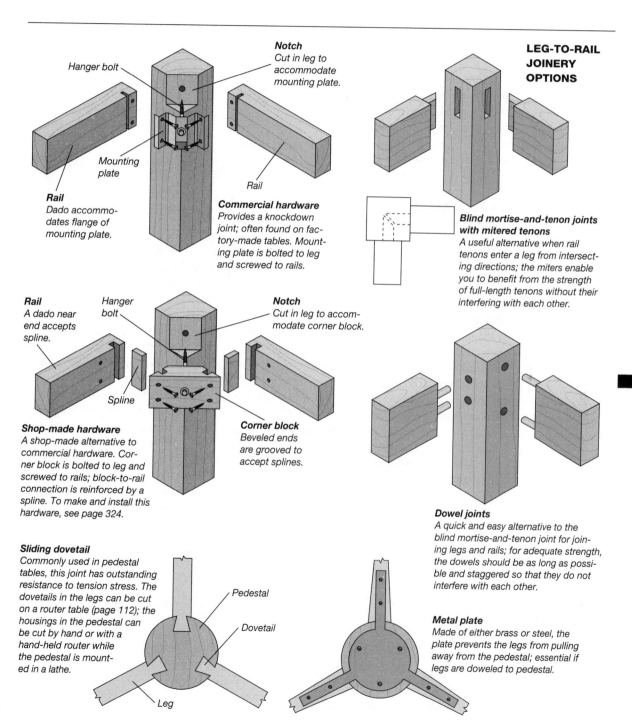

Notch
Cut in leg to accommodate mounting plate.

Hanger bolt

Mounting plate

Rail

Rail
Dado accommodates flange of mounting plate.

Commercial hardware
Provides a knockdown joint; often found on factory-made tables. Mounting plate is bolted to leg and screwed to rails.

Blind mortise-and-tenon joints with mitered tenons
A useful alternative when rail tenons enter a leg from intersecting directions; the miters enable you to benefit from the strength of full-length tenons without their interfering with each other.

Rail
A dado near end accepts spline.

Hanger bolt

Notch
Cut in leg to accommodate corner block.

Spline

Shop-made hardware
A shop-made alternative to commercial hardware. Corner block is bolted to leg and screwed to rails; block-to-rail connection is reinforced by a spline. To make and install this hardware, see page 324.

Corner block
Beveled ends are grooved to accept splines.

Dowel joints
A quick and easy alternative to the blind mortise-and-tenon joint for joining legs and rails; for adequate strength, the dowels should be as long as possible and staggered so that they do not interfere with each other.

Sliding dovetail
Commonly used in pedestal tables, this joint has outstanding resistance to tension stress. The dovetails in the legs can be cut on a router table (page 112); the housings in the pedestal can be cut by hand or with a hand-held router while the pedestal is mounted in a lathe.

Pedestal

Dovetail

Leg

Metal plate
Made of either brass or steel, the plate prevents the legs from pulling away from the pedestal; essential if legs are doweled to pedestal.

LEG-TO-RAIL JOINTS

SHOP-MADE LEG-TO-RAIL HARDWARE

The first step in making leg-to-rail hardware is preparing the corner blocks. Start by beveling both ends at 45 degrees. Then install a dado head on your table saw to cut the grooves for the splines in the beveled ends. Adjust the dado head's width to the thickness of the splines. Adjust the cutting height to slightly more than one-half the spline width. Screw a wooden extension fence to the miter gauge **1**. Align the middle of one of the ends of the block with the dado head and clamp the workpiece to the extension fence. Also clamp a waste piece from the bevel cuts to the extension fence as a stop block. Saw the grooves as shown. Next, use the drill press to bore holes through the block for the screws and hanger bolt that will join it to the rails and leg. Secure the block in a handscrew **2** and clamp

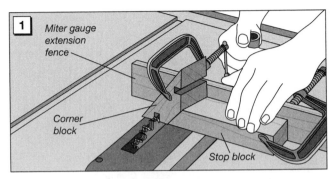

the handscrew to the drill press table so the longer face of the block is facing up. Drill a clearance hole for the hanger bolt through the middle of the block and two holes for screws on each side of the bolt hole; reposition the block on the table as necessary.

To prepare the rails, test-fit the corner block against them and mark the groove locations. Cut a groove in each rail with the same dado head and cutting height you used for the block. Fasten the block to the rails, gluing the splines in their grooves and driving the screws.

To prepare the leg, cut a notch for the corner block. Holding the leg in place against the block, drill a pilot hole into the leg for the hanger bolt. To attach the leg to the block, insert the screw-thread end of the bolt into the leg. Since hanger bolts have no heads, form a temporary head by threading two nuts onto the machine-thread end and tightening them against each other. Use a wrench to drive the screw threads into the leg, then remove the nuts. Slip the bolt through the block and install a washer and nut **3**.

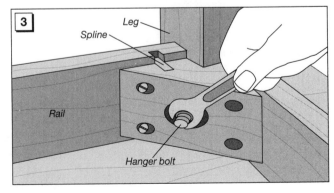

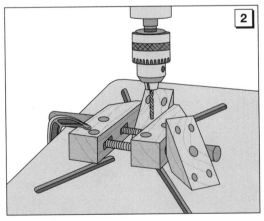

GLUING AND CLAMPING

Gluing and clamping is a critical step in most cabinet-making projects. It can also be an important preparatory step: making wide panels from narrow boards; creating thick leg blanks from thinner stock; and building drawers, doors, and leg-and-rail assemblies. This chapter will show you how to perform these and many other common glue-up tasks.

The diversity of modern adhesives has altered cabinetmaking techniques as much as any other advancement in woodworking. A century ago, finding an adhesive capable of providing a strong, durable bond presented a problem. Today, the challenge is choosing the right glue among a host of options.

This chapter explores the adhesives currently on the market, the applications for which they are best suited, and how to use them. Charts on pages 326 through 329 survey the glues available to woodworkers, explaining methods of use and comparing working characteristics, such as curing time, color, toxicity, spreadability, resistance to moisture, and so on. Porosity, texture, and the presence of natural oils, gums, and volatiles make some species of woods more difficult to bond than others. This topic is dealt with in the chart on page 330.

Regardless of the adhesive or the wood species you select, success at glue-up rests heavily on proper technique. An inventory of essential clamping devices is presented on pages 331 to 333. This is followed by step-by-step descriptions of the techniques normally used to glue and assemble a variety of furniture parts and types. The chapter concludes by examining common gluing and clamping problems and describes how they can be avoided.

ADHESIVES

GLUES FOR WOODWORKING

Until well into the 20th Century, woodworkers could learn everything they needed to know about glues and how to use them in an afternoon. There simply were very few choices. Adhesives such as protein-based hide, fish, and blood glues, and crude milk-based adhesives had been available for centuries. But they were inconvenient to use and lacked reliable resistance to moisture.

Today, the problem with adhesives is that their great diversity and mysterious chemistry can present an overwhelming range of options. Relatively new, ready-to-use yellow glue (aliphatic resin) is now the most popular general-purpose woodworking adhesive. It has many desirable characteristics, including convenience, economy, appropriate tack time, strength, and reasonable sandability. But it is by no means the ideal glue in all situations.

You need to consider several factors to select the right glue for a given job. For example, some glues lack the viscosity to fill gaps and

CHOOSING AN ADHESIVE

ADHESIVE	COMMON USES	COLOR	COST	TOXICITY	RESISTANCE TO CREEP	GAP FILLING
White glue (PVA—Polyvinyl acetate)	Model making, woodworking, and repairs involving porous materials, such as paper, cloth, leather and wood	White; dries clear	Inexpensive	Nontoxic	Good; poor under continuous stress	Fair
Yellow glue (Aliphatic resin)	Formulated to perform better than white PVA glue in woodworking applications	Cream; dries translucent	Inexpensive	Nontoxic	Good	Fair
Weatherproof yellow glue	Like yellow glue; also for outdoor projects	Yellow; dries translucent	Slightly costlier than yellow glue	Nontoxic	Fair	Good
Hide glue	Traditional glue for furniture making and other indoor woodworking projects	Amber; dries clear	Inexpensive	Nontoxic	Good	Fair
Casein	Inexpensive, general-purpose glue for interior woodworking applications	Cream; dries opaque	Inexpensive	Nontoxic	Excellent	Fair to good
Contact cement	For bonding laminates and veneers to substrates; bonds cloth, leather, or plastic coverings to wood	Dries clear	Inexpensive	Strong fumes require a well-ventilated work area.	Poor	Poor

will not hold when bonding coarse-textured materials or loosely fitted joints. Also, many otherwise reliable adhesives lack resistance to moisture or may be affected by the natural oils in some woods such as teak, lignum vitae, and rosewood (page 330).

Aside from bonding strength, consider the appearance, flexibility, temperature sensitivity, and clamping time of a glue. Glues that become brittle when dry sand well, but they also tend to fail under sudden stress. Some glues do not cure well in cold temperatures, and others fail if heated. Glues with long clamping times slow down the completion of a project, yet glues that dry too quickly may not provide adequate time for assembly. And finally, some adhesives can pose a health risk: They may give off irritating volatiles or contain toxic ingredients that prevent their use in making toys or food-related items.

The charts that follow will help you choose the right glue for your needs.

FLEXIBILITY	PREPARATION	APPLICATION	PROS AND CONS
Flexible	Ready-to-use	Spread evenly and press the joint together using clamps or weights	Versatile and convenient to use; sets quickly. Temperatures in excess of 100°F may weaken the joint; will clog sandpaper.
Moderately flexible	Ready-to-use	Spread on and clamp	Heavier consistency than white glues makes it less prone to running and dripping; less affected by high temperatures. Better moisture resistance than white glue, but not waterproof
Moderately flexible	Ready-to-use	Spread on and clamp	Like yellow glue, but weatherproof; fills gaps better. Has slightly longer curing time
Brittle	Available in flakes and ready-to-use form; flakes require a heated glue pot.	Apply to both surfaces and allow glue to become tacky before assembling the joint	A tough, long-lasting glue; does not become brittle. Tannish brown color blends well with most finishes; resists solvents found in most finishes. Not waterproof
Tough	Comes in powder form; mix with an equal volume of water, stirring occasionally until the powder dissolves into a smooth syrup—about 10 minutes	Apply to both surfaces and clamp	Strong; will cure at lower temperatures than hide glue and works well on oily woods such as teak. Only moderately resistant to moisture; once mixed, cannot be stored
Flexible	Ready-to-use	Coat both surfaces and allow glue to cure until it becomes dry to the touch before pressing the surfaces together	Moisture resistant; never becomes brittle. Its ability to bond immediately speeds up assembly time; once laminate and substrate make contact, repositioning is impossible.

(continued)

ADHESIVES

CHOOSING AN ADHESIVE (continued)

ADHESIVE	COMMON USES	COLOR	COST	TOXICITY	RESISTANCE TO CREEP	GAP FILLING
Plastic resin	An inexpensive and general-purpose glue that is resistant to moisture	Tan; dries opaque	An economical moisture-resistant glue	Toxic until cured	Excellent	Fair
Cyanoacrylate	Relatively new to the market and touted as the ideal glue for small repairs, this adhesive will bond to almost any material.	Transparent; dries clear	Cost effective for quick, small repairs	Avoid contact with skin.	Excellent	Poor
Resorcinol	A reliable waterproof glue for exterior applications and marine use	Dark reddish brown; dries opaque	Expensive	Toxic until cured	Excellent	Poor
Epoxy	Used to bond materials with different porosities and surface textures such as metals, ceramic or glass to wood, fiberboard, or particleboard	Varies	Expensive	Avoid contact with skin Moderate (10 min.)	Excellent	Excellent

WORKING CHARACTERISTICS OF NINE COMMONLY USED GLUES

ADHESIVE	WORKING TEMPERATURE	SPREADABILITY	OPEN TIME	SETTING TIME	WET TACK
White glue (PVA — Polyvinyl acetate)	60°- 90°F	Good	Short (3-5 min.)	1 hr.	Moderate
Yellow glue (Aliphatic resin)	45°-110°F	Good	Short (5 min.)	1 hr.	Quick
Weatherproof yellow glue	45°-110°F	Good	Short (5-10 min.)	1 hr.	Quick
Hide glue	70°- 90°F	Fair	Moderate (10 min.)	8-10 hrs.	Quick
Casein	40°-110°F	Fair	Very long (up to 8 hrs.)	6-8 hrs.	Slow
Contact cement	65°-75°F	Excellent	Moderate (5 min. to 1 hr)	5-10 min.	Moderate
Plastic resin	70°-100°F	Excellent	Moderate (10-30 min.)	10-14 hrs.	Slow
Cyanoacrylate	40°- 90°F	Good	Very short (30 sec.)	10-30 sec.	—
Resorcinol	70°-120°F	Good	Moderate (10 min.)	8 hrs.	Slow
Epoxy	Varies	Good	Varies (from 5 to 90 min.)	Varies	Slow

FLEXIBILITY	PREPARATION	APPLICATION	PROS AND CONS
Brittle	Mix powder 2:1 to 3:1 in water, depending upon desired consistency	Brush a thin coat on both surfaces and clamp.	Water in the mixture may raise wood grain; long clamping time.
Very brittle	Ready-to-use	Apply to both surfaces and press the joint together.	Dries in seconds and will bond a wide range of materials; not a very strong or water-resistant glue. Only the gel form works well on porous woods.
Brittle	Mix the powder 3:4 in liquid resin. Cannot be stored; must be used within a few hours of mixing	Lightly coat both surfaces and clamp.	Very strong, dependable, and waterproof; leaves an obvious glue line. Requires a very good fit and heavy pressure
Varies	Mix resin and hardener together.	Varies widely with formulation and fillers added by user	A versatile, waterproof, non-shrinking, and relatively strong adhesive. Resists oils; fills gaps well. Some formulations are fast-setting and must be used within minutes of mixing; others are longer-setting.

CLAMPING TIME AT 70°	CURING TIME	SANDABILITY	STRESS RESISTANCE	MOISTURE RESISTANCE	HEAT RESISTANCE	SOLVENT RESISTANCE
45 minutes to 1 hour*	24-72 hrs.	Fair	Poor	Fair	Poor	Poor
30 minutes to 1 hour*	24 hrs.	Good	Good	Good	Fair	Good
1hour to 90 minutes*	24 hrs.	Good	Good	Weatherproof	Fair	Good
2 to 3 hours	24 hrs.	Excellent	Very good	Poor	Excellent	Very good
2 to 3 hours	24-36 hrs.	Good	Good	Good	Fair	Good
Bonds immediately; no clamping required	—	Very poor	Poor	Waterproof	Fair	Fair
Leave clamped overnight.	24 hrs.	Good	Excellent	Good	Fair	Excellent
No clamping required	—	Excellent	Very good	Very good	Excellent	Excellent
Leave clamped overnight.	10-12 hrs.	Good	Excellent	Waterproof	Fair	Excellent
No clamping required	Varies	Good	Excellent	Waterproof	Ranges from very good to very poor	Excellent

*Leave clamped overnight if the joint will be under continuous stress.

ADHESIVES

The chart below rates a variety of wood species in terms of how easy they are to glue. For many of the species that present difficulties, resins or extractives in the wood inhibit good bonding. For oily and resinous species like rosewood and teak, for example, standard wood glues may not be adequate when the joint relies solely on the strength of the adhesive bond. Some woodworkers prefer to use a specially formulated epoxy, called G-2 epoxy by its manufacturer. For exterior applications, as in outdoor furniture, casein, resorcinol, and plastic resin glues will work well.

Another approach that some woodworkers take with oily species is to plane the mating surfaces or roughen them with a relatively coarse sandpaper just prior to glue-up. Another technique involves wiping off any resins from the surfaces with lacquer thinner, alcohol, or acetone.

GLUING PROPERTIES OF VARIOUS WOOD SPECIES

GLUING PROPERTY	Domestic Hardwoods	Domestic Softwoods	Imported Woods
Bonds easily	Alder	Douglas-fir	Afrormosia
	Ash, white	Cedar, Western red	Avodire
	Aspen	Fir	Balsa
	Basswood	Larch, Western	Banak
	Beech, American	Pine	Bubinga
	Birch, yellow	Redwood	Lauan
	Butternut	Spruce, Sitka	Limba
	Cherry		Mahogany, African
	Chestnut		and South American
	Cottonwood		Meranti
	Elm		Obeche
	Hackberry		Purpleheart
	Hickory		Sapele
	Madrone		
	Magnolia		
	Maple, hard		
	Oak, red and white		
	Poplar, yellow		
	Sweetgum		
	Sycamore		
	Tupelo		
	Walnut, black		
	Willow, black		
Bonds with difficulty	Locust, black	Baldcypress	Ebony
	Osage orange		Lignum vitae
	Persimmon		Rosewood
			Teak

Chart information courtesy Wood Handbook: Forest Products Laboratory, United States Department of Agriculture

CLAMPS AND ACCESSORIES

There are nearly as many types of clamps available as there are clamping tasks, from gluing up a picture frame with mitered corners to assembling a large cabinet with mortise-and-tenon joinery. Ease and success in clamping depends on using the best clamp for the job. The inventory of clamps and clamping accessories below and on the following pages will help you make the right decisions.

Although the range of choices may look bewildering, only a few clamps are really essential in the typical woodworking shop. If you are starting from scratch, buy a pair of 6-inch handscrews, a half-dozen 4-inch C-clamps, seven or eight 3-foot-long bar or pipe clamps, a web clamp, and a couple of spring clamps. However, do not worry about buying too many clamps. Most woodworkers will tell you that you can never own enough of them. And unless your clamps come with padded jaws, remember to place wood pads between the clamp jaws and the workpiece to avoid marring your stock.

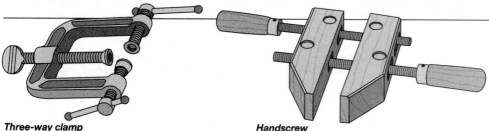

INVENTORY OF GLUING AND CLAMPING DEVICES

Three-way clamp
Ideal for securing edge banding to ends and edges, and assembling frames. Features a C-clamp frame with three tightening screws; in clamping edge banding, the opposing screws fasten the clamp to the faces of the panel and the third screw secures the edge banding to the edge or end.

Handscrew
A traditional woodworking clamp, also known as a screw clamp; ideal for securing angled workpieces. The two screws can be turned independently to draw the jaws together either parallel or at an angle. Available in various sizes with capacities up to about 18 inches. (See page 303.)

Rubber pads
Placed on clamp jaws to prevent marring wood and increase grip.

C-clamp
For clamping short spans; available in sizes from 1 inch to 18 inches. Ideal for face-gluing stock. Standard and deep-throated models available; standard clamp shown. (See page 334.)

Trigger clamp
Similar to a bar clamp, featuring a sliding pistol-grip assembly that enables the clamp to be operated with one hand; padded jaws protect the stock. Available in lengths up to 3 feet; for clamping medium-length spans, as in gluing up drawers.

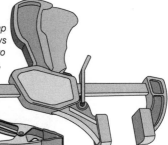

Quick-action bar clamp
A light-duty bar clamp with a sliding screw assembly at one end and a fixed tail stop at the other; available in lengths up to 3 feet. For clamping medium-length spans, as in gluing up drawers.

Spring clamp
Typically used to secure thin stock or molding. Handles are squeezed to open the clamp; plastic tips on the jaws protect the stock. Available in several sizes with clamping capacities ranging from 1 inch to 4 inches.

CLAMPS AND ACCESSORIES

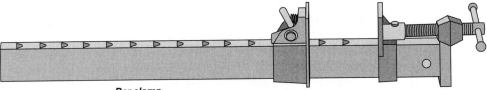

Bar clamp
For clamping wide spans; typical uses include edge-gluing boards into panels (page 334) and gluing up carcases and cabinets (page 336). Metal rectangular bar may be steel or aluminum; available in lengths up to 8 feet.

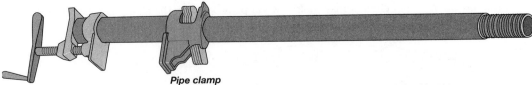

Pipe clamp
For clamping wide spans; converts a length of steel plumbing pipe into a bar clamp. Screw assembly threads to one end of the pipe; tail stop slides along the pipe and is locked in place by clamping pressure. Available in sizes designed to fit either ½- or ¾-inch ID (inside diameter) pipe.

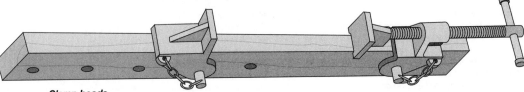

Clamp heads
Convert a board into an adjustable bar clamp. For the type shown, holes must be drilled through the board to accept pins in the headstock and tailstock. Headstock is fixed to one end of board and tailstock is mounted to other end at appropriate hole.

Pipe saddles
Flanges are fastened to a work surface to hold pipe clamps level and stationary.

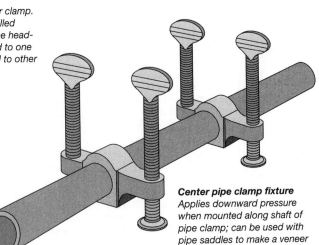

Center pipe clamp fixture
Applies downward pressure when mounted along shaft of pipe clamp; can be used with pipe saddles to make a veneer press. (See page 248.)

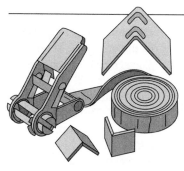

Web clamp

Also known as strap clamp; used for gluing up frames and other light assemblies. A lighter-duty version of the belt clamp featuring a wrench-adjusted ratcheting buckle and 15 feet of 1-inch-wide nylon belt; some models come with four corner brackets that spread clamping pressure. (See page 340.)

INVENTORY OF GLUING AND CLAMPING DEVICES

Corner clamp

For gluing up frames; features two perpendicular screw assemblies that hold miter and butt joints at precisely 90 degrees. Clamp accepts stock up to 3 inches wide; a clamp is needed at each corner of a frame.

Belt clamp

Also known as band clamp; used in gluing up carcases and leg-and-rail assemblies. Canvas belt is wrapped around the work-piece and through the buckle-type tighten-ing mechanism; available with 2-inch-wide belts up to 30 feet long.

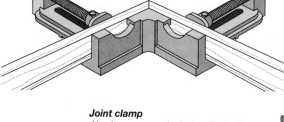

Joint clamp

Also known as a pinch dog. Typically used to secure edge-to-edge or face-to-face butt joints; the tapered points are driven into the ends of the mating boards, drawing the workpieces together. Available in widths ranging from 1 inch to 3½ inches.

Picture frame clamp

For gluing up frames; threaded rods connect four corner brackets that pro-vide even clamping pressure around frames with sides up to 48 inches long. (See page 335.)

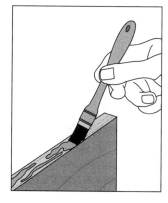

APPLYING THE GLUE

For most glue-up opera-tions, apply a bead of glue on the mating surfaces. Use enough glue so that the surfaces will be evenly and thoroughly covered when you spread the adhesive, but not so much that you make a mess. Some woodworkers spread glue with their fingers, but you risk adding dirt or grease to the glue. A better alternative is to use a small, stiff-bristled brush, as shown at left, a plastic roller, or a rub-ber-bladed printer's brayer. To ensure a strong glue bond, make sure the surfaces are completely coated. For high-viscosity adhesives, such as some epoxies, use a more rigid spreader, like a putty or pallet knife, an old hacksaw blade, or a thin wood scrap.

GLUING UP BUTT AND MITER JOINTS

THREE BUTT JOINTS

Clamping setups for gluing up three common butt joints are shown on this page. For an end-to-face joint 1, align a pipe or bar clamp so that pressure will press the mating surfaces togeth-

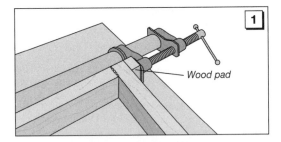

Wood pad

1

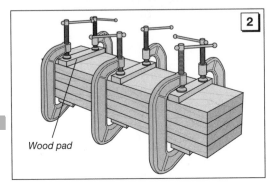

Wood pad

2

er. Use a wood pad to protect the stock and distribute the pressure. Tighten the clamp until a thin glue bead squeezes out and the seam forms a fine even line; overtightening may cause the stock to bow. Because they involve end grain, end-to-face joints are weak. When gluing this joint, generously coat the end-grain surface with glue and allow it to soak in. Next, scrape off the

excess that has not soaked in, recoat the surface with fresh glue, and coat the face-grain surface. Finally, join and clamp the parts. This allows the end grain to absorb all the glue it can before assembly so that it will not starve the joint after assembly. To glue up boards face to face 2, use C-clamps. To apply even pressure along the boards, space the clamps 6 to 8 inches apart and install them in pairs near opposite edges on wood pads. Tighten the clamps until there are no gaps between the pieces and excess glue squeezes out of the joints.

To glue up boards edge to edge 3, use pipe or bar clamps. To keep the clamps from tipping over, cut notches in wood blocks and set the clamps in them *(page 400)*. Arrange the boards so their top surfaces will form a visu-

ally appealing composite and so the end grain of adjacent pieces arcs in opposite directions. This will improve the panel's stability and minimize warping. The more boards you try to glue up, the more difficult it is to keep them in alignment and the more likely it is that some joints will not receive adequate clamping pressure. Do not glue up more than three or four boards at a time. Space the clamps at 12- to 18-inch intervals, alternating between the top and bottom of the panel. Tighten the clamps evenly until a thin bead of glue squeezes out of the joints, always keeping the screw applying pressure in the center of the board edges. To prevent the boards from moving out of alignment, place long wood pads across the top and bottom of the panel at both ends and hold the pads in place with C-clamps.

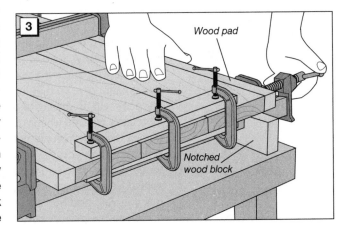

3

Wood pad

Notched wood block

Because face miters involve two end-grain surfaces, the same guidelines for gluing up end-to-face butt joints *(page 334)* apply to face miters. Apply a generous coat of glue to both mating surfaces, let it soak in, scrape off the excess, and then recoat. With miters, it is difficult to apply uniform clamping pressure without using specialized clamps. Although you can use a web clamp to apply pressure around the perimeter of the frame, the picture frame clamp shown at right is the ideal clamp for gluing up a frame with mitered corners. Set the clamp down with the corner brackets spread as far apart as possible. Position the frame in the clamp and slide the brackets flush against the corners of the frame. Then tighten the bracket nuts a little at a time until there are no gaps in the joints. Refer to page 399 for instructions on making and using a shop-made picture-frame clamp.

A FRAME WITH MITERED CORNERS

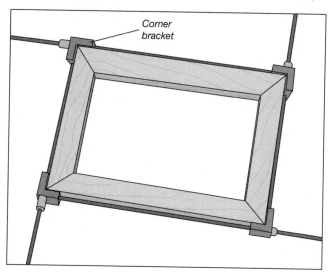

Corner bracket

*QUICK*TIP

A pipe clamp extension

To apply clamping pressure over a longer span than your longest pipe clamp, try the shop-made jig shown at right. Use 1 x 6 stock for the main body of the extension and 2 x 2 stock for the cleat. Saw a semicircular notch near one end of the body to accommodate the pipe clamp's tailstop, then fasten the cleat to the other end. To use the jig, place the cleat against one edge of the workpiece, then place the tailstop in the cutout. Tighten the headstock until it butts snugly against the opposite edge of the project.

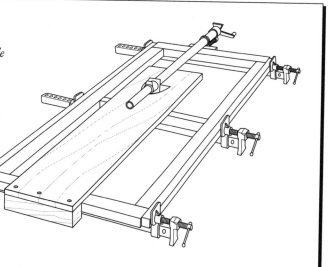

GLUING UP CARCASES AND DRAWERS

CARCASES Since gluing up a carcase typically involves bringing together several joints at the same time, careful preparation is crucial to the operation. Start by assembling the carcase—without glue—to make sure all the joints fit together properly. Once you apply the glue, it is too late to fix the joinery. Then make the necessary preparations: Depending on the tack time of the glue you are using, you will have a limited amount of time to assemble and clamp the carcase. Select the clamps you will need; for the carcase shown in illustration 1, for example, you would need eight bar or pipe clamps for the four corner joints and the two shelves. Set the gaps between the clamp jaws a little longer than the width of the carcase and leave the clamps close at hand. Cut any wood pads you will need, making them as long as the width of the panels; in this example, cut two pads for each pair of clamps. Then apply the glue to the mating surfaces, inserting any dowels or biscuits along the way if they are being used. Begin assembly by fitting the sides onto the bottom. Clamp the bottom loosely to keep the sides from tipping over. Add the lower shelf, then the upper shelf, and finally the top. Tighten the clamps on the top, the bottom, and the shelves—in that order.

For carcases with beveled corners 2, use web clamps with corner brackets. The webs will spread even pressure to all four corners and the brackets will distribute the pressure along the length of each joint. Set the carcase down on its back and fit the brackets on the corners. Wrap the webs around the carcase and tighten them to bring the mating surfaces together.

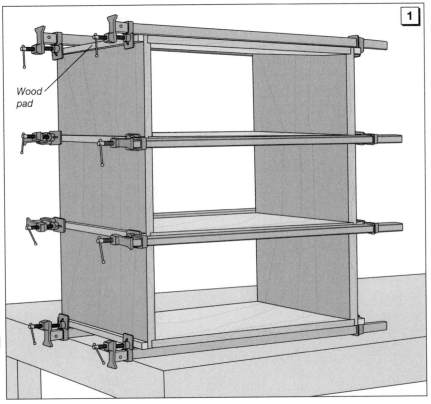

1

Wood pad

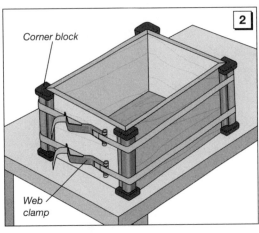

2

Corner block

Web clamp

Most of the guidelines for gluing up carcases apply to drawers as well. The clamping arrangement depends on the joinery used. For the drawer shown at right, the bar clamps secure the sides to the front and back. These clamps should be centered between the top and bottom of the drawer and paired with wood pads as long as the drawer height. The clamps across the top of the drawer are needed to tighten the rabbets joining the front to the sides.

One important difference between carcases and drawers at glue-up is that a drawer bottom is typically a panel that floats in a groove in the drawer sides and front. This complicates the assembly: The glue applied to the corner joints cannot be allowed to ooze into the groove and bond the bottom in place. Allowing the glue to become slightly tacky before assembly will minimize this risk but will in turn shorten assembly time.

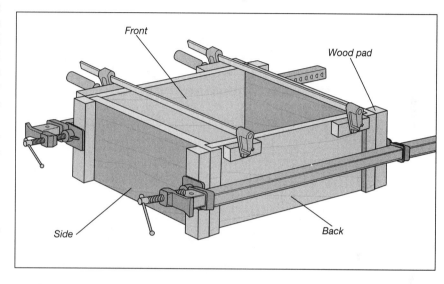

Front

Wood pad

Side

Back

QUICK TIP

Keeping a carcase square

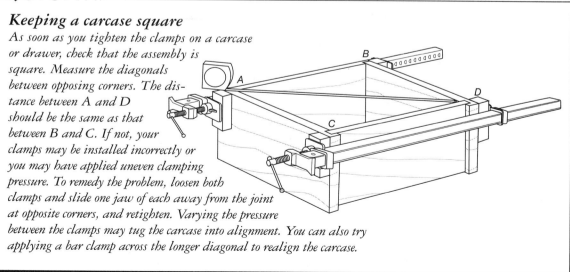

As soon as you tighten the clamps on a carcase or drawer, check that the assembly is square. Measure the diagonals between opposing corners. The distance between A and D should be the same as that between B and C. If not, your clamps may be installed incorrectly or you may have applied uneven clamping pressure. To remedy the problem, loosen both clamps and slide one jaw of each away from the joint at opposite corners, and retighten. Varying the pressure between the clamps may tug the carcase into alignment. You can also try applying a bar clamp across the longer diagonal to realign the carcase.

A
B
C
D

GLUING UP CABINETS AND DOORS

A FRAME-AND-PANEL CABINET

Frame-and-panel cabinets have their own gluing and clamping techniques. For the piece shown below, in which the sides, back, and face frame each have their own stiles, there are two acceptable ways of gluing up. One method involves gluing up the four assemblies as separate units, as you would a frame-and-panel door *(page 339)*. Then glue and fit the assemblies togeth-

er, and install four bar clamps on the corners of the cabinet, as shown, aligning the bars of the clamps with the side rails. It is crucial that the clamps be lined up with the rails; otherwise, the stiles would bow under the clamping pressure, distorting the cabinet.

For the second method, start by gluing together the mating stiles, forming four L-shaped stile assemblies. Then

glue the back and front rails to their respective stiles, inserting the back panel into its grooves in the stiles. For the final assembly, glue the side rails to their stiles, fitting the side panels into place. Use the clamping setup shown. With either method, use wood pads to protect the stock and check the cabinet for square as you would for a carcase *(page 337)*.

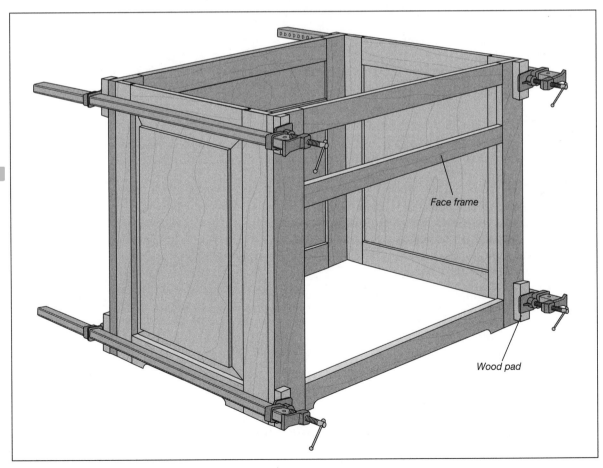

Face frame

Wood pad

Procedures for gluing up frame-and-panel doors or side assemblies for framed-panel cabinets are identical. Set two bar clamps on a work surface. Spread glue on the tenons at the ends of the rails and in the mortises in the stiles. Apply the glue carefully and evenly—just enough to cover the surfaces of the joints completely. Check to be sure that glue has not oozed out into the panel grooves; if so, remove it with a screwdriver or chisel before sliding the panel into place. To prevent glue squeeze-out from bonding the panel in the grooves, you can finish and wax the panel before assembling the frame.

Since doors are held to a piece of furniture by only a pair of hinges and a latch, they must be absolutely flat. Assemble the door and set it on the clamps. Gently press the door flat as you tighten the clamps. Be sure to apply the clamping pressure perpendicular to the seam of the joints to ensure that the door remains square. Check periodically with a try square. Apply just enough pressure to close the joints and squeeze out a bead of glue without causing the door to buckle. Do not overtighten.

A FRAME-AND-PANEL DOOR

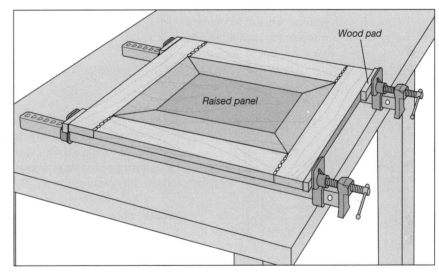

Wood pad

Raised panel

Gluing trim to cabinets presents a challenge because clamping pressure can damage the molding. In addition, the molding's curved profile makes it difficult to secure in place. You can solve both problems by using Styrofoam™ blocks as clamping pads.

Do not glue molding across the grain of a cabinet for more than 3 to 4 inches. A longer piece should be secured with brads. Spread a light coating of glue on the back of the trim, feathering out the coat toward the edges. A slightly starved glue joint in this situation will not be a problem. Rather, you will have less excess adhesive to clean up. Set two bar clamps across the top of the cabinet and set the molding in place. Position the clamping blocks against the molding before tightening the clamps.

GLUING ON MOLDING

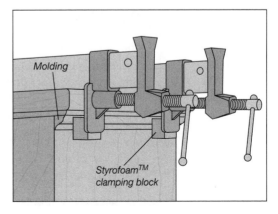

Molding

Styrofoam™
clamping block

GLUING UP LEGS AND RAILS

LEGS AND RAILS

Because leg-to-rail joints must withstand a great deal of stress, they must be well made. The mating parts must fit together tightly, but the glue bond between them is also important. The blind mortise-and-tenon joint, for example, has limited gluing surface between the parts. As a result, the joint must allow for a thin film of adhesive on

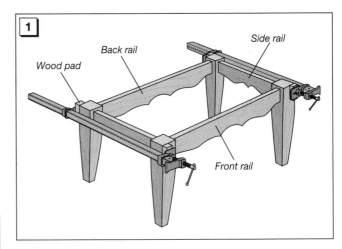

1

Back rail

Wood pad

Side rail

Front rail

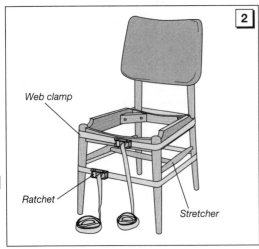

2

Web clamp

Ratchet

Stretcher

all sides. Prior to glue-up, assemble the joint dry to make sure it fits just right; glue alone cannot salvage a poorly fitting joint.

For a table leg-and-rail assembly 1, start by gluing the legs to the front and back rails. Allow these to cure, then join the assemblies to the side rails using bar or pipe clamps, as shown. Protect your stock and distrib-

ute the clamping pressure with wood pads.

Glue up a frame chair using web clamps 2. Assemble the parts, then wrap one web around the legs and seat frame, and the other around the legs at the height of the stretchers. Slip the web through the buckle until it is snug, then tighten the ratchet on the buckle.

QUICKTIP

Shop-made rubber clamp

An old bicycle inner tube can be used as a surprisingly effective substitute for a web clamp. To glue up a chair, loop the inner tube around one leg to prevent the tube from slipping, then stretch it around the remaining legs. Next, pull and twist the tube between two of the legs to create a second loop. Insert a stick through this loop and wind it like a tourniquet until the tube is tight. Use a spring clamp to secure the stick to the tube and prevent the stick from unwinding.

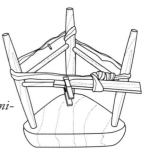

GLUE SQUEEZE-OUT

In practice, you do not know if you have applied the right amount of glue until the clamps are tightened and excess glue squeezes out. Since no two woods share the same porosity and no two joints fit in exactly the same way, there are no hard and fast rules about how much adhesive to apply. In general, however, it is best to slightly overestimate a joint's requirements. In the illustration of three edge-to-edge joints ⬜1⬜, the squeeze-out in the top joint is about right. The glue is

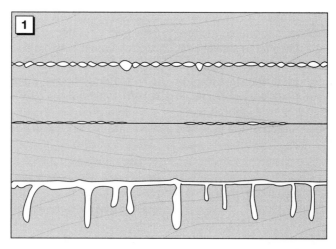

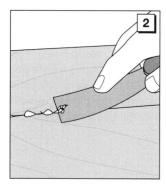

not dripping, but there is a continuous bead along the seam, indicating the entire joint has enough glue. The middle joint very likely has insufficient glue. Although there is some squeeze-out, gaps in the bead indicate that the joint may be starved at these points. The bottom joint obviously has too much glue.

The main problem with excessive glue is the mess.

In most cases, clamping pressure will squeeze out the excess. However, a heavy glue line can make clamping difficult. Until it sets, the glue functions as a lubricant, allowing the mating surfaces to slide. Because glue is less porous than wood, a heavy glue line also makes the seam of the joint more apparent after the finish is applied. And with some joints, like the blind mortise-and-tenon, too much glue can interfere with assembly because the glue cannot readily escape.

There are a variety of ways to clean up glue squeeze-out. If the workpiece is to be planed or painted, wipe off the excess with a damp rag before the glue sets. However, this tends to spread the glue over the surface, reducing the porosity of the surrounding wood. If the surface is to be stained, let the

glue dry and scrape off the bead. You can let the glue set just enough to become gummy and scrape it off with a putty knife ⬜2⬜. Or, allow the glue to cure completely and scrape it off using a paint scraper ⬜3⬜, hand scraper, or chisel.

COMMON GLUING PROBLEMS

DEALING WITH GLUE-UP PROBLEMS

A common problem with edge-to-edge joints—but one that is easily preventable—is the sunken joint, illustrated below. Until the glue cures, the wood on both sides of the seam absorbs moisture from the glue and swells (A). The problem occurs if the panel is surfaced in this swollen state (B). As a result, the wood will shrink as it dries, leaving a valley along the glue line (C). Wait until the glue is completely cured and the moisture content equalized before surfacing.

The moisture content of the wood can affect glue joints in other ways. If the wood is too dry, it can absorb the adhesive too quickly and starve the joint. This condition is also encountered when gluing end grain, which is exceptionally porous. Excessively high moisture content in the wood can also result in a starved joint; the moisture will thin the glue and slow its drying time to the point that clamping pressure drives it out before it can properly set.

Most glues work best if the wood's moisture content is in the 8 to 10 percent range.

Some adhesives, like white glue (polyvinyl acetates -PVA), are sensitive to temperature extremes. At temperatures below 50°F, the solids come out of the solution, resulting in a weak, chalky glue line. At temperatures above 100°F, the glue tends to dry too quickly and may develop a skin before the joint can be drawn together. Also, these glues sometimes fail to bond to oils, gums, and resins in the wood that migrate to the surface. With oily woods, it is best to glue up soon after the mating surfaces are cut. For other ways of overcoming problems gluing up oily woods, see page 330.

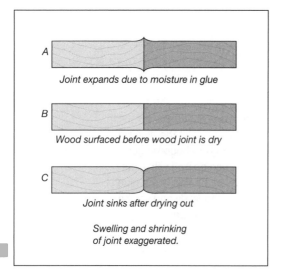

A — Joint expands due to moisture in glue

B — Wood surfaced before wood joint is dry

C — Joint sinks after drying out

Swelling and shrinking of joint exaggerated.

see page 330.

QUICKTIP

Preventing clamping stains

It is a good idea to prevent glue squeeze-out from coming into contact with clamps. Some of the chemicals in adhesives may react with the metal in clamps, producing stains that are very difficult to remove from either the clamps or the wood. To avoid this problem, cut a roll of wax paper into shorter rolls on the band saw. As shown at right, fold a strip of the paper over the bar of the clamp to serve as a barrier.

FINISHING

Finishes both protect wood and enhance its appearance. Choosing among the many options is largely a matter of taste, but the decision should be based on many considerations. If you are reproducing a traditional piece, for example, you should apply a finish that is appropriate for the style of furniture. A glass-smooth, high-luster finish would be expected on a Sheraton or Phyfe piece, but it whispers "fraud" when applied to Shaker or Danish modern designs. This is not to say that old methods and crudely formulated finishing materials are preferable. Modern finishes offer great variety, outstanding durability, and much appreciated convenience. Both old and new approaches to finishing have their place. This chapter explores finishing as a process, explaining both old and new options for achieving different kinds of finishes.

A quality finish starts with preparing the wood's surface with abrasives *(page 344)*, fillers, and sealers *(page 345)*. The porosity,

texture, and natural chemistry of various woods influence what finishes can be used and how the surface must be prepared to accept them. Beginning on page 346, the chapter also discusses altering the color of the wood using dyes, stains, and bleaches. The final step in the process is applying a topcoat to protect the wood and achieve the desired degree of luster. There are a wide variety of topcoats. Shellac, lacquer, and varnish all produce hard films on the surface, and each of these finishes has unique advantages. Shellac and lacquer dry rapidly and are easy to repair, while varnishes provide a more durable finish. Waxes and penetrating oils *(page 351)* are renewable finishes that impart a soft, warm feel and a subtle sheen.

The methods used to apply these finishes are as important as their physical properties. Application tools, techniques and sequences for the various finishes are presented starting on page 352. Steps for overcoming common problems are discussed on page 359.

ABRASIVES, FILLERS, AND SEALERS

The durability and appearance of a finish rests heavily on how the wood surface is prepared to accept it. Planing, shaping, and scraping establish the general contours, but abrasives, fillers, and sealers are often needed to remove or repair blemishes, level the surface, and alter the wood's porosity.

Both natural abrasives, such as flint, garnet, emery, pumice, and rottenstone, as well as man-made varieties, including aluminum oxide and silicon carbide, are available. Although man-made abrasives are generally harder and last longer, natural abrasives are less expensive. To remove paint or sand resinous woods that tend to clog sandpaper quickly, it is more economical to use the less expensive natural abrasives. Harder and finer-textured surfaces typically require harder abrasives and finer final grits.

When preparing a surface for a finish, it is important to sand in stages, gradually progressing from coarser to finer grits so that each grit removes the scratches left by the previous grit. The chart below will help you select the appropriate grit for each smoothing operation. As shown on page 131, always sand with the grain.

Surface defects that are too severe to be sanded away must be filled. Major defects can be plugged with wood inlays or a patching putty formed by mixing sawdust and glue. A variety of fillers is available, each with its own advantages and disadvantages. The chart on page 345 examines the commonly used varieties.

And finally, because wood is porous and there is wide variation in grain texture from species to species, you may need to apply a sealer to the surface. Sealers serve to limit the penetration of stains and prime the surface for a varnish or lacquer. They keep resins, gums, and stains from bleeding into finishes. Sealers also add body to a finish and help it adhere to the wood and prepare the surface for sanding. Consult the chart on page 345 to choose an appropriate sealer for your project. Remember that sealers are not compatible with penetrating oil finishes.

SANDPAPER GRITS FOR SMOOTHING

SMOOTHING OPERATION	TYPE	GRIT NO. USED
Removing saw and other machine marks, and smoothing deep imperfections	Coarse	60
Removing scratches and shallow imperfections	Medium	80-120
Smoothing before finish is applied	Fine	150-180
Polishing after applying finish	Very fine	220-600

CHARACTERISTICS AND USES OF FILLERS

TYPE OF FILLER	DESCRIPTION	ADVANTAGES	DISADVANTAGES	USES
Plastic wood	Ground wood particles and plastic hardener; available in several colors	Ready to use; dries quickly. Compatible with most finishes	Has no grain pattern and resists stains; relatively expensive	Fills cracks, dents, gouges, and large holes
Wood putty	Mixed with water to a dough-like consistency; contains powdered wood and adhesive	Inexpensive and easy to apply; dries quickly. Compatible with most finishes	Has no grain pattern; shrinks about 10%. Requires pigments for tinting; cannot be stored after mixing	Fills cracks, dents, gouges, and large holes
Stick shellac	Colored shellac applied with a heated knife; must match color of wood	Dries immediately to a hard and durable consistency	Has no grain pattern and does not absorb stain; difficult to apply. May be incompatible with alcohol or lacquer-based finishes	Fills dents and gouges
Wax stick	Soft, pigmented wax-like crayon; rubbed on surface and wiped with a soft cloth	Easy to apply; available in many colors. Can be applied after finishing	Has no grain pattern and repels stains; dissolved by some finishes. Never hardens and melts when heated; may be incompatible with lacquer	Fills scratches, and small cracks, and holes

CHARACTERISTICS AND USES OF SEALERS

STAIN OR FINISH BEING USED	RECOMMENDED SEALER	METHOD OF APPLICATION	PREPARATION	PROS AND CONS
Alcohol stain; non-grain-raising stain	Premixed 3-pound-cut shellac	Brush	Denatured alcohol 1:1 or 1:2 with shellac	Brushes on smoothly and is nontoxic; dries quickly, seals knots in wood, and sands easily. Does not resist alcohol or water
Oil-based stain	Boiled linseed oil	Rag	Mineral spirits 4:1 with boiled linseed oil	Easy to apply and penetrates wood surface; dries slowly
Clear lacquer or shellac	Premixed 3-pound-cut shellac	Brush	Denatured alcohol 1:1 or 1:2 with shellac	Brushes on smoothly and is nontoxic; dries quickly, seals knots in wood, and sands easily. Does not resist alcohol or water
Phenolic or alkyd varnish	Premixed 3-pound-cut shellac	Brush	Denatured alcohol 1:1 or 1:2 with shellac	Brushes on smoothly and is nontoxic; dries quickly, seals knots in wood, and sands easily. Does not resist alcohol or water
Polyurethane varnish	Polyurethane varnish	Brush or spray	Mineral spirits 1:1 with polyurethane varnish	Does not mask true color of wood; difficult to apply because it dries quickly

DYES AND STAINS

Dyes and stains are used to add color to wood. Dyes differ from stains in that they are dissolved in a liquid like oil or water, while stains are pigments that are carried in solution. Dyes penetrate the wood, bonding to the wood fibers. The pigments in stains provide a more superficial color: When the solution evaporates, the pigments are left on the surface.

The advantages and disadvantages of the various dyes and stains available have much to do with the solvents used to dissolve or carry them. Water-based dyes penetrate better and are more fade-resistant than alcohol-based ones, but they tend to raise the grain. You usually have to prepare the surface by wetting and sanding it before applying a water-based dye. Alcohol-based dyes do not raise the grain and dry rapidly. They work best when applied with a spray gun. Refer to page 354 for information on using spray equipment to apply a stain or finish.

CHARACTERISTICS AND USES OF SYNTHETIC DYES

TYPE OF DYE	COMPOSITION	PROS AND CONS	APPLICATION
NGR (Non-grain-raising)	Liquid dissolved in anhydrous petroleum distillate	Transparent, does not raise wood grain. Fades when exposed to light. Good for veneers. Not recommended for resinous softwoods such as spruce or pine	Best applied with spray gun. If using a brush or rag, add a retarder to slow drying.
Oil-based	Oil-soluble powder	Penetrating, lightfast, does not raise wood grain. Dries slowly. Good for softwoods. May bleed if used with an oil-based varnish topcoat	Mix with mineral spirits and apply with a brush or rag.
Penetrating oil-based	Liquid dissolved in mineral spirits	Does not raise wood grain. Provides transparent, bright colors. May bleed into oil-based topcoat	Apply with a rag or brush and wipe off once the desired color is obtained. Seal with a shellac wash coat to prevent bleeding.
Spirit-based	Alcohol-soluble powder	Transparent. Dries extremely fast, but may leave streaks if overlapped	Mix with alcohol and apply with a brush or spray gun.
Varnish-based	Liquid dissolved in varnish	Fade-resistant, transparent, non-penetrating. Good for use on woods with uneven porosity such as Douglas-fir and yellow pine	Best applied with spray gun. If using a brush, apply thin coats to avoid brush marks.
Water-based	Water-soluble powder	Bright, transparent colors. Lightfast. Good for open-grained hardwoods. Compatible with most finishes	Mix with water and apply with a brush, rag, or spray gun. Tends to raise grain. Surface may require wetting and sanding prior to application.

Non-grain-raising (NGR) dyes are as easy to use as water-based products without the grain-raising problems. Dyes are also available in oil or varnish bases, and some manufacturers employ a combination of dyes and pigments in their prepackaged stains. Provided the solutions (or vehicles) are the same, most stains and dyes can be blended to adjust the color.

On open-grained, ring-porous woods, such as oak or ash, dyes generally work best, providing a more even color. Stains tend to deposit more pigment in the open grain and therefore exaggerate the figure of porous woods. On fine-textured, diffuse-porous woods such as maple or birch, stains have the opposite effect: The pigment tends to dry on the surface and obscure the figure. One advantage of stains is that they will not accentuate racy grain patterns. If you want to conceal a wood's figure or irregularities in the grain, use a varnish stain, in which the pigment is held in suspension as the film dries.

TYPE OF STAIN	COMPOSITION	PROS AND CONS	APPLICATION	CHARACTERISTICS AND USES OF PIGMENT STAINS
Earth pigment	Powder that can be mixed in various liquids	Lightfast; opaque. Obscures the grain. May be used for tinting varnish	Usually mixed with oil or varnish and applied with a brush or spray gun	
Gel stain	Pigments blended with a petroleum gel	Flexible; easy-to-use. Provides excellent control for touch-up work in hiding blemishes	Apply with lint-free cloth and wipe off to achieve the desired color.	
Glazing stain	Liquid mixed in varnish	Very opaque. Used for graining, shading, and other decorative effects. Should be sealed and protected with a varnish topcoat	Apply with brush or rag.	
Japan color	Concentrated varnish-based liquid pigments	Ideal for tinting other finishing materials such as varnish, stain, or lacquer	Mix with oil or varnish and apply with a rag, brush, or spray gun.	
Oil-based stain	Powder or liquid dispersed in boiled linseed oil	Non-grain-raising. Does not bleed or fade. Transparent. Poor penetration of wood grain.	Stir well and apply with a brush or rag. Wipe off when desired color is achieved.	
Varnish stain	Pigments dispersed in varnish	Fills, colors, and adds a gloss to the surface in one coat. Obscures the grain. Dries fast but does not penetrate	Apply with a brush or spray gun.	
Water-based stain	Pigments suspended in an acrylic/water base	Fade-resistant. Bright colors can be blended to achieve various hues. Useful in matching old or faded finishes, but may raise the grain	Apply with a brush or spray gun. May be diluted to lighten color or wiped to control the amount of pigment left on the surface	

BLEACHING WOOD

Wood is bleached to remove unwanted stains or to lighten its natural color. Virtually any wood can be lightened to an off-white color by bleach. Walnut turns creamy in color when bleached; mahogany becomes pale rose. You can then apply a finish to the wood or stain it to the color that you want. Bleaching has several applications beyond simply suppressing the color of wood. It may be a desirable first step when applying certain stains to some species, such as when staining mahogany blond. Bleaching is also an effective way to downplay the color variations between the heartwood and sapwood in some woods or between two species of different color that you plan to stain to a common color.

The major drawback of bleaching is that the chemicals involved are dangerous. They are poisonous, caustic, and toxic to the skin and respiratory system. In addition, the process is unpredictable; for the home-shop woodworker, obtaining consistent results is difficult.

The process requires a very strong bleach, such as a two-part bleach composed of a caustic lye solution and a solution of hydrogen peroxide. Two-part bleach works by penetrating deep into the surface and breaking down the natural pigments in the wood. Oxalic acid is sometimes used as a stain remover, but another bleaching agent, chlorine, is safer to use. Chlorine bleach is available in various strengths from common household bleach to industrial-strength bleach.

All bleaches, including household bleach, should be handled and used with care. Refer to the safety tips presented below. It is important to follow label instructions carefully for preparing, mixing, and applying bleach. Avoid the fumes and protect your skin and eyes. An inventory of safety equipment is illustrated on page 55.

SAFETY TIPS
- *Wear a respirator when sanding surfaces that have been bleached; the residues that are left on the wood by the bleaching process can be released into the air as hazardous irritants by sanding.*
- *Bleach out-of-doors, or in an area indoors that is well ventilated.*
- *Wear goggles, gloves, a long-sleeved shirt, and an apron to protect your eyes and skin from the bleach.*

- *Always follow the manufacturer's instructions when mixing or applying a bleach; these products are highly reactive, toxic chemicals.*
- *Do not combine one type of bleach with another and never mix a bleach with another chemical; an explosion could result.*
- *Do not mix or store bleach in metal containers, as bleaches may react with metal; use glass containers.*

- *Store bleaches in a cool, dark place and out of reach of children.*
- *Never pour bleach down the drain; consult your local department of environmental protection or public health for proper disposal procedures.*
- *If any bleach contacts your skin, wash it off immediately with water; keep a source of water, either a bucket or a hose, close at hand.*

In spite of the complex changes brought about by modern chemistry, topcoat finishes can still be divided into five basic types: varnish, lacquer, shellac, wax, and oil. Each has played a role in cabinetmaking for centuries. Both varnish and its opaquely pigmented equivalent, paint, were employed by the ancient Egyptians. The use of "natural" lacquer in the Orient goes back almost as far. Shellac, although usually viewed as an "old-fashioned" finish, is a relative newcomer. It was not commonly used in Western Europe until the 17th Century. Both beeswax and oils of various kinds were applied as a crude means of protecting wood as long ago as the Stone Age. Their use in finishing fine furniture has been a well-practiced art at least since the Renaissance.

Varnishes represent the most impervious of the common topcoat finishes. They provide excellent resistance to heat, wear, and moisture, but they cure slowly and turn yellow over time. Varnishes are so varied that they defy description, except in general terms. Basically, varnishes contain film-forming solids dissolved in a liquid (called the vehicle) that evaporates as the varnish is applied. The solids in varnish are composed of natural or synthetic resins. Most varnishes now available are the synthetic-resin type and can be divided into three types: phenolic varnish, alkyd varnish, and polyurethane.

Varnishes are best brushed or sprayed on, but brushing is much easier than spraying. Since varnish takes a relatively long time to cure, brushing leaves you with enough time to apply the finish evenly. When varnish is sprayed, airborne particles of uncured varnish will eventually settle, leaving a sticky film on surrounding surfaces.

Another type of varnish, called wiping varnish, is thinned with mineral spirits so that it can be applied with a rag. These products are often sold as "oil" finishes, but they are actually varnishes. Yet another type of varnish-based product is the oil/varnish blend, which is a mixture of varnish and an oil finish such as tung oil. Oil/varnish blends share some of the characteristics of both ingredients. The oil component slows down the drying time of the finish and results in a less glossy topcoat, while the varnish part of the blend makes the finish more durable and resistant than an oil-only finish. An oil-varnish finish is not as hard as other varnishes.

All varnishes are virtually ready-to-use out of the can, but those that are formulated to provide a satin finish must be stirred periodically. Because these satin varnishes contain powdered silica to cut the gloss, stirring keeps the silica in suspension.

Polyurethane varnishes produce a very resistant finish, but each succeeding coat must be applied before the previous one thoroughly cures or the two coats will not bond. Alkyd- and phenolic-resin "oil" varnishes are generally less expensive than polyurethane types.

Lacquer is another topcoat that provides a hard and durable finish. It resists moisture, heat, and chemicals and dries extremely fast. Lacquer is the topcoat of choice for furniture manufacturers and many professional woodworkers. It is easiest to apply lacquer with a spray gun, but some lacquers are formulated with a retarder that slows drying and enables them to be brushed on. Each succeeding coat of lacquer tends to dissolve the previous coat. It is best to build up the finish by applying several thin coats, beginning with gloss lacquer, because of its greater clarity. The final coat can be a satin lacquer that will soften the shine. The sur-

CHOOSING A TOPCOAT

TOPCOATS

face can then be rubbed with a fine abrasive, such as pumice or rottenstone, to achieve the desired luster.

Shellac is made from resin secreted by the lac bug, an insect native to India and Southeast Asia. The resin is purified and dried into flakes which are then dissolved in alcohol. Modern premixed shellac is commonly available in two forms: yellow and white, which is more refined. Both are sold in various strengths called cuts. For example, a shellac containing 3 pounds of flakes per gallon of alcohol is referred to as a 3-pound cut.

Shellac has its drawbacks: It lacks resistance to alcohol and water, but it is a very convenient finish to use, both as a topcoat and as a sealer. Using shellac to apply a French polish finish (page 358) yields stunning results. Shellac's value as a sealer can be attributed to the fact that it forms a barrier between the natural resins in wood and varnish topcoats that are turpentine- or mineral-spirit-based. Shellac is easy to dilute to any desired consistency, dries quickly, and can be either brushed or sprayed on. Yellow shellac tints wood surfaces with a rich amber hue, while white shellac is virtually transparent.

Wax is typically used as a top dressing over other finishes, but it is easily marred and has low resistance to heat. Various kinds of wax are used in woodworking, including beeswax, white wax, and carnauba. These differ in terms of hardness and luster. Beeswax is exceptionally soft and provides a low, warm sheen, while the harder carnauba is relatively glossy. Waxes may be pigmented to subtly alter the color of the surface, but their chief virtue is that they are renewable finishes that can be easily applied with a rag. The more the rag becomes impregnated with wax, the better it performs as an applicator. Old wax can be removed quickly with a cotton rag soaked in naphtha or mineral spirits.

Penetrating oil finishes are different from varnishes, lacquer, shellac, and wax in that they penetrate the wood rather than forming a heavy film on the surface. Oils are usually applied with a cloth until the wood is saturated; any excess is wiped off. Once dry, penetrating oils provide the wood with varying degrees of protection depending on the kind of oil and how it has been processed. The result is typically a low-luster finish. Traditional oils, such as walnut and linseed, pene-

trate well and produce a warm, mellow luster. But they have low resistance to water and abrasion. "Boiled" linseed oil contains driers, usually in the form of toxic heavy metals, and it therefore should not be used on toys or food-related items, such as bowls or utensils. Tung oil has better resistance to moisture, heat, abrasion, acids, and mildew than other oils, and it can be buffed to a higher luster. Oil finishes are easily renewed; if their luster dulls, a fresh coat will restore it. Oil finishes also tend to darken naturally with age. However, both the luster and patina of a well-maintained oil finish are very attractive.

One issue of great concern to woodworkers is whether a finish is food-safe. Can it be applied to a project designed to come into contact with food? Essentially, all of the wood finishes discussed in this chapter—varnishes, shellac, lacquer, penetrating oils, and waxes—can be considered safe once they are completely cured. Any toxic solvents in a finish evaporate during the curing process, leaving the surface safe. However, one potential danger involves wooden kitchen items like cutting boards, bowls, and utensils. With such objects, small pieces of cured finish may actually be chipped off during use and be inadvertently ingested. To be absolutely safe with such items, it is better to select a finish that carries minimal risk. Safe choices include mineral oil, raw linseed oil (not boiled linseed oil, which contains metallic drying agents), pure tung oil, carnauba wax, paste furniture waxes containing beeswax, and shellac, which is used as a glaze in candy-making.

CHARACTERISTICS OF OIL FINISHES

TYPE OF TOPCOAT	HARDNESS	WATER RESISTANCE	SHEEN	EFFECT ON WOOD COLOR
Boiled linseed oil	Very soft	Very poor	Satin	Dark
Tung oil	Very soft	Fair (3 or more coats)	Satin (5 or more coats)	Medium
Oil/varnish blend	Soft	Fair	Satin	Medium
Polymerized oil	Hard	Good	Gloss	Light

CHARACTERISTICS OF NON-PENETRATING TOPCOATS

TYPE OF TOPCOAT	COMPOSITION	SHEEN	COLOR	DURABILITY	DRYING TIME
Shellac	Natural resin in alcohol	Gloss	White or yellow	Poor; affected by water, alcohol, and heat	Fast (1 to 2 hours)
Lacquer	Cellulose in lacquer thinner	Gloss, semi-gloss	Clear or tinted	Good; moisture resistant	Very fast (30 minutes to 1 hour)
Phenolic and alkyd varnish	Natural and synthetic resins in turpentine or mineral spirits	Gloss, semi-gloss, satin	Clear	Very good; heat-resistant and flexible	Slow (4 to 6 hours); cures overnight
Polyurethane varnish	Polymerizing plastic resins in mineral spirits or hydrocarbons	Gloss, semi-gloss, satin, flat	Clear (yellows over time)	Excellent; resists moisture, heat, and chemicals. Very flexible; has good solvent resistance	Slow (24 hours); resists solvents after curing
Wiping varnish	Natural and synthetic resins in turpentine or mineral spirits	Gloss, semi-gloss, satin, flat	Clear or tinted	Very good; moderately hard and brittle	Slow (4 to 6 hours); cures overnight
Acrylic varnish	Plastic acrylics in water	Gloss, semi-gloss, satin, flat	Clear (remains transparent)	Poor solvent and heat resistance; moderate moisture resistance. Resists scratching	Fast (2 to 4 hours)

APPLYING A FINISH

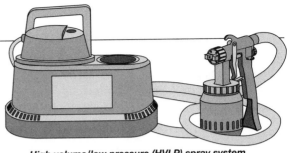

**FINISHING
APPLICATORS**

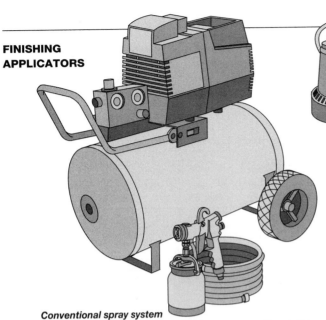

High volume/low pressure (HVLP) spray system
Electric-powered turbine provides a high volume of air to the spray gun. Because the air is supplied at relatively low pressure, there is less overspray and waste, compared to conventional system; also more compact and economical to use than conventional system. Must be used in a spray booth or room to contain and exhaust fumes.

Viscosity cup
Used to measure the viscosity of the finish so that product can be prepared to the proper consistency for spraying. Cup is dipped into the finish; the length of time it takes for the liquid to escape through the hole in the bottom of the cup indicates its viscosity.

Conventional spray system
Compressor forces pressurized air to the spray gun. Air passing through gun creates suction, drawing the finish up from the cup; finish is atomized into a fine mist and sprayed out the nozzle when the trigger is depressed. System features a regulator to control the pressure and volume of air; regulator contains a filter for removing impurities and moisture. Must be used in a spray booth or room to contain and exhaust fumes.

Sash brush
Designed for applying a finish to the muntins of a window sash, but also handy for finishing furniture. As a rule, use natural-bristle brushes to apply lacquer and shellac, and synthetic-bristle brushes for water-based or penetrating oil finishes; either type can be used for varnish.

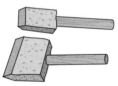

Foam brush
Easy to use, sponge-like applicator ideal for applying a stain or finish to contoured surfaces; inexpensive and designed for onetime use, the foam leaves no brush marks or stray bristles in the finish.

DIFFERENT TYPES OF SYNTHETIC BRISTLES

Blunt cut
Sometimes called straight cut, bristles are trimmed square at the ends; typical of inexpensive brushes, these brushes offer poor flow control.

Flagged bristles
The end of each bristle is frayed into fine fibers; lays down an even coat, minimizing brush marks. Good for applying varnishes.

Tapered bristles
Bristles taper to a fine point comparable to natural bristles; especially good for applying water-based finishes.

Applying a finish with a brush is not as straightforward as it appears. Technique is important. Both the viscosity and drying time of the finish and the size and contour of the surface being covered influence the process. For example, you should "scrub" on a heavy-bodied, slow-drying varnish, applying the finish first across the grain, then leveling it with the grain. For fast-drying finishes, such as shellac and lacquer, flow on the finish, avoiding overlapping the brush strokes, and working in one small area at a time. On large surfaces, work from the center out to the ends, as shown above.

To prevent your main supply of finish from becoming

contaminated with dust particles picked up by the brush, pour some of the finish into a separate large-mouthed container or tray, replenishing it as needed during the project.

Always use good-quality brushes to apply a finish. Good-quality brushes can hold more finish without dripping. Between coats, you can keep a brush suspended in the appropriate solvent to

keep it pliable, but when the project is completed, clean it thoroughly in the solvent, wash it with mild soap and water, rinse it, and hang it up to dry. The chart below summarizes the solvents to use for cleanup. Never store brushes resting on their bristles in solvent. Not only will this damage the bristles, but open containers of volatile solvents can be dangerous.

STAINS	SOLVENT
Water-based	Water
Oil-based	Turpentine or mineral spirits
Alcohol-based	Alcohol
Gelled	Turpentine or mineral spirits
Latex	Water
NGR	See manufacturer's instructions

TOPCOATS	SOLVENT
Shellac	Alcohol
Lacquer	Lacquer thinner
Varnish	Mineral spirits or turpentine
Polyurethane	Mineral spirits or turpentine
Penetrating Oils	Mineral spirits or turpentine

APPLYING A FINISH

SPRAYING TECHNIQUES

Applying a finish with a spray system requires some setup time, but on large projects, spraying is much faster than brushing. With practice, you will also obtain superior results, especially with fast-drying finishes such as lacquer. Set yourself up to work in a spray room or booth that conforms to local regulations. Adjust your equipment following the manufacturer's instructions. Wear a respirator, safety goggles, rubber gloves, and a rubber apron.

To apply a uniform coat, keep the spray gun moving at a constant rate and at a uniform distance from the surface, ideally about 6 to 8 inches. Avoid bending your wrist to direct the spray. Instead, keep your wrist stiff and move your arm so that the spray remains perpendicular to the surface.

To spray a flat surface [1], make straight, overlapping passes. Starting at a corner, move the gun back and forth across the grain, as indicated by the arrows in the illustration. Aim the center of the spray pattern at the outer boundary of the previous pass. Once you reach the opposite end of the surface, immediately repeat the process, this time working with the grain.

To spray the corner of a piece of furniture [2], point the gun directly at the corner so that the spray is delivered equally to the adjacent surfaces.

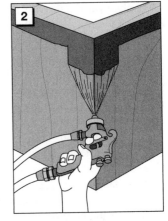

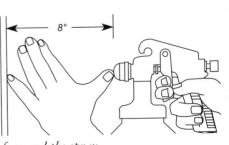

*QUICK*TIP

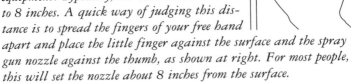

Maintaining the correct spraying distance

The correct distance between a spray gun and a wood surface being sprayed varies, depending on the type of finish and the setting of the equipment. Typically, the ideal distance is 6 to 8 inches. A quick way of judging this distance is to spread the fingers of your free hand apart and place the little finger against the surface and the spray gun nozzle against the thumb, as shown at right. For most people, this will set the nozzle about 8 inches from the surface.

APPLICATION STEPS FOR PHENOLIC AND ALKYD VARNISHES

BRUSHING

1. Dilute the varnish 1:1 with mineral spirits and apply a first coat. Start by brushing across the grain to cover the surface and then with the grain to level the finish and remove brush marks.

2. Let the surface dry, following the label instructions (typically 12 to 24 hours).

3. Sand with 220-grit or finer sandpaper; use 0000 steel wool on contoured surfaces.

4. Apply a second coat of undiluted varnish and repeat steps 2 and 3.

5. Brush on another coat of undiluted varnish and let the surface dry.

6. Sand with 320-grit or finer sandpaper.

7. Repeat steps 5 and 6 as many times as required until the surface is smooth.

8. Let the final coat cure at least 48 hours and rub out the finish until you obtain the luster you want *(page 356)*.

SPRAYING

1. Dilute the varnish to the viscosity recommended by the spray equipment manufacturer.

2. Adjust the spray equipment to low pressure to ensure a light first coat and apply a thin coat to the surface.

3. Let the surface dry, following the label instructions (typically 12 to 24 hours).

4. Sand with 320-grit or finer sandpaper.

5. Adjust the spray equipment to normal pressure and apply another coat. Let dry and sand.

6. Repeat step 5 as many times as necessary until the surface is smooth.

7. Allow the final coat to cure at least 48 hours before rubbing out the finish *(page 356)*.

APPLICATION STEPS FOR POLYURETHANE AND WATER-BASED VARNISHES

BRUSHING

1. Apply a light coat of varnish with the grain. Most polyurethane and water-based varnishes should be applied undiluted; only dilute the product if recommended by the manufacturer.

2. Let the surface dry, following the label instructions (typically 4 to 6 hours).

3. Sand with 220-grit or finer sandpaper.

4. Repeat steps 1 through 3 as many times as necessary until the surface is smooth; do not allow the varnish to cure completely between coats.

5. Allow the final coat to cure at least 24 hours before rubbing out the finish *(page 356)*.

SPRAYING

1. Apply a light coat of polyurethane to the surface. Most polyurethane and water-based varnishes should be applied undiluted; only dilute the product if recommended by the manufacturer.

2. Let the surface dry, following the label instructions (typically 2 to 4 hours).

3. Sand the surface with 220-grit or finer sandpaper.

4. Repeat steps 1 through 3 as many times as necessary until the surface is smooth; do not allow the varnish to cure completely between coats.

5. Allow the final coat to cure at least 24 hours before rubbing out the finish *(page 356)*.

APPLYING A FINISH

APPLICATION STEPS FOR WAXES

RUBBING ON

1. Prepare the surface so that it is smooth, dry and free of oil or other contaminants.

2. If desired, heat the wax and tint it with pigments to make its color more compatible with the wood. **Caution: Wax is combustible; only heat it in a double boiler.**

3. Apply a thin coat of wax with a cloth and let it dry until it forms a blush (15 to 20 minutes).

4. Using a wax-impregnated cotton rag, buff the surface vigorously to remove the blush and achieve the desired sheen.

APPLICATION STEPS FOR SHELLAC

BRUSHING

1. Dilute premixed 3-pound-cut shellac 1:1 with denatured alcohol and apply two or three coats—called wash coats—at 30-minute to 1-hour intervals. Brush with the grain and avoid overlapping your brush strokes.

2. Let the surface dry for 2 to 4 hours.

3. Lightly sand the surface with 320-grit or finer sandpaper and remove dust particles with a clean cloth.

4. Apply additional coats of undiluted 3-pound-cut shellac at 2- to 4-hour intervals. Sand lightly between coats until the surface is smooth.

5. Let the final coat cure at least 24 hours before rubbing out the surface.

SPRAYING

1. Dilute the shellac following the label instructions. Premixed 3-pound-cut shellac is typically diluted 1:1 with denatured alcohol.

2. Adjust the spray equipment to low pressure to ensure a light coat and apply two or three thin coats to the surface at 30-minute intervals.

3. Let the surface dry for 1 to 2 hours. Lightly sand the surface using 320-grit or finer sandpaper and remove dust particles with a clean cloth.

4. Adjust the spray equipment to normal pressure and apply additional coats of undiluted 3-pound-cut shellac until the surface is smooth. Let each coat dry 1 to 2 hours, sand, and remove dust particles before applying additional coats.

5. Allow the final coat to cure at least 24 hours before rubbing out the surface.

Rubbing out a finish

Rubbing out a finish after the topcoat has cured produces a satin sheen on the surface, leaving it clear and smooth. The traditional method involves sprinkling a few drops of a lubricant, such as water, paraffin, or mineral oil, onto the surface and working pumice powder over it with a felt block. Always move the block parallel to the wood grain and wipe the surface periodically to ensure you are not rubbing through the finish. Once a mixture of the lubricant and pumice forms on the suface, wipe it off with a soft, clean cloth. Repeat with rottenstone and more lubricant for a glossier sheen. You can also rub out a topcoat with a commercial rubbing compound using a rag or an electric polisher.

APPLICATION STEPS FOR LACQUER

BRUSHING

1. Apply a sanding sealer that is compatible with lacquer following the label instructions. Shellac can be used as a sanding sealer under lacquer; see page 356. Let the sealer dry and sand with 320-grit or finer sandpaper.

2. Dilute the lacquer with a retarder to extend its drying time, or use a premixed "brushing lacquer."

3. Apply the lacquer with a soft, long-bristled brush. Flow the lacquer on with the grain without overlapping or repeating your strokes.

4. Let the surface dry thoroughly (2 to 4 hours), sand lightly with 320-grit or finer sandpaper, and wipe off the dust particles with a clean cloth.

5. Repeat steps 3 and 4 as many times as necessary until the surface is smooth. Because each coat tends to soften prior coats, extend the drying intervals slightly with each additional application.

6. Let the final coat cure at least 24 hours before rubbing it out *(page 356)*.

SPRAYING

1. Apply a sanding sealer as for brushing lacquer.

2. Dilute the lacquer to the viscosity recommended by the spray equipment manufacturer.

3. Apply a coat and let it dry (typically 1 to 2 hours).

4. Sand lightly with 320-grit or finer sandpaper.

5. Repeat steps 3 and 4 as many times as necessary until the surface is smooth, extending the drying time slightly between each subsequent coat.

6. Allow the final coat to cure thoroughly (at least 24 hours) before rubbing out the finish *(page 356)*.

APPLICATION STEPS FOR OIL FINISHES

WIPING

1. Apply the oil with a cloth rag, saturating the surface.

2. Let the oil soak into the wood for 15 to 20 minutes, then wipe off any excess with a separate clean rag.

3. Let the surface dry thoroughly (typically 8 to 12 hours).

4. Using 400-grit sandpaper, smooth the surface and wipe off any dust with a clean, dry cloth or a tack rag.

5. Repeat steps 1 through 4 until you obtain the desired luster. Fine-textured woods typically require 4 to 6 coats.

6. Recoat the finish periodically (typically once every two years) to maintain the desired luster.

FRENCH POLISHING

Although laborious to apply and not particularly durable, a French polish finish is truly beautiful. You can apply this finish by rubbing the wood with shellac, pumice, and a bit of mineral oil using a cloth pad. Make the pad by placing a wad of wool inside a linen or muslin cover, as shown below. Start by coating the surface with shellac *(page 356)*, let it dry, and dust it lightly with pumice. Then moisten the pad with alcohol or a weak solution of alcohol and shellac and rub the surface using any of the patterns shown below. Regardless of the pattern or combination of patterns you use, keep the pad moving and try to scour the surface uniformly.

During this first stage of the process, the pumice abrades the surface and forms a slurry of pumice, wood particles, and shellac. The constant motion of the pad deposits this slurry in the pores of the wood, filling the surface. As the alcohol evaporates, the pad becomes increasingly more difficult to move. But it will eventually slide more easily as the surface dries. Let the surface cure thoroughly (about 12 hours).

To perform the second stage of the process, prepare a new pad, moisten it with shellac, and place just a touch of mineral oil on the pad cover as a lubricant. Rub the surface vigorously, keeping the pad moving constantly, lifting it periodically to remoisten it with alcohol or the alcohol/shellac solution. Keep rubbing until you obtain the appearance you want. Let the surface dry thoroughly. Once the finish cures, the surface will take on a slightly cloudy appearance. This is caused by the mineral oil. Remove the oil with a clean cloth dampened in alcohol; this will reveal the final luster of the finish. Some finishers use water as a lubricant to avoid this final step, but one risk with this approach is that the water may work through the softened shellac during the rubbing process and raise the wood grain. Also, unless the water evaporates completely during the rubbing process, it may cause the shellac to blush (lose its clarity). You can restore a French polish finish by repeating the second stage of the process.

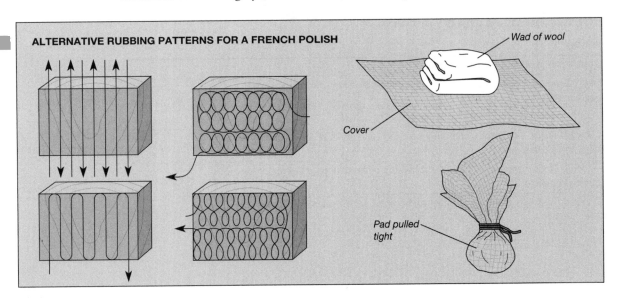

ALTERNATIVE RUBBING PATTERNS FOR A FRENCH POLISH

Wad of wool

Cover

Pad pulled tight

TROUBLESHOOTING A BRUSHED FINISH

OVERCOMING PROBLEMS WITH A BRUSHED FINISH

TYPE OF FINISH	PROBLEM	CAUSE	REMEDY
Varnish	Air bubbles	Friction caused by brushing	Sand surface and thin next coat with about 20% mineral spirits.
	Ridges after applying second coat	Oil contamination in first coat	Wipe off finish before it cures.
	Finish remains tacky; fails to cure	Cold air in shop	Work in heated area.
		Uncured oil on the surface	Allow finish more time to cure.
		The wood, such as teak or rosewood, is naturally oily	Allow finish more time to cure.
Lacquer	Blushing (a cloudy or milky haze in the finish)	Rapid evaporation, often in warm, humid conditions	Add a retarder to slow drying time of next coat.
	Fisheye (round blotches or patches)	Oil contamination on the surface	Sand defects off surface.
	Pinholes (small craters or holes)	Trapped air	Sand defects off surface.
Shellac	Blushing (a cloudy or milky haze in the finish)	Excess moisture in the finish or in the air	Let finish dry overnight.
	Pinholes (small craters or holes)	Air bubbles produced by brushing	Sand pinholes off surface; add alcohol to finish to thin subsequent coats.
	Visible brush marks	Finish too thick	Sand marks off surface; add alcohol to finish to thin subsequent coats.
	Dust remains in the finish	Dust in the shop air	Sand surface and let dust settle before applying next coat.
Water-based finishes	Air bubbles	Air bubbles produced by brushing	Add about 20% water to thin next coat and apply more sparingly.
		Finish not designed to be brushed	Select a finish designed for brushing.
	Finish cures too slowly	Humid conditions in shop	Increase air flow over surface or apply finish in drier conditions.

TROUBLESHOOTING A SPRAYED FINISH

OVERCOMING PROBLEMS WITH A SPRAYED FINISH

PROBLEM	APPEARANCE	CAUSE	REMEDY
Blushing	Cloudy or milky haze in the finish; most common with shellac	High humidity when the finish is applied	Maintain constant humidity and temperature in the shop. Apply finish on dry days. Add a retarder to prevent finish from skinning over too quickly and trapping moisture.
Checking	Grid-like, alligator-hide cracks; most common with varnish	Exposing the finish to sharp changes in temperature	If the finish will be exposed to temperature extremes, use a varnish formulated to produce a more flexible film. Control the temperature in the area where the finished piece will be kept.
Crazing	Fine hairline cracks, often associated with blush or patchy variations in the sheen of the finish	Chemical incompatibility, usually when the sealer and topcoat contain different solvents or have different expansion/contraction properties	Check the labels on the finishing products you are applying to ensure they are compatible. Test for compatibility on a scrap board before applying the finish on the project.
Fisheye	Round blotches or patches	Wax, oil, or other surface contamination that prevents the finish from adhering uniformly	Clean the surface with the appropriate solvent, such as ammonia, naphtha or alcohol, or use a commercial fisheye product.
Orange peel	A pebbly or bumpy surface texture like the skin of an orange	Spraying a finish of incorrect viscosity or from too far away from the surface	Correct the viscosity of the finish or hold spray gun closer to the surface.
Pinholes	Small craters or holes in the finish	Surface contamination, excessive spraying pressure, or too rapid drying	Ensure the surface is free of contaminants. Reduce the sprayer's air pressure or add a retarder to the finish to slow drying.
Run	Drops or runs similar in appearance to raindrops on a window	Applying too much finish	Move the gun across the surface at a faster speed. If the problem persists, check the sprayer feed adjustment or the viscosity of the finish.
Sag	The finish flows to form a wave-like pattern of ridges.	Applying too much finish or spraying the surface at an inappropriate angle	Hold the gun perpendicular to the surface and move it at a slightly faster pace. If the problem persists, check the sprayer feed adjustment or the viscosity of the finish.

HARDWARE

Most woodworking projects require a lot of metal in the form of fasteners and other hardware. But few woodworkers give these parts much thought. They are store-bought, relatively inexpensive in comparison to the cost of quality cabinet woods, and often easy to install. This has not always been the case. Until well into the 19th Century, nails and screws were used sparingly, and showy hardware, such as brass bails and pulls with large back plates, was considered opulent. By the late 19th Century, the Industrial Revolution made metal plentiful and furniture in the revival styles of the Victorian era was often festooned with gaudy hardware. Some would argue that the understated use of decorative hardware in most modern styles represents a reaction to those Victorian excesses.

Hardware is much more than decoration, however. Metal screws, hinges, latches, and drawer slides improve the utility and durability of many woodworking projects. Metal hinges and lid stays can support greater weight than their wooden counterparts, and clever devices like bullet catches let you conceal the way a cabinet door latches. With the advent of modern chemistry, plastic hardware has become available to the woodworker. In some applications, improved durability and pliability make plastic hardware superior to metal. And plastic glides and casters will not mar flooring, since they are softer than metal. Plastic rollers for drawer and door slides reduce friction better than metal parts. You will also find plastic knobs, hooks, catches, and shelf clips in many styles.

This chapter opens with a survey of the fasteners available to woodworkers, including nails, screws, bolts, and knockdown hardware. The remaining types of hardware presented, such as catches and latches, handles, knobs and pulls, hinges, locks, as well as supports, slides, and casters, are all grouped on the basis of function. Each piece is accompanied by a brief description of its typical application. Where possible, examples of both traditional and modern designs are shown.

NAILS

Cabinetmakers working in the 17th and 18th Centuries did not avoid nails because they preferred all-wood joinery. It was because iron and other metals were scarce, while the labor required for the joinery was cheap. Prior to the 19th Century, nails were individually hand-forged. Then "cut" nails appeared—wedge-shaped fasteners stamped from thin sheets of metal and featuring great holding power. The "penny" system that we still use to describe nail sizes originally reflected their cost. Round machine-made "wire" nails were developed in the mid 19th Century and came into common use after the American Civil War.

Because nails are quick and easy to install, they offer a practical way to reinforce joints that are too weak to be held by glue alone. Examples include butt and miter joints involving end grain. However, there are drawbacks to using nails: Often, they must be set below the surface and concealed with a filler *(page 345)*. In addition, chemical reactions between the acids in some woods and the metal in nails can cause corrosive stains.

TYPES OF NAILS

As illustrated below, there are many kinds of nails designed for a broad range of applications. Both the common nail and box nail have large flat heads. Box nails are smaller in diameter than common nails of equal length, making them less likely to split the wood, and are often treated with resin or other coatings to enhance their holding power. The most commonly used nails in cabinetmaking are finishing and casing nails and the brad. Finishing nails are fine-gauge nails that are a good choice with hardwoods that might be split by larger fasteners. Casing nails are slightly heavier-gauge, making them more prone to splitting wood. Their cone-shaped heads lend them greater holding power. Both finishing and casing nails are used for trim work since their heads can be set below the surface and concealed with a filler. Brads are small finishing nails ranging in length from ½ to 1 inch. Small wire nails are sized like brads, but they feature flat heads.

The chart on page 363 illustrates actual sizes for common, casing, and finishing nails from the 1-inch, 2d size through the 3-inch, 10d spike. (The "d" stands for penny.) Although the old "penny" system for expressing nail sizes is still commonly used, it is generally more confusing than helpful. For sizes up to 10d, it is possible to use a formula for calculating the nail's actual length. Divide the penny-size by 4 and add ½ inch. For example, a 10d nail is 3 inches long (10 divided by 4 plus ½ inch = 3 inches). The formula does not work for longer nails.

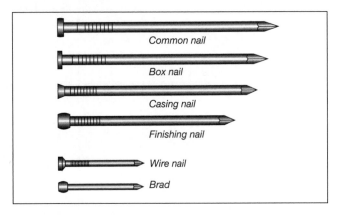

Common nail

Box nail

Casing nail

Finishing nail

Wire nail

Brad

ACTUAL SIZE OF NAILS

Common nails

2d 3d 4d 5d 6d 7d 8d 9d 10d

10d

3"
23/4"
21/2"
21/4"
2"
13/4"
11/2"
11/4"

10d

8d

6d

8d

6d

4d

4d

3d

1"
11/4"
11/2"
13/4"
2"
21/4"
21/2"
23/4"
3"

Casing nails   **Finishing nails**

QUICKTIP

Hiding a nail

To conceal a nail head, you can set the nail and cover the head with filler (page 345). This works well if the surface will be painted, but if you will be applying a clear finish, there is a better way. Before driving the nail, raise a curl of wood using a sharp chisel, a single-edge razor blade, or a commercial blind nailer, like the one shown at right. Then drive the nail flush with the surface under the curl and glue the curl back down to conceal the nail head. To hold the curl in place while the glue dries, weight it down or hold it down with masking tape. Sand the surface lightly to level it and remove any glue, leaving the nail's location virtually invisible.

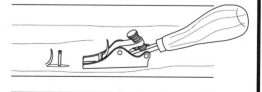

NAILS

SPECIAL NAILS

Skotch fastener
Used to reinforce miters and butt joints; the prongs spread as they penetrate the wood. They have strong holding power, but a drawback is that they are impossible to set or conceal.

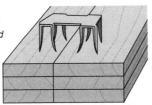

Corner chevrons
Used primarily to reinforce miter joints, chevrons have excellent resistance to shear stress. Drawbacks are that they are difficult to drive and tend to split the wood.

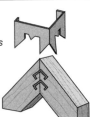

STAPLES

Once used primarily by upholsterers for holding fabric to wooden frames, staples are often used in factories to assemble furniture. They are best installed with an automatic staple gun. Staples have outstanding holding power and are more resistant to pull-through than nails. As shown below, the wedge-shaped points on staples are cut in various ways. This causes the prongs to either flare (left) or crimp (right) as they penetrate the wood.

PINS AND TACKS

Escutcheon pin
A convex-head nail generally used for mounting back plates and other hardware; typically available in solid brass or plated steel and in various diameters and lengths up to ¾ inch.

Wire upholsterer's tack
Similar to the standard upholsterer's tack, but with a nail-like point and a round upper shank that improves its holding power.

Upholsterer's tack
Used to fasten fabric to wood; the large head prevents pulling through the fabric. The sharp, long-tapered point makes them easy to drive with a single blow with a magnetized hammer.

Finish tack
Typically used to fasten seat covers to chair frames; available in various lengths and in a variety of head designs.

CLAMP NAILS

A clamp nail is a splinelike metal fastener that is slightly tapered so that it will draw a joint together as it is driven. As with wood splines, both sides of the joint must be grooved to accommodate the fastener. Clamp nails are available in lengths from ½ inch to 2 inches. They produce an extremely strong joint, but because the grooves must be located with precision, they are used primarily in factory applications.

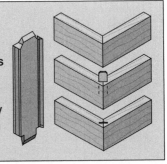

SCREWS, BOLTS, AND NUTS

Screws have been used in woodworking for centuries. However, until the Industrial Revolution, they were individually hand-crafted and designed with blunt tips. Unlike modern screws, they were often imprecisely threaded, difficult to install, and so expensive that they were seldom used except where a removable fastener was required. Today, screws are the most commonly used fastener in cabinetmaking. Because they feature great holding power and can be driven easily with a variable-speed electric drill, they are practical and convenient.

As shown below, screws are available with a variety of head shapes and drive configurations. In addition, there are alternatives to the conventional wood screw, such as drywall screws, and more modern screws with names like "low-root" screws, "cut-thread" screws, and steel screws. Some of the benefits of these designs for woodworking are described on page 116.

TYPES OF DRIVE

Slot
Very common, but screwdriver tip tends to slip out of slot and slot eventually wears under high torsion.

Phillips
Most common type; screwdriver tip fits recess snugly and recess resists stripping.

Square-drive (Robertson)
Very common; resists stripping better than slot-type, but not as well as Phillips.

Hex
Used in industrial applications; not available in wood-screw type. Driven with a hex wrench.

Eight-recess
Used in industrial applications; not available in wood-screw type. Requires a special driver.

Quadrex
Not common; can be driven with either square-drive or Phillips driver tip.

COMMON WOOD SCREWS

ANATOMY OF A CONVENTIONAL WOOD SCREW

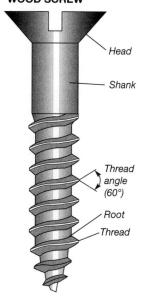

- Head
- Shank
- Thread angle (60°)
- Root
- Thread

TYPES OF SCREW HEADS

Flat
Cone-shaped head lets you countersink the screw so that the top of the head seats flush with the surface or so that the head can be concealed by a wood plug (page 117).

Round
Used in decorative applications or when the screw head cannot be countersunk; the bottom of the head rests flat on the surface.

Oval
Often used with decorative grommet washer as shown for installing trim.

TYPES OF THREADS

Drywall screw
Deep threads let it penetrate some woods without a pilot hole; double-lead threads allow you to drive it faster than conventional wood screws. Heads resist stripping; good for fastening plywood and particleboard. Not available in as many sizes as conventional screws.

Steel screw
Features knife-edge threads with a larger diameter than the shaft so a single drill bit can be used to bore pilot and clearance holes; corrosion-resistant. Coated with a Teflon lubricant to facilitate driving.

Low-root screw
Has a sharp-angled thread to make driving easy and fast; provides good resistance to pullout.

Cut-thread screw
Stronger and can be driven faster than conventional wood screws; resists corrosion. Has great holding power in hard stock.

SCREWS, BOLTS, AND NUTS

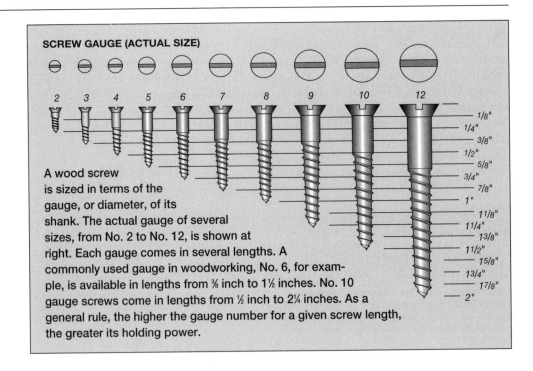

SCREW GAUGE (ACTUAL SIZE)

2 3 4 5 6 7 8 9 10 12

1/8"
1/4"
3/8"
1/2"
5/8"
3/4"
7/8"
1"
11/8"
11/4"
13/8"
11/2"
15/8"
13/4"
17/8"
2"

A wood screw is sized in terms of the gauge, or diameter, of its shank. The actual gauge of several sizes, from No. 2 to No. 12, is shown at right. Each gauge comes in several lengths. A commonly used gauge in woodworking, No. 6, for example, is available in lengths from ⅜ inch to 1½ inches. No. 10 gauge screws come in lengths from ½ inch to 2¼ inches. As a general rule, the higher the gauge number for a given screw length, the greater its holding power.

INVENTORY OF SCREWS AND BOLTS

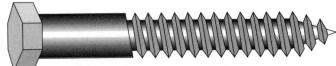

One-piece connector
Has coarse threads and a cylindrical shank; its main advantage is that it aligns parts as it fastens them together.

Lag screw
A heavy-duty hex- or square-head screw tightened with a wrench; generally available in diameters from ¼ to ½ inch and lengths up to about 8 inches or longer. Used in heavy-duty applications, such as hanging kitchen cabinets or securing parts in outdoor furniture.

Round-head machine screw
Tightened with a nut, machine screws are used in assembling knockdown joints.

Hanger bolt
A combination bolt/screw with lag threads on one end and machine threads on the other; used in knockdown assemblies such as mounting leg-to-rail joints. (See page 323.)

Castellated nuts
Available in flat and crowned versions, the notches provide anchorage for a cotter pin which is installed through a hole in the bolt to prevent the nut from turning.

Wing nut
Used in assembling knock-down joints and adjustable assemblies; wings enable nut to be tightened by hand.

Square nut
Cheaper than hex nut; used to tighten machine screws. Available in both flat and crowned versions.

Hex nut
Used to tighten machine screws; available in various sizes and threads.

Knurled nut
A round nut with a knurled outside circumference to provide better grip for tightening by hand; less obtrusive than wing nuts.

Cap nut
Used to cover exposed screw threads; the hex-shaped shoulder enables the nut to be tightened.

TYPES OF WASHERS

Flat
Prevents a nut or round head screw from digging into the surface.

Flush countersunk
Distributes load of countersunk flat-head screw.

Toothed
Geared or scalloped edges bite into the surface to prevent fastener from turning.

Split lock
Similar to a flat washer that has been cut and bent, a lock washer applies springlike pressure against the nut to prevent it from loosening.

Countersunk
Sometimes referred to as a grommet washer; used in decorative applications with flat- or oval-head screws.

---

*QUICK*TIP

Lubricating screw threads

Lubricating screw threads with paraffin reduces friction and makes a screw easier to drive, particularly in hardwood. This helps prevent the head from being twisted off the shank. Do not use oil or other penetrating liquid lubricants as they may stain the wood.

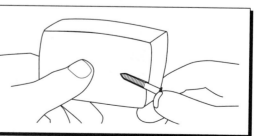

KNOCKDOWN HARDWARE

Most woodworking joints are designed to be both rigid and permanent. In some instances, however, it is preferable to fasten components together so that they can be adjusted or dismantled. Wood joints like the tusk mortise-and-tenon *(page 273)*, for example, can be disassembled, but it is a large and bulky joint that may not be appropriate in some situations. The examples of knockdown hardware illustrated below are all very durable and easy to install and remove. Another benefit of these fasteners is that they reinforce joints that would otherwise be weak, such as butt joints involving end grain or assemblies using materials like particleboard or plywood.

KNOCKDOWN HARDWARE FOR WOODWORKING

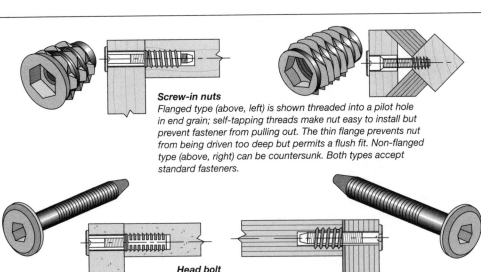

Screw-in nuts
Flanged type (above, left) is shown threaded into a pilot hole in end grain; self-tapping threads make nut easy to install but prevent fastener from pulling out. The thin flange prevents nut from being driven too deep but permits a flush fit. Non-flanged type (above, right) can be countersunk. Both types accept standard fasteners.

Head bolt
Driven with a hex wrench into any of the nuts or connectors shown; has a broad head.

Bolt cap
Mounts like a capped nut to the end of a head bolt to draw two workpieces together; requires access to both sides of the assembly and is tightened using two hex wrenches.

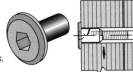

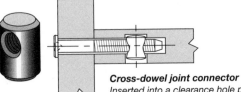

Cross-dowel joint connector
Inserted into a clearance hole perpendicular to the grain of the workpiece; as fastener is driven through mating piece, connector must be held steady with a screwdriver.

T-nut
Requires a clearance hole; spurs on the flange dig into the wood and prevent the nut from turning once it is tapped in place.

CATCHES, LATCHES, AND HASPS

A variety of devices is available for securing a door or lid to a piece of furniture. Early examples of latches, hasps, drop latches, and throw bolts date from medieval times and tended to be heavy and functional. The forged banjo catch shown below, for example, was traditionally used to lock the top of a tilting table in the horizontal position. Although hardware of this type is still appropriate in some applications, modern latching devices tend to be decorative as well as practical and durable.

The type of latching mechanism you choose should complement the hinges *(page 377)* and any pulls or knobs *(page 373)* you are using. Another important consideration is ease of installation. Some devices are flush-mounted while others must be fitted into a mortise and carefully aligned with a strike plate.

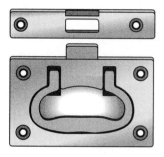

Lift handle with catch
A flush-mounted catch used on large cupboards and chests; catch is mortised flush to the surface and is released from the strike plate when the handle is lifted.

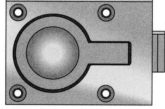
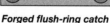

Forged flush-ring catch
Used on cupboards and chests where recessed hardware is desirable; catch is mortised flush to the surface and is released from the strike plate when the ring is lifted.

A SAMPLING OF CATCHES, LATCHES, AND HASPS

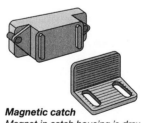

Magnetic catch
Magnet in catch housing is drawn to steel strike plate as the door is closed; oblong screw holes in the strike plate allow for adjustment.

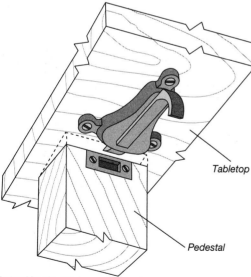

Tabletop

Pedestal

Forged banjo catch
A traditional catch used on tilt-top tables. Catch mounts to underside of tabletop; strike plate is mortised into pedestal on edge opposite hinge. Pulling spring-loaded latch retracts bolt from strike plate, allowing top to be tilted to vertical position; catch locks top in horizontal position.

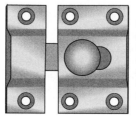

Cast cupboard catch
A traditional surface-mounted catch for kitchen cupboards and cabinets. Knob is slid back to withdraw the bar.

CATCHES, LATCHES, AND HASPS

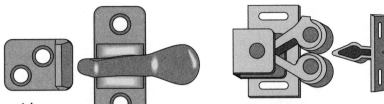

Elbow catch
Spring-loaded arm on the
catch is depressed to release
the catch from the strike plate;
commonly used on one side of
paired doors.

Double roller catch
Spring-loaded arms with neoprene rollers close
over a spear-shaped strike plate; until the development of spring-loaded hinges, this was one of
the most commonly used catches in cupboards
and vanities.

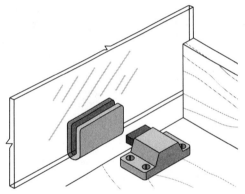

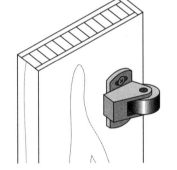

Magnetic touch catch
Used in display cases. U-shaped strike plate
fits over unframed glass door; magnetic spring-
loaded catch releases when door is pressed.

Single roller catch
A spring-loaded neoprene roller mounted on
the door closes over a raised strike plate on
the side of the cabinet; slightly stronger and
more durable than the friction catch.

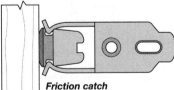

Friction catch
For use on lightweight cabinet doors; a
spring steel stamping closes on a ball-head-
ed screw which functions as the strike plate.
Inexpensive and easy to install and adjust.

Bullet catch
A traditional catch for small cabinets and
cases; the cylindrical spring-loaded bullet
is mortised into the edge of the door and
closes over a round strike plate mounted
to the jamb.

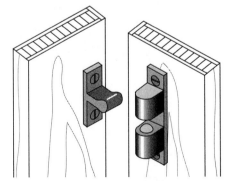

Ball catch
Two spring-loaded balls in the catch
capture the machined brass strike
plate; exceptionally durable and features very smooth action.

Case latch
A small surface-mounted latch used on chests and armoires; latch releases when the U-shaped pivot bar is lifted away from the case.

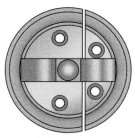

Button-on-plate latch
A surface-mounted turn button-type latch commonly used to secure the two halves of extension tables together; also installed to prevent a door or lid from opening inward. The turn button and attached pivot bar is rotated to release the latch.

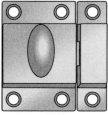

Cupboard latch
Similar to the cast cupboard catch shown on page 369, except that the bar is retracted from the strike plate by turning the knob.

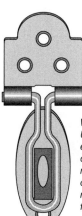

Wire latch
Used on jewelry boxes and other small cases; the wire mounted on the edge of the lid fits over a retainer plate on the face of the box.

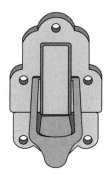

Case latch
Commonly used on heavy cases, the spring-loaded stamped lever snaps over the strike plate.

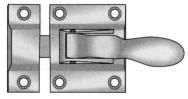

Icebox latch
A surface-mounted cabinet latch similar in action to the cupboard latch, except that the bar is retracted by lifting the spring-loaded lever; the traditional latch for turn-of-the-century iceboxes.

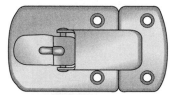

Pressed box snap
Used like the case latch, the box snap releases when the protruding lever is lifted.

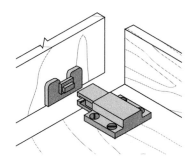

Push latch
Spring-loaded jaws in the latch engage the strike plate when the door is closed; pressing the door releases the latch. Typically used when a knob or pull on the outside face of the door is inappropriate.

CATCHES, LATCHES, AND HASPS

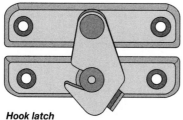

Hook latch
A typical lid latch for pistol boxes and other small cases; the pivoting hook engages a raised button on the strike plate.

Shell latch
For use on small cases and boxes; available in several sizes and designs. The hole in the hinged plate latches onto a raised button on the strike plate.

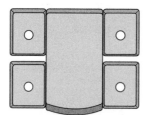

Overlay latch
A low-profile latch used on jewelry boxes and other small cases; the hinged plate mounted on the edge of the lid closes over the strike plate on the face of the box.

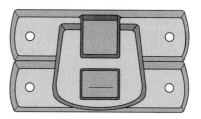

Button-type case latch
A light-duty version of the spring-loaded case latch (page 371); the lever snaps over a button on the strike plate.

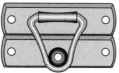

Wire hasp
This light-duty hasp is used on small cases and boxes; usually mounted with escutcheon pins. The wire bail closes over a stud on the strike plate.

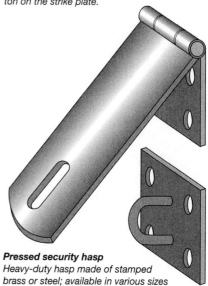

Hook hasp
A light-duty hasp usually made of stamped brass used as a lid latch or on doors; the hook mounted to the hasp arm fits through the ring on the strike plate.

Pressed security hasp
Heavy-duty hasp made of stamped brass or steel; available in various sizes and styles with both fixed and rotating rings on the strike plate.

HANDLES, KNOBS, AND PULLS

O f all the hardware elements used in cabinetmaking, knobs and pulls are chosen almost exclusively on the basis of style. If you plan to do reproduction work, for example, you need to have some knowledge of the types of knobs and pulls that are historically correct for the various periods of furniture making. Most of the major periods are discussed with illustrated examples in the Furniture Styles chapter *(page 21)*. This section offers a sampling of some of the higher-quality knobs and pulls on the market today, many of them relatively faithful reproductions of 17th-, 18th-, and 19th-Century designs.

Knobs and pulls are less prominent on modern furniture. In fact, many recent designs feature surface-mounted doors with beveled edges and spring-loaded, self-closing hinges that render knobs and pulls unnecessary. Still, a host of modern types are readily available in various qualities and price ranges.

REPRODUCTION HANDLES AND PULLS

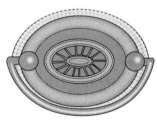

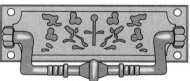

Oval plate handles
The oval back plates with the bail mounted to posts from the outside are typical of the late 18th- and early 19th-Century neoclassical styles of Hepplewhite and Sheraton.

Face-mounted handle
This cast brass bail features a surface-mounted back plate held by screws; typical of late 19th-Century Victorian revival styles.

Teardrop pull
Pull pivots in a post or pin mounted through a rosette back plate; typical of late 17th-Century William and Mary style.

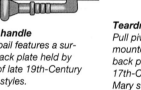

Smooth-faced cast plate handle
Typical of Queen Anne and Georgian style furniture, this bail-type handle features a smooth-patterned back plate, typically polished brass.

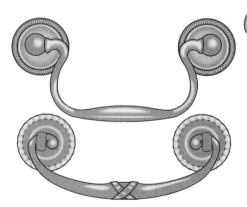

Cast cabinet handles
Often decorated with flowing floral patterns; one-piece and bolted from behind. Typical of late Victorian rococo cabinets and furniture.

Rosette back plate handles
Available in numerous sizes and designs; the posts are seated in round, rosette back plates commonly found in neoclassical styles.

HANDLES, KNOBS, AND PULLS

**HANDLES
AND PULLS**

Pierced forged plate handle
Intricate fretwork patterns usually adorn the back plates; can be used in many applications.

Chased cast plate handle
Available in many styles, the back plate is often embossed, engraved, or cast with various decorative designs.

Flush ring pull
A compact pull commonly used on campaign-style furniture. Mounts flush to surface; hinged ring can be pulled out with a finger.

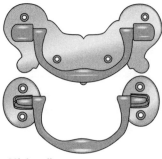

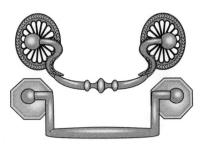

Lift handles
Used primarily on chests; feature bails that stop when raised perpendicular to the surface to facilitate lifting.

Drop handles
Also referred to as ring pulls, these light-duty handles are used in many styles; the shape of the ring and the decorative treatment of the back plate vary widely.

Cast cabinet handles
Available in several styles; can be used in virtually any application.

**A SAMPLING
OF KNOBS**

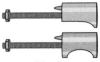

Wooden knob
Inexpensive turned wooden knob available in diameters from ¾ inch to 2 inches; typically used on American Country furniture. Mounted by gluing tenon into a hole bored in the door or drawer face.

Victorian decorative brass knobs
A heavy and ornate solid-brass knob often used with a rosette back plate; screws into face of drawer or door. Available in sizes from ¾ inch to 1¼ inches.

Brass pull knobs
These distinctive Oriental barrel knobs are among many less conventional designs. The lower surface is recessed to provide a finger grip; the spur on the back of the knob digs into the wood to prevent the knob from turning.

Classic brass knob
A back-mounted knob similar to the turned brass knob, but more appropriate for reproduction styles.

Turned brass knob
A plain ball-shaped brass knob turned from solid brass bar stock; tapped to accept a bolt installed into the back face of the drawer or door.

Shaker knob
Similar to the wooden knob, but noted for its distinctive mushroom-shaped profile; may feature a tenon, as shown, and be mounted into a mortise, or be back-mounted with a screw.

Face-mounted handle

Plain versions are often referred to as sash pulls because they are commonly used on windows; easy to install and available in many styles appropriate for cabinets and fine furniture.

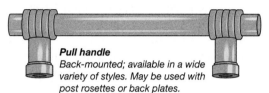

Pull handle

Back-mounted; available in a wide variety of styles. May be used with post rosettes or back plates.

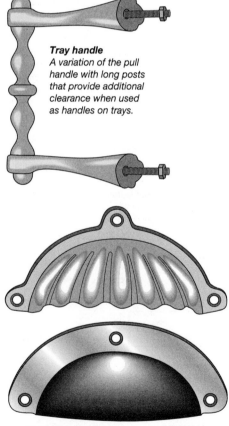

Tray handle

A variation of the pull handle with long posts that provide additional clearance when used as handles on trays.

Ring pull

Features a pivoting ring mounted to a rosette or back plate; comes in a wide assortment of designs compatible with various furniture styles. The low profile is an advantage when a protruding knob or handle is inappropriate.

Shaped wooden pull

Available in simple modern designs or ornately carved with rococo floral patterns; this style is relatively easy to make in the shop.

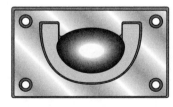

Flush handle

Typically used on chests; a heavy-duty variation of the flush ring (page 374) with a bail-type handle that stops at 90° to the back plate.

Pressed drawer pulls

Cup-shaped surface-mounted drawer pulls come in many styles; commonly used on turn-of-the-century filing cabinets and office furniture. Typically made of stamped brass, but also available in more decorative cast forms.

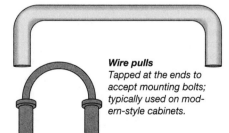

Wire pulls

Tapped at the ends to accept mounting bolts; typically used on modern-style cabinets.

CARD FRAMES AND CORNERS

Card frames are indispensable for labeling the contents of drawers, file cabinets, and cupboards.

Another practical accent is the stamped metal corner often found on 19th-Century steamship trunks and portable furnishings known as campaign furniture. Easy to install, corners are available as decorative embellishments to lend character to chests, cases, and cabinets.

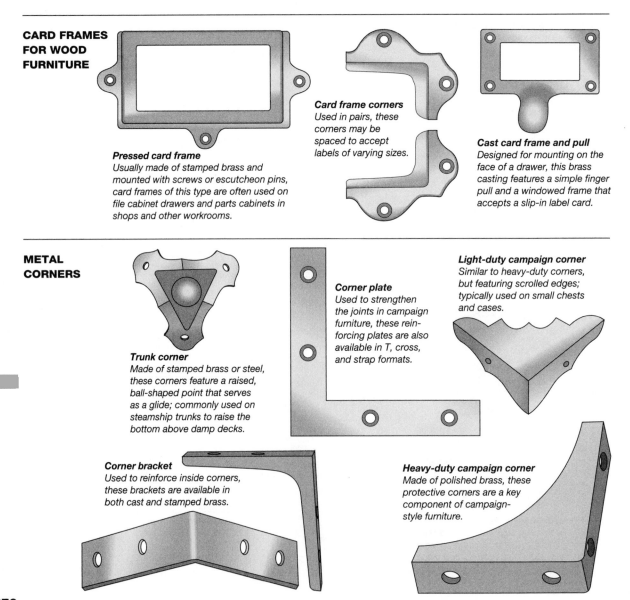

CARD FRAMES FOR WOOD FURNITURE

Pressed card frame
Usually made of stamped brass and mounted with screws or escutcheon pins, card frames of this type are often used on file cabinet drawers and parts cabinets in shops and other workrooms.

Card frame corners
Used in pairs, these corners may be spaced to accept labels of varying sizes.

Cast card frame and pull
Designed for mounting on the face of a drawer, this brass casting features a simple finger pull and a windowed frame that accepts a slip-in label card.

METAL CORNERS

Trunk corner
Made of stamped brass or steel, these corners feature a raised, ball-shaped point that serves as a glide; commonly used on steamship trunks to raise the bottom above damp decks.

Corner plate
Used to strengthen the joints in campaign furniture, these reinforcing plates are also available in T, cross, and strap formats.

Light-duty campaign corner
Similar to heavy-duty corners, but featuring scrolled edges; typically used on small chests and cases.

Corner bracket
Used to reinforce inside corners, these brackets are available in both cast and stamped brass.

Heavy-duty campaign corner
Made of polished brass, these protective corners are a key component of campaign-style furniture.

HINGES

Choosing the right hinge for the job depends on both utility and style. First, hinges must be mechanically correct for the intended application. Traditional furniture styles made lavish use of metal hardware, and this must be considered in the design of a piece. But many styles of modern furniture de-emphasize hinges as style elements. This is reflected in the increased popularity of partially or totally concealed varieties such as knife, soss, and back-mounted offset hinges.

Installing butt hinges that need to be mortised, such as on flush-mounted doors, is a challenging task. You must cut the mortise for each hinge leaf to the correct depth. Also, you must align the hinge pins along the same axis to prevent the hinges from binding and enable the door to open and close smoothly. Fitting and mounting hinges for face-mounted or offset doors *(page 317)* is less demanding. Several of the hinges shown can be used in such applications.

If your project requires hinges, choose the hardware early in the process. Advance planning will enable you to accommodate the hinges and any required mortises during the construction of the piece.

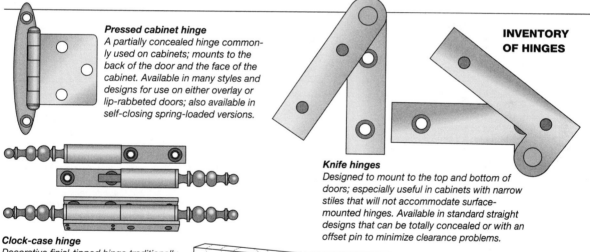

INVENTORY OF HINGES

Pressed cabinet hinge
A partially concealed hinge commonly used on cabinets; mounts to the back of the door and the face of the cabinet. Available in many styles and designs for use on either overlay or lip-rabbeted doors; also available in self-closing spring-loaded versions.

Knife hinges
Designed to mount to the top and bottom of doors; especially useful in cabinets with narrow stiles that will not accommodate surface-mounted hinges. Available in standard straight designs that can be totally concealed or with an offset pin to minimize clearance problems.

Clock-case hinge
Decorative finial-tipped hinge traditionally used on clock cases. Features a pin that permits the door to be lifted off without unscrewing either half of the hinge.

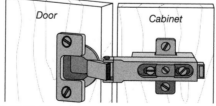

Door   Cabinet

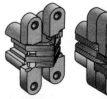

Piano hinge
A continuous hinge commonly used for mounting heavy lids such as on chests. Available in lengths up to 6 feet; can be cut to appropriate length.

Adjustable hinge
Can be used on flush-mounted and inset doors, and is completely hidden when door is closed; features a 100° opening and is spring-loaded to lock in the fully open or closed positions, eliminating the need for catches. Can be adjusted up to ¾ inch horizontally, vertically, and sideways after installation; allows door to be removed without losing adjustment.

Soss hinge
A concealed hinge for use on flush-mounted doors; available in several designs, these hinges are mortised into the edges of the door and stile.

HINGES

INVENTORY
OF HINGES

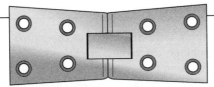

Countertop hinge
A wide, heavy-duty strap-type hinge with a 180°
stop; the leaves are joined by a link plate rather
than a pin. Used to hinge a section of countertop
so that it can be swung over an adjoining section;
mortised flush with the upper surface.

Desk hinge
A narrow back-mounted strap hinge
commonly used on lift-lid desks; mortised flush with the surface.

Card table hinge
A back-mounted hinge used
on fold-down tables; features
a 180° stop that prevents the
table leaf from being raised past
the horizontal position. Mortised
flush with the surface.

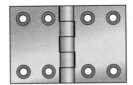

Back-flap hinge
A heavy-duty hinge used
primarily on lids; the wide
leaves provide consider-
able strength.

Decorative hinge
Also known as a butterfly
hinge; a pressed, face-mounted hinge used on small cabinets and cases.

Loose-pin ball-tip hinge
The removable pin in this butt
hinge enables a door to be lifted
off without unfastening either hinge
leaf; one ball threads onto the pin
like a cap nut. Mortised into the
door and stile edges.

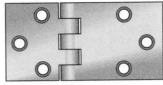

Rule-joint hinge
A back-mounted hinge designed
for drop-leaf tables; mortised flush
with the lower surface. To produce
a rule joint, see page 288.

Lift-off hinge
Similar to a fixed-pin butt hinge,
except that the bayonet-type pin
enables a door to be removed
without unfastening the hinge
leaves; mortised into the door
and stile edges.

Fixed-pin butt hinge
The standard butt hinge traditionally used for flush-mounted doors;
features two flat leaves connected
by a fixed pin. Mortised into the
door and stile edges.

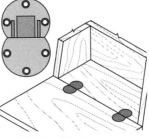
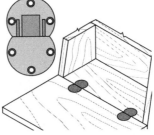

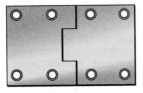

Butler's tray hinge
Traditionally used on butler's
trays to allow the sides and
ends to swing down, forming
a flat table; mortised flush
with the surface.

Fall-flap hinge
Used to raise and lower
the writing surface of a
drop-lid secretary; must
be mortised flush into
the adjoining surfaces.

H hinge
A flat-leaf hinge designed to be
mounted on the face of flush-
mounted doors; available in brass,
wrought iron, and other finishes.
Also available in an offset design
for lip-rabbeted doors.

LOCKS, KEYS, AND ESCUTCHEONS

Keyed cabinet locks are used on display cabinet doors or drawers to safeguard their contents. But function aside, locks and decorative escutcheons are important style elements in many types of wood furniture. Traditional desks and secretaries often have a decidedly unfinished look if these embellishments are omitted. Locks come in many varieties and most of them are reproductions of 18th- and 19th-Century designs. If you wish to incorporate a lock in your project, it is a good idea to explore what is available early in the planning process. This way, you will be able to accommodate the lock and any required mortising as you plan and build the piece.

Lock assemblies often comprise three separate pieces: a bolt assembly mortised into the back face of the door or drawer; a strike plate mortised into the carcase adjoining the bolt; and an escutcheon, which surrounds the keyhole in the front face of the door or drawer.

Pressed escutcheon
Usually made of stamped brass, this type of decorative escutcheon is fastened in place with escutcheon pins.

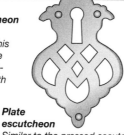

Plate escutcheon
Similar to the pressed escutcheon, but of cast or forged construction and heavier.

Extruded escutcheons
Fit into keyhole; protect the face of the drawer or door from being damaged by the key.

LOCKS, KEYS, AND ESCUTCHEONS FOR WOOD FURNITURE

Covered escutcheon
Available in many styles, this escutcheon features a pivoting cover plate to protect the keyhole.

Door/drawer locks
Used on flush-mounted doors or inset drawers; post and built-in escutcheon must be mortised through surface. Available in both right- and left-hand versions.

Rolltop desk lock
Locks by means of spring-loaded double levers which engage the strike plate.

Jewelry box lock
A small back-mortised lock, usually featuring a center post key.

Escutcheon handle
An escutcheon plate that incorporates a ring pull; usually used on small drawers where a separate knob or handle is inappropriate.

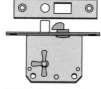

Sliding door/tambour lock
Register pin engages with the strike plate as the door is closed to ensure the hook-type locking mechanism is correctly aligned.

Half-mortise lock
Main part of lock is back-mortised into chest; strike plate is attached to carcase. Often used with an extruded escutcheon.

STAYS AND SUPPORTS

The shelf support hardware shown below provides options for installing adjustable shelving. Other shelf-mounting methods are illustrated on pages 304 and 305.

The purpose of the stays and supports shown on page 381 is to limit the travel of a lid or door. They come in a wide variety of designs for use on chests, desks, and drop-leaf tables. By stopping the swing of a lid or door, they prevent overstressing hinges and lend rigidity to an extended surface such as the drop-lid writing surface on a secretary.

Most stays and supports are surface-mounted and consist of a tension bar or chain attached to the lid and case by swivel flanges. Some need to be mortised into position.

SHELF SUPPORT HARDWARE

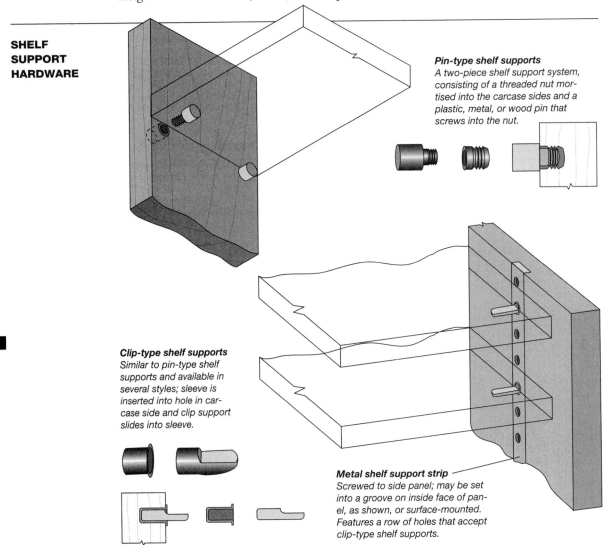

Pin-type shelf supports
A two-piece shelf support system, consisting of a threaded nut mortised into the carcase sides and a plastic, metal, or wood pin that screws into the nut.

Clip-type shelf supports
Similar to pin-type shelf supports and available in several styles; sleeve is inserted into hole in carcase side and clip support slides into sleeve.

Metal shelf support strip
Screwed to side panel; may be set into a groove on inside face of panel, as shown, or surface-mounted. Features a row of holes that accept clip-type shelf supports.

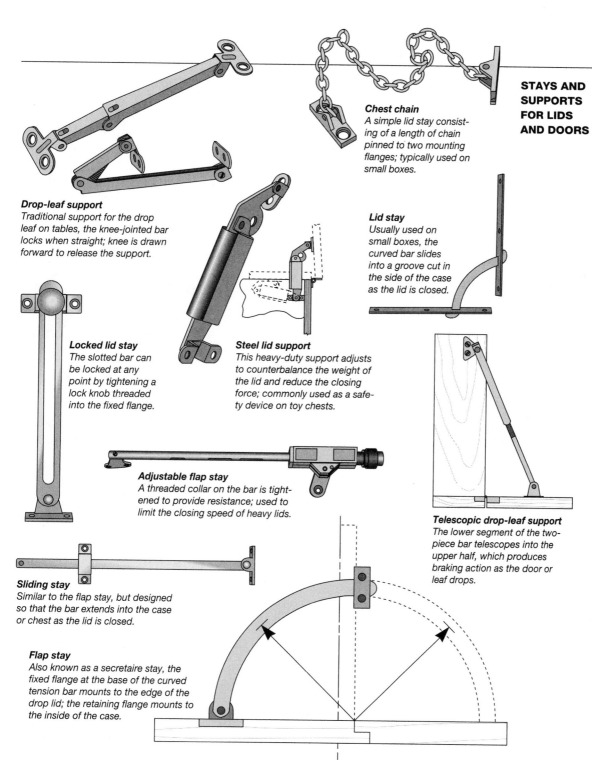

Chest chain
A simple lid stay consisting of a length of chain
pinned to two mounting
flanges; typically used on
small boxes.

Drop-leaf support
Traditional support for the drop
leaf on tables, the knee-jointed bar
locks when straight; knee is drawn
forward to release the support.

Lid stay
Usually used on
small boxes, the
curved bar slides
into a groove cut in
the side of the case
as the lid is closed.

Locked lid stay
The slotted bar can
be locked at any
point by tightening a
lock knob threaded
into the fixed flange.

Steel lid support
This heavy-duty support adjusts
to counterbalance the weight of
the lid and reduce the closing
force; commonly used as a safety device on toy chests.

Adjustable flap stay
A threaded collar on the bar is tightened to provide resistance; used to
limit the closing speed of heavy lids.

Telescopic drop-leaf support
The lower segment of the two-
piece bar telescopes into the
upper half, which produces
braking action as the door or
leaf drops.

Sliding stay
Similar to the flap stay, but designed
so that the bar extends into the case
or chest as the lid is closed.

Flap stay
Also known as a secretaire stay, the
fixed flange at the base of the curved
tension bar mounts to the edge of the
drop lid; the retaining flange mounts to
the inside of the case.

SLIDES AND SWIVELS

Slides and swivels are used to reduce friction in furniture and cabinets with moving parts. This type of hardware includes sliding door tracks, drawer slides, and swivels for shelves and their contents. Before the introduction of metal hardware, tracks and slides were usually an integral part of the cabinetry: Grooves or rabbets were cut into the case or wooden rails were installed to accommodate sliding components. The use of metal and low-friction plastic hardware for this purpose is a relatively new development—and in many ways a vast improvement. The strength and ease of installation of metal and plastic hardware are benefits. (Other drawer-mounting options are illustrated on page 313.)

DOOR TRACKS

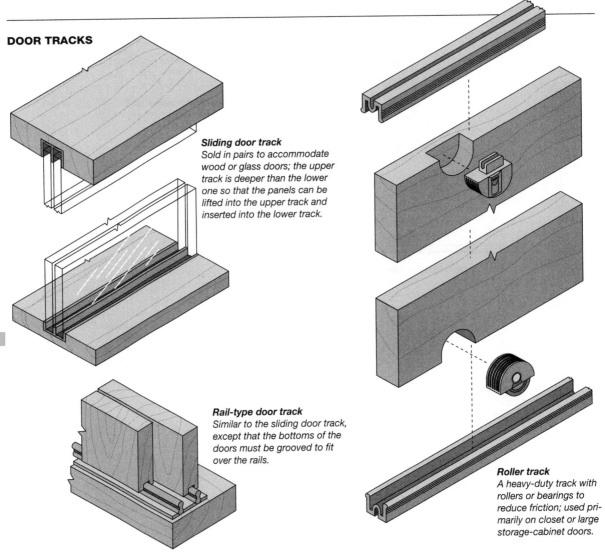

Sliding door track
Sold in pairs to accommodate wood or glass doors; the upper track is deeper than the lower one so that the panels can be lifted into the upper track and inserted into the lower track.

Rail-type door track
Similar to the sliding door track, except that the bottoms of the doors must be grooved to fit over the rails.

Roller track
A heavy-duty track with rollers or bearings to reduce friction; used primarily on closet or large storage-cabinet doors.

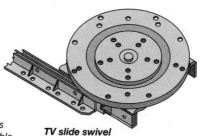

Chair seat swivel
A heavy-duty version of the Lazy Susan bearing designed with a 3° pitch between the mounting plates; used to mount the seats on swivel chairs and bar stools.

"Lazy-Susan" bearing
Consists of two mounting plates separated by ball bearings; enable shelves to be rotated inside their cabinets, making the contents of shelves in corner cupboards more accessible.

TV slide swivel
Typically used in entertainment cabinets to support TV sets; allows the set to be drawn forward and rotated.

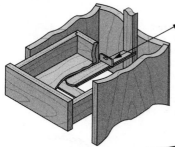

Slide glides
An inexpensive plastic bracket fastened to the back of a drawer and designed to slide over a wooden track fastened to the carcase; bracket reduces friction and prevents the drawer from tipping down when opened.

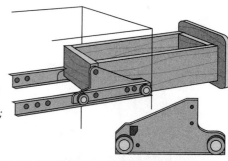

Side-mounted drawer slides
Consists of two tracks with fixed nylon rollers. One track is mounted to the drawer side and the other to the inside of the cabinet; used in pairs to support the drawer on both sides.

Concealed side-mounted drawer slides
A side-mounted system featuring a roller trolley plate mounted to the back ends of the drawer sides; the plate remains in the cabinet when the drawer is opened.

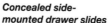

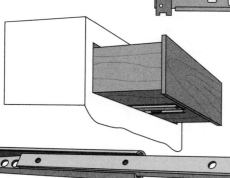

Center-mounted drawer slide
A concealed slide system typically used on kitchen cabinets and vanities. One track mounts to the bottom of the drawer, which slides over the other track mounted to the frame of the cabinet; easy to install, but the drawer must be sized to provide adequate clearance.

CASTERS, GLIDES, AND LEG TIPS

The hardware shown below and on page 385 is both functional and decorative. Casters and glides enable heavy cabinets, tables, and chairs to be moved easily. Leg tips protect floors; and some also incorporate a height adjustment feature to level furniture on uneven floors.

With each of these types of hardware, style is often an important consideration as well.

In some instances, it virtually dictates the type of hardware you select. For example, brass leg tips are an integral part of some neoclassical designs and were used extensively by 19th-Century masters such as Duncan Phyfe. The examples illustrated in this section are an assortment of both traditional and modern designs that are readily available and easy to install.

CASTERS AND GLIDES

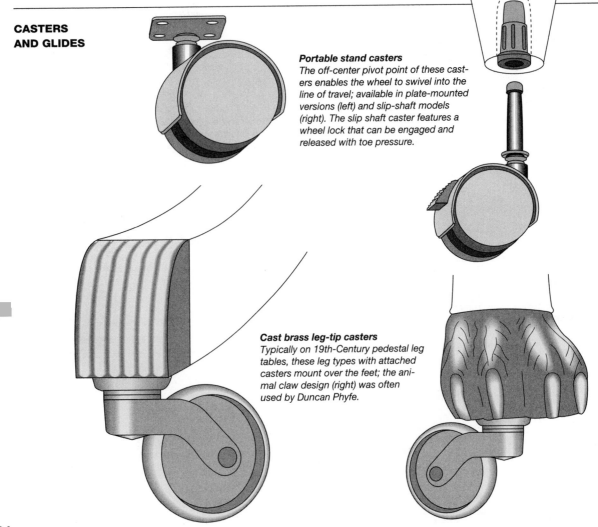

Portable stand casters
The off-center pivot point of these casters enables the wheel to swivel into the line of travel; available in plate-mounted versions (left) and slip-shaft models (right). The slip shaft caster features a wheel lock that can be engaged and released with toe pressure.

Cast brass leg-tip casters
Typically on 19th-Century pedestal leg tables, these leg types with attached casters mount over the feet; the animal claw design (right) was often used by Duncan Phyfe.

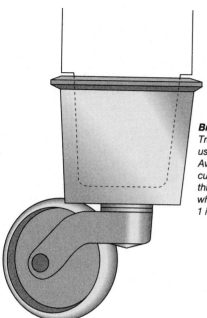

Brass roller casters
Traditional polished brass casters
used on tables and serving carts.
Available with round or square
cup-shaped mountings (left) or
threaded-shaft mountings (right);
wheel diameters range from
1 inch to 2 inches.

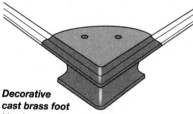

**Decorative
cast brass foot**
Used on small boxes, clock cases, lamps,
and other accent pieces; commonly used
on late 19th-Century Victorian pieces.
Available in plate-mounted versions,
as shown, or lag-shaft mountings.

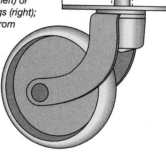

Brass foot cap
Installed over the foot of a
pedestal leg as a decorative
treatment; made of cast brass
and available in animal-claw
and other designs.

Round cast foot cap
Protective cap slips over
the foot of a straight or
tapered leg.

Furniture glide
Enables tables and chairs
to slide easily on uncar-
peted floors without causing damage; available with
nylon or metal heads with
tack-type mountings.

Leveling glide
Similar to standard furniture glides, except
the shaft threads into a flange mounted in
the bottom of the leg; this allows for adjusting the height of the glide.

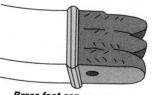

HOOKS

Hooks and pegs for hanging clothes, utensils, and other household items are important style elements in many woodworking projects. Hooks mounted to the inside of wardrobes, on hat racks, or inside cupboards are not only useful, they also add a distinctive look to a piece. Brass hooks in various styles were common fixtures in the entry halls of Victorian homes and peg rails are so tied to Shaker decor that a room without them just does not seem to provide the proper setting for other Shaker pieces.

INVENTORY OF HOOKS

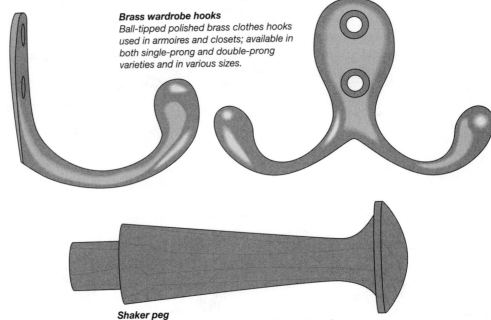

Brass wardrobe hooks
Ball-tipped polished brass clothes hooks used in armoires and closets; available in both single-prong and double-prong varieties and in various sizes.

Shaker peg
Popularized by the Shakers, this mushroom-tipped, turned wooden peg is typically 3½ inches long; the round tenon is tapped into a hole bored in a wall rail. Many Shaker accent pieces, such as shelves, sconces, clocks, small chairs, and other light furniture, were designed to be hung up out of the way on these pegs.

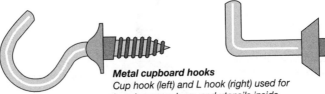

Metal cupboard hooks
Cup hook (left) and L hook (right) used for hanging cups, keys, and utensils inside cupboards; typically made of bent brass wire with screw-thread shanks.

JIGS AND SHOP HELPERS

The jigs present-
ed in this chap-
ter will expand the
capabilities of your
woodworking tools.
Some jigs will help
you perform certain
tasks more efficiently
and accurately, or will
eliminate the need to
change a tool's standard adjustment. Others
enable repetitive tasks to be carried out quickly and with consistent results. Still others are
designed to make operations safer. Some jigs
accomplish all of these objectives at once. A
jig can take the form of a hastily fashioned
guide aimed at solving a onetime problem; or
it can be a truly ingenious contraption destined for repeated use. One feature all of the
jigs in this chapter share is that they are relatively simple to build and convenient to use.

Since most jigs must be custom-made
to fit a specific tool, this chapter describes
design principles and explains how a jig is

supposed to work.
Many of the illustra-
tions of the jigs sug-
gest dimensions for
building them. You
may need to adapt
these dimensions to
suit your tools and
the particular needs
of your projects.

The chapter organizes the jigs according
to their purpose. For example, jigs used for
cutting with power saws and handsaws are
grouped together, beginning on page 388.
Drilling jigs are shown on pages 395 and
396, while gluing and clamping devices are
described starting on page 397. Jigs designed
to be used with the router are presented on
pages 402 through 405. The balance of the
chapter shows how to build and use a range
of useful shop accessories, ranging from simple push sticks and featherboards to relatively
complex, freestanding shop aids like router
tables and roller stands.

CUTTING JIGS

BENCH HOOKS

Jigs that hook against the edge of a workbench are handy because you need only one hand to steady the jig, leaving your other hand free. Two useful and easy-to-make bench hooks are shown at right and on page 389. To make perfectly square crosscuts with a handsaw and cut several workpieces to the same length, you can use a cutting board-type bench hook ☐1. The jig features a sturdy base and an adjustable stop block for setting the cutting length. Use ¾-inch plywood for the base and fence. Use a router to cut the slot through the fence for the bolt that will hold the stop block in place. Then fix the fence flush with the back edge of the base using glue and screws. Make the lip and stop block from ¾-inch-thick hardwood. To mount the stop block to the fence, position it against the fence and mark the location of the slot on it. Then drill a bolt clearance hole through the block at the mark. Fasten the block to the fence with a 2-inch-long carriage bolt, a washer, and a wing nut. Glue and screw the lip to the underside of the base flush with the front edge. Use a carpenter's square to lay out the 90-degree kerf on the base and cut the kerf with a backsaw.

To use the cutting board, set it on a workbench with its lip butted against the front edge. Align the cutting mark on your workpiece with the right-hand end of the fence, slide the stop block against the end of the stock, and tighten the wing nut to lock the block in place.

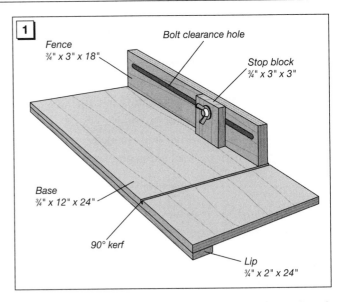

1

Fence
¾" x 3" x 18"

Bolt clearance hole

Stop block
¾" x 3" x 3"

Base
¾" x 12" x 24"

90° kerf

Lip
¾" x 2" x 24"

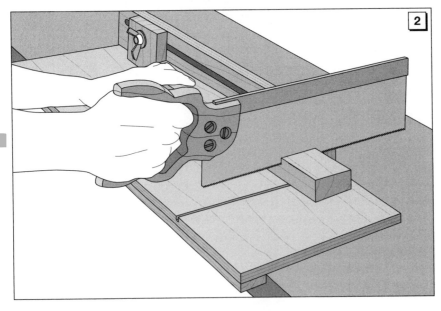

2

Then, holding the workpiece against the fence 2, butt the handsaw blade against the fence and make the cut.

A variation of the bench hook is the sharpening box shown in illustration 3. This jig will hold a sharpening stone steady for honing a hand-tool blade, such as a chisel or plane iron. Cut the base and lip from solid wood, then mark the outline of the stone on the top surface of the base. Use a router fitted with a straight bit to cut a recess for the stone within the outline; the recess should be slightly deeper than one-half the thickness of the stone. Use a chisel to square the corners of the recess. Fasten the lip to the underside of the base, flush with the front end, using glue and screws. To use the jig, insert the stone in the recess and secure the base to your bench with the lip flush against the edge.

BENCH HOOKS

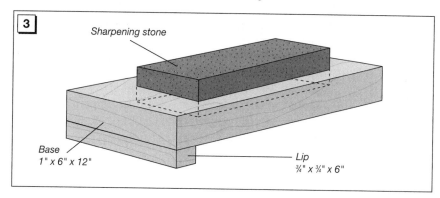

3

Sharpening stone

Base
1" x 6" x 12"

Lip
¾" x ¾" x 6"

QUICKTIP

Table saw inserts

Table saws come with an insert that is slotted to accommodate a standard blade at its highest setting. This insert may not provide adequate support when you are sawing thin or narrow stock. You can make your own insert for such situations from a rigid material like plastic, hardboard, or wood that is the same thickness as the original insert. Cut the shop-made insert to fit the saw table, using the original insert as a template. Drive setscrews through the insert to serve as leveling screws, as shown at right. To slot the new insert, lower the blade below the table, slip the insert in place, and position the rip fence over it. Since the opening in most saw tables is wider to the left of the blade than to its right, place the fence to the left of the blade for this operation. Turn on the saw and slowly raise the blade to the cutting height you will use for your project.

End-view cross section   Blade slot

Leveling setscrews

CUTTING JIGS

CIRCLE-CUTTING JIG FOR THE SABER SAW AND ROUTER

Some saber saws and routers come with a circle-cutting guide that fastens to the tool's base plate *(saber saw, page 121; router, page 108)*. However, commercial jigs are typically too short for cutting circles larger than about 24 inches in diameter. To cut larger circles, you can make a jig from ½-inch plywood 1. For the saber saw, remove the blade from the saw and outline the front of the tool's base plate at one end of the plywood piece. Reinstall the blade and cut out the pattern, leaving a notch for the blade. Screw the jig to the saw's base plate. (With most models, you will have to drill clearance holes through the base plate.) Next, mark a line along the arm of the jig in line with the front of the blade; make sure the line is parallel to the edges of the jig.

To adapt the jig for a router, set the tool's base on the arm and mark the screw holes and bit clearance hole. Mark a line along the arm of the jig in line with the center of the bit clearance hole. Drill the holes and fasten the jig to the router.

To use the jig with a saber saw, secure your workpiece good-side down and butt the inside edge of the blade against the stock. Measure the radius of the circle from the blade along the line on the jig and drive a finishing nail through the jig and into the stock at this point. The nail will serve as a pivot point at the center of the circle 2. Keep the jig flat on the workpiece as you cut the circle. Clamping the workpiece good-face down ensures that the nail will not mar the good surface. Also, since saber saws cut on the up stroke, any fraying will be on the back side of the workpiece. As an alternative, you can glue a roofing nail to the surface, point up, with cyanoacrylate glue. This avoids marring either surface. When you are finished cutting, simply pop the nail off and scrape the surface clean. Paired with a router, the jig works like the one shown on page 403.

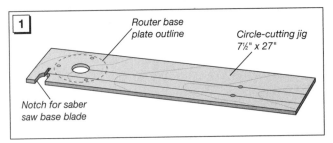

1

Router base plate outline

Circle-cutting jig 7½" x 27"

Notch for saber saw base blade

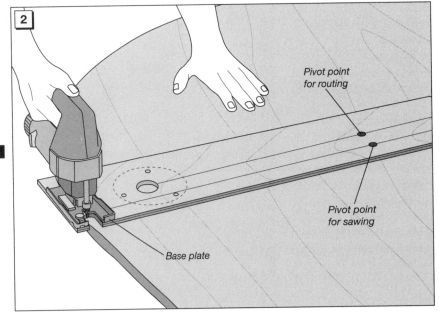

2

Pivot point for routing

Pivot point for sawing

Base plate

Making a taper cut on the table saw requires the use of a jig. Commercial taper jigs like the one shown on page 147 are available, but the shop-built jig shown at right 1 is easy to make and equally effective. Begin by cutting the base from ¾-inch plywood; for maximum stability, the base should be slightly larger than the workpiece. Next cut the hold-down bracket from ¾-inch-thick stock; make it about 4 inches wide and slightly longer than the base. Rip a narrow strip along one edge, stopping the cut to form a lip. Make the handle from two wood scraps and a length of dowel.

To assemble the jig, set the workpiece on the base with the cutting mark lined up with the edge of the base. Butt the hold-down bracket against the workpiece so that the lip supports the trailing edge of the stock and screw the bracket to the base. Fasten a toggle clamp to the bracket to secure the workpiece and screw the handle to the base along the back edge. To cut the taper, align the cutting mark with the saw blade and posi-

tion the rip fence flush against the back edge of the base. Feed the jig and work-

piece across the table, keeping the jig butted against the fence throughout 2.

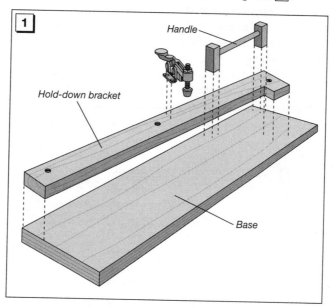

Handle

Hold-down bracket

Base

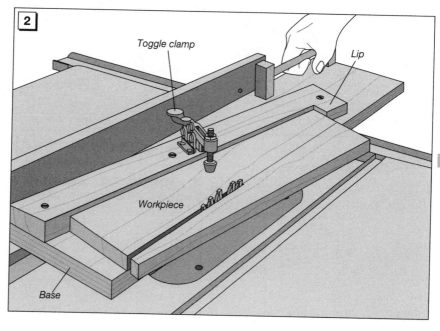

Toggle clamp

Lip

Workpiece

Base

CUTTING JIGS

**CROSSCUT-
TING JIG**

The fence of the miter gauge supplied with most table saws is typically too narrow to provide adequate support when crosscutting long boards. You can build a crosscutting jig as a substitute for the miter gauge in such situations. Equipped with two runners that slide in the table's miter slots, the jig ensures that the workpiece will be square to the blade. The jig is shown in an exploded view in illustration 1 and assembled in illustration 2. The dimensions provided will tailor the jig to a typical 10-inch saw. To fit the jig for a smaller saw, such as an 8-inch bench-top model, size the base, fence, support lip, and runners appropriately.

Cut the base from ½-inch plywood. Fasten the support lip to the base flush with its leading edge using glue and screws; countersink the screws, making sure none of them is near the

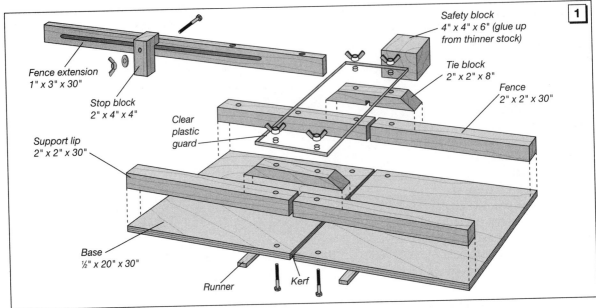

Safety block
4" x 4" x 6" (glue up from thinner stock)

Tie block
2" x 2" x 8"

Fence
2" x 2" x 30"

Fence extension
1" x 3" x 30"

Stop block
2" x 4" x 4"

Clear plastic guard

Support lip
2" x 2" x 30"

Base
½" x 20" x 30"

Runner   Kerf

1

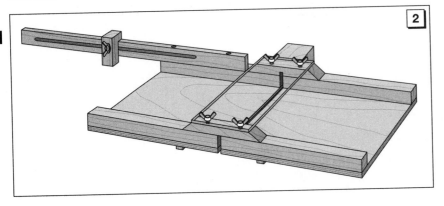

2

middle of the edge where it may get in the way of the blade. Cut the runners from hardwood, making them as long as the width of the base; rip and place them to fit in the miter slots. Drill counterbore holes through the runners about 2 inches from each end and fit the strips in the slots. With the runners extending off

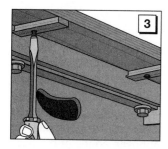

3

the back edge of the saw table ⬛3⬛, set the base squarely on the runners and drive the back-end screws. Next, slide the base across the table so that the runners extend off the front edge and install the front-end screws.

To install the jig's fence, slide the assembly back clear of the blade, raise the blade to a height of about 1 inch, and cut a kerf about two-thirds of the way across the base. Use a carpenter's square to set the fence perpendicular to the kerf ⬛4⬛. Clamp the fence to the base and fasten it in place

along the trailing edge. Bevel the tie blocks and screw them to the top edges of the support lip and fence. Then complete the kerf all the way across the base. Use carriage bolts, washers, and wing nuts to attach the clear plastic blade guard to the tie blocks. Fasten the safety block to the fence as a reminder of the blade's location; the block will cover the blade at the end of the cut. Place your hands on either side of the block when using the jig.

For repeat cuts, use the fence extension, which is fastened to the fence. Mount a sliding stop block on the extension as you would on the bench hook shown on page 388. To use the jig, position the stop block on the extension for the appropriate cutting length. Then, hold the workpiece flush against the jig fence, butt the end against the stop block, and feed the jig across the saw table ⬛5⬛.

CROSSCUTTING JIG

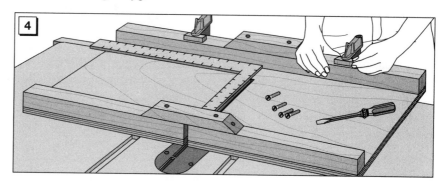

4

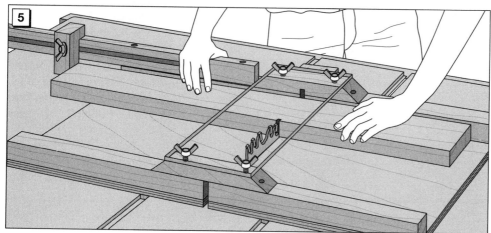

5

CUTTING JIGS

TENONING JIG

Most commercial tenoning jigs for the table saw feature a runner that slides in the miter slot *(page 141)*. The shop-made jig shown in illustration ☐1 rides along the rip fence to guide the workpiece past the blade. Made entirely from ¾-inch plywood, the jig will enable you to cut both parts of open mortise-and-tenon joints.

Cut the pieces of the jig to size, referring to the illustration for suggested dimensions. Make the body long enough to resist rocking as you feed it across the table. The width of the spacer, less the combined thickness of the two brace pieces, should be the same as the saw's rip fence. The height of the brace pieces should enable the spacer to just clear the top of the rip fence with the base flat on the table ☐2. Fasten the body and front brace to opposite edges of the base with glue and countersunk screws, using four evenly spaced rectangular supports to hold the body and brace perpendicular to the base. Cut an oval handle in the second support from the rear of the jig, as shown. Next, screw the spacer to the brace pieces and fasten the vertical support guide to the front of the body; use a combination square to make certain the guide is perpendicular to the bottom edge of the body. Screw a wood block to the body behind the guide and fasten a toggle clamp to the block to secure the workpiece to the jig.

To use the jig, set it astride the rip fence and clamp the workpiece to the jig, making sure the edge of the stock is flush against the vertical guide. Position the rip fence so the cutting mark on the workpiece is lined up with the blade, then feed the jig along the rip fence, as shown.

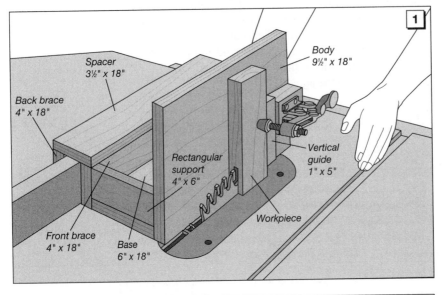

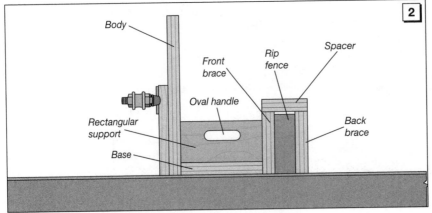

DRILLING JIGS

The jig shown in illustration [1] enables you to bore a row of angled holes on the drill press with the workpiece tilted perpendicular to the way the machine table normally tilts. Cut the base and tabletop from ¾-inch plywood so that each piece is about 1 inch longer and wider than the drill press table. Drill two holes through the base so that it can be bolted to the machine table. Cut the fence from ½-inch plywood and rout three slots through it. Fasten the fence to the top parallel to the edges, using bolts, washers, and wing nuts so that its position on the top can be easily adjusted. Join the base and top along the front edge using a length of piano hinge. Make the adjustable brackets from hardwood; use a router fitted with a ¼-inch straight bit to cut a slot in each bracket for a hanger bolt. Fasten the brackets to opposite edges

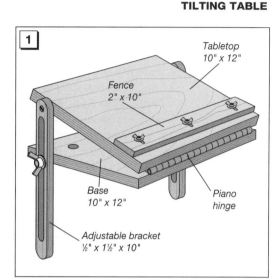

1

Tabletop
10" x 12"

Fence
2" x 10"

Base
10" x 12"

Piano
hinge

Adjustable bracket
½" x 1½" x 10"

of the tabletop with screws; use hanger bolts, washers, and wing nuts to attach the brackets to the base.

To use the jig, bolt its base to the drill press table. Loosen the wing nuts securing the brackets to the base, pivot up the top to the desired angle, and tighten the wing nuts. Set the workpiece on the tabletop and position the first hole outline under the bit. Loosen the wing nuts holding the fence in place and butt the fence against the workpiece. Making sure the fence is square to the edge of the top, tighten the wing nuts and drill the holes [2].

2

DRILLING JIGS

DRILL PRESS EXTENSION TABLE

The drill press extension table shown in illustration 1 can make quick work of boring dowel holes in the sides of a bookcase for shelf pins. Featuring a removable insert, it can also be used as a table for drum sanding. Use ¾-inch plywood for the base, the fence, and the lip. The larger the base of the jig, the more support it will provide for long and wide panels. Cut a hole in the base large enough to accommodate your largest sanding drum. Use a hole saw to make inserts to reduce the hole size to fit your smaller drums. Rout two slots through the fence and fasten it to the base, using bolts, washers, and wing nuts so that its position can be easily adjusted. Use glue and screws to attach the lip to the base flush with the front edge.

To use the jig for drilling, butt the lip against the front edge of the machine table and seat the workpiece on the base, aligning the first hole outline under the bit. Loosen the wing nuts securing the fence to the base, butt the fence against the workpiece, tighten the wing nuts, and clamp the jig to the machine table. After drilling each hole, slide the workpiece along the fence and bore the next one 2.

To use the jig for sanding, remove the insert and clamp the jig to the machine table with the hole directly under the sanding drum. Adjust the height of the table so that the bottom of the drum is slightly below the top of the base.

1

Wing nut

Removable insert for sanding drum

Base
8" x 24"

Lip
1" x 12"

Fence
3" x 24"

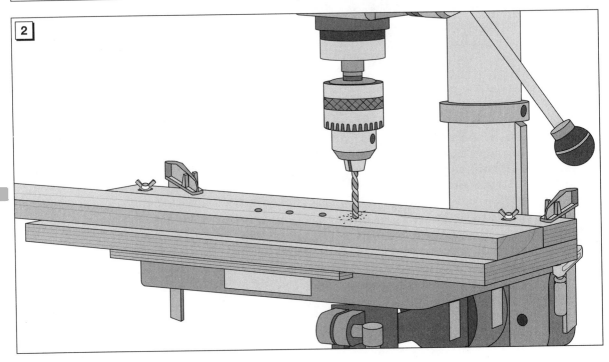

2

GLUING AND CLAMPING JIGS

Sawhorses make very convenient racks for edge-gluing, particularly in shops with few work surfaces. The simple trestle design shown in illustration 1 employs sturdy mortise-and-tenon joinery, which enables the horse to be lightweight and easy to assemble. The dimensions provided are optional, but the height of the horses should be compatible with the height of the other work surfaces in the shop so that they can be used together, if necessary. Use 1½-inch-thick hardwood stock for the crosspiece, legs, and stretcher and 1-inch-thick hardwood for the feet. Use blind mortise-and-tenons to join the legs to the crosspiece, the pinned version of the joint to connect the stretcher to the legs, and a bridle joint to attach the legs to the feet.

To adapt a pair of sawhorses for edge-gluing boards, cut two 2 x 6s at least as long as the boards you will be gluing up as clamp holders. Then cut notches across one edge of the holders to accept the bars of the clamps you will be using; the notches should be about ¼ inch shallower than the height of the bars. Space the notches 6 to 8 inches apart. Cut notches into the oppo-site edge of each holder to fit over the crosspieces of the sawhorses.

To use the gluing horses, set two of them on the floor so that the crosspieces are parallel and fit the clamp holders in place. Set the bar clamps in the notches, jaws up 2. Follow the instructions presented on page 334 for applying glue to your workpieces and for spacing and tightening the clamps.

EDGE-GLUING SHOP HORSES

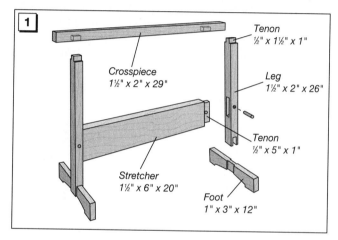

1

Crosspiece
1½" x 2" x 29"

Tenon
½" x 1½" x 1"

Leg
1½" x 2" x 26"

Tenon
½" x 5" x 1"

Stretcher
1½" x 6" x 20"

Foot
1" x 3" x 12"

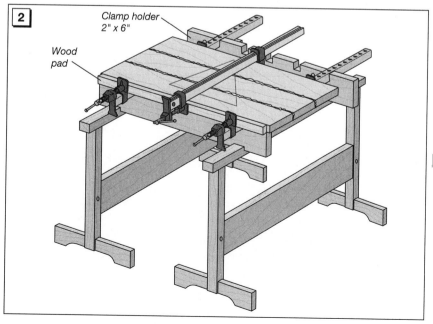

2

Clamp holder
2" x 6"

Wood pad

GLUING AND CLAMPING JIGS

WEDGE CLAMPS FOR EDGE-GLUING

The shop-made wedge clamps shown in illustration ☐1 will enable you to edge-glue boards without using commercial bar or pipe clamps. The jig can be made with standard hardware and a few boards. Make the bars from 1 x 2 hardwood, cutting them several inches longer than the combined width of the boards you will glue up. Bore a series of holes through the bars for carriage bolts; locate a hole about 1½ inches from each end and a row of holes at 1½-inch intervals in between. Stack the bars together with their edges and ends aligned and bore the holes on the drill press to ensure that corresponding holes line up. Cut the spacer blocks and wedges from stock of the same thickness as the boards being glued up. Bore a hole through the middle of each spacer. Cut each wedge from a 12-inch length of 6-inch-wide stock that is the same thickness as the stock being glued. Rip the pieces diagonally from corner to corner, then trim the points, leaving a small square section at the narrow end.

To use the wedge clamps, wax the bars to prevent glue from adhering to them. Then loosely fix the bars and spacers together at the back edge of the stock being glued up using washers, wing nuts, and carriage bolts at least 2 inches longer than the thickness of the stock. Use one clamp for every 12 to 18 inches of board length. Pivot the top bars out of the way, apply glue to the edges of the stock, and assemble the panel on the bottom bars. Pivot the top bars back into position and install the front-end spacers with bolts, washers, and wing nuts, leaving enough room between the spacers and the panel for the wedges. Tap the wedges in place from opposite sides of the bars to press the boards together ☐2. Once the wedges are snug, finish tightening the wing nuts.

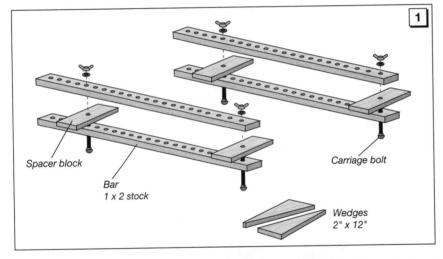

1

Spacer block

Bar
1 x 2 stock

Carriage bolt

Wedges
2" x 12"

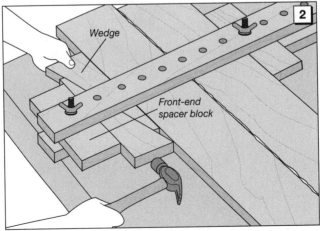

2

Wedge

Front-end
spacer block

Frames with mitered corners can be secured at glue-up with commercial clamps (*page 335*), but the shop-made jig shown in illustration 1 will do the job equally well. It features four arms joined in pairs that enable a single clamp to hold the frame in alignment and distribute uniform pressure to the four corners. Use nominal 1 x 3 hardwood to make the arms and pivot blocks, and ¾-inch plywood for the corner brackets, cutting the arms long enough to accommodate the size of the frame to be glued up. Drill a row of clearance holes for 2-inch-long machine bolts through each arm, spacing the holes about 1½ inches apart. To prepare the corner brackets (*inset*), cut a 90-degree wedge from an end of each one, creating a V. Then bore a clearance hole through each bracket for the bolts and another hole at the apex of the V. This second hole will prevent glue squeeze-out from adhering to the brackets when you use the jig. Wax the top surfaces of the arms to prevent glue from sticking to them and assemble the jig using bolts, washers, and wing nuts. Position the corner brackets on the arms so that the pivot blocks will be about 1 inch apart when you glue up the frame.

To use the jig, apply glue to the contacting surfaces of the frame and position the frame on the arms, seating its corners in the Vs of the brackets. Then squeeze the pivot blocks together with a handscrew to close up the joints 2. Make sure the frame remains flat on the arms of the jig; avoid overtightening.

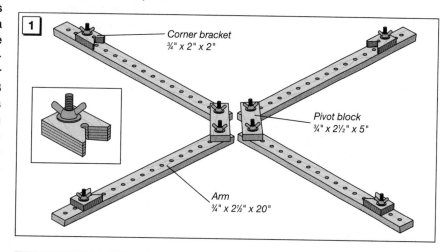

1
Corner bracket
¾" x 2" x 2"

Pivot block
¾" x 2½" x 5"

Arm
¾" x 2½" x 20"

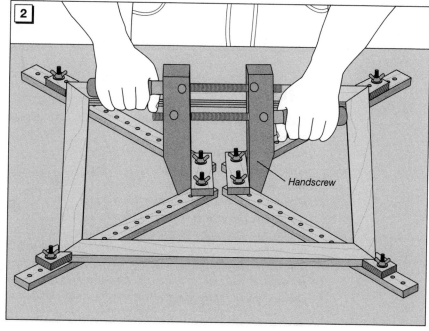

2
Handscrew

GLUING AND CLAMPING JIGS

NOTCHED BLOCKS FOR BAR CLAMPS

Bar clamps have a tendency to fall over, particularly when being used to edge-glue several boards together. If you do not have a glue rack like the one shown on page 397, the simple notched blocks shown below 1 will keep your clamps from moving. To make the blocks, cut a 1 x 2 into 6-inch lengths, then notch one edge of each block to accommodate the clamp. As shown in illustration 2, use one block to prop up each clamp you are using on the underside of the boards, placing the block near the handle-end of the clamps. The other end of the clamp can simply rest on the work surface. Refer to page 334 for detailed instructions on edge-gluing boards.

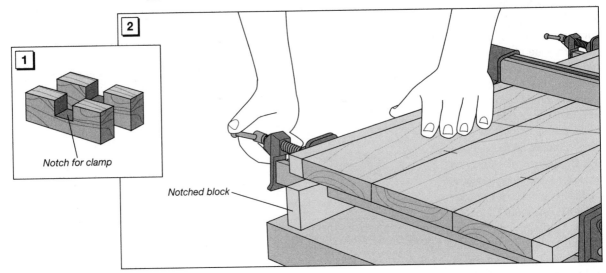

Notch for clamp

Notched block

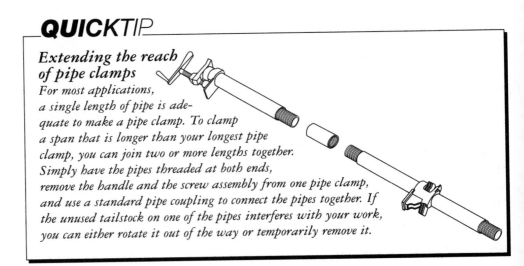

QUICKTIP

Extending the reach of pipe clamps

For most applications, a single length of pipe is adequate to make a pipe clamp. To clamp a span that is longer than your longest pipe clamp, you can join two or more lengths together. Simply have the pipes threaded at both ends, remove the handle and the screw assembly from one pipe clamp, and use a standard pipe coupling to connect the pipes together. If the unused tailstock on one of the pipes interferes with your work, you can either rotate it out of the way or temporarily remove it.

In assembling carcases, holding the corners square as clamping pressure is applied can be a cumbersome task. The squaring jig shown at right ⬚1 is easy to make and simple to use. Begin by cutting the body of the jig into a triangle with one 90-degree angle and equal adjoining sides. (The remaining corners of the triangle should each be 45 degrees.) Trim off the tip of the 90-degree angle so that the joint you are gluing will be visible when the jig is placed over the corner. Cut the lips from 1 x 4 stock and screw them to the short sides of the body.

Use two squaring jigs for each carcase you are gluing up. Once you have assembled the carcase, loosely install bar clamps on opposite sides to hold the joints together as shown in illustration ⬚2. Then place a squaring jig on one corner, making sure the body is flat on the top edges of the carcase. With the lips butted against the sides, secure the jig in place with C-clamps. Install a second jig on the opposite corner of the carcase, then tighten the bar clamps. The jigs will keep the assembly square.

CARCASE-SQUARING JIG

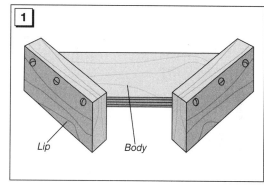

Lip   Body

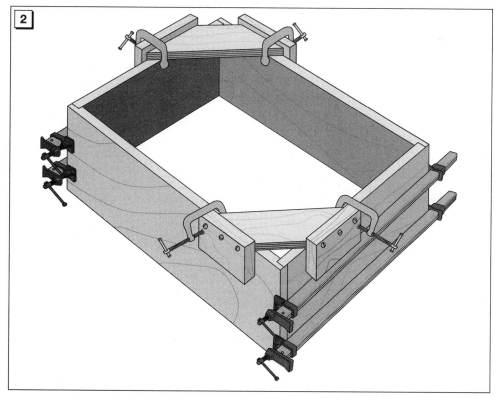

ROUTING JIGS

MORTISING JIG Routing a mortise in the edge of a workpiece can be done with a hand-held router equipped with an edge guide *(page 110)* or with the

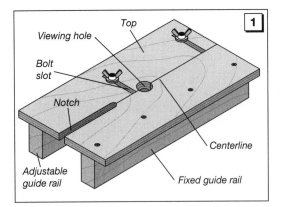

Top
Viewing hole
Bolt slot
Notch
Adjustable guide rail
Centerline
Fixed guide rail

1

jig shown in illustration 1. The jig adjusts to center the bit on the surface of the workpiece. Cut the top from ½-inch plywood and the guide rails from 2 x 4 stock. Make the top about 16 inches long and wide enough to accommodate the thickest stock you will be mortising. To prepare the top, mark a line along its center, then rout a notch about one-third of the way along this centerline from the front end. The width of the notch should match the diameter of the pilot bearing or template guide you will use when cutting the mor-

tises. Next, mark two perpendicular lines across the top from the centerline to a point about 2 inches from one edge. Locate one line at the center and one about 1 inch from the unnotched end. Rout a slot along each line for hanger bolts. Then drill a viewing hole through the top between the bolt slots to help you align the jig over the workpiece. To attach the adjustable guide rail to the top, position the top on the rail and mark the slot locations on the rail's edge. Bore a pilot hole for the hanger bolts at each mark. Drive the bolts into the rail, set the top in place, and use washers and wing nuts to secure it. Fasten the fixed guide rail to the top with screws, making sure it is parallel to the notch.

To use the jig, hold your workpiece on edge and set the jig down on top of it. Slip plywood spacers in between the workpiece and the fixed guide rail until the mortise outline is centered under the notch. Slide the adjustable guide rail over next to the workpiece. Tighten the wing nuts to lock the rail in place. Clamp the whole assembly in a vise to hold it as you rout 2. To help you rout the mortise to the right length, you can clamp stop blocks to the top of the jig.

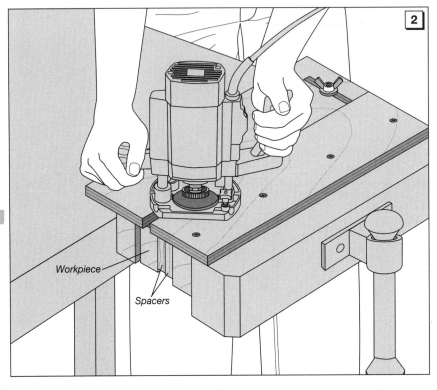

2

Workpiece
Spacers

The shop-made circle-cutting jig shown at right will enable you to rout larger circles than is possible with the commercial guide supplied with most routers. Use metal rods that are the same diameter as the predrilled holes in the router's base. Cut them long enough to accommodate the largest circle you plan to rout. Use 1 x 3 stock for the pivot block.

To assemble the jig, rest the router on a flat surface and slip the rods through the holes in the router base plate. Then hold an edge of the block against the ends of the rods and mark their location on the block. Drill 1-inch-deep holes into the block for the rods and fix them in place with epoxy. Bore a clearance hole for the pivot screw through the center of the block.

To use the jig, secure the stock good-face down to a work surface with cleats and screw the pivot block to the center of the circle to be routed. Slide the router along the rods so that the bit aligns with the circumference of the circle. Tighten the setscrews to lock the rods to the router base. Turn on the router, plunge the bit into the stock, and cut the circle, as shown.

If you are routing only partway through the stock and must secure it good-face up, glue a plywood spacer to the center of the circle. Then screw the pivot block to the spacer and add a spacer of the same thickness to the router's base plate. Once you are finished routing, carefully scrape the spacer from the workpiece. This way, you will not have to drive a screw into the good face of the stock.

CIRCLE-CUTTING JIG

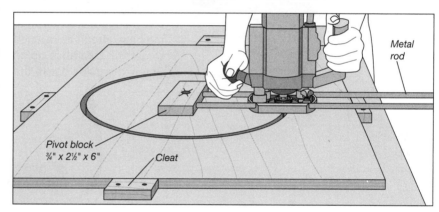

Metal rod

Pivot block
¾" x 2½" x 6"

Cleat

QUICKTIP

Hardboard compass jig

A strip of perforated hardboard can be used with a router to cut perfect circles. Cut the strip a little wider than the router's base plate, making sure that one row of holes runs down the center of the strip. Attach the jig to the workpiece and the router using the existing perforations; also cut a bit clearance hole through the hardboard directly under the bit. Rout a circle as you would with the jig described above.

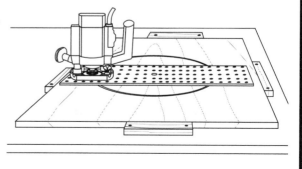

ROUTING JIGS

JIG FOR ROUTING EQUALLY SPACED DADOES

The simple jig shown in illustration 1 will enable you to cut equally spaced dadoes with a router. Cut the base from ½-inch plywood and the guide from hardwood. Make the bar a little longer than the width of the base and its width equal to the diameter of the dadoing bit you will use; make it slightly thinner than the depth of the dadoes to be cut.

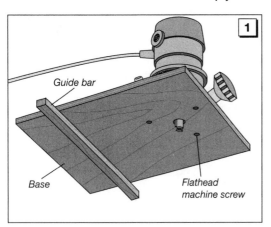

Guide bar

Base

Flathead machine screw

To assemble the jig, drill a bit clearance hole through the base and fasten the router to the base with countersunk flathead machine screws driven from underneath. (If you are using a plunge router, you can plunge the bit through the base after it is installed to cut the clearance hole.) Screw the guide bar to the bottom of the base so that the gap between the bar and the bit equals the desired spacing between the dadoes to be routed.

To cut the first dado, clamp the panel down. Holding the guide bar flush against the end of the workpiece and the base flat on its face, feed the router across the surface. To rout the remaining dadoes, slip the bar into the last dado cut and repeat 2, repositioning the clamps as necessary.

You can easily reposition the guide bar on the base to change the spacing between the dadoes to be routed.

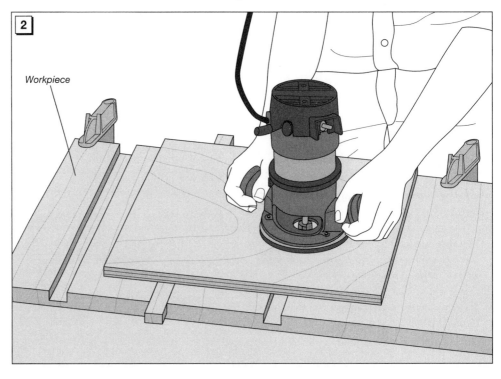

Workpiece

To rout dadoes that are perfectly square to the edges of a workpiece, use the T-square jig shown in illustration 1. Make the jig from 3-inch-wide strips of ¾-inch plywood. For most applications, make the guide 24 to 28 inches long and the crosspiece at least 12 inches long.

To assemble the jig, fasten the guide arm to the crosspiece with glue and countersunk flathead screws. Use a try square to ensure that the two pieces are perpendicular to each other. To cut the alignment notches, clamp the guide arm to the face of a piece of scrap with the crosspiece butted tightly against the scrap's edge. Guide the router along the arm to cut a notch into one side of the crosspiece; cut the notch with a bit you commonly use (½ inch, for example). Install a bit with a different diameter in the router (¾ inch, for example) and repeat to cut a notch into the crosspiece on the other side of the arm. Finally, drill a ½-inch-diameter hole through the arm near one end to hang the jig up.

To use the jig, secure the workpiece and clamp the jig on top of it so that the crosspiece is butted tightly against an edge and the appropriate notch is aligned with the dado mark on the stock. Feed the router across the workpiece 2, keeping the base tight against the guide arm throughout the cut.

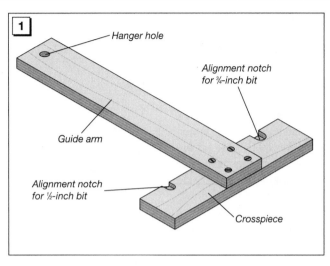

DADOING GUIDE

Hanger hole

Alignment notch for ¾-inch bit

Guide arm

Alignment notch for ½-inch bit

Crosspiece

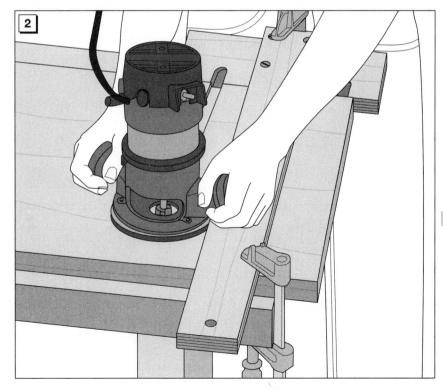

SHOP ACCESSORIES

PUSH BLOCKS AND PUSH STICKS

Push blocks and push sticks for feeding stock across the table of a stationary power tool come in many forms. These devices enable you to control a workpiece while keeping your fingers a safe distance from the cutter. Although many models are available commercially, they are also easy to design and make. The push block shown in illustration 1 features a broad base designed to hold

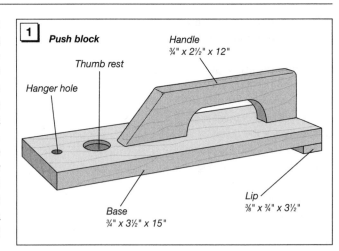

1 *Push block*

Handle
¾" x 2½" x 12"

Thumb rest

Hanger hole

Base
¾" x 3½" x 15"

Lip
⅜" x ¾" x 3½"

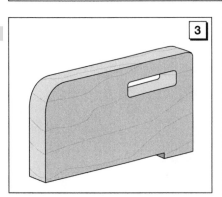

2

14"

45°

Hanger hole

Notch

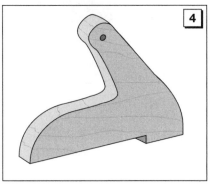

3

4

a workpiece flat on a table; it is especially useful when flattening the face of a board on a jointer *(page 164)*. Use standard 1 x 4 stock or ¾-inch plywood for the base and fashion the handle from solid stock, rounding the edges for a comfortable grip. Fasten the handle along the center of the base using countersunk screws driven through the bottom. Then glue the lip to the underside of the base, flush with the back end. Bore

a hole through the base near the front end for hanging the jig up and a shallow 1-inch-diameter hole directly in front of the handle as a thumb rest. The thumb rest will enable you to apply downward pressure on the workpiece.

Push sticks for feeding stock across a saw table can be cut from ¾-inch plywood or solid stock and shaped to suit the job at hand. The design shown in illustration 2 is ideal for ripping on the table saw. The longer bases of the push sticks in illustrations 3 and 4 are better for applying heavy downward pressure on the workpiece. Whichever design you select, include a notch that is large enough to feed the stock without contacting the saw table. Also locate the handle so that your fingers will remain well away from the blade.

Featherboards are used to keep a workpiece flush against the fence or flat on the table of a stationary machine. However they are designed, all featherboards have flexible fingers cut into one end. When the jig is clamped in place, the fingers press against the workpiece. Designed to flex only in the feed direction, the fingers prevent the stock from being kicked back toward the operator.

Most commercial featherboards must be clamped to the saw table. The shop-made featherboard shown in illustration 1 has the advantage of being anchored in the miter slot of a table saw. In addition, its fingers are tapered on both sides, enabling it to be used on either side of the blade. Make the jig from ¾-inch-thick hardwood. Cut one end to a point and notch this end to create fingers that are about 2½ inches long. Next, bore a hole for a dowel through the edge near the other end. Also cut a ¼-inch-wide slot down the middle of the featherboard from the straight end to just beyond the midpoint. This slot will house the machine bolt that anchors the jig to the miter

bar. Once the slot is cut, glue the dowel into its hole. To make the miter bar, rip a piece of hardwood to fit snugly in the miter slot and cut it about 6 inches long. Drill a ¼-inch clearance hole in the center of the bar for the bolt and countersink the bottom end of the hole. Cut the expansion slot in the bar on the band saw, as shown. Fasten the miter bar to the featherboard with a flathead bolt, washer, and wing nut.

To use the featherboard, position the saw's rip fence for the desired cutting width and butt the workpiece against it. Fit the miter bar into the miter slot and rotate the featherboard so that its fingers press against the workpiece 2 . As you tighten the wing nut, the cone-shaped head of the

bolt will be drawn upward, expanding the miter bar and fixing the featherboard in place. Feed the workpiece between the rip fence and the jig, as shown.

SELF-LOCKING FEATHER-BOARD

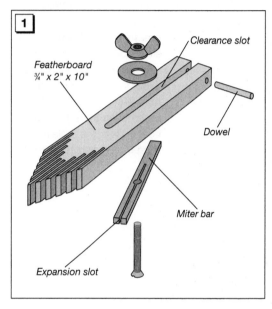

Featherboard
¾" x 2" x 10"

Clearance slot

Dowel

Miter bar

Expansion slot

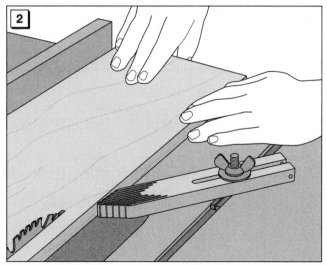

SHOP ACCESSORIES

The adjustable shooting board shown in illustration [1] will enable you to use a hand plane to joint the edges of a workpiece perfectly square to the faces as well as plane an accurate bevel. The jig features two stop blocks: one for planing square-end stock and a removable one for mitered workpieces. Cut the base, table, and stop blocks from ¾-inch plywood. Before assembling the jig, bevel the front edge of the table at a 45-degree angle and cut a ⅛-inch-high flat section at the top of the beveled edge; the bevel and flat section ensure that the sole of the plane will run true to the base when the table is tilted up. Drill two clearance holes for bolts through the table about 1 inch from each end. Insert T-nuts in the holes; the nuts will accommodate bolts for supporting the table at the desired angle. Then fasten the square-end stop block to the table, driving the screws from underneath. Attach the table to the base using a length of piano hinge.

To use the shooting board, screw on the removable stop block if you are planing a mitered end, secure the base on a work surface and place the workpiece on the table with one end butted against the stop block. To joint the edge of a board square to the face, simply leave the table flat on the base. Place a support board or two on the base to raise the plane to the workpiece. To plane a bevel on the edge of the workpiece, thread a bolt (with a wing nut and washer already threaded onto it) into the T-nuts at each end of the table. Adjust the bolts to hold the table at the desired angle and tighten the wing nuts to fix the bolts in place. Use the holes near the hinge to plane greater bevel angles; the holes near the beveled edge of the table are best for lesser angles [2]. Check the angle of the table at both ends with a sliding bevel.

Hold the stock with one hand and guide the plane along the length of the workpiece with the other. The edge of the workpiece should extend slightly beyond the edge of the table, and the side of the plane should be flat on the base (or support board).

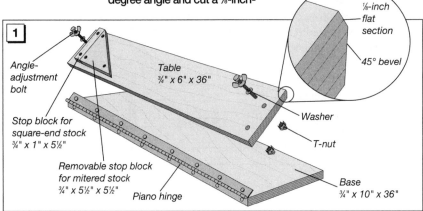

⅛-inch flat section
45° bevel

1

Angle-adjustment bolt

Table
¾" x 6" x 36"

Stop block for square-end stock
¾" x 1" x 5½"

Removable stop block for mitered stock
¾" x 5½" x 5½"

Piano hinge

Washer

T-nut

Base
¾" x 10" x 36"

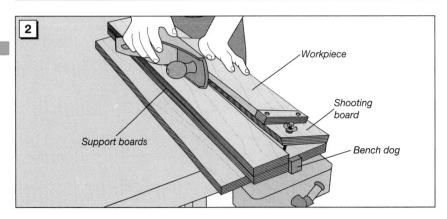

2

Workpiece

Shooting board

Bench dog

Support boards

The wheeled caddy shown in illustration 1 makes it easy to move bulky materials, such as plywood sheets, around the shop. This jig is simple to make from a few wood scraps, a pair of old wagon wheels, and some hardware. Cut the sides from ½-inch plywood and the spacer from ⅞-inch-thick hardwood. Bevel the inside faces of the sides' top edges to make it easier to slip the plywood into the caddy. Then glue the sides to the spacer, aligning the bottom edges of the three pieces. Once the glue is dry, cut off the bottom corners of the assem-

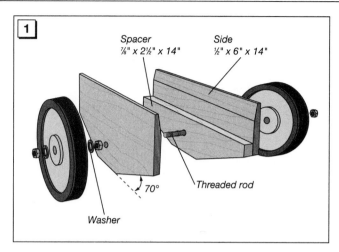

1

Spacer
⅞" x 2½" x 14"

Side
½" x 6" x 14"

70°

Threaded rod

Washer

bly at an angle that will enable the corner to rest flat when the caddy is tipped forward. Then drill a clearance hole t hrough

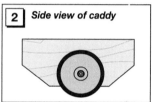

2 Side view of caddy

the assembly for the threaded rod that will serve as the wheel axle; locate the hole so that the wheels will contact the floor when the top of the caddy is parallel to the floor 2.

Install the wheels with the rod, threading nuts onto the rod on both sides of each wheel. Add washers on the outside of the wheels to prevent the nuts from gouging the wheels. To use the caddy, set a plywood panel on the floor on edge, raise one corner, and slip the caddy under the middle of the sheet 3.

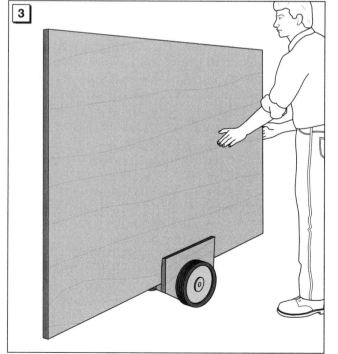

3

TOOL EXTENSIONS AND TABLES

ROUTER TABLE

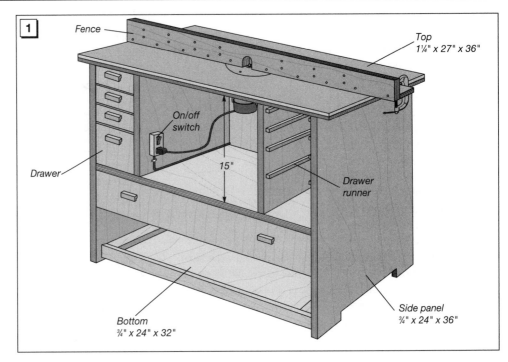

1

Fence

Top
1¼" x 27" x 36"

On/off
switch

Drawer

15"

Drawer
runner

Bottom
¾" x 24" x 32"

Side panel
¾" x 24" x 36"

The router table/cabinet shown in illustration 1 is a relatively ambitious project, but well worth the effort. A well-constructed table enables the router to be used as a mini-shaper. The version shown is sturdier than the average commercial model and incorporates a number of useful features, such as a pivoting fence and drawers for storing bits and accessories. The dimensions provided are optional, but make sure the overall height is comfortable and the cabinet is deep enough to provide adequate stability. The drawers shown are side-mounted

to the cabinet: Runners attached to the cabinet sides and dividers fit into grooves cut in the drawer sides. See pages 310 to 313 for additional information on making and mounting drawers. You can also design a router table with shelves, rather than drawers, to simplify construction. Keep in mind that the most important part of a router table is the top. If you do not need a table/cabinet with drawers or shelves, simply build the top and secure it to any level work surface, such as sawhorses *(page 397)* or a table saw extension table.

Use ¾-inch plywood and solid-panel construction *(page 296)* for the cabinet, attaching the sides to the top and bottom with dado or biscuit joinery. Make the space for the router below the top at least 15 inches high and wide; this will give you enough room to adjust the router's cutting depth. Once the cabinet is assembled, cut an 8-inch-diameter hole through the middle of the top to clear the router body 2. Then cut two more panels to the same dimensions as the top: one from ¼-inch plywood and one from ¼-inch tempered hardboard. Face-glue the two

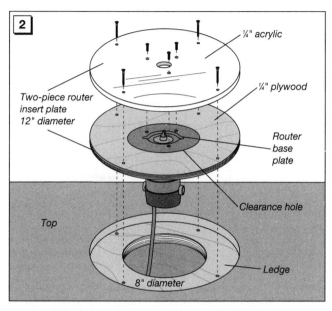

2

¼" acrylic

¼" plywood

Two-piece router
insert plate
12" diameter

Router
base
plate

Clearance hole

Top

Ledge

8" diameter

Build the fence for the table from two 4-inch-wide strips of ¾-inch plywood cut to the same length as the length of the table **3**. Cut a notch into an edge of each piece at the middle to clear the bit. Then fasten the strips together with glue and countersunk screws, forming an L-shape. Reinforce the fence with triangular supports; screw down three supports on each side of the notches, as shown. To install the fence, set it across the top of the table so that its front edge bisects the bit clearance hole in the top. Drill a clearance hole for a bolt through the fence near the left-hand end and through the top. Attach this end of the fence to the top with a carriage bolt, a washer, and a wing nut. To adjust the width of cut, pivot the right-hand end of the fence to the desired position and secure it to the top with a C-clamp.

panels together and cut a 12-inch-diameter hole through the middle of the assembly. Glue and screw the two panels to the top (with the hardboard panel facing up).

To make the insert plate, cut a piece of ¼-inch-thick acrylic and another of ¼-inch plywood to fit into the circular recess in the top. Bore a 1-inch-diameter bit clearance hole through the center of the acrylic piece and countersink clearance holes for the screws you will use to attach the router base to the insert. Cut a clearance hole for the router base through the plywood piece. Then screw the two pieces together face to face and fasten the assembly to the table with the

acrylic piece facing up, forming the insert plate. Fasten the router to the plate. As an added convenience, attach a combination switch/receptacle to one of the cabinet dividers below the router, plug the device into a nearby wall outlet, and plug the router into the switch/receptacle. Use the device to turn the router on and off when you are using the table.

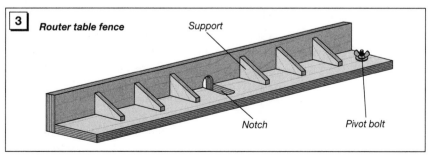

3 *Router table fence*

Support

Notch

Pivot bolt

TOOL EXTENSIONS AND TABLES

ROLLER STAND The shop-made roller stand shown in illustration [1] will work as well as a commercial model and is simple to build. With a center post that slides within a hollow column, the roller can be set to any convenient height. Cut the post from 2 x 2 hardwood and counterbore a hole for a carriage bolt through its middle. Cut the roller support to accommodate a wooden roller and fasten the roller to the support. Drill a hole through the roller and into the support for a dowel that can be used to lock the roller and keep it from turning, enabling the jig to be used as a simple stand. Then join the top end of the post to the roller support using a wedged mortise-and-tenon joint. Box in

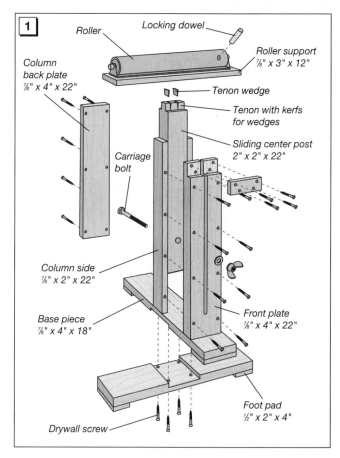

[1]

Roller

Locking dowel

Roller support
⅞" x 3" x 12"

Column
back plate
⅞" x 4" x 22"

Tenon wedge

Tenon with kerfs
for wedges

Sliding center post
2" x 2" x 22"

Carriage
bolt

Column side
⅞" x 2" x 22"

Front plate
⅞" x 4" x 22"

Base piece
⅞" x 4" x 18"

Foot pad
½" x 2" x 4"

Drywall screw

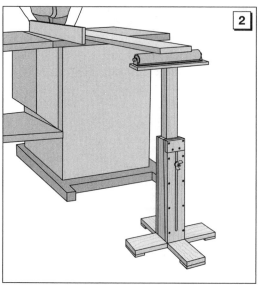

[2]

the center post in a four-sided column so that the post will slide snugly down the center. Cut a slot in the front plate of the column to provide clearance for the end of the bolt and cut a tie block to reinforce the column and close off the top of the slot. Use glue and screws to mount the column to the base, which consists of two boards joined with half-laps. Fasten foot pads to the base

pieces to provide stability. To install the center post, insert the bolt through the counterbored hole, slip the post into the column, and screw the tie block in place. Slip a washer over the bolt and thread on a wing nut.

To use the stand with a table saw [2], loosen the wing nut, raise the post so that the top of the roller is at or slightly below the level of the saw table, and tighten the nut.

A

ABC fire extinguisher
A dry-chemical fire extinguisher effective against three classes of fires: burning wood, paper, or other combustibles (Class A); oil or grease fires (Class B); and electrical fires (Class C).

Air-dried lumber
Lumber that has been seasoned by exposure to the air.

Alternate top bevel with raker (ATB/R)
A circular saw blade designed with four alternately beveled cutting teeth followed by a flat-top raker tooth to remove debris from the kerf.

American Country furniture
A style of furniture produced primarily by amateur cabinetmakers in frontier America from the 17th through the 19th Centuries.

Amperage
The strength of an electrical current; one ampere (or amp) represents the current produced by one volt of electricity in a conductor providing one ohm of resistance. An ohm is a unit of measurement for the amount of resistance in a circuit.

Arbor
A round shaft or spindle to which a cutter can be attached.

Arithmetic progression
A mathematical relationship used in designing furniture; obtained by increasing the dimensions of the elements in a piece by a constant value. An example is a piece that is 12 inches deep, 24 inches wide, and 36 inches high; each dimension is created by adding 12 to the previous one.

Art deco
A style of furniture produced in the 1920s and 1930s characterized by curved veneer surfaces and decorative banding.

Art nouveau
A design movement originating in 19th-Century France that generated individual furniture pieces of unique but highly varied styles. Many feature fluid, vinelike forms.

Auger-type bit
A drill bit designed for use with a hand brace incorporating a threaded pilot point, a spiral shaft, and a square shank.

B

Back saw
A short, fine-toothed handsaw with a reinforcing spine along the top of the blade; used primarily for fine joinery work.

Bastard-cut file
A relatively coarse file with teeth cut diagonally across the blade.

Bead
A molded profile with a convex shape generally used to decorate an edge.

Bench dog
A metal or wood peg that fits into a hole in a workbench to hold a workpiece in place; can be square or round.

Bevel
A cut at an angle from face to face along the length or width of a workpiece.

Bird's eye
A type of figure in wood characterized by small circular swirls resembling a bird's eye; most commonly found in maple.

Biscuit joint
A butt joint reinforced by means of a football-shaped "biscuit" of compressed wood; also known as a plate joint.

Blade heel
The tendency of a table saw or radial arm saw blade to rotate at an angle other than 90 degrees to the saw table when crosscutting or ripping; produces crooked kerfs and may cause kickback.

Blast gate
A piece of plastic or metal inserted in a section of dust collection pipe to shut a tool off from the system.

Board foot
A volume of wood equaling 144 cubic inches; the standard board foot is a piece that is nominally 1 inch thick x 12 inches wide x 12 inches long.

Bore
The arbor hole in a circular saw blade.

Box joint
A type of joint consisting of a series of interlocking fingers used to connect the corners of boxes and small drawers; also known as a finger joint.

Brad
A small finishing nail measuring up to 1 inch.

Burl
Wood cut from abnormal bulbous growths on a tree; because of its structural frailty and dramatic figure, it is used primarily as veneer.

GLOSSARY

Burr
A sharp raised ridge of metal produced when sharpening the cutting edge of a scraper.

Butt joint
A method of joining two workpieces in which the edge, face, or end of one board is set squarely against the edge or face of the other.

Chamfer
A narrow bevel, usually at a 45-degree angle, used to relieve the sharp corner of a board.

Chest-on-frame construction
An enclosed cabinet or chest of drawers set on an open frame; typical of 17th-Century furniture styles, such as William and Mary.

Chippendale style
Any of several styles of furniture developed by the 18th-Century English cabinetmaker Thomas Chippendale; the term is most commonly associated with his rococo designs.

Clear
A lumber term referring to a piece of wood without defects.

Clearance hole
A hole that is bored to accept the shank of a screw or bolt.

Closed coat
A piece of sandpaper whose surface is completely covered by abrasive particles; tends to clog more easily than open-coat papers, in which the particles are more spread out.

Compound cut
A cut made at an angle other than 90 degrees to both the face and the edge of a board.

Concave
An inward-curving shape.

Convex
An outward-curving shape.

Core stock
The composition of the interior of a plywood or particleboard panel; can be veneer, particleboard, or lumber.

Counterbored hole
A hole that enables a screw head to be recessed below the surface of a workpiece so that a wood plug can be used to conceal the fastener.

Countersunk hole
A hole that enables a screw head to sit flush with the surface of a workpiece.

Crosscutting
Sawing wood at a right angle to the grain.

Crotchwood
Wood cut from a log radial to the junction of a branch.

Cutoff
A short section of wood produced by crosscutting a board.

Cutting list
A written list including the quantity and dimensions of the parts in a project.

Dado head
A table saw blade or set of blades, shims, and chippers that cut a rectangular channel in a workpiece; can be adjusted to saw dadoes of varying widths.

Dedicated circuit
An electrical circuit providing power to a single tool or appliance.

Deflection
The amount of displacement—or sag—in a shelf caused by the weight it is supporting.

Density
A wood's weight relative to an equal volume of water; refers to the hardness of a wood sample.

Diffuse-porous wood
Hardwoods such as maple, birch, and yellow poplar that contain pores of comparable size equally distributed between the annual rings.

Double-cut file
A file with two sets of teeth in parallel rows arranged diagonally; the second set is laid over the first at about a 90-degree angle.

Dovetail joint
A very strong and attractive method of joining wood at corners by means of interlocking pins and tails.

Dowel center
A cylindrical metal pin with a raised centerpoint that is inserted into a dowel hole to locate a matching hole in a mating workpiece.

Dozuki
A type of Japanese saw used for fine joinery work; equivalent to the Western-style backsaw.

Drawer stop
Any device installed in a carcase to limit the inward travel of a drawer or prevent it from being pulled out completely.

Dressing
Shaping the cutting edge of a tool blade to restore the correct bevel.

Drop-leaf table
A table with one or more hinged leaves that can be folded down when they are not needed.

Dust frame
A horizontal divider between the drawers in a carcase.

E

Earlywood
Wood tissue along the outer edge of an annual ring produced early in the growing season by trees in temperate climates.

Edge banding
A strip of wood glued to the edge or end of a panel; often used on plywood to conceal exposed laminations.

Edge-gluing
Joining two or more boards edge to edge to create a panel.

End grain
The surface of a board perpendicular to the grain.

Equilibrium moisture content (EMC)
The amount of moisture in a piece of wood when it is neither absorbing or releasing moisture into the surrounding environment; EMC is expressed as a percentage of the wood's oven-dry weight.

Every-tooth set (ETS)
A type of band saw blade in which the teeth are bent alternately to the left or right.

Expansion slot
A slot extending from the rim of a circular saw blade toward the arbor designed to prevent the blade from warping as the blade's temperature increases.

F

Face frame
A flat frame attached to the front of a carcase; used to conceal exposed edges in plywood panels and to lend rigidity to the carcase.

Face vise
A vise mounted to the front of a workbench to hold a workpiece against the edge of the bench.

Face veneer
Veneers used on the outside faces of plywood panels; not necessarily cut from the same species as the core veneers.

Featherboard
A block of wood with flexible fingers cut into one end; clamped to the table or fence of a stationary saw to press a workpiece flat on the table and flush against the fence as it is fed into the blade.

Fiberboard
A type of manufactured panel made from wood fibers and resin binders.

Fiddleback
A decorative wood figure characterized by wavy grain; commonly used in musical instruments.

Figure
The appearance of the surface of a piece of wood as a result of its grain structure, texture, or color variations.

Filler
Any product used to fill pores, defects, or other irregularities in the surface of a workpiece.

Finial
A decorative turning used at the tip of a post.

Flat grain
Refers to the surface of a board that has been sawn so that the face is tangential to the growth rings.

Flitch
A slab or block of wood used in carving or turning.

Flute
A straight groove milled along the shaft of a bit to produce a cutting edge or to facilitate the removal of debris.

Fluting
Parallel grooves cut in a leg or post for decoration; used to convey the image of a fluted column in neoclassical furniture styles.

GLOSSARY

Forstner bit
A bit designed to bore flat-bottomed holes.

Frame-and-panel construction
A method of building carcases in which panels are contained in frames consisting of vertical stiles and horizontal rails; the panel rests in grooves cut in the frame and is free to move—or "float"—as it expands or contracts with changes in humidity.

Frame chair
A style of chair constructed by joining a back and leg frame to a seat frame.

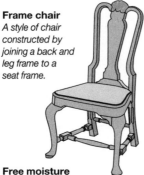

Free moisture
The excess moisture contained in green wood that is not absorbed—or bound—in the tissue itself.

French polish
A finishing technique employing shellac and pumice which are rubbed into the wood using a cloth pad, creating a deep, lustrous glow.

French Provincial
A simplified and less ornate rococo style of furniture developed in rural France during the 18th Century and popular among French colonists in North America.

Frog
The platform on the body of a plane to which the cap and iron assembly is attached.

G

Geometric progression
A mathematical relationship used in designing furniture; obtained by making one part of a piece relate to a second part in the same ratio that the second relates to the third, and so on. An example is a piece that is 8 inches deep, 16 inches wide, and 32 inches high; the dimension of each element after the first is twice the preceding one.

Georgian
English furniture styles popularized during the reigns of George I through George III; commonly refers to the more ornate examples of early 18th-Century furniture following the Queen Anne style.

Golden mean
A method of proportioning the elements in a piece of furniture; obtained by bisecting a dimension so that the relationship between the length of its smaller and larger segments is the same as the relationship between the larger segment and the original dimension.

Gothic revival
A style of furniture incorporating medieval motifs; one of several revival periods popularized during the reign of Queen Victoria.

Grade
The quality of lumber according to established standards regarding visual and structural defects; separate standards exist for hardwoods and softwoods.

Grain
The direction of the fibers and other anatomical features in wood.

Grit
The size of the abrasive particles used in making sandpaper; measured by the finest mesh of screen the particles will pass through.

Gullet
The space between the teeth of a saw blade.

H

Hanger bolt
A fastener with machine threads on one end, lag threads on the other, and an unthreaded section in between.

Hardboard
Any of several forms of dense fiberboard; generally available in ⅛- and ¼-inch-thick panels measuring 4 feet x 8 feet.

Hardwood
With minor exceptions, the wood from a deciduous tree.

Heartwood
The wood tissue near the center of a log; typically darker in color and more durable than the surrounding sapwood.

Hepplewhite style
A style of neoclassical furniture designed by the late-18th-Century English cabinetmaker George Hepplewhite.

High-speed steel
A steel alloy used to produce tool bits and blades because of its durability when exposed to heat and abrasion.

Hold-down device
Any clamp or other device designed to secure a workpiece in place while it is being machined.

Honing
Using an abrasive stone to sharpen a tool's cutting edge.

Hook angle
The angle between the face of a circular saw blade tooth and the radius of the blade.

Hygroscopic
The tendency of a substance, such as wood, to absorb and expel water as humidity levels change in the surrounding atmosphere.

I

Inlay
A strip of decorative veneer or other material glued in a groove cut into the surface of a workpiece.

Interlocking grain
Wood tissue formed by successive layers of vascular cells running obliquely across each other as they grow in alternating spirals up the trunk of the tree.

Isometric drawing
A system of drawing which represents an object pictorially (approximately as it would appear in a photograph).

J

Jacobean
A style of furniture popularized in England during the reign of James I in the 17th Century; characterized by Mediterranean design motifs, heavy oak construction, and dark color.

Jointing
The process of truing a workpiece by making an edge or a face perfectly flat and straight and usually square to an adjoining surface.

Joists
Horizontal framing members in building construction that support floors; typically 2 x 10s.

K

Kerf
The groove left by a saw blade.

Kickback
A dangerous situation (particularly on the table saw) in which a power tool throws the workpiece back at the operator.

Kicker
A strip of wood attached to the side panel of a carcase and positioned flush against the top of a drawer to prevent it from tilting down when opened.

Kicker —

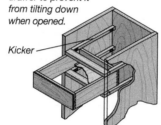

Kiln-dried lumber
Lumber that has been seasoned in a kiln to control the speed of the drying process.

Knockdown
A design that features hardware or joinery that enables a piece of furniture to be easily disassembled.

L

Lapping
Removing the burr from the cutting edge of a tool blade that results from the honing process.

Latewood
Wood tissue produced by a tree during the latter phase of the growing season; typically harder, less porous, and stronger than earlywood tissue.

Lineal foot
A measurement referring to the length of a board regardless of its thickness or width.

Lumber rule
A specialized measuring stick used by lumber graders to quickly calculate board feet while examining a board for defects.

M

Marquetry
The use of wood veneers with varying colors, textures, and figures to create inlaid pictures and patterns on the surface of a workpiece.

Medium-density fiberboard
A type of manufactured sheet material made from a wood fiber and resin composite.

Microbevel
A secondary bevel honed on the primary bevel of a blade's cutting edge at a slightly steeper angle than that of the primary bevel.

Miter
A cut that angles across the face of a workpiece, typically at 45 degrees.

Mixed hardwoods
A lumber trade term used to describe a shipment of lumber containing more than one species of hardwood.

Moisture meter
A device that relies on electrical current to determine the moisture content of a wood sample.

GLOSSARY

Molding head
A solid metal wheel attached to the arbor of a table saw or radial arm saw that holds a set of three identical knives; used to mill molding profiles into a workpiece.

Molding
A decorative strip of wood featuring a contoured profile.

Mortise gauge
A hand tool featuring an adjustable arm and scribing pins used to lay out mortises.

Mortise-and-tenon joint
A method of joining wood in which a protruding tenon on one board fits into a hole—or mortise—in another board.

Mullion
A wood strip used as a vertical divider in a piece of furniture.

N

Neoclassical
Any of several styles of furniture incorporating classical decorative motifs, such as the designs of Hepplewhite and Sheraton.

Nominal
The width or thickness of lumber based on its original dimensions when green. The actual width and thickness of a board will be less than its nominal dimensions as a result of shrinkage and milling; a plank that is nominally 2 x 4, for example, is actually 1½ inches by 3½ inches.

Non-grain-raising (NGR)
A type of stain formulated to evaporate without causing the wood to swell.

Non-piloted bit
A router bit without a bearing to guide the cut.

O

Open coat
A piece of sandpaper with abrasive particles that are thinly spread out to prevent clogging.

Orbital action
In power sanders, refers to the oscillating action of a sanding disc that is elliptical rather than straight; in saber saws, refers to a blade that moves backward and forward, in addition to up and down, to minimize tearout.

Orthographic drawing
A drawing technique used in most blueprints and plans in which objects are drawn to scale in two dimensions; two or more individual views of the object are provided, each illustrating the object from a different direction.

P

Pantograph
A design and layout device used to duplicate, enlarge, or reduce an original pattern.

Particleboard
A type of panel manufactured from wood particles and adhesive fillers; often used as corestock.

Patina
A change in the color or appearance of wood over time, usually resulting from the polymerization or oxidation of natural compounds in the wood.

Pattern routing
A routing technique in which a piloted bit or template guide follows a template fastened to the workpiece, reproducing the template's outline on the workpiece.

Perspective drawing
A drawing technique in which an object is rendered much as the eye would see it.

Phillips tip
A screwdriver with a cross-shaped tip for driving screws with cross-shaped recesses in their heads; this type of tip is less likely to skip than a slotted tip.

Piloted bit
A router bit with a bearing attached to the shaft that tracks along the edge of the workpiece to guide the cutter.

Pilot hole
A hole drilled into a workpiece to accept the threaded portion of a screw; the hole is slightly smaller than the diameter of the fastener to minimize the risk of splitting without reducing the fastener's holding power.

Pitch
A black or dark resinous substance in wood.

Plain-sawn
A method of sawing lumber from a log that yields mainly tangentially cut boards; the term is also used to describe a board with annual rings that are more or less parallel to the faces.

Plate joint
See biscuit joint.

Platform chair
A chair design in which the back and legs are separate assemblies anchored to a solid seat.

Plinth
A block or square base at the bottom of a pedestal or column.

Plumb
Perfectly vertical.

Plunge cut
A cut in which the bit or blade is held above the workpiece at the start and pivoted into the stock.

Plunging bit
A router bit designed for making plunge cuts.

Plywood
A manufactured panel usually made from several layers of veneer. The grain in each layer is at 90 degrees to that in the layers on either side.

Pocket hole
A hole drilled into a workpiece at an angle, typically used to join a tabletop to its under structure.

Points per inch (PPI)
On a saw blade, the number of tooth tips in 1 inch of blade length; the number of PPI is always one fewer than the number of teeth per inch (TPI).

Pressure-treated lumber
Lumber that has been saturated with chemical preservatives to enhance its durability when used outdoors.

Pull stroke
The direction of travel of a handsaw—back toward the operator; used as the cutting stroke with most Japanese saws.

Pumice
A fine abrasive powder made from volcanic ash used with a felt block in rubbing out finishes.

Push stick
A safety device used to feed a workpiece across the table of stationary machines, keeping the operator's hands a safe distance from the cutter.

Push stroke
The direction of travel of a handsaw—away from the operator; used as the cutting stroke with most Western-style saws.

Q

Quarter-sawn
A method of cutting lumber from a log that produces boards whose annual rings are more or less perpendicular to the boards' faces.

Queen Anne
A style of furniture first popularized in England during the reign of Queen Anne and used extensively by Colonial America cabinetmakers during the first half of the 18th Century; characterized by cabriole legs and graceful contours.

Quill stroke
The downward movement of the spindle and bit of a drill press.

Quilted figure
A decorative undulating grain pattern primarily found in bigleaf maple native to the Pacific Northwest.

R

Radially cut
See quarter-sawn.

Rail
A horizontal member of a frame-and-panel assembly.

Raised panel
A panel with beveled edges that fit into grooves cut in the rails and stiles of a frame.

Rasp-cut file
A file with coarse, individual teeth designed for rough shaping of wood.

Reaction wood
Abnormal wood tissue produced by stresses in leaning tree limbs and trunks; reaction wood is extremely unstable and produces boards that are prone to warping.

Release cuts
Straight cuts made through the waste portion of a workpiece enabling a saber saw or band saw blade to more easily follow a curved cutting line without binding.

GLOSSARY

Retarder
A chemical additive mixed with a finish or adhesive to slow its drying time.

Ribbon-striped grain
The figure pattern exposed by radially cutting (quarter-sawing) woods, such as elm and mahogany, with interlocked grain; characterized by alternating light and dark longitudinal bands.

Ring-porous wood
A wood such as oak, ash, and elm with end grain characterized by a band of large pores along the outside edge of each annual ring; ring-porous woods are also commonly referred to as open grained.

Ripping
Cutting wood with the grain—usually along its length.

Rococo
A style of furniture characterized by flowing curves, cabriole legs, and floral motifs popularized in France, but adapted into several 18th- and 19th-Century styles, such as Chippendale, French Provincial, and late Victorian Rococo.

Rolltop
A curved, retractable cover commonly employed on desks.

Rotary-sliced
Veneer produced by peeling a thin layer of wood from the circumference of a log.

Rottenstone
A very fine powdered stone used to rub out finishes and dull the gloss.

Rough lumber
Lumber that has not been milled or surfaced.

Rule joint
A joint in which a convex cut in one workpiece mates with a concave cut in another; the joint is held together with a hinge and is commonly used on dropleaf tables.

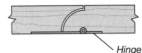

Hinge

Runner
A wood strip that runs in a groove used to support drawers in a carcase; runners may be fastened to either the drawer or the carcase.

Runout
The tendency of an arbor or drive shaft to spin slightly eccentrically.

Ryoba
A Japanese saw that features crosscut teeth on one edge and rip teeth on the other edge.

S

Sanding sealer
A primer applied to a workpiece to reduce the permeability of the surface; typically used as a barrier between bare wood or a stain and the finish.

Sapwood
Wood tissue between the bark and heartwood of a log. Usually softer and lighter in color than the heartwood; sapwood becomes heartwood as the tree ages and impregnates this tissue with extractives.

Saw set
A tool used to bend the teeth of a saw blade, making the kerf produced by the blade slightly wider than the blade itself, minimizing binding.

Seasoning
The processing of wood, either by air drying or kiln drying, to reduce its moisture content and inhibit decay.

Sensitizer
A compound in wood that can cause an allergic reaction.

Shaker
A style of furniture developed by members of a 19th-Century American religious movement; characterized by its extreme simplicity and emphasis on utilitarian function.

Sheraton
A style of neoclassical furniture developed by the English designer Thomas Sheraton; characterized by novel, space-saving features, beautiful inlays, and use of the lyre as a decorative motif.

Shoulder line
A layout line pinpointing the shoulder of a tenon or dovetail.

Side chair
A type of chair, usually without armrests, used primarily with dining tables.

Single-cut file
A type of file with a single set of teeth arranged in diagonal, parallel rows.

Skip-tooth blade
A band saw blade with widely spaced gullets as if every other tooth had been removed; designed primarily for resawing.

Slip seat
An upholstered chair seat.

Slurry
A mix of solids suspended in a liquid.

Smooth-cut file
A file with closely spaced teeth, producing a relatively fine cut.

Softwood
Wood produced primarily by nee-dle-bearing evergreen trees such as pine, fir, spruce, and hemlock, but also cedar, cypress, and redwood.

Soldering
The bonding of two metals using an alloy with a low melting temperature.

Solid-wood lamination
A part assembled by gluing togeth-er strips of wood; often used to cre-ate curved workpieces.

Spindle
A turned wood cylinder, often employed decoratively in chair and table construction.

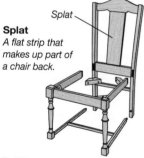

Splat
A flat strip that makes up part of a chair back.

Splat

Splitter
A table saw accessory used to hold a saw kerf open so the blade will not bind.

Spontaneous combustion
A fire that ignites as the result of a chemical reaction, generally in com-bustible substances that have been improperly stored or disposed of, such as oil-soaked rags.

Square-drive tip
A screwdriver with a square tip for driving screws with square recesses in their heads; also known as a Robertson tip, this type of tip is less likely to skip than a slotted tip.

Squeeze-out
A bead of glue forced out of a joint as clamping pressure is applied.

Starved joint
A weak glue joint resulting from an insufficient quantity of glue; can be caused by excessive clamping pressure.

Sticker
One of a series of wood strips placed at intervals between the boards in a drying pile to space the layers and allow for air flow.

Stile
A vertical member in a frame-and-panel assembly.

Stopped groove
A channel cut in a workpiece that does not extend the full length of the board.

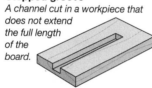

Stopped rabbet
A steplike cut in the edge or end of a board that does not run the full width or length of the board.

Stretcher
A supporting member connecting the legs of a chair or table to pro-vide stability.

Stropping
Drawing the honed edge of a blade across a leather strap—the final step in sharpening.

Substrate
The corestock panel to which veneer is applied.

Sunken joint
A depression along a glue joint typi-cally caused by sanding the joint while the wood is still swollen from moisture in the glue; when the glue cures, the wood shrinks, creating the depression.

Surfaced lumber
A plank that has been planed smooth on one or more of its surfaces.

Sustainable yield
The harvesting of timber at a rate that does not exceed its rate of regrowth.

T

Tack time
The amount of time it takes an adhe-sive to form a bond before it is com-pletely cured.

Tail vise
A vise mounted to the end of a workbench to secure stock along the front edge of the bench top.

Tangential
A term used in the lumber trade to describe the surface of a board that has been cut perpendicular to the radius of the log so that the annual rings on its end grain arc more or less from edge to edge.

Taper
To cut a workpiece so that it is wider at one end.

Tearout
The tendency of a cutter to fray or splinter the workpiece, typically at the end of a cut.

GLOSSARY

Teeth per inch (TPI)
The number of teeth per linear inch of saw blade; the number of TPI is always one more than the number of points per inch (PPI). Typically, the greater the number of teeth, the smoother the cut a blade will make in dense material.

Tempered hardboard
Fiberboard that has been processed to increase its strength, density, and resistance to moisture.

Template
A pattern used as a guide in laying out or cutting duplicate workpieces.

Through-and-through cut
A method of cutting lumber in which all the boards are cut parallel to the diameter of the log.

Toe kick
An indentation along the bottom of kitchen cabinets installed to provide room for the toes when standing up close to the countertop.

Tongue-and-groove joint
A joinery technique that consists of a tongue on one workpiece that fits into a groove in an adjoining board.

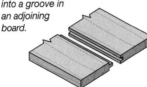

Torque
The amount of force needed to turn an object.

Trim
A wood strip applied to a project, typically for decorative purposes.

Tudor
A style of 16th-Century furniture popular in England under the Tudor monarchy, primarily the reigns of Henry VIII and Elizabeth I; characterized by oak construction and generally rectangular shapes.

Turning
Making or shaping a workpiece on the lathe.

Tyloses
A rigid foamlike substance in the pores of some species of wood, such as white oak, which helps to make the wood less permeable to liquids.

U

Underlayment
Plywood or other manufactured board used as a base material under finish flooring, such as carpeting.

V

Vehicle
The liquid, typically a volatile solvent, that carries the solid compounds in a finish or adhesive.

Veneer
A thin sheet of wood applied over a substrate; also, the layers in manufactured panels, such as plywood.

Viscosity
The thickness of a liquid.

Vitrification
The melting and hardening of a substance, such as the silica in clay, to form a dense surface; used to make some types of grinding wheels.

Void
A gap or hollow space within a material, such as a plywood sheet.

Volatile
An unstable compound, such as the solvent in a finish or adhesive, that evaporates when exposed to air.

W

Waferboard
Panels fabricated by bonding wood shavings and wood chips; commonly used as an inexpensive underlayment.

Wall studs
Vertical framing members in building construction that support walls or partitions; typically 2 x 4s or 2 x 6s.

Wash coat
A coat of thinned finish or sealer used to change the appearance or porosity of a surface; generally the first coat when applying a finish.

Wet tack
The time it takes for an adhesive to become dry to the touch.

Winding stick
A narrow board placed on a board face to check for twists.

Windsor chair
A style of platform chair featuring turnings and bentwood parts to form the back and legs.

ACKNOWLEDGMENTS

By providing materials and offering information, dozens of companies and individuals helped make this book possible. The editors wish to thank the following:

Jon Alley, Churchville, Pa.; American National Standards Institute, New York, N.Y.; American Plywood Association, Tacoma, Wash.; Architectural Woodwork Institute, Centerville, Va.; Black & Decker/Elu Power Tools, Towson, Md.; Glenn Bostock, Pipersville, Pa.; Cooper Industries, Cooper Hand Tools Division, Raleigh, N.C.; Jim Cummins, Woodstock, N.Y.; Delta International Machinery Corp./Porter Cable, Guelph, Ont.; DeVilbiss Ransburg Industrial Coating Equipment, Barrie, Ont.; Diamond Machining Technology Inc., Marlborough, Mass.; Michael Dunbar, Portsmouth, N.H.; Ben Erickson, Eutaw, Ala.; Forest Products Laboratory, Madison, Wisc.; Ted Fuller, Guelph, Ont.; Garrett Wade Company, Inc., New York, N.Y.; Frederic Hanisch, Quakertown, Pa.; Hardwood Plywood & Veneer Association, Reston, Va.; Human Factors and Ergonomics Society Inc. Santa Monica, Calif.; Richard Jagels, Dept. of Forest Biology, University of Maine, Orono, Maine; Frank Klausz, Frank's Cabinet Shop Inc., Pluckemin, N.J.; Neil Koury, Falk Canada, Montreal, Que.; Lee Valley Tools Ltd., Ottawa, Ont.; Leichtung Workshops, Cleveland, Ohio;

Leigh Industries Ltd., Port Coquitlam, B.C.; Giles Miller-Mead, Brome, Que.; Chris A. Minick, Stillwater, Miss.; National Fire Protection Association, Quincy, Mass.; National Hardwood Lumber Association, Memphis, Tenn.; National Institute of Occupational Safety and Health, Cincinnati, Ohio; National Particleboard Association, Gaithersburg, Md.; Northeastern Lumber Manufacturer's Association, Cumberland Center, Minn.; Julius Panero, New York, N.Y.; Andrew Poynter, A & M Wood Specialty, Cambridge, Ont.; Richard's Engineering Co., Vancouver, B.C.; Tim Rinehart, Woodcraft Supply Co., Parkersburg, W.V.; Robert Bosch Power Tools Inc., (Canada) Mississauga, Ont.; Robert Larson Company Inc., San Francisco, Calif.; Ryobi America Corp., Anderson, S.C.; Tom Searles, American Lumber Standards Committee, Germantown, Md.; Sears, Roebuck and Co., Chicago, Ill.; Simonds Industries, Fitchburg, Mass.; Skil Power Tools Canada, Markham, Ont.; Unicorn Abrasives of Canada Ltd., Brockville, Ont.; Watson-Guptill Publications, New York, N.Y.; Winterthur Museum, Winterthur, Del.

The following persons and companies also assisted in the preparation of this book:

Frances Brochu, Lorraine Doré, Graphor Consultation, Linda Jarosiewicz, Andrew Jones, Rob Lutes, David Simon

Cover photography

Front: Robert Chartier
Back: John La Pine

INDEX

INDEX

INDEX

INDEX

INDEX

INDEX

435

INDEX

W-X-Y

Waferboard, 203, **203**, 422
Wall studs, 60, 422
Walnut wood, **182**, **183**, **184**, **198**, *234*
Wardrobes. *See also* Armoires
  Hepplewhite, *30*
Wash coats, 422
Washers (fasteners), *367*
Washstands, American Country, *37*
Water-based varnishes, 349, **351**, **355**
Waterstones, **78**, **79**, 80, *80*
Wax finishes, 349, 350, **356**
Wenge wood, *235*
Wet tack, 328, 422
Willow wood, *235*
Winding sticks, 190, *190*, 422
Wood, 179. *See also* Lumber; Wood species for bookshelves, **8-9**
  crotchwood, 245, *414*
  cutting into lumber, 186-87, *186-87*
  density, *414*
  diffuse-porous, 217, 347, *414*
  grain, 208, *209*, 254, *254*, *416*
  grain, fiddleback, 244, *415*
  grain, quilted figure, *419*
  grain, ribbon-striped, 208, *420*
  hardwood, 180-81, *181*, *416*
  heartwood, 180, *180*, *416*
  latewood, 181, *181*, *417*
  moisture content, 179, 206-207, *206*, *207*, 261, *261*, *342*, 415, *416*, *417*
  properties, finishing, **184**
  properties, gluing, **330**, 342
  properties, physical, **182**
  properties, sawing, **73**
  properties, working, **183**
  reaction wood, 197, 214, *419*
  ring-porous, 245, 347, *420*
  sapwood, 180, *180*, *420*
  shrinkage, 242, **242**, *243*, *243*
  softwood, 180, *181*, *421*
  toxicity, 185
  tree anatomy, 180-81, *180*, *181*, 186, *186*, *187*, *192*
  tyloses, 227, 422
Wood species, 208
  afrormosia, *210*
  agba, *210*
  alder, **184**, **198**, *211*
  amburana, *209*
  ash, **182**, **183**, **184**, **198**, *211*
  aspen, **182**, **183**, **184**, **198**, *212*
  baldcypress, *237*
  balsa, *212*
  basswood, **182**, **183**, **184**, **198**, *213*
  bayo, *213*
  beech, **182**, **183**, **184**, **198**, *214*
  birch, **182**, **183**, **184**, **198**, *214*
  bocote, *215*
  bubinga, *215*
  butternut, **182**, **183**, **184**, *216*
  catalpa, **198**, *216*
  cedar, **182**, **183**, **184**, **198**, *237-38*
  chactacote, *217*
  cherry, **182**, **183**, **184**, **198**, *217*
  chestnut, *218*
  coffeetree, Kentucky, *222*
  Douglas-fir, **182**, **183**, **184**, **198**, *238*
  ebony, *218-19*
  elm, **182**, **183**, **184**, **198**, *209*, *219*
  goncalo alves, *220*
  hemlock, **198**
  hickory, **182**, **183**, **184**, **198**, *220*
  holly, *221*
  jarrah, *222*
  lacewood, *223*
  lauan, *223*
  lignum vitae, *224*
  locust, *224*
  mahogany, *225*
  maple, **182**, **183**, **184**, **198**, *209*, *225*
  mesquite, *226*
  myrtle, *226*
  oak, **182**, **183**, **184**, **198**, *209*, *227*
  olivewood, *228*
  osage orange, *228*
  padauk, *229*
  pecan, **182**, **183**, **184**, **198**, *229*

INDEX